A
MONOGRAPH
ON THE
SILK FABRICS OF BENGAL

A
MONOGRAPH
ON THE
SILK FABRICS OF BENGAL

N.G. MUKERJI, M.A., M.B.A.C. and P.H.A.S.

GYAN

Published by

Gyan Publishing House
5, Ansari Road
Daryaganj, New Delhi-110002
Phone: 011-47034999, 9811692060
E-mail: books@gyanbooks.com

Distribution Network
gyanbooks.com
India, USA, Canada, UK, Australia, France

ISBN : 978-81-212-9659-5 (PB)
First Published, 1903

2nd Impression 2023

Printed at: Gyan Press, Delhi.

A MONOGRAPH ON THE SILK FABRICS OF BENGAL
Author: N.G. MUKERJI

A

MONOGRAPH

ON THE

SILK FABRICS OF BENGAL.

BY

N. G. MUKERJI, M.A., M.R.A.C. AND F.H.A.S.,

OF THE BENGAL PROVINCIAL CIVIL SERVICE, AUTHOR OF THE HANDBOOK OF SERICULTURE AND HANDBOOK OF INDIAN AGRICULTURE.

1903.

Published at the BENGAL SECRETARIAT BOOK DEPÔT,
Writers' Buildings, Calcutta.

OFFICIAL AGENTS.

In India—

MESSRS. THACKER, SPINK & CO., Calcutta and Simla.
MESSRS. NEWMAN & CO., Calcutta.
MESSRS. HIGGINBOTHAM & CO., Madras.
MESSRS. THACKER & CO., LD., Bombay.
MESSRS. A. J. COMBRIDGE & CO., Bombay.
THE SUPERINTENDENT, AMERICAN BAPTIST MISSION PRESS, Rangoon.
MRS. RADHABAI ATMARAM SAGOON, Bombay.
MESSRS. R. CAMBRAY & CO., Calcutta.
MESSRS. S. K. LAHIRI & CO., Printers and Book-sellers, College Street, Calcutta.
RAI SAHIB M. GULAB SINGH & SONS, Proprietors of the Mufid-i-am Press, Lahore, Punjab.
MESSRS. V. KALYANARAMA IYER & CO., Book-sellers, &c., Madras.
MESSRS. D. B. TARAPOREVALA, SONS & CO., Book-sellers, Bombay.
MESSRS. G. A. NATESON & CO., Madras.
MESSRS. A. W. HAMILTON & CO., 11 Edmondstone Road, Allahabad.

In England—

MR. E. A. ARNOLD, 37 Bedford Street, Strand, London.
MESSRS. CONSTABLE & CO., 2 Whitehall Gardens, London.
MESSRS. SAMPSON LOW, MARSTON & CO., St. Dunstan's House, Fetter Lane, London.
MESSRS. LUZAC & CO., 46 Great Russell Street, London.
MESSRS. KEGAN PAUL, TRENCH, TRÜBNER & CO., Charing Cross Road, London.
MR. B. ALFRED QUARITCH, 15 Piccadilly, London.
MESSRS. P. S. KING & SON, 2 & 4 Great Smith Street, Westminster, London.
MESSRS. H. S. KING & CO., 65 Cornhill, London.
MESSRS. WILLIAMS AND NORGATE, Oxford.
MESSRS. DEIGHTON, BELL & CO., Cambridge.

On the Continent—

MESSRS. R. FRIEDLÄNDER & SOHN, Berlin, N. W., Carlstrasse, 11.
MR. OTTO HARRASSOWITZ, Leipzig.
MR. KARL HIERSEMANN, Leipzig.
MR. ERNEST LEROUX, 28 Rue Bonaparte, Paris.
MR. MARTINUS NIJHOFF, The Hague.

TABLE OF CONTENTS.

INTRODUCTION.

PAGE.

PART I.

THE MULBERRY AND THE MULBERRY SILK-WORMS.

PART II.

SILK YARNS.

PART III.

THE SILK-WEAVING INDUSTRY.

PART IV.

SILK-WEAVING AND DYEING.

PART V.

INFERIOR SILKS.

LIST OF ILLUSTRATIONS.

Also 16 sheets of coloured plates illustrating silk-dyeing and silk-fabrics.

INTRODUCTION.

THIS Monograph has been prepared according to the directions contained in the Revenue Department Circular No. 10, dated the 29th November 1898, which requires that the Monograph "should give a complete review of all branches of the silk industry." All the other branches, however, have been treated here only as subsidiary to those of silk weaving and silk-fabrics, that the main character of the Monograph may be maintained.

2. The silk-weaving industry of Bengal is of greater magnitude than even the manufacture of raw silk, which forms the main staple of European export. From the Vedic times silk fabrics have been enjoined to Hindus for use on ceremonial occasions. One of the verses of the Rig Veda* is referred to by orthodox pandits as enjoining the use of silk cloths for the marriage ceremony, and, as a matter of fact, Hindus all over India use silk cloths for every religious ceremony, and those who can afford it, regard it as incumbent on them to wear it daily at the time of worship. Foreign silks and silks containing an admixture of other fibres are prohibited for such ceremonial purposes, though as articles of luxury, foreign silks were in use even in ancient times. The use of unmixed silk is prohibited among Muhammadans, specially of the stronger sex, but they, as also the Parsis, use a good deal of cheap silk on ceremonial occasions, in imitation of the Hindus. The silk-manufacturing industry has thus a peculiar vitality of its own, which is not shared by the cotton-manufacturing industry, and the general notion that silk and cotton weaving industries of India have equally suffered and have suffered for the same reasons, is not correct. The recent decline in the silk-weaving industry is chiefly in the direction of foreign export. European countries no longer depend on Indian calicos and silks. But the manufacture of those fabrics which are required for native use continues as vigorously as ever, and the Census figures for 1901 show that the silk weaving industry of Bengal has had a remarkable development during the last decade. The costliest silks, embroidered with gold and silver threads, are not manufactured in Bengal, but chiefly in Benares. The raw material used, however, in the Benares looms, is largely imported from Bengal, and as the Benares embroidered silks are extensively used by the higher and middle classes of Bengal, the silk industry of Benares is intimately connected with that of Bengal. The same may be said of the silk-weaving industry (based on European principles) of Bombay, though the raw material in use in Bombay is largely derived from China also. Bombay silks are largely used by women of the middle classes of Bengal. But the whole rank and file of the Hindu population of Bengal and other parts of India *have to use indigenous silk fabrics* on certain occasions, however coarse or cheap these fabrics may be, and it is for this reason that there is a large internal trade in silk fabrics, specially of the cheaper kinds.

3. The information for this Monograph has been derived from the following sources:—

(1) The district reports or monographs based mainly on the personal observations of officers, usually of the grades of Covenanted Assistant Collectors and Uncovenanted Deputy Collectors, who were specially deputed by their Collectors for the purpose of preparing these district monographs.

* Kshoumé basané basáná-magni-mádhiyátám (=The bride is to worship the fire decked in silken cloth).

(2) The Bengal Administration Reports for 1896 to 1901.
(3) The Census Reports for 1891 and 1901.
(4) The Report of the Bengal Chamber of Commerce for 1901.
(5) The Annual Statement of the Director-General of Statistics for 1902.
(6) Some account of silk in India, by I. Geoghegan.
(7) Silk in India, by L. Liotard.
(8) Dr. Watt's Dictionary of Economic Products.
(9) My own personal observations, which have been mainly recorded in the Hand-book of Sericulture which has been published by Government.

The subject will be dealt with in five parts. The first part will refer to the first raw material, viz., the mulberry and the silk-worm; the second part will deal with silk yarns; the third part, with commercial and industrial questions; the fourth part, with weaving proper; and the fifth part, with the *Tasar* and *Endi* or *Eri* silk industries. All the parts, however, will be treated from the point of view of the silk fabrics.

A
MONOGRAPH
ON THE
SILK FABRICS OF BENGAL.

PART I.

THE MULBERRY AND THE MULBERRY SILK-WORMS.

CHAPTER I.

LOCALITIES WHERE SILK IS PRODUCED.

Chittagong Division.

Presidency Division.

WITH the exception of the Chittagong Division, all other divisions of Bengal have reported the existence of the silk-weaving industry. In the Presidency Division the industry is reported to be at present confined to Murshidabad. In this district mulberry-growing and cocoon rearing are particularly common in the *thanas* of Burwa, Burwan, Gowas and Raghunathganj, while silk-weaving is carried on mainly within the jurisdictions of the *thanas* of Sujaganj, Doulatbazar, Bhagawangola, Gowas, Manullabazar, Asanpur, and Mirzapur. The town of Mirzapur produces the most superior silk fabrics in the whole of Bengal. Among other important silk-weaving centres may be mentioned Baluchar, Islampur, Kadai, Saidabad, Beldanga, and Hariharpara. Berhampur and Jeaganj are the two chief centres of silk trade where the wealthy merchants reside. During the last decade the industry continued to decay in the department of cocoon-rearing and also in that of *corah*-weaving. The Census figures for 1901 show 41,615 persons as being dependent on this industry in Murshidabad, against 55,142 which was the number according to the Census Report for 1891. Studying the Census figures in detail, however, one would be struck with the rapid strides the silk-weaving industry of Murshidabad, as a whole, has made within the last decade, though this improvement has gone on *paripassu* with the decline in the cocoon-rearing industry. Nadia and Jessore were at one time recognized as silk-producing districts. Mulberry-growing and cocoon-rearing still prevail in the northern part of the district of Nadia. In Khulna there has never been any silk-rearing, though an experiment on a small scale, conducted for three years from 1891 to 1894, was sufficient to demonstrate the possibility of growing the mulberry and the mulberry silk-worms exactly in the same way as it is done in the northern districts. It remains to be seen if local enterprise will prompt the utilization of the mulberry trees which were planted at this time and which are only just ready for rearing silk-worms. The presence of about 100 large mulberry trees within two or three miles of the Sadar station ought to be a sufficient inducement for some poor man, acquainted with the art of rearing silk-worms and making thread, to take up the industry, if facilities are put by local bodies in the way of such a man to do so. The Chairman of the District Board of Khulna, having lately addressed the writer of this Monograph on this subject, the matter may be mentioned here in case it should lead to any practical result in the future. A similar experiment was conducted from 1892-95 in the Magura subdivision of Jessore, but this has given rise to no local enterprise. In the 24-Parganas the cocoon-rearing industry still lurks in some villages in the neighbourhood of Dattapukur. It may be also mentioned here that at Ultadanga, near Calcutta, an enterprising Muhammadan gentleman has set up a silk-weaving mill on European principles, which is said to be in a flourishing condition. But as this is not, strictly speaking, an indigenous industry, nothing further need be said about this enterprise.

Burdwan Division.

2. In the Burdwan Division, silk-weaving is reported to be carried on in all the districts. The following interesting history of the silk industry in the district of Hooghly has been furnished by Babu Sukumar Haldar, Subdivisional Officer of Jahanabad:—

"Local tradition points to the existence of an important silk industry in the Jahanabad subdivision as far back as the seventh century. It would appear from old records that at a time not long after the transfer of the Dewani of Bengal to the East India Company, the Company had a factory at Khirpai (now in the Midnapore district), the place which was the head-quarters of this subdivision at the time of its formation in 1845. It is difficult to ascertain the precise date of the establishment of the factory, but it was certainly in existence in 1795, and probably existed prior to 1765, the date of the cession of the Dewani to the Company (*vide* Mr. Toynbee's sketch of the administration of the Hooghly district, paragraph 91). It would appear that the Company, until the winding-up of their commercial affairs, held the absolute monopoly of the silk industry in this district.

"Proofs are not wanting that the industry was in a flourishing condition before it was taken in hand by the East India Company. Dewanganj, on the right bank of the river Dwarkeswar, was the centre of an important silk industry, which still survives, though in a state of decadence. In those early times the trade was almost exclusively an inland one, and was chiefly in the hands of Bunniahs from Upper India. Camels were the only means of transport; and traces of an elevated highway used by the caravans of these merchants are still in existence. The character and extent of the trade at this time cannot be ascertained with any accuracy, but there is reason to believe that the trade was an important one.

"Under the East India Company the trade was a river-borne one. Mr. C. Touchet, the Commercial Resident of Radhanagar, writing in 1795, states that Ghatal on the Silye in Midnapore was the port of Khirpai, Chandrakona, and Dewanganj. It would appear that during the rains when the river Dwarkeswar was navigable, the silk goods were sent down the river (which from the point of confluence with the Silye near Ghatal assumes the name of Rupnarain) in boats from Dewanganj. During the dry season the goods were despatched by pack-bullocks to Ghatal, a distance of eight miles. There was at this time great activity in inland as well as in river-borne trade. In consequence, however, of the monopoly acquired and jealously guarded by the Company, the old direct inland trade with Upper India was seriously paralysed and, perhaps, temporarily extinguished.

"For the subsequent history of the industry under the Company, I cannot do better than reproduce the following account from Mr. Toynbee's sketch:—

"The cloth factories in the Hooghly district were gradually abolished, and the buildings and sites were sold off between 1830 and 1836. The silk filatures in the Midnapore district appear to have been kept on for some time longer. The commercial concerns of the Company were gradually wound-up by the Board of Salt, Customs and Opium, and the post of Resident appears to have been abolished about 1830. The cause of this collapse was the competition of the Manchester cotton goods which the Collector says could be sold at *less than half* the price of the cloths made at the Company's factories. The native cloth industry still struggles on in this district, but it cannot survive for many more years, and most of the weavers have already taken to other pursuits and become absorbed in the general population. (Paragraph 92.)

"After the winding-up of the East India Company's commercial concerns, the silk factories were taken up by Messrs. Robert Watson and Company. A part of the industry which still survives continues to be in the hands of that Company in the Midnapore district.

"The history of silk in Jahanabad is the history of an effete industry. Dewanganj, the only place where it survives to any appreciable extent, is noticed by Hunter in his *Statistical Account of Bengal* only in connection with brass work.

"In the District Census Report, 1891, the Magistrate (Mr. H. G. Cooke, c.s.) thus briefly notices the silk industry:—

"Some mention may be made of the traces of former European enterprise in indigo and silk. These industries have absolutely disappeared, but it is not an uncommon thing to come across traces of considerable factories and filatures now in ruins. . . . . There was at one time a very flourishing silk trade in Jahanabad and its neighbourhood, but since the importation of European goods, this industry only exists in name. The decline of this trade dates so far back that it scarcely affected the density of the population in the two previous decennial periods. (Paragraphs 11 and 57).

"The manufacture of silk textures is at present confined to Bali, Dewanganj, Kalagachia, Radhabullabpur* in thana Goghat, and Kishorepur in thana Khanakul, in the subdivision Dewanganj being the chief centre.

"Silk filatures are at present confined to Gheso, Raghunathpur, Ghoshpur, Thakuranichak, Kagnair, Dhangari, Ghoradaha, Jagatpur and Henosundarpur, all in thana Khanakul.

The thread is utilised in the manufacture of fabrics at Ghatal and places outside the limits of this subdivision. The number of spinners is returned by the police to be 860, which I consider to be an overestimate.

"The silk weavers of Bali, Dewanganj, &c., neither manufacture their own thread nor buy from these spinners. They buy their thread from dealers in Midnapore."

The statement that the silk industry of Midnapore is still in the hands of Messrs. Robert Watson & Co. is not correct, as the only European Company that is at present working silk in that district is that of Messrs. Louis, Payen & Co., the French Company.

3. The Hooghly report does not mention the fact of silk printing on corahs obtained from the district of Murshidabad being carried on on a fairly extensive scale at Serampur, where some silk-weaving also is still done. The census figures would also lead one to infer that the silk-weaving industry of Hooghly was in a more flourishing condition in 1901 than in 1891.

4. In the Burdwan district the silk industry is carried on in the Sadar Katwa and Kalna subdivisions, but not in the Raniganj subdivision.

5. The industry is carried on in the following villages :—

In Satgachia thana in the Sadar subdivision—

At Memari	By about	50	families.
At Radhakantapur	,,	34	,,
At Tantigantar	,,	8	,,
In Golsi thana—			
At Khana	,,	19	,,
At Jaikrishnapur	,,	19	,,
In Sahebganj—			
At Jagdabad	,,	22	,,
At Panchkula	,,	25	,,
Total ...		173	families.

6. In Kalna subdivision no weaving is carried on, but cocoons are reared to a certain extent, and a good deal of *Tasar* yarn is also manufactured. Cocoons are raised at Serampur, Kaknail and Khaiduttpara. Spinning is carried on at the above-mentioned villages, and also at Satni, Sigubagh, Hamedpur, Gachee, Pathangram, Khanpur, Hat Tare, Nakdaha, and Hapania. Employment is given to about 3,000 people, mostly engaged in cultivation, who eke out their agriculture by raising cocoons and by spinning the thread. By caste they are chiefly Satgopes, Chandals, Gandhabanias or Mussalmans; the only exception to the rule is one Babu Gour Mohan Bhattacharjee, M.A., Head-Master of the Patuli Entrance School, who has been trying to revive the mulberry silk-rearing industry of these villages in correspondence with the writer of this Monograph. The silk industry was originally introduced into this subdivision from Murshidabad on the failure of the cotton industry; the credit of this being due to one Radhikananda Rai, of Amdanga, a servant of one of the Nawab Nazims of Bengal.

7. In the Katwa subdivision *Tasar* alone is grown, and a description of the *Tasar* silk industry of Katwa will be found in its proper place (Part V). According to the Census figures of 1901, the silk-weaving industry of Burdwan has undergone a considerable decline within the last decade.

8. In the district of Midnapore mulberry cocoon-rearing is carried on in Ghatal and Tamluk subdivisions, chiefly within the jurisdiction of Ghatal, Daspore and Garhbeta *thanas*. The village of Chandrakona, in Ghatal subdivision, is almost as important a centre for silk-weaving as Mirzapur and Baluchar in the district of Murshidabad and Shibdanga in the district of Maldah. The products of the native reel from all parts of Midnapore, and even from parts of Howrah, are utilized in the looms of Chandrakona and the neighbouring villages. The Census figures show that the silk industry of this district is declining very fast.

9. In Howrah, the silk-rearing industry is of minor importance. It is carried on by about 600 persons altogether, who are mostly Kaibartas, Bagdis

and low-class Muhammadans, living in the jurisdiction of the different *thanas* of the Ulubaria subdivision, viz., Ulubaria, Bagnan, Amta, Jagatballabpur, Sankrail and Shyampur. They carry on cocoon-rearing and silk-spinning on a very small scale, and they also follow other agricultural pursuits The mulberry is grown chiefly on both sides of the Damudar and the Kana *nadi*, and it is only in the jurisdiction of the *thana* Jagatballabpur that cocoon-rearing and spinning are carried on on any considerable scale.

10. In Birbhum, the cocoon-rearing and spinning industries prevail in the Rampurhât *thana*, the silk factory of Ganutia belonging to the Bengal Silk Company being the centre of these industries; while the principal villages where mulberry silk-weaving is carried on are Baswa, Bishnupur and Margram, also within the jurisdiction of the Rampurhât *thana*. The silk-weaving industry of Birbhum is of less magnitude and importance than the silk-spinning industry, but the "Baswa-Bishnupur silks" enjoy more than a mere local repute. If the Census figures for 1901 can be depended upon, the silk industry of Birbhum is declining very fast.

11. The silk-weaving industry of Bankura is of greater importance than the cocoon-rearing and spinning industries, and the Census figures show that the industry has made considerable progress in this district during the last decade. Only a portion of the raw material used in the looms of the Vishnupur subdivision is produced locally, the balance being imported from Midnapore. Silk-worms are reared and silk spun in the following villages: Dhanda, Punishole, Kesavpur, Chinganu, Tilaghagri, Simlapal, Pakhurduba, Pathardoba and Barakhulia. The Government sericultural experiments conducted in the villages near Garhbeta attracted the attention of the cocoon-rearers of Bankura, who are eager to profit by the introduction of Pasteur's system in their midst. They come to fetch seed from those cocoon-rearers of Garhbeta who are following this system with profit, and they hope by-and-bye to have a seed-rearing establishment at Punishole. The silk-worm epidemics have been the principal cause of the great contraction of the silk industry within a very few years both in Midnapore and in Bankura, and as both districts still contain large numbers of people who depended at one time on sericulture but who have now taken to other pursuits, the resuscitation of the silk industry in these two districts, if taken in hand within a few years, is not such a difficult matter to accomplish.

Rajshahi Division.

12. In Rajshahi, mulberry cultivation, cocoon-rearing, silk-spinning, and silk-weaving, are still regarded as industries of very considerable importance. To feed the European silk factories cocoons are now imported from the neighbouring district of Maldah, as the local produce is found insufficient for local demands. The various sericultural industries in this district are carried on chiefly within the jurisdiction of Charghat, Puthiya, Bagmara, Panchupur and Fanar *thanas*. Within the jurisdiction of Godagari, Boalia, Lalpur and Nattor *thanas*, the industries are of less importance. In the remaining five *thanas* of the district, sericulture is not carried on. The system of taking cocoons and yarns to *hâts* prevails in the district of Rajshahi, Maldah and Bogra. In Bagmara *thana* there are fifteen of these *hâts*, of which the principal are those of Taherpur, Ekdala and Mohanganj. In Panchupur *thana* there is Suktigachi *hât* and in Tanore *thana* the *hâts* are at Kesur, Jahanabad, Raighati and Dhorsa. In Boalia *thana* there are five *hâts:* Talaimari, Binodpur, Parila, Godagari and Kharkhari. The *hât* system of buying and selling cocoons and yarns does not appear to exist in Charghat, Lalpur and Puthiya. European factories do not make use of the *hâts* in obtaining supplies of cocoons but depend in this matter on their agents or *paikars*, the cocoons not bought by the filature *paikars* going to *hâts* for sale to native filatures. Weavers sometimes go in quest of yarns to the spinning centres or villages instead of to the *hâts*. The chief centre of spinning and weaving in this district is Mirganj in *thana* Charghat. The principal village of this centre, where the best *matká* silks are woven, is Dákrá. Mirganj *matkás* or Dákrá *matkás* are well known even in the Calcutta market. The principal trade centre for yarns and fabrics produced in this district is a portion of the sadar station (Rampur Boalia), known as Resampati.

13. In Bogra, mulberry is grown only in the western portion of the district in a few villages surrounding the sadar station. The mulberry bush is considered unsuitable for the portion of the district east of the Karotoya, known as Pali, while the western tract, called Barind, is considered suitable. Barind is a part of the ancient province of Barendra, which included the district of Rajshahi. This tract is distinguished by the reddish and sticky appearance and the hardness of the soil. The tract known as Pali is alluvial, consisting of loose, sandy soil, which is considered specially adapted for the castor oil plant. Hence the rearing of *Endi* or *Eri* silk-worms (the *Attacus Ricini*) is carried on chiefly in the Pali tract, while mulberry silk-rearing is confined to a portion of the Barind. Mulberry silk-rearing was in a flourishing condition when there were some European factories in this district. The last of these, viz., the one at Nowdapara, about 3 miles away from Bogra town on the western bank of the Karotoya, ceased working about 30 years ago. It is said, there had been a European factory at Kharna and another at Sajapur long before this time. At present the decayed industry of Bogra depends entirely on the neighbouring district of Rajshahi, where cocoons and yarns produced in Bogra are sold, mostly at the *hât* at Tahirpur.

Bhagalpur Division.

14. In Maldah, cocoon-rearing and silk-spinning are carried on more or less extensively throughout the district; while silk-weaving is carried on at Shibganj, 24 miles from the sadar station, at Shahpur near Bholahat, where there is a silk factory belonging to the French Company, at Sajapur near the ruins of Gour, and at old Maldah, which is 4 miles from the sadar station. The silk industry of Maldah has slowly but steadily improved during the last decade, and the Census figures show 43,498 persons as being dependent on this industry in 1901 against 42,896 in 1891, but the development, as in the case of Murshidabad, Rajshahi and Birbhum has been mainly in the department of weaving.

15. Mulberry silk-rearing is a very important industry in the districts of Murshidabad, Rajshahi and Maldah. In the districts of Midnapore and Birbhum, it is also an industry of some consequence. In Bankura the silk-weaving industry still holds its own, though cocoon-rearing has dwindled down into insignificance. In the districts of Nadia, Howrah and Bogra, cocoon-rearing is carried on only in a few villages, while in the districts of Hooghly, Burdwan and 24-Parganas only a vestige of the industry is left.

16. Rangpur, Dinajpur, Purnea and Bhagalpur were recognised in the eighteenth century among the mulberry silk-producing districts of Bengal. Patna produced better silks than Murshidabad in the middle of the seventeenth century.* In those days Santipore also ranked with Maldah and Cossimbazar as silk-weaving centres.†

CHAPTER II.

Mulberry and Mulberry-Growers.

No reliance can be placed on the figures furnished by the different districts as to the acreage under mulberry in Bengal. The Agricultural Statistics of the Lower Provinces of Bengal and the Season and Crop Reports of Bengal published by the Department of Land Records and Agriculture do not take separate cognizance of this crop. The most recent figures that I could lay my hands on are those furnished by a Note on the Outturn of the *Rabi* Crops in Bengal for 1895-96, prepared by the Department of Land Records and Agriculture. These put side by side with the figures obtained from the Census Report

---

* *Vide* Mr. C. R. Wilson's brochure, entitled "Reports and Letters concerning the Company's Affairs in Bengal, 1661 to 1685":—"There are better Taffaties made at Pattana than Casumbazar, which are sold from 9 to 10 as. the long yard, but no great quantities, but if followed a good quantitie might be procured."

† *Vide* Geoghegan's "Silk in India":—"The trade of the East India Company in Indian silk was, however, inconsiderable till about the middle of the last century. At that time the cultivation of the domesticated kinds of silk-worms seems to have prevailed in very much the same regions of Bengal proper as at the present day. It was to be found in the districts of Rangpur, Dinajpur, Purnea (these two including what is now Maldah), Rajshahi, Murshidabad, Birbhum, and parts of Hooghly, Midnapore and Howrah" (page 2, para. 6).

"At the Cossimbazar, Maldah and Santipore factories, silk goods were manufactured" (page 14, para. 29).

of 1891 relating to the number of mulberry-growers and cocoon-rearers give the results tabulated here:—

District.	Area under mulberry.	Number of mulberry and cocoon growers.	Acreage per individual.
1	2	3	4
	Acres.		Acres.
Birbhum	2,000	8,249	$\frac{1}{4}$
Bankura	200	978	$\frac{1}{5}$
Midnapore	18,500	3,566	5
Hooghly	200	83	2
Murshidabad	62,900	31,698	2
Rajshahi	800	8,793	$\frac{1}{11}$
Maldah	50,000	38,433	$1\frac{1}{3}$
Total ...	134,600	91,800	$1\frac{1}{2}$

18. Allowing four individuals per family the above table gives 6 acres of mulberry as the average possession of each family of mulberry-grower and cocoon-rearer. This is far too excessive an estimate. To the above table must be added a few hundred acres of mulberry for the districts of Bogra, Nadia, Howrah, Burdwan and 24-Parganas. The census figures for 1891 and also for 1901 for silk-worm-rearers and cocoon-gatherers for these and probably other districts are too low, and the actual number of mulberry-growers and cocoon-rearers must be over 100,000 (*vide* Tables A and B in Part III). Some of these are accustomed to call themselves cultivators and many of them are mainly cultivators, though they grow mulberry or rear cocoons also. This would account for there being more mulberry land than the census figures for mulberry-growers and cocoon-rearers would warrant one to expect. The estimates given in the above table of mulberry land in Maldah, Midnapore and Murshidabad are, however, far too high, 50,000 acres of land shown against Maldah would produce 15,000,000 maunds of mulberry leaf per annum, raising 750,000 maunds of cocoons. The district report or monograph on silk fabrics, dated the 1st May 1899, estimates the annual produce of cocoons in Maldah at 70,000 maunds only—a quantity which would go to produce about 4,000 maunds of silk. This is a good approximation, and it agrees with my own estimate. The produce of native spinning establishments is about 2,000 maunds per annum (*vide* page 215 of Hand-book of Sericulture), and of the European filatures about 1,600 maunds. The figures of export of raw silk from Maldah in Table P (Part III) afford no reliable guide as to the production of silk in the European filatures of Maldah, as most of it is sent through the Sardah factory (Rajshahi) to Calcutta. A few thousand maunds of Maldah cocoons also find their way to Rajshahi and Birbhum, which would make perhaps another 400 maunds of silk. This total of 4,000 maunds of raw silk could be produced out of 5,000 acres of mulberry. But, as a matter of fact, the silk-worm epidemics and the fly-parasite make only a third of the cocoon crops successful, and the crop of cocoons actually obtained is probably derived from three times as much mulberry land as would be required if there were no failures. Fifteen thousand to twenty thousand acres of mulberry is perhaps a closer approximation than 50,000 acres for Maldah. This also gives $\frac{1}{2}$ an acre per individual or 2 acres per family as the average possession of mulberry land, which is a fairer estimate than 6 acres per family. For Murshidabad, the district monograph considers 50,000 *bighas* (about 16,000 acres) as too high an estimate, and I have no hesitation in discarding the figures given in the above table (62,900 acres) and adopting 16,000 acres as a closer approximation for this district. Ten thousand acres for Midnapore also is nearer the mark than eighteen thousand acres. So, while some addition would have to be made to the above tables on account of those silk districts for which no returns for the mulberry crop have been furnished and also on account of some mulberry-growers and cocoon-rearers being regarded as cultivators or persons belonging to other professions or trades, a considerable deduction must be made on account of exaggerated estimates for Maldah,

Murshidabad and Midnapore. Instead of 134,600 acres, I would estimate the total quantity of mulberry land in Bengal at the present time at only 60,000 acres. Monsieur Natalis Rondot, the greatest authority on sericultural statistics, estimates the annual production of raw silk in India at 625,000 kilogrammes. This quantity of raw silk would be produced from about 12,000,000 kilogrammes of green cocoons. Now, assuming there were no epidemics and no loss, this quantity of cocoons could be raised with 6,000,000 maunds of mulberry leaf (one maund producing 2 seers of green cocoons). Six million maunds of mulberry is the normal produce of 20,000 acres of land. I have already said that silk-worm epidemics and the fly-parasite make only about a third of the cocoon crops successful. The actual acreage of mulberry that produces the outturn alluded to is, therefore, about 60,000 instead of 20,000, even on the assumption of the whole of the estimated production of raw silk being from Bengal, which is not quite the case.

19. In the Census Report for 1891 the number of mulberry-growers in Bengal has been put down at 12,004. The small figures shown against some of the districts, *e.g.*, 5 males and 5 females for Murshidabad, evidence conclusively that the number is meant to include only those who subsist entirely on mulberry-growing. The Census Tables for 1901 ignore mulberry-growers as a special class.

20. Many high-caste men and men holding other occupations in the silk districts of Bengal have plots of mulberry which cocoon-rearers resort to when their own supply falls short. Every cocoon-rearer has his own mulberry field which he uses for rearing silk-worms, and only when his own supply happens to fall short at the very last, that he runs to non-cocoon-growers who have mulberry land. His own mulberry costs him about 4 annas a maund, but he has to pay as much as Rs. 4 or Rs. 5 a maund sometimes for what he buys from mulberry-growers. As his needs at the last are very pressing, he willingly pays the high price for it, or pledges, by handing over a token (usually a blade of grass), to the mulberry-grower, to pay the price demanded as soon as his crop is ripe. Sometimes the cocoon-rearer cannot redeem his pledge and, as a rule, the mulberry-grower does not press for payment when the cocoon-rearer loses his worms at the last through some epidemic. But, on the whole, the mulberry-grower gets unusually high prices for his crops, and a *bigha* of mulberry in a silk district is considered a little fortune. If the number of mulberry cocoon-rearers is estimated at 80,000 (*vide* Table A) in Bengal, the total number of mulberry-growers, including cocoon-rearers and others, must be over 100,000, representing about 25,000 families. The census figures for 1901 work up to a lower figure, viz., 55,256 inclusive of dependents. The census figures for silk-worm-rearers and cocoon-gatherers are evidently too low (*vide* page 68), and the number of cocoon-rearers and mulberry-growers in Bengal must be about 100,000. Many of these would call themselves only cultivators, and they would thus be excluded from the tables referring to the silk industry. The social position of mulberry-growers who carry on no other profession is higher than that of cocoon-rearers, spinners or weavers. The social position of mulberry-growers, who follow other professions and only add mulberry-growing to their ordinary avocations, is determined by their principal profession. A zemindar or a silk factor may derive part of his income by sale of mulberry, but he would not be recognized as a mulberry-grower. A cocoon-rearer with 2 or 3 *bighas* of mulberry is not necessarily a more substantial man than one who owns only 2 or 3 *bighas* of mulberry but does no cocoon-rearing. Cocoon-rearing may or may not be remunerative, as the silk-worm epidemics make the industry a most precarious one; but mulberry-growing is scarcely attended with any risk. For miles and miles it is known, so and so have mulberry land, and even if one among a hundred cocoon-rearers within this tract makes a miscalculation and finds at the end that his home leaf will not suffice, the few mulberry-growers would have every time a crowd of persons offering to buy his mulberry, one man one load, another two, another four, and so on. It is only when silk-worm epidemics do very great havoc that the loss of cocoon-rearers is generally shared by the comparatively few mulberry-growers also. But as the latter can better afford to lose occasionally, mulberry-growing is regarded as a safe and profitable industry. The average rental of mulberry land is about Rs. 10 per acre per annum. There are some mulberry lands,

even in the district of Maldah (where the highest rents are paid), which are rented at 6 annas to 8 annas per *bigha, i.e.*, Rs. 1-2 to Rs. 1-10 per acre per annum. But in the principal *joars* or cocoon-rearing centres, the rent is sometimes as high as Rs. 12 or Rs. 15 per *bigha* or about Rs. 40 per acre per annum. The average purchase value of mulberry land is about Rs. 100 per acre; but I have known an acre of mulberry fetching as much as Rs. 300. Each acre produces about 300 maunds of mulberry leaf per annum, inclusive of stalks, which are cut with the leaves and given to silk-worms. If the mulberry-grower realizes an average price of Re. 1 per maund for his crop, and spends as much as Rs. 150 per acre in cultivation, &c., even then he can secure a clear profit of Rs. 150 per acre per annum. This is considered a fair estimate of profit in the silk districts for mulberry-growing as distinguished from cocoon-rearing.

21. As a rule, mulberry is cut four times a year. In Bogra and in parts of Rajshahi, leaves are stripped from the stalks twice and the stalks with leaves cut twice. In Midnapore the bushes are allowed to grow in size for two or three years and leaves only are stripped.

22. Two kinds of mulberry are recognized in the silk districts, the *kajli* or *bara tunt*, and *pheti* or *chhota tunt*. Botanically there is no difference between the two and they all come under *Morus alba*, variety Indica. The former has whole (*ovate-lanceolate*) leaves and the latter split (*palmate*) leaves. The leaves of the former are also thicker and slightly rougher. The difference is entirely due to the difference of soil. Stony soils, such as occur in parts of Birbhum and Midnapore, produce the whole-leaved variety. Stiff clay has also a tendency to make a palmate-leaved stock to be converted into the lanceolate type. Sandy soils produce palmate and lighter coloured leaves. The *pheti* variety is better suited for rearing the *chhotapalu* variety of silk-worms, and the *kajli* variety for the *barapalu* variety. The *nistari* variety is reared indifferently on both varieties.

23. A detailed description of the Bengal system of mulberry cultivation is given in Part I, Chapter II, of the Hand-book of Sericulture, and the subject of the present Monograph does not admit of the reproduction of that chapter here.

24. Before concluding this chapter, however, it should be noted that various kinds of mulberry are found wild throughout the Himalayas at an altitude of between 500 to 4,000 feet above the level of the sea, and that there are references in old Sanskrit literature to sericulture having been carried on in ancient times by certain mountain tribes, among whom Paundrakas are specially mentioned in the Institutes of Manu. The recognized silk-worm-rearing castes of Bengal still call themselves Pundás, and they probably came originally from the hilly regions of the Himalayas, where the mulberry grows wild. The western portion of the Himalayas, from Kashmir to Kumayun, the climate of which is less damp than that of the eastern portion, is still to be regarded as more naturally suited for sericulture than any other part of India. In a paper published by Government some years ago on "The Genesis of the Silk-worm," I endeavoured to show that the sericultural industry of India is traceable not to China but to the Himalayan country; that it travelled not from north-east to south-west but from north-west to south-east. Perhaps one more fact, culled from ecclesiastical history, will vividly bring into prominence the importance attached to the silk-weaving industry in the north-western corner of India in the first century of our era. The first Indian Bishop (Agæus) from whom "all Persia, Assyria, Armenia and Media, the regions about Babylon, Huz and Gala, to the borders of India, and as far as Gog and Magog (the country north of the Caucasus), received the priesthood" was "a weaver of silk clothing."—(The Syrian Churches and Gospels by Etheridge, p. 18.)

CHAPTER III.

Cocoon-rearing and cocoon-rearers.

The varieties of mulberry silk-worms reared in Bengal are: (1) the *Nistari* or *Madrasi* (*Bombyx crœsi*), which is suitable for the warm and rainy seasons, (2) the *Chhota-palu* or *deshi* (*Bombyx fortunatus*), suitable for the cold season, (3) the *Barapalu* (*Bombyx textor*), which is an annual variety, of which the egg-stage continues for 10 months instead of 8 to 16 days as in the case of the

Chhota-palu and the *Nistari*, and (4) the *Cheena-palu* (*Bombyx sinensis*), which is reared chiefly in the Tamluk subdivision of Midnapore. The *Bara-palu* is reared in the spring (February and March) in parts of Murshidabad (near Jangipur and Kandi), in Birbhum, and in Midnapore. The Midnapore *Bara-palu* produces indifferently white, greenish, salmon-coloured and bright yellow cocoons The *Bara-palu* cocoons of Murshidabad and Birbhum are a select class of beautiful white cocoons, which yield the yarn which is in high demand among the best weavers. What is called *dhali* (white) silk is made out of thread spun from white *Bara-palu* cocoons. There is another class of polyvoltine *dhali* cocoons in Midnapore, called *bulu* (evidently corruption of 'blue'), the colour of which is somewhat greenish and not silvery white as is the colour of *Bara-palu* silk. These *bulu* cocoons were originally selected out of *Nistari* and *Cheena* varieties, light-coloured cocoons often occurring among these species. The *Bara-palu* silk goes almost entirely to feed the native looms, and there is neither supply nor demand for this in the European factories at the present time. It is curious how this superior staple has come to be neglected by European traders, while it was this that chiefly attracted the early traders from Europe. The three kinds of Native reeled silk mentioned in Mr. C. R. Wilson's little brochure, entitled Reports and Letters concerning the Company's Affairs in Bengal, 1661-1685, are *putta*, *puttany*, and *dolleria*. *Putta* is evidently derived from Sanskrit *patta* (silk), and yellow cocoons and silks are still called *pat* in some parts of Bengal and Assam. A common saying among cocoon-rearers is "*Late pate challish din*," *i.e.*, it takes forty days for yellow cocoons to form from the time of the moth's piercing the seed cocoons to the time of the new cocoons being formed. *Puttany** as explained in Mr. Wilson's brochure, was a term applied to fine reeled silk. *Dolleria* must be what is now called *Dhali* silk or *Bara-palu* silk. The very first reference preserved for us of transactions in silk by the East India Company refers also to *Dhali* silk. Geoghegan alludes to this in the following lines:—

"Thus under date 18th and 19th November 1679, he (the Chief of the factory at Fort St. George) writes:—'White silk bought at Serpore and tannee (thani?) silk examined; to be packed with coarse silk ropes, which may be sold in England at good profit'" (page 2, para. 3).

25. Later on the *Bara-palu* silk was largely exported by the East India Company from the Cossimbazar circle. "The first kind," says Geoghegan, "was the large or annual worm (*B. textor*), yielding its yearly supply in March, its silk being of a high quality. This worm predominated in the Cossimbazar circle, where it yielded the greater part of the March crop of silk, but was found also in Huripal, Jangypore, Radnagore, and Sonamukhi. The Jungypore Resident in 1819 complains of the cultivation of this worm having become extremely precarious and uncertain, and attributes this to degeneracy in the stock" (page 15, para. 31).

26. For quantity or proportion of silk, the *Chhota-palu* (*B. fortunatus*) ranks next to the *Bara-palu*, though the fibre of *Nistari* is softer and finer. The *Nistari* (*B. crœsi*) is oftener reared than the other varieties, but the cocoons yield a smaller proportion of silk. The respective qualities of the three principal kinds of Bengal cocoons for textile purposes may be best ascertained from the following figures:—

	Bara-palu.	Chhota-palu.	Nistari.
(1) Average length of fibre in a cocoon in metres ...	270	215	210
(2) Weight of unreelable portion in each cocoon in millegrammes	20	16	16½
(3) Weight of reelable silk in each cocoon in millegrammes	60	45	36
(4) Proportion of reelable silk in the fresh cocoon per cent.	8	7¼	6
(5) Diameter of fibre (*bave*) in millemetres	16½	20⅓	20
(6) Average weight of test skeins of fibre (*bave*) 476 metres long, in deniers	2⅓	2	1⅗
(7) Tenacity of fibre (*bave*) in grammes	6⅓	6⅕	4
(8) Percentage of elasticity of *bave* ...	16	12½	12
(9) Percentage of loss in weight due to "boiling off"	24	30	25

27. The above figures are most convincing with regard to the high intrinsic merit of the *Bara-palu* cocoon and silk as compared with the other two ordinary

* See also paragraph 85 of Geoghegan's "Silk in India." The *chasas* or rearers of the silk-worm wind off the cocoons in earthen basins (with the aid of cowdung as fuel instead of wood) upon the common Bengal *nuttahs* or reels made of bamboo, the thread so reeled being called *putney*.

varieties. Picked *Bara-palu* cocoons may yield as much as 14 per cent. of silk; but the average actually obtained specially in Midnapore, where the annual worms are more largely reared than anywhere else, is much smaller, about 7 per cent. In Midnapore, the *Chhota-palu* or *deshi*, *Nistari* or *Madrasi* and *Cheena*, cocoons are small, and they yield much smaller proportions of silk than they do in the northern districts. The yield of silk obtained from the other three varieties of cocoons in Midnapore are—

Chhota-palu	... ...	5½ to 6¼ per cent.
Nistari	... ...	5 to 6¼ „
Cheena	... ...	5¼ to 6¼ „

28. Usually three or four crops of cocoons are reared during the year out of eight that are possible, viz., three of *Nistari* and one of *Chhota-palu*. There are exceptions to this rule, *e g.*, in Bogra the *Chhota-palu* is the principal crop and in Midnapore the *Nistari*. It is not ordinarily feasible to take all the eight crops though the polyvoltine silk-worms, *Nistari*, *Chhota-palu* and *Cheena*, breed eight times in the year. The parasitic fly (*Trycolyga Bombycis*) would make silk-rearing impossible if all the crops were taken in the same locality. The practice therefore prevails of silk-worms being reared during one *bund* and mulberry being attended to during the next, when in some distant *joars* (silk-rearing centres) silk-worms would be reared. The seed is thus perpetually kept up one *bund* in one *joar* and another *bund* in another, and cocoon-rearers of one *joar* go to a distant *joar* for seed, and they walk sometimes 60 or 80 miles before they light upon good seed. There are, however, some recognised seed-rearing *joars*, where, at particular seasons, cocoon-rearers resort to, in preference to others. Thus, there are the Bachra and Bhattamati *joars* in Murshidabad, the Baralpar *joar* in Rajshahi, the Khanna *joar* in Bogra, Dhantala Ganipur *joar* in Malda, and Rarh *joar* in Birbhum, where thousands of cocoon-rearers can be seen going to in quest of good seed. Exchange of seed is also recognised as beneficial to the health of silk-worms. In Malda, Rajshahi and Bogra, the practice prevails of going to *hâts* for seed. But it is considered safer to go to the proper *joar* and buy seed, after seeing the worms ripening in a faultless manner. In Murshidabad, the principal cocoon-rearing *bunds*, or seasons, are Aghrani (November), Chaitra (March), and Srabani (July); while the three principal *bunds* in Malda are Kartika (October), Baishakhy (May) and Bhadruria (August). In parts of Rajshahi, the Maghi (January) *bund* is of the first importance, as at the end of this *bund* cocoon-rearers from Murshidabad, &c., come to Rajshahi for Nistari *sunch* (seed-cocoons); while the Ashwinè (September) *bund*, for *Chhoto-palus*, is of considerable importance for parts of Birbhum and for Bogra, whence *Chhoto-palu* seed for the early November *bund* is taken to other districts. From June to September two crops are usually taken in succession: one of which is more important than the other. The parasitic fly does the second crop a great deal of harm, but the growth of mulberry at this time of the year being very vigorous it pays taking a second crop.

29. The following estimate of production of cocoons in the different districts is somewhat conjectural, but is based on the suppositions (1) that an average of eight maunds of cocoons are raised per family of cocoon-rearers, or two maunds per individual per annum; and (2) that the census figures for cocoon-rearers are somewhat low, persons belonging to other professions, but doing cocoon-rearing also, not being generally included in the census figures for cocoon-rearers:—

District.		Produce of green cocoons. Mds.
Burdwan	... ...	20
Birbhum	... ...	16,000
Bankura	... ...	2,000
Midnapore	... ...	37,000
Hooghly	... ...	200
Howrah	... ...	100
24-Parganas	... ...	20
Nadia	... ...	200
Murshidabad	... ...	72,000
Rajshahi	... ...	18,000
Bogra	... ...	400
Malda	... ...	70,000
	Total ...	215,940
	Or, roughly speaking ...	220,000

30. The above quantity would produce about 12,000 maunds of raw-silk (filature-reeled and *Khamru*), of which about 5,000 to 6,000 maunds are used in the country looms. Besides raw-silk, however, inferior silks (*Tasar*, and *Endi*) and a great deal of 'waste,'—altogether not less than 12,000 maunds of Bengal silk, are used in India for weaving purposes. The averages during the last decade have been somewhat higher, and the estimate is rather too cautious than liberal.

31. Cocoon-rearing is done in almost the same way all over Bengal, the variations in methods and appliances being insignificant. Mud-walled houses are the best for rearing worms, but those who cannot afford such houses do the rearing in mat-walled houses. The seed cocoons are placed, thinly spread out, on *dalas*, or flat bamboo trays, which in some districts are circular and in others square or oblong. In eight or nine days in the hot weather, and in 15 or 16 days in the cold weather, the moths come out, and they remain paired for the greater part of the day: that is, until they are separated in the afternoon. Unless they are separated the males do not allow the females to lay eggs uninterruptedly. The males are known from their smaller size and their constant fluttering of wings. After being separated, the males are thrown away and the females left to lay eggs on the *dala*. In the case of the *Bara-palu*, the female moths are transferred to a piece of rag, and they deposit their eggs there. Pieces of rag with eggs adhering to them by means of a natural gum are folded up and kept inside a *handi*, or earthen vessel, the mouth of which is closed by means of an earthen cover and sealed with mud. If the moths cut out of the *Bara-palu* cocoons for three or four days successively, three or four pieces of rag with eggs are obtained. The vessel in which they are kept is of sufficient size to prevent asphyxiation of the eggs. It is kept suspended from the roof in a cool part of the house. The moths finish depositing the eggs in about 24 hours, and on the 3rd or 4th day the female moths are thrown away. In the case of the polyvoltine silk-worms (*Nistari*, *Chhoto-palu*, and *Cheena-palu*), the eggs are left on the *dalas* on which they are laid, and allowed to hatch there, the hatching taking place in eight to nine days in the hottest weather, and in 16 or 18 days in the coldest. The *Bara-palu* eggs do not hatch till next spring, the eggs remaining in the *handi* from the end of March to the end of January, *i.e.*, when the weather begins to get warm. The fixed day for opening the *handi* is the *Sripanchami*, or *Saraswati Puja* day. The hatching of *Bara palu* eggs does not take place so evenly and completely as that of the polyvoltine silk-worm eggs. It goes on for 8, 10, or 12 days, and the cocoons afterwards go on forming for a similar period. This is a great disadvantage, and when there is any epidemic among the worms ripening first, the late worms fall a complete victim to it. After the worms have hatched out, the same system of rearing is followed in the case of every kind of mulberry silk-worm. Tender leaves of mulberry are cut up very fine and sprinkled over the newly-hatched worms. Three or four hours afterwards the worms are removed to another *dala* with the help of a little brush made with grass or feathers. The worms with the refuse leaves are then made into a neat flat circle or *châki* (disc) of uniform depth of about $\frac{1}{12}$th of an inch, and fresh leaf, finely cut up, is sprinkled over this *châki*. Feeding is done at 5 or 6 A.M., 10 A.M., 3 P.M. and 8 or 9 P.M. Sometimes, specially in the wet season, only three feeds are given. In the dry season five feeds are sometimes given in the early stages of the worms. Regularity of feeding is regarded as very essential. The refuse leaf is cleaned once in four or five days, *i.e.*, a day before and a day after each moulting period. The moulting period lasts each time from 20 hours in the hot weather to 48 hours in the coldest weather, when the worms are left without food and untouched. Feeding is recommenced when the worms are well out of the moult. The special art in rearing silk-worms consists in stopping feeding at the right time and recommencing feeding at the right time. One often sees an old and experienced woman being called in at these critical periods to judge whether feeding should be stopped or whether feeding should be recommenced. Women do most of the work in connection with the rearing-house, while men look after the mulberry, cut and bring it home for the silk-worms, and assist the women at feeding and cleaning. After the fourth moult the worms become very voracious, but the regular three or four feeds are adhered to, and it is not considered right to give extra feeds at this last stage. Three to nine days intervene between moult to moult

according as the season is warm or cold, and the last stage before the worms make their cocoons lasts from five to twelve days according to the season. *Bara-palus* eat for four or five days more and *Chhota-palus* two days more than the *Nistaris*, and the *Nistaris* two days more than the *Cheena-palus*, before they commence making cocoons. So, altogether from the time the worms hatch out of the eggs to the time they begin making cocoons, the *Nistari* silk-worms have constant care bestowed on them for 20 days in the hottest weather and 55 days in the coldest weather; the *Chhota-palus* 22 days in the hottest weather and 57 days in the coldest weather; and the *Cheena-palus* for 18 days in the hottest weather and 53 days in the coldest weather, and the *Bara-palus* (which are reared only once a year in the spring) for 30 days. When ready for spinning the silk-worms cease eating, look about restlessly, spit out silk-fibre and appear translucent. They are then picked and placed on *chandrakies*, —*called also talias, chánches* or *fingás* (Fig. 1).

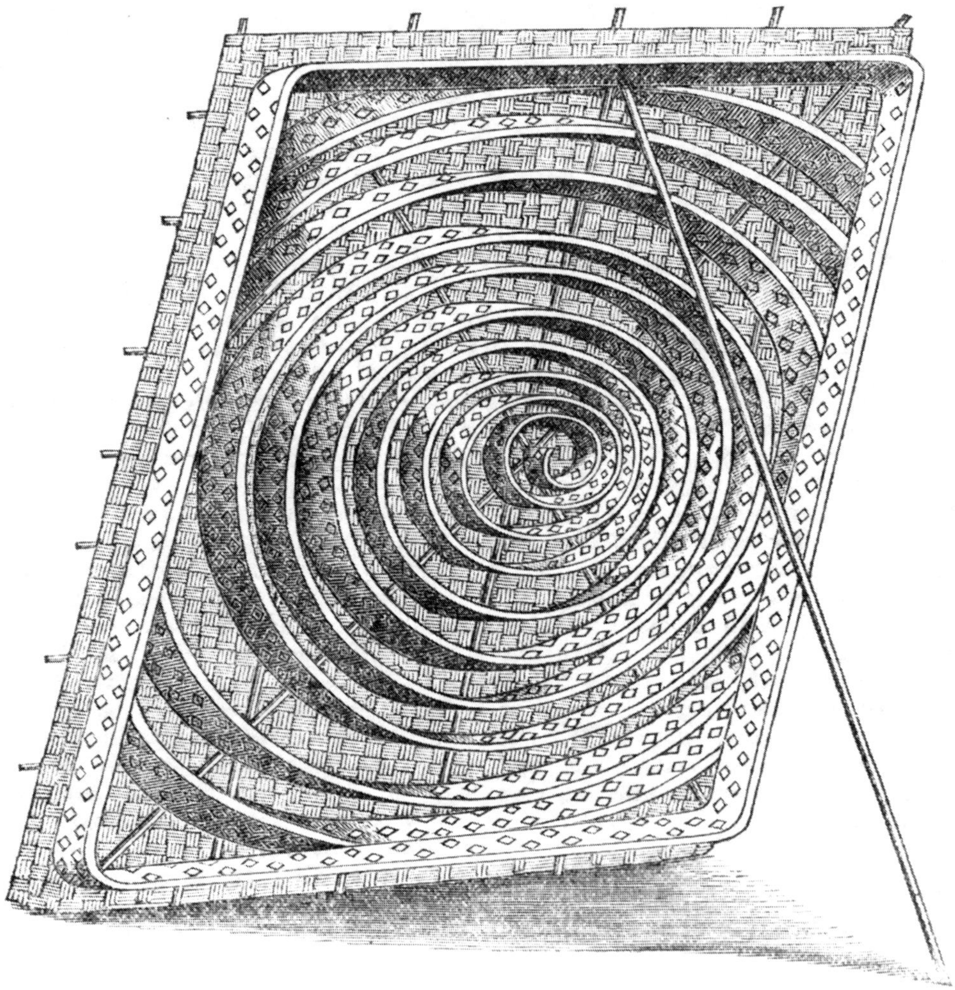

Fig. 1—Chandraki or spinning mat.

32. The spinning of cocoons on these bamboo screens is finished in two days in the hot weather and four days in the cold. The screens are put out in the morning sun, and in the cold weather fire is kept in the room at night to hasten spinning. The most insidious and general of all the silk-worm epidemics, viz., *Pebrine*, requires to develop for 30 days before it proves fatal to the silk-worm. So when the seed is badly diseased the worms die off simultaneously in the cold weather, sometime after all the care has been bestowed on the worms. In the case of the *Bara-palu* the death from *Pebrine* (when diseased seed is used) taking place invariably on the very day of ripening, the event appears most weird and ghastly; and hence there is a strong objection on superstitious ground against rearing the *Bara-palu*. Even in the case of

the other silk-worms the phenomena connected with the epidemics are at times so unexpected and inexplicable to the cultivator that he attributes them to supernatural agencies. The silk-worm rearer feels he is surrounded at all times by *devatás* and hobgoblins, and he is a most superstitious and usually a most unreasonable person to deal with. At one time, I remember, in connection with the experiments with which I was entrusted, a belief spread among a number of villagers in Malda that the microscope caused cholera. I traced the origin of this belief to a Malda boy who had been learning to use the miscroscope having died of cholera. Another cocoon-rearer whom I trained in connection with these experiments lost two wives in succession, and he was shunned for a long time as a man who was under a curse for using sulphur for fumigating his rearing-house and appliances. Burning of sulphur is considered an act of desecration by the *Pundas* of Malda, who believe this substance to be some kind of uterine discharge of the goddess Bhagabati. Cocoon-rearers have been fast giving up their superstitions since they have come to recognise the benefit of these experiments. They see that all those trained men who ignore the old superstitious rules, get nevertheless very good crops. These old rules, which are observed during rearing, consist in, not shaving, not giving clothes to the washerman, not eating curries in which oil, turmeric and chillies have been used, not anointing the body with oil, not wearing shoes, keeping strangers out, preventing owls from flying over the rearing-house, abstaining from conjugal association, giving wrong information about the progress of the worms,* &c.

33. The hereditary silk-worm-rearing caste of Bengal is known as the Punda caste, who live mainly in Malda, but who are also found in parts of Murshidabad and Rajshahi. They are the best, the most intelligent, and the most prosperous of all cocoon-rearers. Other castes have also taken to cocoon-rearing, and Muhammadans, though very slovenly in their work, form the largest proportion of cocoon-rearers in almost all the districts, specially in Rajshahi, Bogra and Midnapore. Cocoon-rearers are sometimes called *tuntias*, *tuntia-kaibartas*, *tuntia-chashas*, *tunt* being the Bengali word for mulberry, and *kaibartas* and *chashas* being a generic name for cultivators. The total number of cocoon-rearers in Bengal (including those who add cocoon-rearing to other professions) is about 90,000. All the lower castes among Hindus rear silk-worms, and it is only the highest castes, viz., Brahmans and Kayasthas that consider it derogatory to rear cocoons. Cocoon-rearers are considered higher up in the social ladder than most cultivators, and, as a rule, they employ labourers of other professions for ploughing, digging and other works, which are recognised as menial. They are not, however, at the present time more prosperous than other cultivators, and their somewhat superior status implies past prosperity rather than present affluence. They are perhaps heavier in debt than other cultivators, and their struggle for life is made more poignant on account of their being still recognised as belonging to the middle rather than the lower classes of society. A cocoon-rearer, burdened as he is with debts, usually wears shoes or slippers, and when he goes out takes a *chaddar* to cover his body. The cocoon-rearer, in spite of the silk-worm epidemics, actually handles more coin at times than the ordinary cultivator ever gets the opportunity of doing. The average quantity of silk-worms reared by a family of cocoon-rearers is three *gharas*, or 48 trays, each tray being about 5 feet in diameter. If two out of his four cocoon crops are a decided success, he may succeed in selling them both for seed. Every cocoon-rearer has this chance, and many get the chance a dozen times during their life. Three *gharas* of silk-worms turning out successful, yield an average quantity of from 100 to 150 *kahans* of cocoons according to the season, the larger quantity in the cold weather when worms are kept thicker on *dalas*. Each *kahan* (=1,280) of good cocoons selling for seed may fetch Rs. 2, and the two successful crops in the year may bring to the cocoon-rearer as much ready money as Rs. 400 to Rs. 600, the produce of only 2 acres of mulberry. If he and the members of his family work in the mulberry field and in the rearing-house, as they nearly always do, his outgoings are very little. But, as a rule, the cocoon-rearer sells his 100 *kahans*

---

* The following wrong information contained in the District Monograph from Bankura was probably supplied by a cocoon-rearer, when he had cocoons in his house:—The *Tutias* of this district generally purchase cocoons for reproduction from men of eastern districts such as Dacca and Pabna. Advances are given to these men for supplying the cocoons at the proper seasons of the year." No cocoon-rearing is done in Dacca or Pabna. The superstition that lying is beneficial for a trade occurs also among those castes of Calcutta who deal in dyes and paints.

for Rs. 50, and he gets altogether about 100 *kahans* out of his four crops, expecting each time to get as much, and probably buying two or three loads of extra mulberry each time and spending Rs. 10 or Rs. 15 on mulberry alone, and the rest in paying rent and keeping himself and his family in that state of semi-respectability to which he is born. He finds it impossible to get on without incurring debt or taking to some other calling considered less respectable. The cocoon-rearer, all over Bengal, is in this struggling condition and he has been so for twenty or thirty years past. A ray of light has dawned on him in recent years, and there is a general feeling among his fellow caste men that better days are again in store for them.

34. It is needless to enter here into a description of the various silk-worm diseases and pests, as they have been fully described in the Handbook of Sericulture recently published by Government.

CHAPTER IV.

Decline of the cocoon-rearing industry and efforts at improvement.

There have been ups and downs in the cocoon-rearing industry of Bengal from the days of the East India Company, that is, the earliest days from which we have a continuous record of this industry. Epidemics among silk-worms are not a new thing in Bengal, nor are efforts at improvement in the direction of avoiding epidemics of recent growth. Mr. Atkinson, Resident of Jungypore, writing in 1796, mentions about the degeneracy of the *Bara-palu* silk-worm (see Geoghegan's "Some Account of Silk in India," page 2). In 1819 the Jungypore Resident again "complains of the cultivation of this worm having become extremely precarious and uncertain and attributes this to degeneracy in the stock" (page 15). "According to Mr. Atkinson the '*desi*' worm had also degenerated" (page 16). In 1830, in the evidence taken before the Select Committee of the House of Lords, the degeneracy of the silk-worms was distinctly asserted.

"The preponderance of authority," sums up Mr. Geoghegan, "is certainly in favour of the view that the Bengal species have degenerated ; but the subject does not seem to have been very carefully investigated, and Mr. Turnbull of Ghattal maintains that the fact of degeneracy has yet to be proved. Most of those engaged in silk manufacture assume this point and confine themselves to discussing the remedies. These are various. It seems generally admitted that the attempts to introduce exotic breeds have not of late years succeeded. It would also appear that though there has sometimes been a large mortality among silk-worms, no epizoic, such as the *Muscardine* and the *Pebrine,* which have devastated France and Italy, has as yet appeared in India. Mr. Gallois, of Midnapore, appears to think the cause of degeneracy may be in the mulberry being too long cultivated in one spot. Mr. Perrin, of Berhampore, on the other hand, extols the native mulberry cultivation as careful and judicious. Mr. Marshall urges an attempt to improve the stock by offering prizes for the best method of selection. Most authorities agree that the natives stint the worms, and Mr. Atkinson long ago saw the difficulty of dealing with this tendency on their part. Mr. Malcolm, of Ramnagar, in the Kandi subdivision of Murshidabad, maintains that the worm has been injured by being forced into too rapid reproduction of itself; that whereas 20 or 25 years ago there were but four breeds or "bunds" in the year, there are now from six to eight. It may be the worm has been forced in this direction, but I do not find that the bunds are anywhere given as less than five, even so long as 50 years ago." (Geoghegan, page 34.)

36. From the very earliest days, therefore, of European dealings in Bengal silk, the chief difficulty has been the 'degeneracy' of the silk-worms, that is, their proneness to die off from diseases. If the cocoon crop had been as certain as the jute, or the sugar-cane, or the rice crop, trade in Bengal silk would not have had those ups and downs and that continuous depression in the foreign trade during recent years. Cocoon-rearing is much more profitable than any other agricultural industry, provided the crop can be assured. The remedies suggested according to Mr. Geoghegan's summary just quoted are :—

(1) Introduction of the superior European or Chinese cocoons (Bombyx mori).
(2) Arresting the silkworm epidemics.
(3) Improvement in the system of mulberry cultivation.
(4) Better and more liberal treatment of the worms.
(5) Taking fewer "bunds" or crops.

37. All these important questions have been fully discussed in the Handbook of Sericulture, and it is unnecessary dealing with them here. An historical

sketch of all the efforts at improvement, may, however, prove interesting. Experiments have been conducted to solve all the above and other questions from the earliest days of British enterprise in Bengal, and the only improvement successfully introduced at a very early period was an improvement in reeling. The Novi pattern of reeling (the main principle of which was the crossing of threads on the same reel) was successfully introduced in 1770 by Messrs. Wiss and Robinson, "assisted by a staff of reelers and mechanics chosen from Italy and France, and provided with tools, implements and models" (Geoghegan's Report, page 3). The efforts of the Bengal Government to introduce the *B. mori* of China in 1771 and the subsequent attempts of Messrs. Frushard and Captain Kyd in the same direction, were unsuccessful. The efforts of Government in 1771 to introduce the China mulberry and a more rational system of mulberry cultivation also failed. The Hon'ble A. Ramsay, in his evidence given in 1830, speaks of the obstructiveness of the people's habits. "The Court of Directors wished the natives to use the old leaves in preference to young leaves, but the natives were averse to it, and it could never be carried into effect" (Geoghegan, page 4).

38. In 1796 Mr. Atkinson again advocated the introduction of a superior race of silk-worm and a better system of management.

39. In 1812, with the help of Dr. Roxburgh, Government initiated a plan of improvement in the method of mulberry cultivation and of rearing of silk-worms. But no important results were achieved. In 1826, the Resident of Santipore was allowed to incur an expenditure of Rs. 25,000 (sicca) in a trial of 'neez' cultivation, that is, cultivation of mulberry and rearing of worms in large nurseries with hired labour, under the direct personal supervision of the Resident.

"The experiment which was carried on till 1830 unfortunately failed entirely in producing a supply of silk, and not only so, but entailed considerable pecuniary loss, outstanding balances of a dubiously recoverable sort having been allowed to accumulate to a large extent The plan was, therefore, abandoned" (Geoghegan, page 10).

40 In 1832 the Italian "silk-worm bred at St. Helena" was imported by Government and distributed to the Residents of Boalia, Sonamukhi, Haripal, and Kumarkhali and to the Agri-Horticultural Society who had an experimental station at Akra. Two varieties of mulberry were also imported from St. Helena at the same time. Nothing came of these experiments. The transfer of the silk trade from the hands of Government to those of private companies was completed between the years 1834-37. The result of all attempts at improvement during a whole century that the silk trade was under the direct control of the Hon'ble East India Company is thus summed up by Geoghegan:—

"The only direction in which any effective improvements had been introduced was that of reeling and drying. The method of cultivating the mulberry and the kinds cultivated were in 1835 just what they were a century before. Attempts had been made to introduce new stocks of worms; but the worms introduced from China had not thriven, and in respect to their breeds, the attempts do not seem to have been made with energy enough to have warranted any expectation of success." (Geoghegan, page 27.)

41. Since Government gave up the direct control over the silk trade of the Province, experiments at improvement were conducted mainly through the Agri-Horticultural Society of India. There was an attempt to introduce the *Morus Multicaulis* variety of mulberry; there were also experiments, at crossing the indigenous varieties of silk-worms with foreign varieties and also at the introduction of the Japanese bivoltine silk-worm, conducted by Mr. Bashford, Captain Hutton and M. de Cristoferis. Mr. Bashford succeeded in producing fine cross-bred cocoons, but when he distributed his stock to native breeders, it degenerated rapidly and produced very flimsy cocoons. Captain Hutton subsequently expressed his opinion that crossing would be of no use. Captain Hutton's own conclusions from his experiments were, that the climate of Bengal was not suitable for sericulture, and that the western parts of the Himalayas were marked out by Nature herself as the best tract for carrying on sericulture to perfection. M. de Cristoferis' experiments showed that the Japanese bivoltine silk-worm soon degenerated into the polyvoltine in the climate of Bengal and produced cocoons inferior to those indigenous to Bengal, though the worms continued free from disease. An attempt to introduce sericulture in Behar, conducted in 1867 and subsequent years, also proved futile. The difficulty they had to contend with were the difficulty of getting good seed and the occurrence of sudden mortality among their worms, sweeping off apparently the

whole stock and compelling them to indent on Bengal for a fresh supply. (*vide* Geogheghan, p. 31). "In Cuttack, sericulture has been carried out an an experiment since 1877 at Government expense, under the supervision of the Executive Engineer of the Mahanadi Division." (Liotard's Memorandum on "Silk in India, 1883," p. 21.). The reference here is no doubt to the experiments of Mr. J. Cleghorn of the Public Works Department. Mr. Cleghorn's experiments were not altogether fruitless. He published his studies of the life-history of the parasitic fly, and brought to light the great destruction caused by it. He produced some valuable races of beautifully white cocoons, both annual and polyvoltine. He also claimed to have discovered a simple means of avoiding or destroying the fly-pest. But as he could not be induced to part with his secret for less than a lakh of rupees, nothing is known with regard to his method of coping with one of the chief enemies of sericulture in Bengal. The fine races of cocoons he was rearing in conjunction with the Secretary of the Agri-Horticultural Society were not given out to the world either, and Mr. Cleghorn's researches and experimonts have, therefore, left little of practical value behind.

42. Next may be mentioned the experiments of Messrs. Keighley, Blechynden and Anderson, at Ghatal and at Alipore. These were based on the supposition that M. Pasteur's system of selection of healthy 'seed,' which involved the use of very high power microscopes, was not practicable in Bengal where the peasantry, who had the management of silk-worms, was much less intelligent than the Italian or the French peasantry.

43. Side by side with these experiments conducted by Messrs. Cleghorn, Keighley and others between 1886 to 1892, Government initiated experiments with the object of introducing M. Pasteur's system among the Bengal cocoon rearers. These experiments were initiated by Sir Edward Buck, Revenue Secretary to the Government of India, at the instance of Sir Thomas Wardle, President of the Silk Association of Great Britain and Ireland. A preliminary study of the conditions prevailing in Bengal from December 1886 to March 1888, conducted by Mr. J. Wood-Mason, Superintendent of the Indian Museum, and the writer of this Monograph, left no doubt that it was the European epidemics, *Muscardine* and *Pebrine*, (which were being successfully dealt with in France and Italy), that had been doing their work of destruction among the Bengal silk-worms also. The writer of this Monograph was thereupon deputed to study the practical methods by which these silk-worm epidemics were being dealt with in Europe. The experiments were renewed by Government in August 1890 on a more solid foundation than had hitherto been possible, owing to the uncertainty that had prevailed on many points. It was demonstrated that the peasantry of Bengal were able to carry out M. Pasteur's system successfully and profitably. Not only were the principal silk-worm epidemics, *Pebrine* and *Muscardine*, dealt with in connection with these experiments, but all the diseases and pests of the silk-worm and the mulberry plant were studied and remedies capable of easy adaptation by the Bengal peasantry, devised. It may be specially mentioned that methods of avoiding *Grasserie* (which occurs in an epidemic form among Bengal silk-worms, but not among the silk-worms in Europe), and also the fly-pest, were discovered by the writer of this Monograph in connection with these experiments. The cocoon-rearers who were taught these methods no longer consider the cocoon crop uncertain and precarious, and year after year they are now getting full crops which they had never done before. As early as 24th August 1892, Mr. C. W. Marshall, Manager of the Bengal Silk Company, communicated to Government, through Messrs. Lyall, Marshall and Company, his appreciation of the results of these experiments. He wrote: "I believe Mr. Mukerji has succeeded in his work, and now rears seed which can be depended on." In his letter No. 1448A., dated the 10th September 1896, Mr. P. C. Lyon, Director of the Agricultural Department of Bengal, reporting on the conduct of these experiments to Government, gives pretty fully, not only his own views, but also the views of the principal European silk factors regarding the value of these experiments. The following extract from this report may be found interesting:—

"While Government interference does not seem to be called for to assist the trade in supplying the manufacturers of silk with the particular silk referred to by Mr. Wardle, or to maintain its quality, there appears to be no room for doubt that the operations, hitherto under the superintendence of Mr. Mukerji, have had considerable effect in eradicating disease among silk-worms, in diffusing healthy seed over the silk districts, and in thus improving the outturn and consequently the profits of silk-worm rearers. That such results will tend to popularize the silk industry among cultivators, and to revive it to a great extent in the districts in which it has fallen into disrepute, is more than probable.

"On this subject I have consulted Mr. R. A. Lyall, of Lyall, Marshall and Company, the most important firm in the silk-trade in Calcutta, and he has been kind enough to obtain for me the opinions of his agents and correspondents in the silk districts, as to the value of the work done by Mr. Mukerji and his assistants. This question has been very frequently discussed before, and Government has already on its files correspondence showing that Mr. Mukerji's opinions have often been severely criticised by experts in India, and that his work has not always been approved by them. On the other hand, Government is also aware that much of the criticism has been directed to minor details, and that in main principles there has not been much difference between Mr. Mukerji and those who have opposed him.

"As the result of my present enquiries I may quote the following views, which have been expressed on the above subject.

"Mr. H. C. Fraser, Manager of a Silk Concern in Berhampur, writes:—

" I believe that there is a future for the seed-rearing nurseries, such as that established at Kagachira in Malda by Dandadhar Das.

"'The advisability of Government aid in this direction is doubtful, and I am not prepared to speak authoritatively, but my private opinion is that, with a little encouragement, many others might be induced to follow Dandadhar's example, when it is proved to them that there is money in it, as there undoubtedly is.

"' The seed cocoons (not eggs) supplied by this man, have a good reputation, and if only a few more men were induced to go in for the same thing, trained properly and assisted at the first go-off with microscopes, &c., I feel sure that the cocoon-rearers would take to it gradually, as they said clearly that profit accrues.'

" 'Mr. T. G. Rice, Manager of the Bengal Silk Company's filature at Gonatea, writes:—

"' I am of opinion that the nurseries Mr. Mukerji has established in the different districts will eventually prove of great benefit.

"'The Kagachira nursery in Malda has now pretty firmly established its reputation, and the rearers in Malda are eager to get this seed, and, in fact, are beginning to take it from nurseries in other districts as well, in preference to the ordinary seed. This is a very hopeful sign, it will be a great point gained, and may gradually lead to the rearers adopting the scientific methods of rearing.

" I think these nurseries should be increased and encouraged as much as possible. The danger is that, before the rearers come to have confidence in the seed—this will be a matter of time—the men in charge of the nurseries may get disheartened, and may get careless with the rearing, and one or two failures of seed taken from them would ruin all that has been gained.'

" Mr. J. Fraser-Forbes, Manager for the same Company at Sarda, Rajshahi, writes:—

" Mr. Mukerji seems to be more successful in Malda than anywhere else, the rearers round about here are very conservative, and wont be convinced that there can be any good in anything new. I think if his methods were carefully carried out on a large scale, some good might result, but anything that involves extra care, or expense, is not likely to quickly find favour with Bengalis.'

"Mr. Lyall himself, after pointing out to me that the above gentlemen are practical men on the spot who thoroughly understand their business, writes:—

" From what I saw, when working the Rearing house at Alipore with Messrs. J. A. Anderson and J. C. Hodgson, I am strongly of opinion that it will not be possible to get the silk-worm rearers as a class to adopt the methods of the Silk Committee, as described in the pamphlet I gave you. They are too wedded to their ancient ways, and will not give them up.

" All that is needed is carefully-selected seed, good mulberry, careful and frequent feeding, plenty of ventilation, and extreme care as to cleanliness—all very simple, but involving a lot of care, attention and time.

"'If it is admitted that we cannot get the rearers to adopt our method, the next question is what else can be done?

'Like Mr. Fraser and Mr. Rice, I think a system of nurseries, scattered over the silk districts, would gradually effect improvement in the seed. One man, you will observe, has established a nursery in Malda, and I am told he is making it pay. Once this is known and recognised, others will follow his example. I believe this man is one of Mr. Mukerji's pupils. In Europe, silk-worm rearing is a large and profitable industry of itself, and there is no reason why it should not become so here, if the people would take it up in the right way. I do not refer to the rearers as stated above. I do not think they ever will, but men such as the man Dandadhar Das, referred to in Mr. Fraser's letter, might. How men are to be got to take it up is a matter for careful consideration.'

"I also enclose copy of a communication received by Mr. Mukerji from Mr. Fraser-Forbes, and enclosure, on the subject of the work done in the Noadapara nursery (Rajshahi).

'I am bound to add that none of gentlemen consulted think that it would be worthwhile to place Mr. Mukerji on special duty again to carry out these operations.

" We have, therefore, to consider whether it is worthwhile for Government to persevere in its efforts to stamp out silk-worm diseases, by inducing the people to rear healthy-seed, and whether the lines on which we are at present proceeding are the right ones.

"The conservatism of the silk-worm rearers is, of course, no new thing. The same spirit is encountered throughout India by all who promote agricultural improvements of any kind. And the practical lesson, which is taught by it everywhere, is the same as that indicated by Mr. Lyall. It is useless to ask them to join with us in experimenting. However certain the results may be, they will only appreciate the work when the solid results appear. We must not appeal to their intellects, but direct to their pockets.

"And it is on this ground that I would now propose to Government to maintain the work which is in progress, and to sanction a small yearly expenditure for the extension of nurseries and the practical instruction of silk-worm rearers in the various *joars*. However, opinions may differ as to the value of Mr. Mukerji's personal work; he may, at least, claim to have established three facts fairly clearly:—

" (1) that the seed produced under his instruction is a great improvement on the ordinary native seed;
" (2) that the cultivators are beginning to appreciate this and are buying increasing qualities of this seed; and
" (3) that his pupils in independent charge of private nurseries, originally started by him, are making the business pay.

" And as a deduction from these facts, I think we may reasonably hope that, if we proceeded quietly and preseveringly to open out nurseries in each of the more important *joars* (or silk-worm seed centres) to train men in each, and then leave those men in charge, we shall probably do a great deal to revive an industry which was once a source of considerable profit to Bengal, but has nearly died out in recent years.

" It seems clear that if our operations are to be confined to a more demonstration and pioneer movement in two or three isolated places, we shall never have a real chance of success. It is only by plodding steadily on, and by gradually persuading the people, in each silk centre of the practical value of the knowledge we have acquired, that we can do any good. If we stop now, the spread of knowledge will cease abruptly as the men whom we have trained will do their best to keep the monopoly of seed-rearing in their own hands, and will have no inducement to instruct others.

" The cost of the operations that I would propose will not exceed Rs. 3,000 per annum, and they can be supervised by one of the Assistant Directors of Land Records. They will take their place, in future, among the ordinary experimental operations of this Department, and their special character will disappear.

"In making these recommendations I have not been unmindful of the lengthy correspondence that has passed on the subject of these operations during the past two years, but hope that the determintion that was then expressed, to put an end to the heavy expenditure we were annually incurring on silk experiments, will not apply to the comparatively modest proposals which are now made."

44. As appendix to this report of the Director of Agriculture is published a letter, dated the 4th August 1896, from Mr. F. A. M. Dixon, silk factor of Matihar, addressed to Mr. J. Fraser-Forbes, General Manager of the Bengal Silk Company. This letter may be fully quoted here:—

"In reply to your's of 23rd ultimo, I have to state that I went out to the Noadapara nursery on the 25th July last, and again yesterday. On the first visit, I saw the worms before they had spun, and was very much taken with all I saw, and the clean way in which everything was kept. On making enquiries from the man in whose house the worms are being reared, he told me that since he had taken to Babu N. G. Mukerji's system of rearing he had not lost a single *bund*, and that although one lot had a very bad attack of *muscradine*, the Babu in charge had cured all the worms attacked, in a short time, by the use of sulphur. He spoke very highly of this new way of getting rid of this disease, and said that, had it not been for the sulphur, he would have had to throw all his worms away. He also said that great benefit had been derived from the use of sulphate of copper for disinfecting the house in which the worms were reared. Yesterday I saw the cocoons, and they were a very nice lot of *desi* ones. He told me that he had sold more than half of the 1½ maunds he had reared for seed, and was sure he would get rid of the remainder, as men were coming from long distances, now that they were beginning to know about the seed, one man having taken as much as Rs. 10 worth. He is selling the seed at 12 *puns* for the rupee. As I have said above, I was greatly taken with all I saw, and the only drawback is that a more central place was not chosen. This place is quite out of the way, and nowhere near any of the big centres where cocoons are reared For instance, it is over 25 miles away from Tahirpore, and more from the people living north of that place. It is too far for people to come and see what is being done, and return home the same day. The Babu in charge told me that the Tahirpore Raja had promised to erect a place for seed-rearing at Tahirpore this coming October, and I strongly advise the offer be taken up, and a place started there as soon as possible. Another might with advantage be built at Doorgapore, and one also a little to the north of Madarigunge I am sure that great benefits would be derived from the rearing sheds, and specially to the north, where, as you know, the rearers are a very ignorant set, and take very little pains with their worms. I feel sure that had Mr. Mukerji commenced operations to the north of this at first, instead of going to the Berhampore side (where they know more or less what they are about), rearers would not have thrown up rearing cocoons to the north in the way they have done.

"In conclusion, I would strongly recommend these rearing sheds being started to the north as soon as possible, so that the ignorant raiyats can see how things should be done. I am sure they would take to the new system at once, and be sure of good crops of better cocoons."

45. On the transfer of the writer of this Monograph to Sibpur as Agricultural Lecturer, the silk merchants of Bengal formed themselves into a Committee in 1898 to carry out the system thus initiated by Government with the help of the men trained by him, and the expenditure of the departmental grant of Rs. 3,000 has been since entrusted to this Committee. The system is slow, but it is the only sure and satisfactory way of introducing scientific methods of sericulture in Bengal, and the Committee must be prepared to work away with perseverance and confidence, starting seed-nurseries in one *joar* after another, helping trained cocoon-rearers (but not outsiders) to establish these nurseries, until all the *joars* have been supplied with centres of instruction and of supply of healthy seed. There is danger in helping non-professional or non-caste men to establish these *grainages*, as this has the effect of exciting the jealous opposition of professional cocoon-rearers, who, instead of deriving benefit from such establishments, do their best to boycot them and to bring discredit on the seed issued from them. Everything should be done with a view to grafting the new methods on to the existing system and never to excite the jealousy or the opposition of the cocoon-rearing cultivators, who are only too ready to believe that the ultimate object of a Committee of silk factors is to take away from their hands the lucrative trade of seed-rearing, and to make them (the rearers) dependent on the *grainages* owned by the Committee for good seed. The operations of the Silk Committee are at present confined to the districts of Murshidabad, Birbhum, Malda and Bogra. In the district of Rajshahi a distinct movement among Native zamindars, initiated by the late Mr. N. K. Bose, Collector of the district, resulted in a sericultural school being established. About Rs. 30,000 were contributed by the zamindars, and the District Board of Rajshahi and the Agricultural Department of Bengal have liberally subsidised the institution. The whole of the Hand-book of Sericulture in Bengali is taught in this school, and students do all the work with their own hands, from the planting of mulberry to the weaving of silk cloths. The school has now worked for two years, and it shows continued progress. Thirty-six pupils, most of whom are actually connected with one or other branch of the sericultural profession, were in training in this school in 1899; the number in the previous year having been 15. The following extract from the report of the Secretary of the school, forwarded with the District Monograph from Rajshahi, will be found interesting:—

"The proposed school, at the suggestion of Mr. Bose, who took an abiding interest in its welfare, was made over to the District Board of Rajshahi, and a Committee, consisting of its Chairman and Vice-Chairman, the Chairman of the Rampur Boalia Municipality, the Principal of the Rajshahi College, and some of the leading donors and supporters, with an Honorary Secretary, was formed to start and manage the school, according to the scheme prepared at their request by Professor N. G. Mukerji, M.A., who then held the office of the Assistant Director of Land Records and Agriculture to the Government of Bengal.

"The foundation-stone was laid by Mr. Bose on Jubilee-day, amidst great public rejoicing, on a piece of land measuring about 3 bighas, 2 cottahs, 15 chitaks, the proprietory right of which was made over to the school by Raja Promoda Nath Roy of Dighapatiya, and the Government of Bengal, in its Department of Land Record and Agriculture, having placed the services of Babu Sitanath Guha, a trained sericultural overseer, at the disposal of the school, on condition of paying only Rs. 15 a month towards his salary, the institution was started from January 1898, with the help of the District Board promising to pay Rs. 1,200 a year, and the leading zamindars of the district came forward to support the movement with donations amounting to Rs. 32,000, part of which was paid down in cash.

"With a view to introduce the scientific knowledge and encourage the students who would be likely to profit by it, the Committee resolved to charge no tuition-fees, but to support the students with scholarships and help them with prizes to start seed nurseries in the district. The District Board of Rajshahi sanctioned eight scholarships of Rs. 8 each a month, the Berhampore Silk Committee sanctioned three scholarships of Rs. 6 each a month, and Babu Rabindra Nath Tagore granted four scholarships of Rs. 5 each a month. At the suggestion of Mr. P. C. Lyon, Director of Land Records and Agriculture to the Government of Bengal—who has evinced a great interest on the welfare of this school—the Honorary Secretary started a Prize Fund to which Mr. Lyon contributed Rs. 25, Mr. Fraser-Forbes, Manager of the Bengal Silk Company at Sardah, Rs. 50, and the Rampur Boalia Municipality, Rs. 75, with the object of enabling two of the best students of the school to start seed nurseries in the district. As the Prize Fund fell short of the requirements, the District Board of Rajshahi and the Department of Land Records and Agriculture were pleased to make a grant of Rs. 160 and Rs. 50, respectively, at the suggestion of the Honorary Secretary.

"The training under the scheme, prepared by Professer Mukerji, consisted, in the first year, in theoretical and practical lessons in the cultivation of mulberry-rearing and reeling of the Bengal and Assam silk-cocoons, and manufacture of course silk pieces from the thread of pierced cocoons locally known as *mutka*. As this scheme required two complete years to finish the sericultural training, the attention of the Committee was drawn to it, and a modified scheme was adopted to divide the school into two independent departments—(1) Sericultural, and (2) Weaving, and to complete the training in either, in the course of one year only, leaving it optional with the students at the end of the year to leave the school or join the other department. The Sericultural Department under this modified scheme imparts in one year sound theoretical and practical training in the cultivation of mulberry-rearing, of Indian and foreign silk-cocoons and in the reeling of silk threads; while the Weaving Department, during the same period, imparts practical lessons in bleaching, dyeing, and weaving of various silk stuffs

"Altogether 15 students (Hindus and Muhammadans) joined the school as regular students during the first year of its existence. They were examined twice during the year, and at the final examination held in January last by Professor Mukerji and the Honorary Secretary, 13 students passed the test: 11 being placed in the first, and two in the second division. The first two students—Ekramuddin and Ebadulla—have been awarded a prize of Rs. 175 each for starting seed nurseries in the interior of the district. Four students have obtained employment under the Berhampore Silk Committee on Rs. 15 a month each; and two students have been employed on Rs. 8 a month each by Babu Rabindra Nath Tagore for introducing the rearing of the Assam silk-cocoons in his zamindari in the district of Nadia. Besides these regular students, several casual students and visitors interested in the industry, both literate and illiterate, received instruction at the school as well as through correspondence. A few associates in different parts of India also received casual help from the school for introducing the industry in their localities.

"Pandit Sital Prosad Upadhaya, in the employ of the Hon'ble Raja Rampal Singh, after a course of training at this school for three months, returned home and started a nursery at Fort Kalakanker, in the district of Partabgarh in Oudh, where he is successfully rearing the Assam silk-cocoons. Mr. O. Lloyd, Superintendent of the Oxford Mission Industrial School at Baliganj in Calcutta, who came to this school with a Native Christian pupil for a short time, is doing useful work, and rearing Assam silk-worms in Calcutta. Mr. Lawrence, in the employ of Babu Rabindra Nath Tagore, is rearing, successfully, Assam silk-worms at Silaidaha, in Nadia, and the Honorary Secretary—being invited to visit his nursery and advise generally upon starting a rearing establishment on a large scale—testified to his success and skill. Mr. R. S. Joshi, Superintendent of the Government Experimental Farm at Nagpur, in the Central Provinces, Mr. Pink of Dehra Dun, and Mr. Eusafali of Hamirpur, North-Western Provinces, received written instructions, and are rearing the Assam silk-cocoons at their respective stations. Seed was supplied to these places from the school in the beginning, and arrangements have been made to encourage an exchange of seed between them and the school."

46. One point of somewhat general interest I may notice here in connection with the progress of this school during these two years, viz., the prominent place occupied by Muhammadan pupils in this school. In going through the annual examination papers of the pupils, I was struck with the capability of the Muhammadan pupils in taking in every detail of the work. The Hindu pupils wrote neater hands, their composition and style of writing were better, but the Muhammadan pupils showed greater familiarity with the subject, though their composition and spelling were abominable. With the march of technical education, the Muhammadans of Bengal are likely to show a keener appreciation of the benefits of education than they have done in the past. In connection with the working of this school, it may be also mentioned, there is some danger in admitting non-professional or non-caste men as pupils, and helping these with microscopes, &c., to start grainages in the midst of professional cocoon-rearers. In reviving an existing industry, it is a bad policy creating a new guild or craft, and putting it virtually in a position of antagonism to the existing caste or craft. Educational qualifications should not be given prominence to in the admission of pupils into this school, but rather caste or professional qualifications.

47. As the net result of the sericultural experiments conducted for ten years by the writer of this Monograph may be mentioned, besides the establishment of a Silk Committee and of the Sericultural School of Rajshahi, the successful working of fifteen seed-rearing stations by professional cocoon-rearers themselves, without any subsidy or help from Government, except at the outset, when they were taught the new methods and given microscopes and a few other appliances free of charge. These nurseries are scattered all over Bengal, seven of them being in Malda, two in Birbhum, three in Murshidabad, two in Rajshahi,

and one in Midnapore. The owners of the nurseries are carrying on the work with profit to themselves and benefit to their fellow-cocoon-rearers, and their methods of work are being extensively imitated by their relations and fellow-caste men. These trained cocoon-rearers have a sixteen-anna crop every time now, and some of them take as many as eight crops in the year. Five or six years ago they were poor and struggling cultivators, but now they are men of considerable substance, who are looked upon with jealous eyes by money-lenders and zamindari officials.

48. As a further result of these experiments may be pointed out the revival or initiation of the silk industry in Baroda, Kashmir, Mysore, Gurdaspur (in the Punjab), and Kalakankar (in Oudh), where men instructed by the writer of this Monograph have been employed in carrying on sericultural enterprise on the most approved principles. I will conclude this chapter by quoting an extract from a letter, dated 4th April 1901, addressed to me by Mr. J. Partridge of Yelelauka (Bangalore), who has been having successful crops of cocoons every time since he has adopted the method of work recommended by me:—

"I am meeting with success each crop. I have now on their fourth moult 60 trays and cannot see a faulty worm. I have to thank you and only you for the good luck attending my endeavours. I follow your instructions fully, and so far as disinfections are concerned, I freely use the sulphate of copper after each crop . . . . There is therefore no possibility of things going wrong, when once you have seed free from disease. Sericulture is a splendid opening, and I am glad I started it."

PART II.

SILK YARNS.

CHAPTER V.

Matká and Khamru-spinning.

The cocoons, after they are finished spinning, are taken down from the *chandrakies* and either (1) taken to the nearest *hát* for sale, or (2) killed by exposure in thin layers to the sun and reserved for sale until *paikars* or agents of European filatures come round, or (3) steamed in a basket covered-up with cloth under which a pot of water is kept boiling, and reeled off into silk, or (4) if they were formed in a very healthy manner, they are bought up for seed by travelling rearers going about in quest of seed, from village to village and sometimes from *joar* to *joar*. In some districts, *e.g.*, Malda, Bogra, Birbhum and parts of Rajshahi, spinning of silk is done by cocoon-rearers themselves, and they are more or less independent of the local cocoon-market for the time. If they get a good price they sell off their cocoons, or else they convert them into silk.

50. *Matká-spinning.*—Then there are the pierced cocoons, which accumulate in every cocoon-rearer's house after his seeding is done, that is, after the moths have cut out of the cocoons and laid eggs. These empty cocoons cannot be reeled off into silk in the same manner as whole cocoons with dead chrysalids inside them can be reeled off. Whether a rearing succeeds or fails, there are always the few seed-cocoons. Each cocoon-rearer makes, on an average, four attempts every year to rear cocoons, and each time he uses an average quantity of one kahan (1,280) of seed-cocoons. Many Malda and Murshidabad rearers use as much as five or six kahans of seed each time, but the majority use only half a kahan of seed for a crop; and I take the average to be one kahan per crop or four kahans per annum. If there are 100,000 cocoon-rearers in Bengal, or 25,000 families rearing cocoons, 100,000 kahans of empty cocoons accumulate each year. These weigh about 10,000 seers, the greater portion of which is spun into a coarse thread and utilized for weaving *matká* cloth. *Matká*-spinning and *matká*-weaving give occupation to the poorest of women and the least artistic among the weavers. The *matká* cloths, however, that are made in Rajshahi are not so coarse as Murshidabad or Malda *matkás*, and a better class of weavers are employed in that district in *matká*-weaving. The empty cocoons are kneaded with a little clay, or with a paste made by pounding peas with water. They are left soaked in this thin paste for a little while, and then they are taken up one by one with the left hand, while a strand of fibres is drawn out of it with the thumb and index finger of the right hand and attached to a spindle variously called *teko*, *tékia*, *takur*, *jámta*, or *jámtákur*. The fibres are kept twisting with the revolution of the spindle. When the portion drawn out has been thus twisted into a single and firm thread, it is collected at the base of the spindle, and another strand of fibres drawn out of the cocoon and twisted as before. When one cocoon is finished, another is taken up, and the fibres from this are joined on to the fibres of the previous cocoon, and the operation is continued until about 400 cocoons are spun in one day. Women doing the work during their leisure time at home, do the spinning of about 400 cocoons per day, not at one sitting but as they get time. It takes six or seven hours' continuous work spinning 400 cocoons in this manner. When the day's spinning is done, the thread is taken out of the spindle and gathered on to a *látái* or *nátái* which is

represented in the figure (Fig. 2) as lying beside the woman engaged in spinning.

Fig. 2.—Matka-spinning.

A woman spins only about an ounce of thread every day, and, when four or five ounces accumulate in the *látái*, the thread is taken out, a band put on it to prevent the mass getting tangled, and it forms what is called a *bándil* or bundle. When several of these bundles or short skeins accumulate, they are taken to a local *hât* for sale. A seer of *matká*-thread sells for Rs. 2 to Rs. 6, according to the rate prevailing at the time. The profits of *matká*-spinning industry are extremely low; and it is only old and feeble women, as a rule, who carry on the industry. The only thing to recommend it to them is its ease and inexpensiveness. The woman can do the work at her leisure, in the midst of her ordinary domestic duties, and the appliances required are only a *tákur* and a *látái* and a mud vessel to hold the cocoons. The former consists of a thin bamboo stick, about 10 inches long, of which the upper end is cut to form a hook, and to the lower end of which is attached a stone or earthenware disc which acts as a fly-wheel. The other implement, the *látái*, is a skeleton bobbin made of bamboo *laths*, about six inches in diameter, conical at one end and having a long shaft or handle going lengthwise through the middle, which helps in the easy turning of the *látái* when the thread is taken on to it from the *tákur*. Both these implements can be made at home by a poor woman, or a *látái* can be bought for a pice or two. The earthen vessel may cost another pice, and it is only the cocoons that have to be reckoned in the calculation. If the woman belongs to a family where cocoon-rearing is done, as she usually does, she does not need to buy even the cocoons. The cocoons, the continuity of the thread of which has been broken by moths cutting out of them, cannot be reeled in filatures, and there is no very great demand for them. They are collected in some villages and sold in some *hâts* at about 4 annas per *kahan*, or Rs. 2-8 per seer. When a woman has to buy a *seer* of pierced cocoons, she has to pay about Rs. 2-8 for it. She spins about an ounce of thread per diem, using $1\frac{1}{16}$ ounces of cocoons. It thus takes her about a month spinning a *seer* of pierced cocoons. Thus, after a month's toil, she may make a rupee or two by an outlay of Rs. 2-8 and another two or three pice worth of *dál* (pulse).

51. *Matká*-spinners are amongst the poorest of the poor, and they are usually Muhammadan women who attempt to keep up their *purdah* respectability by means of this sedentary toil which brings such poor return. There is no means of judging how many *matká*-spinners there are in Bengal. The census figures (Tables A and B of Part III) include *khamru* and filature spinners and winders, and it is therefore not possible to say how many of the 19,904 persons returned as silk-carders and spinners are *matká*-spinners. Further the census figures do not give an adequate idea of the number of persons who actually do spinning or carding. Cross-division in sericultural industry is unavoidable. Mulberry-growers are generally also cocoon-rearers, and cocoon-rearers are also generally silk-spinners, at least in some districts, and silk-spinners are usually cocoon-rearers in every district. In census operations, a person is regarded as depending on agriculture, or mulberry cultivation, or

cocoon-rearing, or silk-spinning, according as the principal occupation of the person is agriculture, or mulberry-growing, or cocoon-rearing, or silk-spinning. The same may be said of silk-weavers. They may be principally cultivators, or they may depend entirely on weaving, or they may return themselves as cotton-weavers, though they use the same looms for weaving silk and cotton fabrics. We can get some idea, however, of the number of individuals who can entirely depend on *matká*-spinning if we go back to the consideration of the amount of seed-cocoons used in the country. One hundred thousand individuals depending upon cocoon-rearing, means about 25,000 families. Each family using, on the average, 4 *kahans* of seed-cocoons per annum, gives us 100,000 *kahans* as the total quantity of pierced mulberry cocoons available in Bengal. One spinner, if wholly occupied in spinning every day in the month, would spin about 10 *kahans* per month, or about 120 *kahans* per annum. This gives us a smaller number than 1,000 as the total number of individuals who may depend upon *matká*-spinning. As a matter of fact, however, there are 800 to 1,000 *matká*-spinners in the district of Murshidabad alone, as I ascertained after an elaborate enquiry during the last famine, when these poorest class of people suffered most. All the other silk districts put together would probably have another 2,000 *matká*-spinners, and I estimate the total number of *matká*-spinning women in Bengal as 3,000. There are more *matká*-spinners in Murshidabad and Rajshahi than in the other districts. It is only for a few days in every *bund* that *matká*-spinning is done, and women are never employed all the year round in this industry. This is how 3,000 women do the work that could employ only about 800 of them fully.

52. *Khamru-spinning.*—A little more than half the quantity of mulberry cocoons raised in Bengal is spun into thread by the country method of reeling. This is called *khamru*, *khangru* or *bánk* silk. *Bánk* is a name of the machine by which *khangru* silk is made. The machine is more commonly known as *ghái*, which properly means simply the pan in which cocoons spin in hot water. *Gháis* are chiefly worked by Muhammadans, but in Malda and Birbhum silk-spinning on the native method is largely done by Hindus. The processes employed are mainly the same in every district. In Malda there are regular native filatures consisting of 40 or 50 *gháis*. In some of these, six skeins of silk are turned out at a time on each reel, while in others four, and in others two as in European filatures. In some places single *gháis* are the rule (Fig. 3). In Rajshahi the *ghái* is usually double (Fig. 4.)

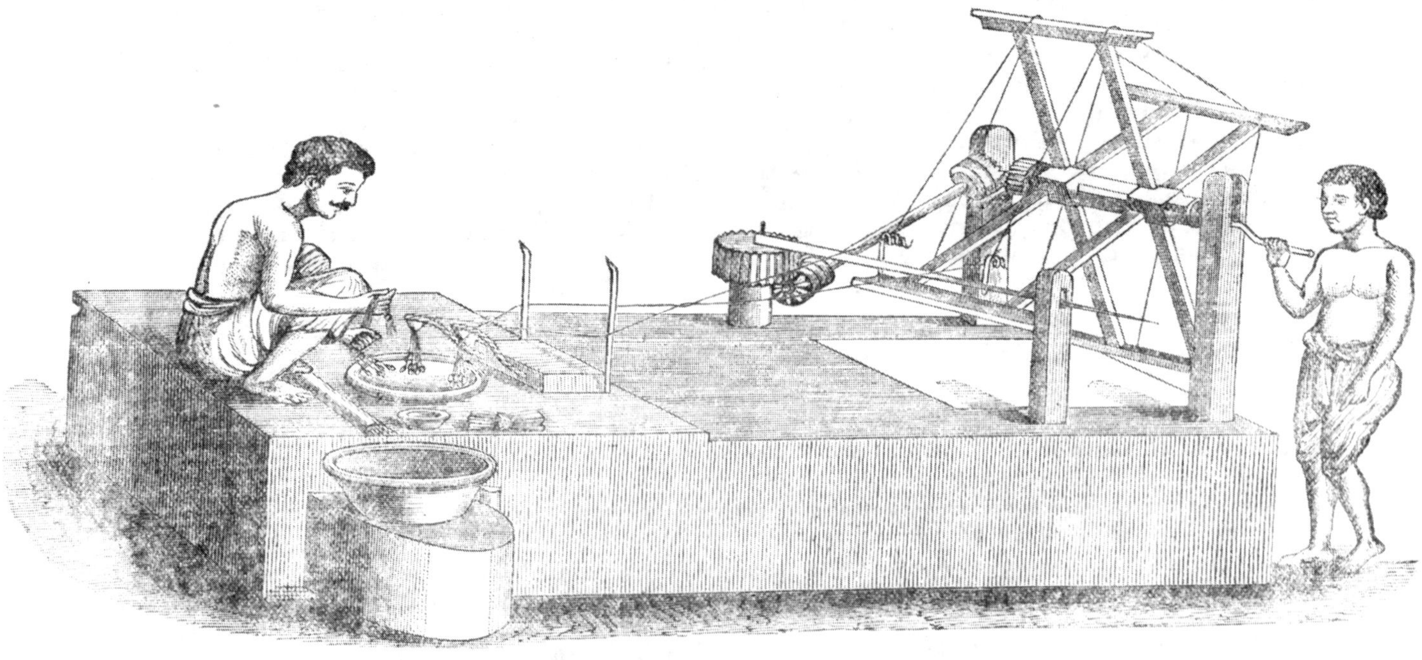

Fig. 3.—The single-*ghái* of Murshidabad.

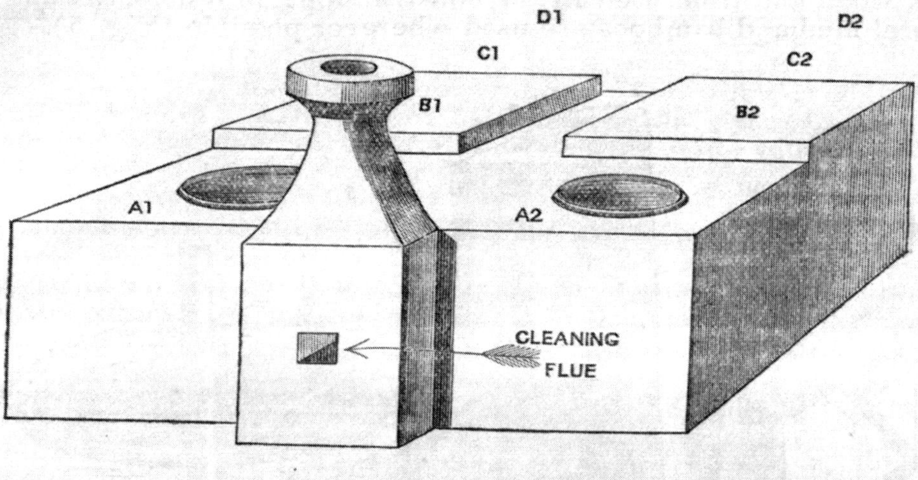

(1) The double *ghái*.

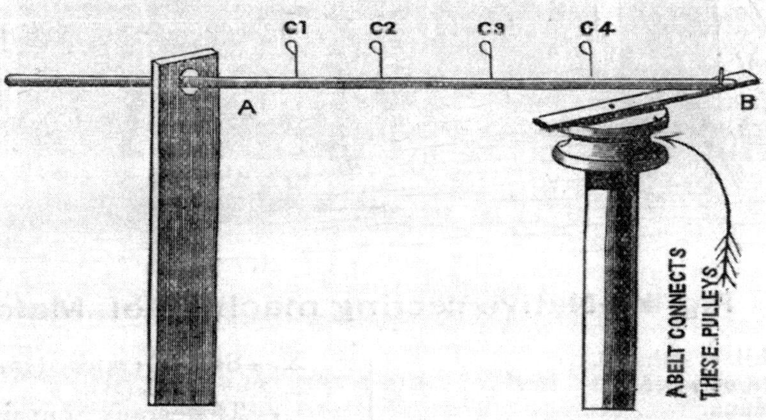

(2) The Khelná on ára.

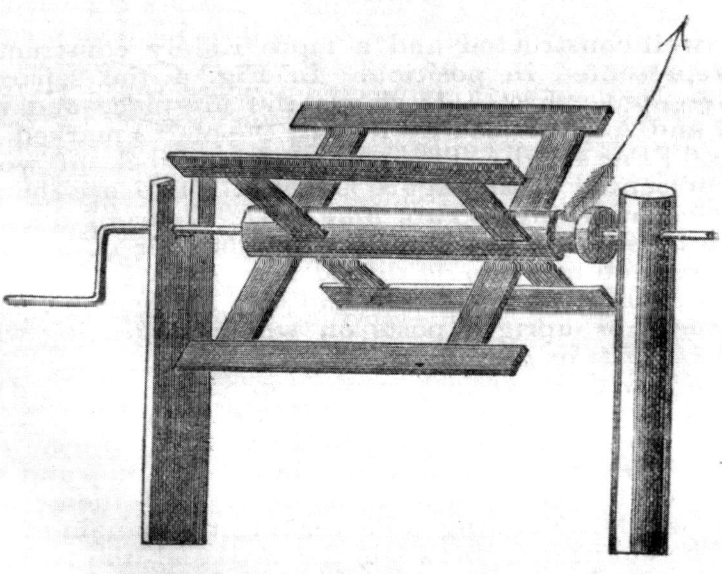

(3) The Tahbil.

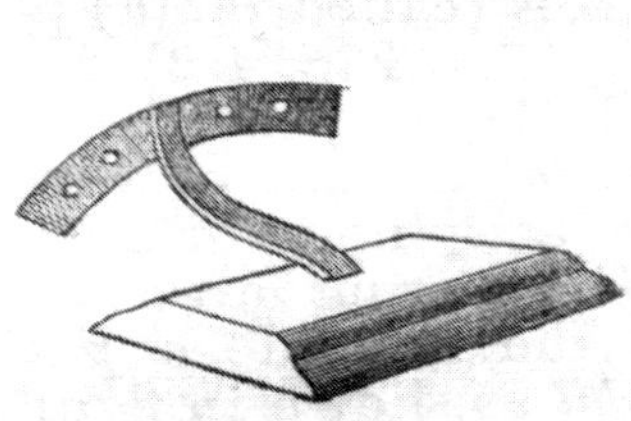

(4) The *Banti-kal*.

Fig. 4.—Native reeling machine of Rajshahi shown part by part.

53. In some places, as in Murshidabad and Rajshahi, there is more masonry, wood and iron used in the construction; in others, as in Bogra and Midnapore, mud and bamboos are used wherever possible (Fig. 5).

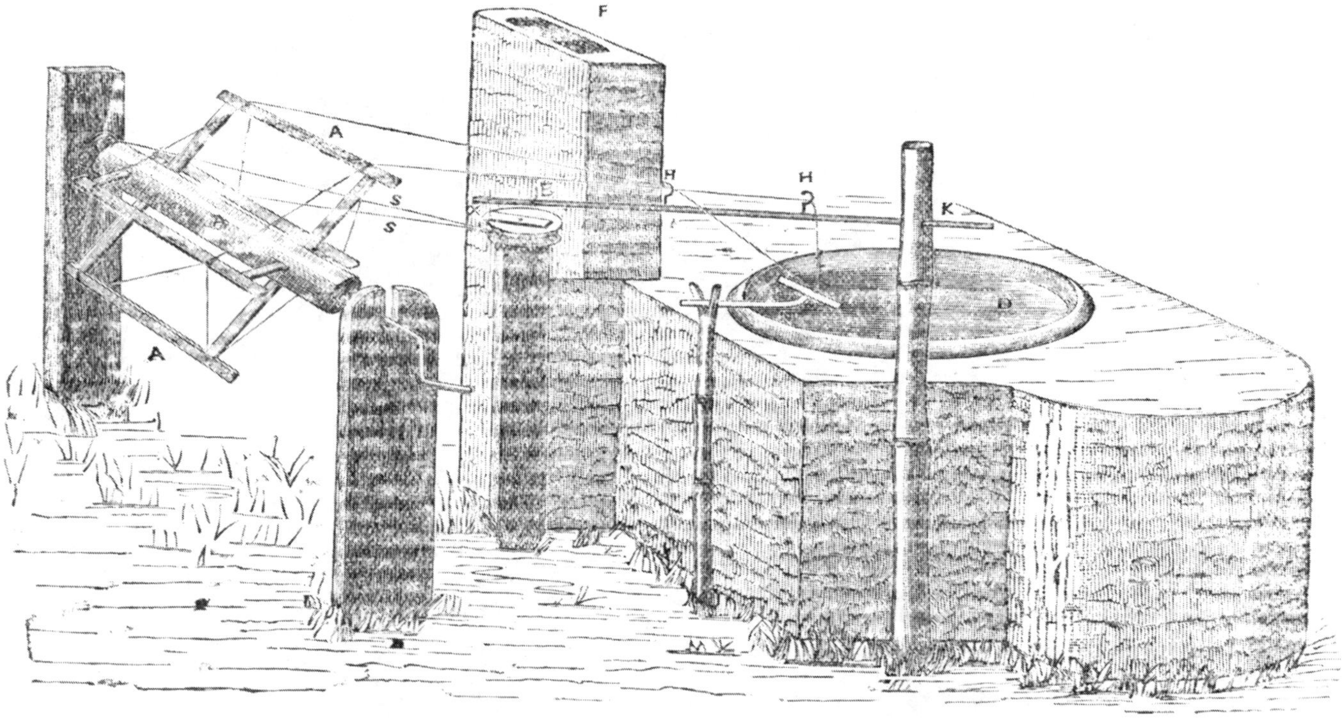

Fig 5.—Native reeling machine of Malda.

A.—Taphil or tahabil.
B.—Jántá or wheel.
K.—Kheláná.
N.—Kal.
D.—Karai.
S.—Strap or string.
H.—Iron hooks for conducting thread to reel.
X.—Small crank (*kheláná**r** tár*) on wheel (B).
This crank imparts a reciprocatory motion to the kheláná in order that the thread may be evenly distributed on the reel (A).
F.—Flue.

54. In Figs. 3 and 5, a well-constructed and a more rudely constructed single *ghái* are respectively represented in position. In Fig. 4, the separate parts of a double *ghái* are represented. Fig. 4(1) shows the fire-place and the two *gháis*, *karais* or basins (A1 and A2) warmed by it. At the places marked B1 and B2 two *bantikals*, are placed [Fig 4(4)]. This consists of a block of wood to which an iron portion as represented in the figure is fixed. The arc-shaped portion has two, four or six holes according as two, four or six skeins of silk are reeled off at a time. Through these holes the fibres from a number of cocoons in the basin are passed and carried on as a single thread to the *tahbil*, *tohbil* or reel, which is separately shown in Fig. 4(3). At C1 and C2, *i.e.*, beyond each set of basin and *kal*, stand *árás* or upright posts on which in gearing with wheels (called jántá) play the *khelánás* or *ghargharis*.

55. Fig. 4(2) shows one *árá* with its *kheláná* on the top of it. Beyond C1 and C2, &c., that is, beyond the two *árás* of a double *ghái* at (D1 and D2) stand two *tohbils*, one of which is separately represented in Fig. 4(3). Each *ghái* has a spinner or reeler (*katani*) sitting with his face towards the flue and the basin looking after the boiling of the cocoons and the reeling of them; and on the far side a *pákdár* or winder standing and turning the handle of the *tohbil* as shown in figure 3. The connection between the *árá* and the *tobhil* is established either by toothed wheels as shown in figure 3, or by means of a string passing through the groove of the wheel (*janta*, on the *árá*, and another on the offside of the axis of the reel as represented in figure 5.

56. The owner of a native *ghái* begins by steaming the cocoons. Cocoons are killed by exposing them to the sun for a few days, or, when no sunlight is available, they are killed in the process of steaming. Whether the chrysalids are alive or dead, the cocoons are placed in a basket, and the basket is placed on the basin in which water is kept boiling. The whole is covered with a blanket or a thick cloth. After about half-an-hour the steamed cocoons are ready for reeling. The steaming makes the cocoons easier to reel. Steamed cocoons are not exposed to the sun nor allowed to get too dry, but they can be kept ready for reeling for a week, if necessary, spread out in a cool room. The steamed cocoons are reeled by first putting them in the basin in boiling water, and working them with a brush or bundle of sticks (represented in figure 3), so that each cocoon gets dipped in the boiling water and its end attached to the brush. When nearly all the ends have got attached to this brush they are taken up with the left hand, and with the right hand the cocoons are lightly shaken, so that a greater length of the fibres works off. A few, ten, or twelve, or twenty, according to the size of silk wanted, that work off very easily, are then separated out of the whole lot of cocoons in the basin, and these are divided into two equal lots of 5, or 6, or 10 cocoons, the end of which are passed through the two eyes or holes of the *kal*. Where there are four eyes (as in Fig. 4), 20, 30, or 40 cocoons are divided into 4 equal lots, and the ends of these are taken out separately from the whole lot on the left hand of the spinner, and passed through the holes of *kal*. There are usually two upright wires on the *kal* to keep the two lots of fibres separate during the reeling. These also serve to give two *croiseurs* to the fibres, one between the holes of the *kal* and the upright wires, and the other between these wires and the reel. The friction caused by these *croiseurs* agglutinate the fibres together, and make them pass on to the reel as two firm and single threads. It should be noted, however, that crossing the threads before they pass on to the reel is a European innovation introduced into Bengal in 1770, and it is still rather the exception than the rule in the reeling of *khámru* silk (*vide* Fig. 5). As the real is turned by the *pákdár*, the cocoons in front of the *katáni* get worked off. The *katáni* sees that any cocoons that get entangled, or that jump up, are instantly separated out, ends of new cocoons thrown along with the fibres which are being reeled, as the old cocoons work off, and thus he goes on feeding cocoon after cocoon while the reeling is going on. When there is any interruption or break, the *pákdár* assists him in re-establishing order and union, and the work is continued as before. When one lot of cocoons is finished, another lot is subjected as before to boiling, heating with the brush, and reeling, until the day's work is done. There are little twisted wires or guides (*khelánar-tár*) on the *khelaná*, or piece of bamboo or wood, which moves in an eccentric manner on the *jántá*. The thread passing through these wires on to the reel do not pass straight to the reel and get laid on the reel exactly on the same spot. The movements to and fro of the *khelaná* causes each thread to be laid over a width of 3 or 4 inches of the reel. Getting laid on the reel in this wide manner, the thread gets dry more easily, and when there is a break the end is also found out more easily. In *Khámru*-reeling, however, they do not take the trouble of finding out the end when there is a break and putting a knot, as is done in European filature, but the union is effected anyhow. It is, therefore, more troublesome unwinding a skein of *Khámru* silk than a skein of filature-reeled silk. *Khámru* silk is also much coarser and uneven than European filature-reeled silk. In filatures 4 to 6 cocoons are usually reeled off together to form a single thread, while in Native *gháis* 8 to 20 cocoons are used. The cocoons used in European filatures are also more select; cheaper cocoons, and the rainy season cocoons (which do not work off easily) being chiefly used for the *gháis*. The oridinary price of *Khámru* silk is Rs. 10 to 12 a seer In Bankura Rs. 13 to Rs. 14 a seer, and in Burdwan Rs. 14 to Rs. 16 per seer, is the usual price. The *Khámru* silk of Malda is highly prized by Native weavers, specially for the weft, the weft (*bharná*) silk of Malda usually selling a rupee per seer higher than the *táná* or warp-silk. Mirzapore weavers of Murshidabad prefer Malda *Khámru* to that reeled in their own district. At Bashwa Bishnupur, and other villages of Birbhum, where silk-weaving is done, they use the *Khámru* of their own district. At Vishnupur in Bankura, and Chandrakona in Midnapore, a good deal of *Khámru* silk is employed in Native looms. But

half the total quantity of *Khámru* silk produced in Bengal is bought up by dealers from Benares, Nagpur, Karachi, Mysore, Sholapore, and other parts of India where there is silk-weaving. Only an insignificant quantity of filature-reeled silk is used in Native looms. Weavers of Murshidabad call filature-reeled silk "Latin silk," owing probably to the fact of its being produced on the improved 'Novi' pattern introduced by Italian artizans in the filatures of the Hon'ble East India Company. It is for some exceptionally fine fabrics such as silk muslins, that the weavers use 'Latin silk,' for which they pay Rs. 17 to Rs. 20 per seer, instead of Rs. 10 or Rs. 12.

57. The *Khámru* silk-spinning industry of Bengal is at present in a very flourishing condition. The Bombay plague has, no doubt, put some check on this industry, but it is likely to be only a temporary check. The silk-weaving industry of other parts of India is also in a flourishing condition. The quantities of raw-silk imported from foreign countries (Table K) into India has practically remained the same during the last 30 years, while the demand for *Khámru* silk, in the silk districts of Bengal, specially Malda, Birbhum, and Rajshahi, has gone on increasing. Of the two million pounds of foreign raw-silk from China, etc. that are used in India, Bengal uses only about five thousand pounds (*vide* Table M), while she exports by coasting steamers only to the other Indian ports about 250,000lbs. of raw-silk per annum (*vide* Table G); and nearly as much goes by rail to the other Provinces (*vide* Table Q). Malda produces about 2,000 maunds of *Khámru* silk; Murshidabad, about 800 maunds; Rajshahi, about 1,500 maunds; Birbhum, about 500 maunds; and Midnapore and the other districts put together, about 1,000 maunds,—the total quantity being five to six thousand maunds per annum and the tendency has been upwards during the last 8 or 10 year—though, as I have already said, the plague has somewhat impeded the progress of this branch of the silk Industry. In Malda, *Khámru*-reeling prevails in all the *joars*, chiefly in the villages close to English-bazar, and in English-bazar itself. In Murshidabad, *Khámru*-reeling prevails chiefly in the Jangipur and Kandi subdivisions, and in Birbhum, in all the villages where cocoon-rearing is done. With regard to the localities where *Khámru*-reeling is done in Rajshahi, the following extracts from the District Monograph will be found interesting :—

"*Ghais* are found in the same villages as looms and also where there is weaving, but those who work them are Musalmans. Out of 41 reelers, 21 bear the name of Paramanik, and the remaining 20 one of the following: Sarkar, Mandal, Mullah, Sirdar Saha, Sheikh, or Chaukidar. In Dakra itself there are 14 *ghais* to 12 looms. In Dakra and ten neighbouring villages, which together constitute the greatest reeling centre, there are 104 *ghais*. All these villages are in thana Charghat. There are others too for which figures are not available in this thana, such as Belgharia; in Boalia, such as Kadirpur, and in Lalpur, such as Kalidaskhali, Kamaldear, and Gargari. In the latter village there are four or five filatures, and in one house there are as many as six *ghais*.

"From Lalpur and Charghat a great deal of *khangru* is exported across the river into the Murshidabad district, where it is sold at Islampur and Berhampur. Some goes direct to Calcutta, and a large proportion comes to the silk merchants of Rampur Boalia.

"There is a quarter of the town called Resampati, where most of these dealers live in large brick buildings, and form a small but wealthy community of both Hindus and Musalmans. There is one *bapari*, known as Meajan Dalal, who buys *khangru* for most of the silk merchants, as it is brought in from the mufassil villages. The chief business of these silk merchants is to act as commission agents for up-country weavers. Hence we find that the places to which they consign their *khangru* are chiefly Benares, Amritsar, Lucknow, Delhi, Agra, and also Bombay and Calcutta. To these places principally and to a few other towns, the quantity of silk thread reeled in native filatures and exported from Rampur Boalia alone by steamer for the year 1898-99 exceeded 1,500 maunds. No figures are available to show how much *khangru* finds its way out of the district through other channels of export, but from a comparison of the number of villages whose produce comes to Boalia with the remaining villages, containing native silk filatures (not under European control), it is probable that 1,500 maunds represent about two-thirds of the total produce of the district."

58. What is said here about the export of *khangru* or *khamru* silk to other parts of India applies equally to Murshidabad and Birbhum.

59. In Bogra "there are only about a dozen skilful labourers who can reel silk. Most of them belong to the village Barbakpur, also called Barapur, near Nowdapara, where there was once a silk factory. These reelers are all Muhammadans. Reeling of silk is not their only occupation. They live by cultivation and field-work, and silk-reeling takes only a part of their time."

60. In Bankura all the silk reeled "is sent to Vishnupur for sale. The principal traders dealing in silk thread at Vishnupur are Chandra Sekhar Banerji, Nafor Tanti, Sundar Rakbit, Kartik Chand, and Behari Tanti. They also import silk from Midnapore district. Silk thread is sold at Rs. 14 per seer, generally on credit of one month."

61. In Midnapore this, as other branches of the silk industry, is in a declining condition.

62. This chapter may be brought to a close by the following extract from the *Handbook of Sericulture* (pages 216 to 219):—

"For the last few years the native silk-reeling industry has been steadily improving. At times the price of this inferior silk goes up higher than that of the superior raw silk turned out from European factories. This absurdity can be explained only by the ignorance of native silk merchants regarding the state of the European silk market. The silk-reeling industry of Bengal suffers considerably by the absurd procedure of native silk merchants. At one season when the market price in Europe for the superior filature silk of Bengal was Rs. 14 per seer, these native silk merchants were buying the inferior *khamru* silk for Rs. 15-8 per seer. Under such circumstances native silk-reelers began buying cocoons at a higher price than European silk factors. The latter saw that they could not make any profit buying cocoons at Rs. 40 or Rs. 41 per maund. Cocoon-rearers in Malda also made up their minds not to sell their crops for less than Rs. 40 or Rs. 41 per maund. The factories were closed for some time. The native silk-reeling went on briskly for a few days, while most of the cocoons remained locked up in the houses of silkworm-rearers. In a month the price of the *khamru* silk came down from Rs. 15-8 to Rs. 12-8, and only those few silkworm-rearers who had succeeded in selling their crop for Rs. 40 or Rs. 41 per maund made a profit. Most of the cocoon-rearers who had kept their crop locked up for two months got more heavily involved in debt to the money-lenders, and finally sold their April and May crops of cocoons at the low price prevailing during the rainy season. Native silk merchants and silk-reelers should accept as just the prices at which European factors buy cocoons or sell their silk, if such disappointments are to be avoided. European silk factors make exact calculations as to the price of cocoons they ought to pay after consulting the state of the European market at the time. Native silk merchants and silk-reelers should simply follow them in this matter. If they do not, they may make an accidental profit, but they are more likely to lose. Buying cocoons at the same price at which European factors buy them, native silk-reelers can make sure of their profit, as, for various reasons, *khamru* silk is worked cheaper than the filature-reeled silk:—(1) The yield of *khamru* silk is larger. (2) A spinner can turn out three times as much *khamru* silk as filature silk. (3) As six skeins of *khamru* silk are turned out at a time in some parts of Malda instead of two, the number of winders required is also less in the case of the *khamru* silk. (4) The establishment charges of a European factory are considerably larger."

63. For the above reasons, the manufacture of *khamru* silk proves more profitable to the native reeler than that of the filature silk, notwithstanding the higher price which is or ought to be obtained for the latter. From a maund of green cocoons $2\frac{1}{2}$ to $3\frac{1}{2}$ seers of *khamru* silk is obtained, the outturn of filature-reeled silk being about half-a-seer less in either case. The cost in reeling off a maund of green cocoons into *khamru* silk is Rs. 3-8 to Rs. 4. The cost of reeling a maund of poor cocoons is the same as that of reeling a maund of good cocoons, though the produce in the two cases differs a great deal in value. To the European factor a seer of silk costs about Rs. 2 in reeling. A maund of green cocoons yields two to three seers of 'waste silk' as a bye-product to the native reeler. Those two to three seers of 'waste' sell for Rs. 3 to Rs. 3-8. The cost of reeling native silk is therefore sometimes defrayed by the sale of the bye-product, and any excess in the sale-price of the silk turned out above the purchase-price of cocoons yields a net profit. If a maund of green cocoons has to be bought for Rs. 40, that is, if the cocoons are very superior, three seers at least of *khamru* silk can be expected as the produce. But the average price of superior cocoons should be taken as Rs. 30 per maund. The three seers of *khamru* silk can be sold at Rs. 30 to Rs. 46, according to the fluctuations of the market. The weft silk, again, can be sold for Re. 1 to Re. 1-8 more per seer. Native silk-reelers usually pay higher wages to their spinners and winders than European silk factors. In Malda the spinner in a native reeling establishment gets Rs. 6 Rs. 10, and the winder from Rs. 4 to Rs. 6 per month. European factors, however, have to advance money in engaging spinners and winders. It is for this reason they are able to secure spinners for Rs. 5 to Rs. 6 a month, and winders for Rs. 3 to Rs. 4. The spinner and winder in a native silk-reeling establishment work much harder than in a European filature. In the hot season they begin work at 4 in the morning, and go on until 1 P.M. In the cold season they work from 6 A.M. to midday, and again

from 1-30 P.M. till 4 P.M. In European factories regular work goes on only for eight hours in the day. The weft *khamru* silk is reeled out of 8 sers of green cocoons (about three seers of dry cocoons) by each spinner per diem. If he has to make warp silk, he has to reel off 10 seers of green cocoons (about $3\frac{1}{4}$ seers of dry cocoons) before he gets leave for the day. *Khamru* silk is sold by $82\frac{1}{3}$ tola weight. Filature silk is sold by $72\frac{3}{4}$ tola weight. With one maund of *khamru* silk are obtained 25 to 30 seers of 'waste.' This waste is not clean like the filature waste, but full of chrysalides. In filature the quality of cocoons is fairly judged form the 'waste' they produce. If on reeling 11 *kahans* of cocoons 1 seer of silk is obtained in a filature, *i.e.*, if the cocoons are tip-top in quality, 11 seers of waste are expected with a maund of this silk. If the cocoons are poor, and they go 20 *kahans* to the seer, 20 seers of waste are expected with a maund of this silk. The filature 'waste' which is clean sells for Rs. 80 to Rs. 100 a maund in the Calcutta market, while the *khamru* 'waste' sells from Rs. 38 to Rs. 60 per maund. In filatures each spinner makes 4 skeins of silk per day, which weigh from 3 to 4 chitaks. In *khamru*-reeling establishments each spinner turns out 12 skeins per day. If these are of weft silk, they weigh 8 to 9 chitaks: if they are of warp silk, they weigh 10 to 14 chitaks. The comparison here instituted will show that, on the whole, it is more profitable for the native reeler to reel coarse *khamru* silk. Bengal *khamru* silk is not exported to Europe, but coarse silk is exported to Europe from China and Japan, and it is advisable to export *khamru* silk also to Europe. But it will scarcely find a market unless it is re-wound before export. In the manufacture of the *khamru* silk thread, the winder turns the reel very fast. When a thread happens to break, he makes the re-attachment anyhow without putting a knot, and the winding of the reel goes on as before after a moment's interruption. Such being the case, it costs a great deal unwinding the *khamru* silk from the skeins into bobbins. The cost of labour in Europe is so great that *khamru* silk will fetch very little price unless it is exported in a re-wound state. A great deal more of *khamru* silk is produced in Bengal than filature silk. The competition between European factors and native reelers is therefore very keen. The best way for the European factors to avoid the evil resulting from this competition is to recognise the *khamru* silk as an article of export, to buy up large quantities of it, to re-wind it, and then send it to the European market. The effect of such a procedure will be two-fold—(1) to give the native silk-reeling industry a still greater impetus, and (2) to combine it with European enterprise. That a very wide field is likely to be opened out in Europe for the coarse *khamru* silk is the opinion of some of the best manufacturers of England, France, and Italy.

64. No time should be lost in taking advantage of an enterprise that is likely to develop export trade in a new direction, while giving an impetus to an already-flourishing native industry. For such manufacturing purposes (*e.g.*, for manufacturing shoe-maker's twine), where coarse sizes are preferable to fine sizes, the native-reeled silk, if exported re-wound and twisted, if possible, would be preferred to the more expensive filature-reeled silk.

CHAPTER VI.

SILK SPINNING—FILATURE SYSTEM.

65. The raw silk of superior quality—superior, that is, to *khamru* silk—is nearly all exported to Europe. This silk is spun in filatures, the largest of which are owned by the Bengal Silk Company and Messrs. Louis, Payen and Company. Many small filatures producing silk of nearly as good quality as that produced in European filatures are owned by native merchants, such as the Debkunda filature, owned by Haji Naku Mondal. The principal filatures of the Bengal Silk Company are those of Sardah and Matihar in Rajshahi, Baragharia in Malda, Ganutia in Birbhum, Babulbona and Rangamati in Murshidabad, and Ghatal and Chatteraganj in Midnapore. The principal filatures owned by the French Company are those of Kajla and Talaimari in Rajshahi; Bholahat in Malda; Gadi, Bajarpara, Gouripur, Sujapur, and Narayanpur in Murshidabad, and Gorelle in Midnapore. Mr. Fergusson of Berhampore owns a factory at Beldanga and another at Jangipur, in the district of Murshidabad, and also the

factory of Sirool in Rajshahi. The produce of the filatures owned by native merchants are bought up by the European silk factors on a system of contract. The tendency of late years, when prices of Bengal silk have gone down very much in the European market without any fall in the price of cocoons, has been to reduce establishment charges by concentrating the work in a few factories, while at the same time keeping up the quantity as in former years. This has resulted in the majority of silk filatures in Bengal being closed. The following account of the present state of the filature industry in Murshidabad, furnished in the district monograph, may be read with interest:—

"After the rearing comes the preparation of the silk from the cocoon. Last year's district administration report records that there were 48 filatures in the district, which turned out some 484,597 lbs., valued at Rs. 28,80,955. Of these, some 26 are the property of European firms, the rest belong to natives. Generally speaking, the outturn of the European is greater than that of the native filatures.

"According to the annual statement of important industries of the district for 1897, the average daily number of persons permanently employed throughout the year in these factories reaches a total of 3,151. At certain seasons of the year, generally speaking from January to March, April to September, and during December, the average daily number of persons temporarily employed is more than three times as great.

"*Large owners and centres.*—The Bengal Silk Company and Messrs. Louis, Payen and Company are the largest filature owners in the district. Mr. Rice, the Manager of the former, and Mr. Gourju of the latter have their head-quarters at Berhampore. Haji Nakibuddin and Haji Moniruddin are owners of large native filatures in the thana of Burwa. Again, turning to the annual statement of important industries, I find that amongst the largest European filatures are those of—Choa, with an outturn in 1897 of 19,393 lbs; Gadi, with an outturn of 34,045 lbs.; and Faridpur, with an outturn of 21,334 lbs. All these are in the Sadar division. In Kandi subdivision that of Bajarpara produced 23,863 lbs. In Jangipur the filatures of Chila and Balighatta produced 15,502 and 82,313 lbs. respectively. Among native filatures, those of Beldanga and Debkunda, in the Sadar division, produced 9,734 and 8,526 lbs. respectively, while in the Kandi subdivision the outturn of the Shomepara filature was 3,588 lbs."

66. For Rajshahi the following account has been furnished:—

"To show the extent of the silk industry as a whole, native and European, in this district, a brief statement of the numbers of the factories in each concern and their outturn for the year 1898 is appended:—

	Number of filatures.	Outturn. lbs.
Bengal Silk Company ...	Sardah, Matihar, and eight subordinate filatures ...	98,732
Louis, Payen and Company ...	Kajla, Khojapur, and Sahibganj ...	45,120
Watson and Company ...	Sirool	11,600
Total—Three ...	Fourteen	155,452

"In other words, three companies owning fourteen factories produced 69 tons 7 cwt. 3 qr. 14 lbs. in the year 1898."

67. Two thirds of the cocoons produced in this district find their way to these filatures.

68. The district monograph from Midnapore contains the following very short notice on this subject:—

"Some factories have been established here, among which are those at Guruli-Nimtola and Moheshpore in Daspore thana, and Gurpartabpore, Ramchundrapore, and Moherajpore in in Ghatal thana. In them raw-silk is reeled off cocoons and woven into cloths. One seer of cocoon yields from two to three tolas of yarn, which sells at about Rs. 15 per seer of 80 tolas. The yarn is either exported or sold to weavers for weaving into cloths. Each spinning wheel turns out about two to three *chitcks* of yarn."

69. The quantities of raw silk exported in the palmy days of the East India Company, *i.e.*, from 1812 to 1835, and in subsequent years up to 1876, have not been approached of late years; but otherwise there is nothing much to complain of regarding the quantity of silk produced in filatures and exported to Europe. The competition with China, Japan, France, and Italy is now keener than ever; the improvements effected in all branches of sericulture in France, Italy, and Japan within the last 20 years are enormous; and the struggle the European silk factors have had during these 20 years in keeping up the quantity is very great. But so far the struggle has been well

maintained, and some improvement even is noticeable. The regular export of raw silk from Bengal may be said to have commenced in the year 1772. The annual average of export for the 20 years from 1773 to 1792 was about 409,000 lbs. During the next 20 years 1793—1812) the average annual export was 438,554 lbs. The next period of 22 years (1813 to 1834), at the end of which Government gave up all direct control over the silk trade, saw the average annual export of raw silk attain to 982,761 lbs. The next period of 20 years, from 1836 to 1855, saw the average rising to a still higher figure, viz., 1,435,225 lbs. The next period of 20 years, from 1856 to 1875, saw a still higher average, viz., 1,690,836 lbs, which was the maximum reached. To study the march of export in raw silk from this time onwards it is best to take into account much shorter periods—

			lbs.
The average annual export of raw silk from ...	1876 to 1880	was	1,074,837
	1881 to 1885	,,	480,992
	1886 to 1890	,,	486,517
	1891 to 1895	,,	601,171
	1896 to 1900	,,	632,164
	1901 and 1902	,,	643,713

70. The upward tendency since 1889 has been very distinct (*vide* table C of Part III); and if the methods of amelioration are persevered in, I have no doubt, the improvement can be maintained. Every department of the silk industry depends for its health and vigour on the state of the cocoon rearing industry. Cocoons will necessarily become cheaper if crops become certain and plentiful; and it is cheaper cocoons that are needed to make cheaper silk, both raw and manufactured. Bengal silk is always acceptable, specially in England, if it can be supplied cheap. The Imperial sentiment is operating here, as in every-thing else in the British Empire, and England is interesting herself more and more in the raw-silk from Bengal. France is no longer the principal patron of Bengal silk, and England is striving to assume the same unrivalled position with reference to Bengal silk which she held 30 or 40 years ago. The nature of the present competition between England, France, and Italy in this respect can be judged from the following figures:—

Export of raw-silk in bales.

	To England.	To France.	To Italy.
1891	1,362	1,242	194
1892	1,125	1,256	723
1893	1,927	1,663	686
1894	1,186	952	334
1895	1,380	2,052	475

71. The figures compiled from the Bengal Administration Reports for 1896-97 to 1900-1901 are given in Table E. In 1896-97 the amount of raw silk and waste exported to England was 5,064 maunds or 416,713 lbs., while in 1897-98 it rose to 9,432 maunds (753,080 lbs). The quantity exported to all other countries taken together in 1896-97 was 9,152 maunds, while in 1897-98 it fell to 6,871 maunds. From 1875-76 down to 1896-97 France invariably imported larger quantities of raw silk and 'waste' from Bengal than England, and even Italy occupied for some years a higher place than England. For the first time during the last 30 years, therefore, England assumed the first place once more in 1897-98. This is as it should be, and if the tendency continues, there is no reason why Bengal silk should not continue to flourish, though it may never regain the position it occupied from 1813 to 1875, when Bengal silk stood unrivalled in the competition even with Chinese and Italian silks. Table E, however, is not altogether hopeful on this point. Mr. Liotard writing in 1883 made the following cogent remarks regarding the fall of Bengal silk being due to England's failure to patronise it:—

"It will have been seen from this series of tables that of Indian raw silk, the United Kingdom was by far the largest consumer 13 years ago (viz., 99½ lakhs of rupees in

1870-71), but that the exports thither declined rapidly till they came down to Rs. 11 lakhs in 1875-76, to Rs. 4½ lakhs in 1880-81, and to about Rs. 3 lakhs in 1882-83. It is chiefly this decline, this abandonment of the Indian supplies by the United Kingdom, that has brought about the fall in the Indian raw silk trade."

72. England's behaviour in this respect is all the more regrettable, since other European countries did not see any reason for abandoning Bengal silk in the same manner as England did. The cocoon crops of France and Italy began steadily to improve from 1876, and yet France went on importing almost as much silk from India, and Italy imported more and more of it.

73. The raw-silk of export is made in large factories, and more carefully, though, on the main, the principle of reeling resembles more the old native method than the present methods which have come into vogue in Italy and France. The principal differences between the *khamru* and the filature methods are—

(1) The boiling and heating of water is done in filatures from a central boiler with steam, and not by fire kept under each basin as is done in the native *ghais*.

(2) The discipline under which the spinners and winders are kept by constant check of their work by means of special testing machinery and a special supervising staff renders the silk turned out of evener size than *khamru* silk.

(3) When there is a break a knot is put, which is not done in *khamru* silk.

(4) Crossing of two adjacent threads to give them roundness and firmness is invariably done in filature-reeling, though it is only rarely done in *khamru*-reeling.

(5) Filature silk is finer than *khamru* silk.

74. The following extracts from the "Handbook of Sericulture" will give an idea of the system of filature-reeling in vogue in Bengal :—

"*The Oven.*—In Part II of this book it has been said that cocoons require to be killed by heat or with carbon-bisulphide before they are reeled. Even when they have been killed, they require to be steamed, except in the rainy weather, when cocoons killed in the sun are exposed to the action of heat and moisture simultaneously, which does away with the need of subsequent steaming. The combination of heat and moisture makes the fibres on the cocoons to swell up and become loose and easily reelable. Even in the rainy weather it may be necessary to bake the cocoons in a steaming oven, simply to kill them, when the rays of the sun or carbon-bisulphide is not available for this purpose. At other seasons the object of putting cocoons into an oven is not simply to kill them. They are, therefore, steamed in the oven even when they have been killed in the sun before they can be properly reeled. Where large quantities of cocoons require to be killed, steaming ovens must be provided. When small quantities of cocoons only have to be reeled, the steaming can be done by introducing the cocoons in a basket or in an earthen vessel having holes at the bottom, and putting the basket or the earthen vessel on the reeling basin, where water is boiling, the basket or the earthen vessel being covered up with a blanket, to keep the steam in as much as possible. A properly constructed oven has this advantage, that the temperature inside it can be made to exceed 100°C., while the temperature of the steam got from the boiling basin is ordinarily 100°C. Exposure of cocoons to a temperature of 160°C. for 5 minutes kills them effectually. A short exposure of living cocoons to 100°C. leaves those inside a heap alive. Moths coming out of such cocoons afterwards make them 'waste.' Killing cocoons in the sun in the rainy season does not do any harm to the silk fibre, but in those seasons, when the air is naturally dry, killing the cocoons by exposure to the sun lessens the elasticity of their fibre. Cocoons should, therefore, be killed in those seasons either in a steaming oven or with carbon bisulphide. The kind of ovens constructed in this country in connection with filatures is not altogether suitable for the baking of cocoons. These are hemispherical in shape, constructed with bricks, and have a small removable door in front of each. They are first heated with fuel burnt inside. The fire is then extinguished by sprinkling water from outside, the charcoal and ashes being removed immediately afterwards, and cocoons arranged in baskets put in. The little moveable door is then fastened on, and the cocoons kept inside in the hot and steamy atmosphere of the oven for 10 or 12 hours. They are afterwards taken out and spread in thin layers on *machans*, and distributed as required to the reelers. In Europe there is a long cavity under the oven. In this cavity is put fuel (wood or coal) and a boiler in contact with it. A tube from this boiler opens into the oven above. The cavity underneath the oven leads into a flue, which goes up the further end of the oven, then along the top, until it terminates in front in the form of a chimney. The cavity or flue going round three sides of the oven, heat is radiated into the oven from the three sides. This makes the temperature of the oven stand at over 160°C. Putting fuel inside the oven, bringing charcoal and ashes out, and sprinkling water are not required for an oven of this kind. The killing of the chrysalides is also effected in about three minutes in such an oven.

At the entrance to the oven just described, a couple of rails are fixed in the ground. A truck laden with cocoons is rolled along these rails, shut in for three minutes in the oven, and then rolled back. Another truck laden with baskets of cocoons is in the meantime got ready and rolled in as before. If the oven is made 12 cubits long 3 cubits wide and 4 cubits high, 5 maunds of cocoons can be smothered at a time, or 50 maunds (10 truckfuls) per hour. An oven like this worked for eight hours a day can kill and steam 400 maunds of green cocoons per diem. Sometimes the accumulation of cocoons in a filature is so great that it seems desirable to introduce the European system of baking in this country. If a much larger quantity of cocoons arrives in a factory in one day than what has been spoken of as being easily capable of being smothered during the day, those must be baked first that are not safe to keep over for a day or two. A handful of cocoons out of each lot coming into a factory should be held close to the ear and shaken. If the shaking gives one the idea that the sound has a dry character, or when a rustling sound is heard from inside the cocoons when they are simply held close to the ear, those cocoons should be killed that very day, or else moths are likely to emerge next morning and spoil some of the cocoons. If there is any doubt in the matter, a few cocoons may be cut open, and it may be seen whether the chrysalides have got their eyes quite distinct, and also whether the contour of the wings are quite plainly seen. When these signs appear, the cocoons should be killed the same day. Steamed and unsteamed cocoons should not be kept in the same room, as this may lead to occasional mistake in steaming cocoons.

"A more detailed description of the methods actually followed in the large filatures for killing, drying, and ovening cocoons may be of interest.

"*Killing and drying.*—A special method is adopted for killing the cocoons of the rainy bunds and the November bund. When sunny days are available, the cocoons with live chrysalides inside them are exposed to sun for a day or two immediately after they are brought to the filature. If it is wet at the time, they are spread out in the cocoon-godown; and before the moths cut out, they are killed in a stove-room called *atasghar*. This room is kept hot with a big stove, the fire-place of which is at a low level and in one corner of the room, so that coal is fed from outside this room. Two pipes or flues from this stove go in a curved manner along the length of the room and up to the roof, where they end in chimneys, whence the smoke goes out. On the opposite wall to which the door of the stove is placed is a huge door through which an iron truck laden with flat trays of cocoons goes inside the stove-room or comes out of it along iron rails. The trays are made of wood or iron, and each time the truck is charged with about 600 *kahans* of cocoons in 60 or 65 trays. The cocoons are kept in the stove-room at a temperature of 150° to 160°F. for four or five hours, after which they lose nearly the whole of the moisture. There is a small trap-door at one end of the room to which a thermometer is attached, and which is opened every now and again for inspection. Out of this opening a few cocoons are also brought out with the help of a stick and cut open. Excessive heat or too long heating spoils the cocoons. In the hot weather, when two or three days' exposure to the sun is sufficient, the cocoons are not put in the stove-room. After sunning or stoving the cocoons, as the case may be, they are spread out on bamboo shelves (*máchâns*) and stirred every now and again, and after seven or eight days they are put out once more in the sun for a short time.

"*Ovening.*—Three or four days before the cocoons are reeled, a week's supply of cocoons (about 2,000 *kahans*) is ovened at once. The oven or *tundul* is a hemispherical masonry structure, hollow in the interior, having a masonry floor and a small trap-door. Wood is burnt inside this oven, and when a blazing fire has been made and the oven has become very hot, the fire and cinders are brought out and water is sprinkled thoroughly all over the inside without loss of time. In December 12 or 14 *kulsies* of water are thus used, and in April 24 or 25 *kulsies*. In the rainy bunds cocoons do not need ovening, as the fibre in these bunds is naturally soft and open. The cocoons arranged in baskets are put inside the oven as soon as sufficient water has been sprinkled inside the oven, and immediately the trap-door is made firm. The ovening continues for 10 or 12 hours. No sunning is required after ovening, as the object of ovening is to give the cocoons a mellowness, which is lost by sunning or drying. In December the ovened cocoons are spread out on bamboo shelves, but in April they are spread out on the floor that they may not lose the mellowness through excess of drought. The ovened cocoons are distributed among the reelers.

"*Method of reeling.*—It is impossible to learn reeling of thread from cocoons simply by reading books. It is altogether a matter of practice. One should learn to reel silk at an early age. In youth it is easier to bring muscles and nerves under control, and apply them to special kinds of work. In silk-reeling factories, therefore, small boys and girls are usually employed for winding the reels. They begin by learning to wind the reel and to put knots on to the reeled thread when it happens to break, and they gradually get to do the unravelling of the ends of the cocoons with bundles of sticks, and to throw them off their fingers for the purpose of reeling. In Bengal it is usual to employ one reeler and one winder for reeling four skeins of thread per diem. This is waste of labour. Two winders can be employed for winding a whole series of reels, while an extra man can be employed to walk up and down, putting knots on to threads that happen to break. This system has come into operation in some of the Bengal filatures. There are three main arrangements in a reeling machine:—(1) A basin, where hot water is kept, where the cocoons spin, and whence the fibres are carried off. (2) Two perforated porcelain eyes or discs attached to the end of two wires just above the basin. These are fixed to a block of wood, into which also are fixed vertically two brass wires or rods. The ends of a number of cocoons are passed through one of the eyes or discs and attached to one side of the reel. The ends of a similar number of cocoons are then passed through the other eye or disc and attached to the other side of the reel. When this is done the two lots of fibres will be found stretched in a parallel way from the basin to the reel. If the reel is turned under such circumstances, the fibres from the cocoons will work off and be laid on the reel in two loose bundles. The fibres going to form the two threads reeled off from the two sets of cocoons are agglutinated together by the two sets being crossed with each other a number of times, the vertical brass rods serving to keep the two 'croisures' or crossings intact by keeping the threads separated between them. The first croisure lies between the two porcelain discs and the two vertical brass rods, and the second croisure between these vertical rods and the reel. The two sets of fibres from the cocoons form into two single threads by means of these croisures, and they are gathered on to the reel as single threads. (3) The reel. When this is turned with a handle, the fibres from the two sets of cocoons are worked off from the basin into two threads. When a cocoon has been worked off in this way, another is made to supply its place out of a lot of ready-boiled cocoons. To avoid the two adjacent threads from a basin being laid on the reel exactly on the same spot, a rod or lath is made to work laterally with the help of an eccentric arrangement connected with the reel by means of toothed wheels. On these laths are fixed two glass or brass guides, through which the two threads are made to pass. The top end of these guides being twisted in the shape of corkscrews, the thread reeled off pass in contact with them without getting detached, so that the two threads are laid on a width of 3 or 4 inches of the reel, when the lath moves right and left at each turn of the reel. The thread reeled off being laid in this wide manner, results in two advantages—(1) When the thread happens to break the end is more easily found out on the reel. (2) The threads get dry in the skeins while the reeling is going on (Fig. 3).

"We may conclude this chapter by giving an estimate of cost and outturn of a filature of 100 basins conducted on the Bengal (European) system :—

		Rs.	A.	P.
(1) Purchase of cocoons, at 3½ kahans per basin per day, for 250 working days ($100 \times \frac{7}{2} \times 250 = 87{,}500$ *kahans*), at 11 annas a kahan		60,156	4	0
(2) One hundred reelers, employed for 250 days, on Rs. 6 per month		5,000	0	0
(3) One hundred winders, employed for 250 days, on Rs. 4 per month		3,333	5	3
(4) Two coolies for pumping water, for 250 days, at Rs. 5 per month		83	5	3
(5) Coal, 35 maunds for each maund of silk turned out and 2½ maunds for the stove-room for each maund of silk turned out (say, 136½ maunds out of 87,500 kahans of cocoons), *i.e.*, 5,126¾ maunds, at Rs. 40 per 100 maunds		2,050	12	0
(6) Fuel for ovening, &c., 500 maunds, at Rs. 25 per 100 maunds		125	0	0
(7) Repair of filature		300	0	0
(8) Establishment charges—	Rs.			
European Assistant, including commission ...	4,000			
Gomastah	480			
Clerk	240			
Godown-keeper (also clerk)	180			
Hazirnabish (roll-caller)	84			
Chaukidar	72			
Two *barkandazes* or peons	120			
Three filature *sardars* or foremen	180			
Oven *sardar*	72			
Engine lascar	72			
Carpenter	120			
Sweeper	72			
		5,092	0	0
(9) Contingent expenses		1,200	5	6
Total expenditure ...		77,941	0	0
"Outturn—				
136½ maunds of 10—12 denier silk, at Rs. 800 per maund		1,09,200	0	0
45½ maunds of *chasam* or tape-waste, at Rs. 100 per maund		4,550	0	0
Nine maunds of *gudar* or coarse *chasam*, at Rs. 40 per maund		360	0	0
34 maunds of *topa* or unreelable portions of cocoons, at Rs. 7 per maund		238	0	0
Total outturn ...		1,14,348	0	0
Deduct expenses ...		77,941	0	0
Net profit ...		36,407	0	0

"According to the above calculation of expenditure, each seer of silk (and a filature seer is only 72¾ tolas) costs over Rs. 14; and if the price realised is only Rs. 12 or Rs.13 per seer, as sometimes happens, instead of a net profit a net loss would be the result."

75. The number of silk-carders and spinners in Bengal inclusive of dependents is over 19,000 (vide Table A). It includes *matka* and *Khamru* spinners, but not cocoon-rearers, who are also spinners. So the figure gives no clue for finding out how many filature-spinners are at present employed in Bengal. The amount of raw-silk exported to foreign countries, which is all filature-reeled silk (very little of which is used in the country), offers, however, a clue for ascertaining the number of spinners and winders employed in filatures. Assuming 600,000 lbs. as the amount of filature-reeled silk turned out *per annum* of 200 working days, and ⅜ lbs. as the amount turned out *per diem* by two men, *i.e.*, one spinner and one winder, we get the total number of employed hands in filatures as 16,000, that is, 8,000 spinners and 8,000 winders. But as in some filatures, where better mechanical arrangements have been introduced, one winder is employed for several spinners, the number of winders is perhaps 6,000 instead of 8,000, and the total number of hands employed about 14,000. The filature-spinners and winders come from the lowest grades of Hindu and Muhammadan (chiefly Muhammadan) societies. They work on a system of advances, and they get very small wages—Rs. 4 to Rs. 6 per month—for those days when they actually work.

CHAPTER VII.

Unwinding and Throwsting.

76. *Phirán, or unwinding.*—Native weavers, as a rule, employ *khamru* silk in their looms. It is only rarely that they employ European filature silk, or 'Latin' silk, for turning out some very superior fabric. In weaving 'pakwan' silks (*i.e.*, silks made out of twisted thread), the weaver first unwinds the skeins to a number of *latais* (fig. 6), and then gets this unwound raw-silk twisted, and

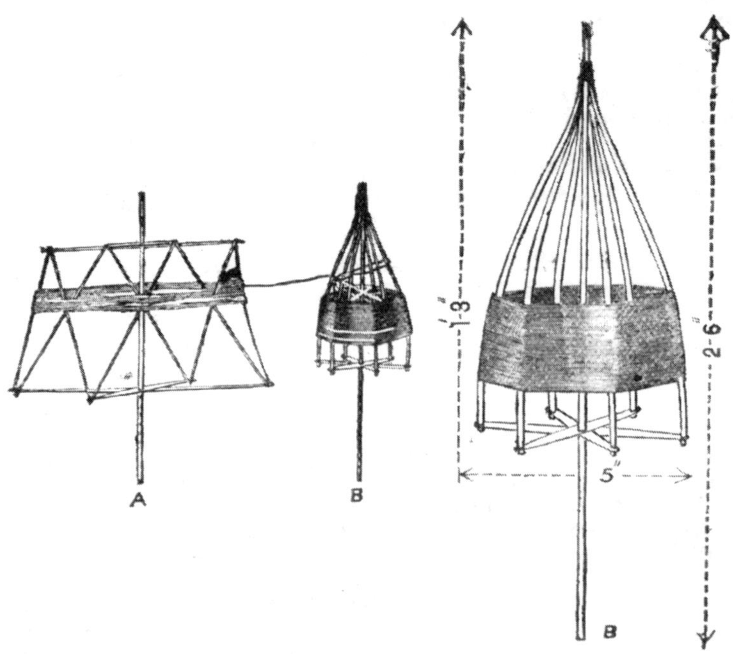

Fig. 6.—Unwinding of skeins.

finally gets it warped before he commences weaving. In weaving *khám* silk (*i.e.*, those made out of raw or untwisted silk), the weaver gets the thread unwound and gathered on to *latais*, and then warped before commencing weaving. If the thread is bleached, dyeing is done after warping. The thread for the weft is gathered on to *latais* from the skeins, two or three fibres from the skeins of a raw silk going to form a weft-thread. The weft-thread is taken out of *latais* and bleached and dyed, if necessary. In other words, whether the raw silk is used in a twisted or untwisted condition, whether it is bleached or not, whether it is dyed or not, it must be unwound before it is used. The unwinding is done with two objects—(1) to gather the thread of the same thickness or 'size' in the same *latai*, and (2) to get one uninterrupted thread in each *latai*. The skeins of raw silk are loosened out and put round a frail bamboo wheel called '*polti*' or '*chorki*' (fig. 6 A.). The end of the skein is attached to a *latai*, and the thread transferred to this *latai* (fig. 6 B) by keeping it turning with the right hand, while the thread is made to pass between the thumb and the index finger of the left hand. The stick passing through the axle of the 'polti' being loosely planted in a hole in the ground or in the hollow of a thick piece of bamboo, the turning of the *latai* with the right hand makes the thread come out unwound from the skein. The thread passing through the fingers of the operator, he can judge of its thickness. Thread of the same thickness is wound on to one *latai*, so that three or four *latais* are sometimes employed for unwinding one skein of native-reeled silk. In unwinding the thread, the clue is lost from time to time. To get back the clue or end, some waste takes place. European filature-reeled silk is easily unwound, as it is fairly even in thickness throughout, and a whole skein can be gathered on to one *latai*. One *tola* or half a *tola* of silk per seer is wasted in unwinding filature silk, and half a chitak to one chitak is wasted per seer in unwinding the *khamru* silk. It costs about 8 annas per seer to get raw silk unwound. Women are usually employed in this work.

77. *Throwsting or twisting.*—The raw-silk gathered on to *latais* may be used for warping in untwisted condition for manufacturing *khám* silks, or silks of poor quality. For manufacturing superior silks, twisted thread is employed. Superior silks are therefore styled *pakwan* (*i.e.*, twisted). The native process of twisting is extremely simple and inexpensive. In other words, the total cost of the tools and appliances used in twisting silk thread is less than one rupee. But to get a seer of silk thread twisted by this process costs about two rupees. In Europe, labourers are paid nearly ten times as much as in this country, and yet getting a *seer* of raw silk twisted in Europe costs only about eight annas. The machinery used in Europe for twisting silk thread is not so complicated that it cannot be constructed even in country places in India. The chief obstacle to the employment of the Bengal raw silk in Europe is the greater cost it entails in unwinding. The Bengal raw-silk should be re-wound and twisted in this country before export. Re-wound raw-silk has indeed begun to be exported by the French firm. If the export takes place in the form of thrown-silk, the difference of Rs. 6 or Rs. 7 per *seer* between European and Bengal silk is likely to disappear. Indeed, one of the principal ways of ameliorating the export trade in Indian raw silk would be the recognition of Organzine and Trame as the staples of export, instead of raw-silk. Doubt may be reasonably entertained with regard to the advisability of introducing the complicated power-looms of Europe into this country under existing conditions, but there is no doubt it is high time that the comparatively simple machinery required for throwing or twisting silk should be introduced. European methods, indeed, should be introduced into this country, as a rule. China and Japan have been able to develop their silk industry considerably by the adoption of European improvements. That the old methods are the best for India alone can never be accepted as a sound theory. With regard to the Japanese enterprise, one fact only may be pointed out as quite conclusive: we are now buying Japan-made handkerchiefs and other silk articles even at Berhampore. These are quite European in style and finish. Japan silks are finding their way into the English market also, to the great detriment of the silk-weaving industry of England.

78. *The native process of twisting.*—In twisting silk by the native process, the *látais* are planted loosely in holes in the floor (fig. 7). The threads are

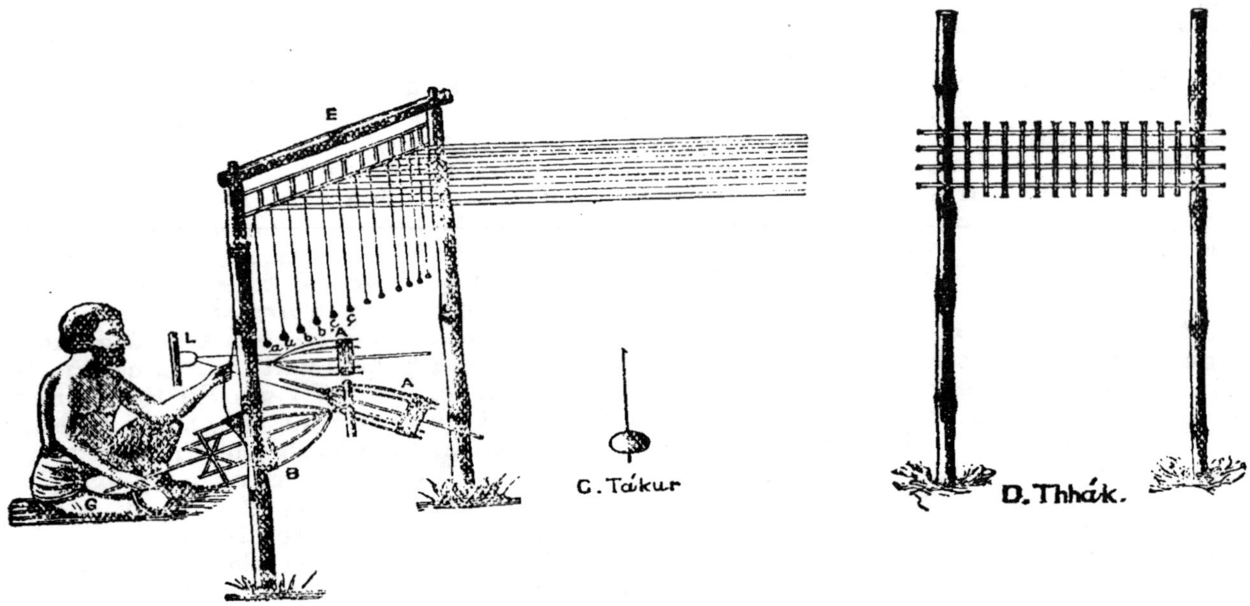

Fig. 7.—The Twisting of raw-silk.

passed through an iron guide (L), called *Loibangri khunti,* firmly planted in the floor; they are then carried up in front of the operator through a bamboo and cane erection (E), called *Dôl* (fig. 8), and then through the first space of the

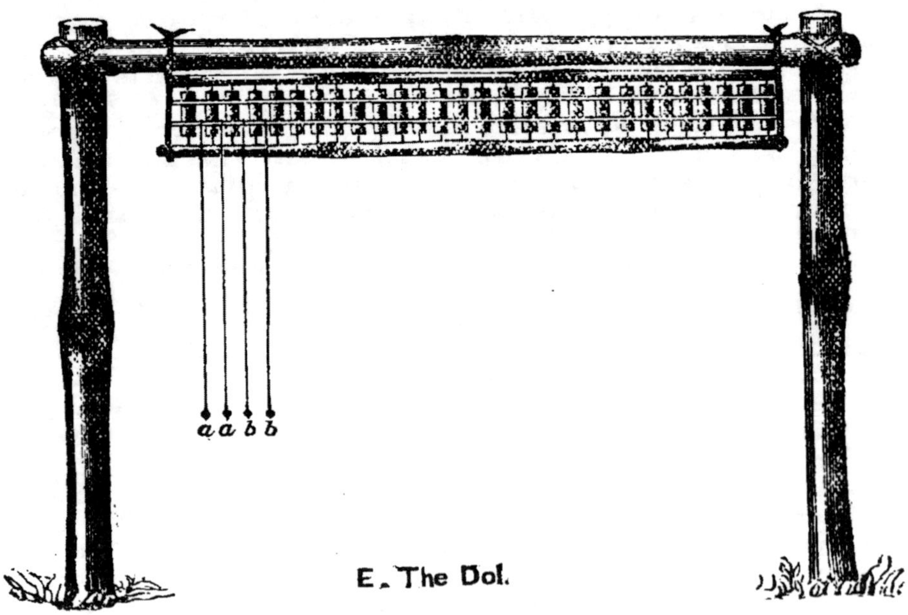

Fig. 8.—The Dôl.

upper-most series of a number of *thháks* or bamboo erections (D), back through the first spaces of the lower series of spaces of the same *thháks* and the second space of the *dôl*, when the threads are snapped at the iron guide, and a *tákur* tied at each end, as at *a, a,* the two ends being then made to hang vertically at equal heights from the floor. Another length of thread is then taken exactly in the same way from the *látais*, passed through the guide, the third space of the *dôl*, the second spaces of the upper and lower rows of the *thháks* and the fourth space of the *dôl*, two *tákurs* being again tied at the two ends in front of the operator, as at *b*, *b*. In this way seven lengths of threads with 14 *tákurs* attached to their ends remain hanging in front of the operator. One of these *tákurs* is separately shown in the figure 7C. From the *dôl* to the last *thhák* being 27 yards, 378 yards of thread are twisted at the same time by each operator. The distance between the *dôl* and the last *thhák* is sometimes more and sometimes less, and sometimes 16 *tákurs* are used instead of 14. There are usually 9 *thháks* when the distance between the *dôl* and the last *thhák* is 27 yards. The *tákurs* are simply slender pins of bamboo with mud weights attached to their bottom, which help to keep the threads straight while the twisting is going on. The operator keeps rubbing the pins of the *tákurs* successively between the palms of his hand, so as to make them spin fast and uninterruptedly, which serves to twist the threads. When the *tákurs* are only 9 inches from the *dôl*, by the shortening of the threads by 9 inches, as the result of twisting, the operator considers the twisting done. The seven pieces of twisted thread are then gathered on to a *látai* (B) as one continuous piece by knotting them together. More thread is then twisted exactly in the same way. Two to three lengths of raw silk are usually twisted together. In other words, the pieces of thread passing through the same spaces of *dôls* and *thháks* are taken from two to three *látais* at the same time, and not, as a rule, from one *látai*. In the native system of weaving the weft is never made of twisted thread.

79. The illustration here given represents the system actually carried on by Kusi Mandal of Sibganj, one of the principal *chambulias* or silk-twisters of Maldah. In principle, the method of twisting adopted at Baluchar and Khágrá (two other principal silk-twisting centres) in Murshidabad, is also the same. In Murshidabad the *dôl* from which the loose ends of the silk threads suspend consists of two bamboo upright posts and a bamboo cross-piece (as shown in the figure) to which a number of U-shaped pieces of cane are attached. From sixteen U-shaped canes 8 single, double, or treble pieces of raw silk hang down, the two ends of each piece of thread being attached to *tákurs a*, *a*, *b*, *b* (as in the figure). In another detail also the Murshidabad arrangement slightly differs from the Maldah arrangement. The upper and lower spaces of the *thháks* have *churis* or common glass bangles tied to them, so that the silk threads pass through in contact with the smooth surface of U-shaped canes and the glass bangles instead of with bamboo tubes and laths. Silk fibre gradually cuts through bamboo, but it does not cut through cane or glass. The *chámti* or piece of leather (G) shown strapped at the operator's thigh helps to make the rotary motion of the *látai* to which the twisted thread is gathered, easier. The *chámti* is sometimes dispensed with. There is always a boy assisting the operator in carrying one end of each piece of thread from *thhák* to *thhák*, and also when the twisting is finished and when the piece of twisted thread has to be gathered into the *látai* (B). As only one *thhák* (instead of nine) is shown in the figure, and that even not *in situ*, the work of the boy has not been represented here.

80. Silk-twisters are called *chambuliás*, and there is a *Chambuliá-párá*, or silk-twisters' quarter at Berhampore. They are either Hindus or Muhammadans—usually the latter. There are *chambuliás* also at Baluchar, Jangipur, and Shibganj. Their total number is perhaps less than 1,000. In social position they occupy a place intermediate between weavers and spinners, that is, they are considered better off than spinners, but not so well off as weavers.

81. In Bogra and other districts, where the number of weavers is comparatively small, a separate Chambuliá class does not exist, and the twisting is done by each weaver on his own account. The processes of unwinding and throwsting are thus described in the Bogra Monograph:—

"After purchasing the thread the weaver puts the skein on to a big *cherkhi*, mounted on two upright posts fixed on a block of wood, so that it may turn on the reel, which is now horizontal, without anybody holding it.

"The weaver then reels off the thread on to *latáis*. If the cloth to be woven be very fine, the threads are not joined: otherwise two or three such reels are suspended from the ceiling of the house according to the thickness of the thread required. The operator sitting below takes down the ends of the threads, and joins them so as to form one thread. This joint thread is then twisted with the right hand on the left forearm. As the process goes on the operator keeps the prepared thread on a thing called *Khatia* (fig. 9), which consists merely of two small upright posts fixed on a block of wood. The thread is arranged on this in the shape of an elongated 8."

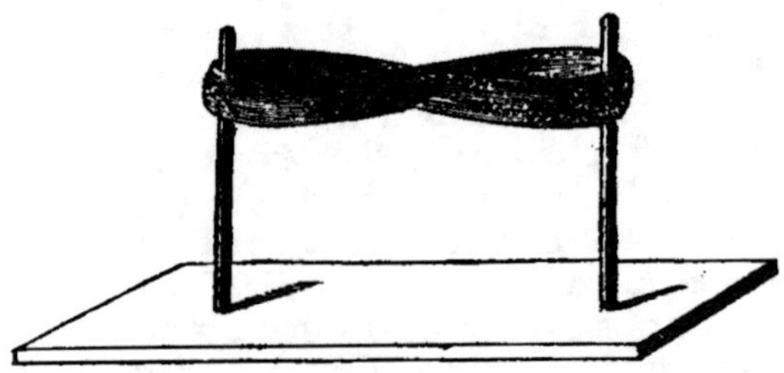

Fig. 9.—The Khatia.

PART III.

THE SILK-WEAVING INDUSTRY.

CHAPTER VIII.

SILK-WEAVERS.

82. IT is best to deal with this subject district by district after discussing the common features of the industry in the different districts of Bengal.

83. Weavers are more wholly dependent on weaving than spinners on spinning, or cocoon-rearers on cocoon-rearing. About half the cocoon-rearers of Bengal are also cultivators in the ordinary sense. It is only the old caste of *Pundas*, who more or less depend exclusively on cocoon-rearing. Carders and spinners are usually too poor to own land, and when they are not spinning *matká* or working in filatures, they are usually employed as servants or labourers. But there are scarcely an eighth part of weavers owning land, and they belong to a grade of Hindu society (when they are Hindus) in which working as servants or labourers is considered degrading. Muhammadan weavers, called *jugis* or *jolas*, are more independent in this matter, but even they cannot help imitating Hindus in this as in many other social customs. Weavers are considered superiors to cultivators in social position, and a family of weavers will suffer a great deal of privation and incur a good deal of debt before it chooses the lower position in society. Families of weavers struggling away for two or three generations and yet pursuing their calling is an ordinary affair in the silk districts. But silk-weavers as a class are far more prosperous than cotton-weavers, though in the districts where silk-weaving is not a speciality silk-weaving and cotton-weaving are pursued indifferently by the same families, as occasion arises, the same looms being used for both purposes. Silk-weaving proper is done in all the districts by adult males, but women and children assist them in preparing the thread and fixing the warp.

84. Weavers are usually their own dealers, that is, when a number of pieces accumulate on their hands they take them to the nearest towns for sale, and what they cannot dispose of in this way, they take to their *mahajans* or money-lenders by way of part-payment of their debts. The *mahajans* are well acquainted with the prices of yarn, the cost of bleaching, dyeing and weaving, and they acquire the pieces at cost price after a most detailed calculation. Besides getting silks cheap, they charge the weavers heavy rates of interest—12 to 36 per cent. per annum. The progress of the silk-weaving industry, as of many other industries in Bengal, is greatly impeded by the grabbing policy of rich money-lenders, who get all the good out of an industry, leaving the actual workers poor. But in silk-weaving there is fortunately another class to be reckoned with, viz., the silk merchants, European and native. *Mahajans* are indifferent whether they are paid back in money or in kind, and they are no more interested in silks than in jewellery, or in grain, or in land. They are utterly indifferent if their grabbing policy only results in the decay of a particular industry. There will be people always ready to borrow money, whatever they may pledge against the loan, and nothing comes amiss to the *mahajans*. The silk merchants, on the other hand, are interested in the welfare of the silk industry, and they pursue a more liberal policy. They make advances of money, buy articles at more reasonable prices, and they compete one against another to the benefit of weavers. At Berhampore, Rampur Boalia, and English Bazar, there are many rich silk merchants who keep up regular places of business, and make purchases for various parts of India and also for foreign countries.

85. There is one well-known family of actual silk-weavers at Berhampore—the family of Tanti Ram Babu, who are now zamindars and also exporters of silk. Babu Shoshi Bhushan Chowdhury is the present representative of this family. Rai Mukunda Lal Barman Bahadur, who died lately, was also a rich silk merchant of Berhampore. His firm deals principally with the

Mahratta country. The French firm of Messrs. Louis, Payen & Co. also deals in silk piece-goods. I have known one very talented weaver (Mrityunjoy Sarkar of Gankar-Mirzapur) rising from the ranks within the last 13 years and aspiring to the position of a silk merchant until death removed him also from the field of competition. In 1887, when I first knew him, he was a servant of Joykisto Mandal, getting Rs. 6 a month, but when he died the other day he left a brick-built two-storied house behind him. Other Mirzapur weavers recognised him as their master, as he was the means of introducing many improvements in the silk-weaving industry of the Jangipore centre. The caste system viewed in the light of trade-guild is a great lever for industrial improvements in this country, and any system of technical education that may be introduced in the country should fully utilize the existing system.

86. In Murshidabad about 15,000 persons depend on silk-weaving, and there are over 2,500 looms at work. Most of the Murshidabad weavers are Hindus, and the majority belong to the Tanti caste. There are also some *Kaibartas*, *Vaishnavas*, *Mals*, *Bagdis*, *Chandals*, and Muhammadan *jugis* engaged in this industry. Dubraj, the most famous weaver of this district, who also died within the last four years, belonged to the *Chamar* caste, and he actually began life as a maker of *tom-toms* or native drums and other articles in which leather or skin is employed. He then changed his profession entirely and became the leader of a gang of *impromptu* singers (*kabis*). Though he could neither read nor write, he was able to compose verses *impromptu*. Later in life he became apprenticed with a famous Muhammadan weaver of Baluchar, who knew the art of constructing looms for bringing out figured patterns; and Dubraj was the only master-weaver in this department of the industry until death removed his most interesting figure from the recent sericultural history of this district. But Dubraj's case is an exception rather than the rule. Families of weavers adhere to their ancestral occupation in Murshidabad as elsewhere. If Dubraj had belonged to the weaver caste, there would have been no occasion for any anxiety that his art should not die with him. The majority of weavers in this district belong to what may be termed "the intermediate class," a large number to the lowest, but none to the highest, with the sole exception of Tanti Ram Babu's family. In their house also the family traditions are kept up, and here a number of looms may be always seen at work. The other native silk merchants of Berhampore are not weavers, but only exporters. These are S. S. Bagchi, Durga Sankar Bhattacharjya, Kalidas Premji, Dharamsi Kanji, and Gopaldas Makundalal (to which firm the late Rai Makundalal Barman Bahadur belonged). Though some of these call themselves silk manufacturers, they are really silk-merchants or dealers. S. S. Bagchi, the winner of the Gold Medal, at the International Exhibition of Paris, does some amount of directing, which has resulted in the improvements which have characterised of late years, the silk weaving industry of Jangipur.

87. There are many weavers in the district who employ their fellow-caste-men on a system of contract. They each keep 40 or 50 families of weavers employed, and they exercise a kind of supervision over the actual work of these families, with the object of keeping up their own reputation for the quality of their goods. Joykristo Mandal of Gankar-Mirzapur and Butakrishna Ranu of Islampur-chak are weavers of this class. These also in time are likely to be reckoned as silk merchants, like Babu Shoshi Bhushan Chowdhury of Berhampore. Besides Berhampore, Mirzapur, and Islampur, there is another recognised silk-weaving circle in Murshidabad, viz., Baluchar. There is no substantial weaver in this circle, though Dubraj, the most ingenious weaver of the district (but a poor man), belonged to it. The persons who are recognised as the silk merchants of this circle are Bisen Chand Babu and Khetu Babu. They are not silk merchants properly so called, but they add ordinary *mahajani* business, which all rich *Jains* more or less delight in, to their function as silk-exporters. This is one cause of the low condition of the Baluchar silk industry. Another reason for the Baluchar weavers not getting on so well now as they did in times gone by, is the change in public taste. The figured *saris*, etc., of Baluchar were at one time very fashionable, but now they are rather despised as being ugly and unsuitable for personal wear; and as they are far more expensive than *phulkaries* of the Punjab, they cannot be used for mere decorative purposes. The silks known as 'Baluchar silks' are not actually woven

at Baluchar, and there are no weavers at Baluchar. The weavers live in the neighbouring villages of Bahadurpur (where Dubraj had his looms), Amai-para, Ramna-para, Ram-dahar, Baligram, Bag-dahar, Belia-pokhur, Am-dahar, and Ran-sagar. As the Mirzapur (Jangipur) silk-weaving industry is in a comparatively flourishing condition, weavers of the Baluchar circle are gradually giving up weaving of figured fabrics and taking to weaving plain and check fabrics in imitation of Jangipur weavers. This is a good policy under existing circumstances, however much the death of the artistic weaving of Murshidabad with the master-weaver, Dubraj, may be deplored. The weavers of the Gankar-Mirzapur (Jangipur) circle are better off than the weavers of any other part of Murshidabad. Next to them come the weavers of the Islampur-chak circle. Next come the weavers of the Berham pore circle, and last of all the weavers of the Baluchar circle. But the *matkâ* weavers of the Berhampore circle are the poorest of all. They live in two villages—Goaljan and Neyalishpárá—across the river, opposite Berhampore. The average earnings of an adult male weaver are from Rs. 8 to Rs. 15 per month, and of a woman or child about Rs. 4, these last getting food in addition. In the Baluchar system of weaving figured silks, children are largely employed to assist weavers; a man and a boy being required to weave a piece of figured silk, while other kinds of fabrics are woven by a single person. Mr. A. R. Edwards, Assistant Collector of Murshidabad, who wrote the district monograph of Murshidabad, says:—

"A weaver, whose cottage I visited, told me that he can earn about 6 annas a day, and his boy about 4 annas, but there are times at which he can get no work. Another said his profits on a piece of work which took him one and-a-half days to finish amounted to 6 annas. There is no doubt that as a class their condition is not prosperous, and that they are deeply involved in debt. They do not, as a rule, work for themselves, but for dealers who advance them material and pay them so much for their labour. Some of these dealers employ a very large number of weavers. I am told in Kandi subdivision some weavers found the industry so unprofitable that they have entirely given it up and in many cases taken to agriculture. Others in the same subdivision have abandoned the weaving of silk for that of cotton. At present the price of cotton yarn is low and the demand for goods fairly great, so that industry is found to be more paying."

88. These remarks, though probably applicable to the *matká* weavers of Goaljan and Neyalishpárá, and weavers of figured fabrics of Baluchar, or to the few silk-weavers who are found in the Kandi subdivision, do not apply to the great body of Murshidabad weavers, who are on the whole, prosperous, many living in brick-built houses. The *matká* weavers also have constant occupation; and though the profits of their rude industry are very small, and though very few own lands, they are an independent class of men In famine times, however, *matka* weavers (who being landless buy food-grains) suffer very much owing to the smallness of their income, and being weavers they are ashamed to dig or to work as field-labourers, or to earn famine-wages by twisting jute-string. The average income of Rs. 8 to Rs. 15 per month, specially when women and children can earn separate wages is considered a good income in this country, and as a class, therefore, silk-weavers cannot be regarded as indigent.

Hooghly.

89. The following extracts from the Hooghly report give an idea of the existing status of the silk-weavers of that district:—

"In the Census of 1891 the workers and dealers in silk fabrics were returned at 505 for the district. As no silk and *tasar* fabrics are manufactured in any part of the district outside the Jahanabad subdivision, the figure represents the manufacturers of that subdivision."

"The decline in the silk trade has been to some extent compensated by the gradual extension of the *tasar* industry to the western part of the subdivision, which borders on the subdivision of Ghatal (Midnapore) and Bishunpore (Bankura), which are noted for *tasar* manufacturers."

"About 210 people of the Tanti caste are engaged in the silk industry proper, the rest in the *tasar* industry."

"The silk industry in this subdivision has its centre at Bali. There are at present only seven firms (*kuthis*) or individual dealers, five of the *kuthis* or wholesale shops being owned by bunniahs of Agra and the Punjab.

"The only kind of silk fabric manufactured is *rangin-kapar*, or coloured silk, which is made for export to the Punjab.

"These wholesale dealers are only agents of, or order-suppliers to, up-country firms, and receive a commission at the rate of two per cent., payment being made on arrival of goods at destination. It is said that camels were formerly sent by the Punjab merchants for this traffic."

"It is estimated roughly that goods to the value of Rs. 40,000 are annually sold by the agents or middlemen to the up-country merchants."

"The fabrics made at Bali are now used only on marriage and ceremonial occasions. It is said that only three years ago, when there was an unusually long *akal* or prohibited season for marriages in the Punjab, there was a serious depression of the industry here."

"The Tantis depend almost entirely on the product of the loom, and very few of them possess agricultural lands. Several families have emigrated to and have settled in Calcutta."

Burdwan.

90. In Burdwan, the average wages of a weaver are said to be Rs. 8 to Rs. 12 per month, and it goes up sometimes to Rs. 15. The silk-weavers of Burdwan may also therefore be said to be in fairly easy circumstances. The following extract from the Burdwan report will be found interesting in connection with the question of the income and social position of silk-weavers :—

"The yarn costs about Rs. 15 to Rs. 16 a seer. This is manufactured into articles which sell at the rate of Rs. 8 or Rs. 9 per piece of 10 cubits, of which $2\frac{1}{2}$ to 3 pieces can be manufactured in a month. Thus Rs. 20 to Rs. 27 would be the gross income per month to make $2\frac{1}{2}$ to 3 pieces; Rs. 12 or Rs. 13 worth of yarn would be used, and thus the average net income, would be Rs. 8 to Rs. 12 a month. *Garad* silk requires more skill and care than *tasar* silk but the wages obtained are quite as high. The cocoons cost Rs. 12, and Rs. 2 go to the women for making the yarn, and there are incidental expenses for dyeing, etc., which make the cost about Rs. 15 a seer, which is about the same as for *garad* silk. The same quantity is woven, and pieces 7 cubits long are turned out to the number of three to four per month. Thus the wages vary between much the same limits. It is said that a thoroughly energetic and skilful man could make Rs. 15 a month, but, on the other hand, the ordinary weaver's wages are nearer the lower limit than the higher.

"The caste rank of the weavers is, as has already been said, fairly high, being inferior only to Brahmins, Baidyas, and Kaysthas. Financially their position is not very high, and is sinking along with their industry. Some families, *e.g.*, the Bisni Shana families of Memari are wealthy, but their position is not due to the silk trade, but to outside causes."

91. In the silk districts proper (Murshidabad, Rajshahi, Maldah, Birbhum, and Midnapore), the yarn does not cost Rs. 15 to Rs. 16 a seer, but only Rs. 10 to Rs. 12, and the *saris* and other 10-cubit pieces turned out by the best weavers of Murshidabad sell not for Rs 8 or Rs. 9 per piece, but for Rs. 13 to Rs. 15. The profits of the best Murshidabad weavers are therefore larger.

Midnapore.

92. The condition of Midnapore silk-weavers is, however, deplorable. Midnapore silk fabrics have not the same reputation as Jangipur silks, and fabrics almost of the same quality can be had very much cheaper at Chandrakona (Ghatal) than at Mirzapore (Jungipore). The profits of the Midnapore silk-industry are therefore less, though there being a fairly large number of weavers concentrated in two villages, the competition is great. The monograph from this district has the following remarks on the condition of silk-weavers :—

"In Ghatal thana men of the Kaibarta caste, numbering about 200, and in Daspore thana those of the weaving (*Tanti*), *Sunri*, *Vaishnava* and other castes, numbering about 700 in all, work in silk. They are not in prosperous circumstances, as the industry is declining."

Birbhum.

93. The Birbhum report has the following remarks on this subject :—

"About 300 or 400 families in this district have taken up this industry for their livelihood. Most of them come from Boswa, Bishunpur, Margram, and some petty villages round Ganutia Silk Factory and other petty villages scattered over many parts of the district. The manufacturers generally come from the following classes :—(1) Tanti, (2) Jugi, (3) Joláh, and some Dhopás in villages Raipur and Mirzapore in Bolpur thana.

"The castes employed in this business are regarded as coming between the artisan caste and the labouring castes. Their social position is, therefore, an inferior one. Their industrial position is gradually falling, as the business seems to have been in a declining condition."

Birbhum-made silks being of an inferior quality to Murshidabad and Midnapore-made silks, the profits of the Birbhum silk-weavers are less.

Bankura.

94. In Bankura, however, silk-weavers are better off. There is more local demand for Vishnupore (Bankura) and Memari (Burdwan) silks than for Birbhum silks, as the

quality of the former is superior. "At Vishnupur," says the district monograph, "there are about 60 families engaged in the manufacture of silk fabrics. Of these, 6 belong to the Rajak (washerman) caste; the rest are all Tantis."

Bogra.

95. In Bogra there are only about a dozen silk-weavers properly so-called. The Bogra silk has only a local demand, not sufficient to keep even these few weavers fully occupied. They are, however, considered of good social position. They take pride in their work, and they do not let their women go out to work, which is a sign of respectability.

Rajshahi.

96. In Rajshahi silk-weaving proper is hardly ever done. This district, however, is famous for its *matká* weaving. There are about 30 families of weavers at Dakrá who produce the famous Mirgunge or Dakrá *matkás*. Some of these are made so fine that they look like fabrics made out of reeled silk. *Khamru* silk is occasionally mixed with *matká* thread for turning out *matkás* of superior quality specially ordered. The weavers are mostly Tantis. Mr. H. L. Salkeld, Assistant Collector of Rajshahi, writes in the monograph furnished by him:—

"There are very few Musalman silk-weavers in this district. I have only heard of one at Paikpara, police-station Lalpur, in the course of my enquiries; but in cotton-weaving many are engaged. Silk-weaving on a small scale, by one person, seems to be combined with other occupations."

97. The Maldah monograph has the following remarks on this subject:—

Maldah.

"In Maldah there are over 2,500 silk-weavers. The weavers are all Tantis by caste. They are not badly off. Muhammadans have lately taken to silk-weaving in this district."

CHAPTER IX.

Silk fabrics.

98. It will be best to treat this subject also district by district. The largest variety of silks is woven in the district of Murshidabad, which is the heart of the silk-weaving industry of Bengal. The fabrics woven in the other districts of Bengal have their counterpart in Murshidabad, except a class of fabrics woven in Maldah, but now almost defunct. No specimens of these Maldah fabrics have been supplied with the district monograph, and I have not any of these in my own collection. A fuller description of Murshidabad silk fabrics may precede the mere enumeration of the fabrics in the other districts. The only district monograph accompanied with samples of fabrics is the one from Manbhum. With the exception of the seven samples of *Tusser* from Manbhum, shown in the sample sheets, all the samples shown at the end of this chapter are from my private collection obtained principally from the district of Murshidabad. The Murshidabad silk fabrics have been thus fairly well illustrated, which is another reason for dealing with them first.

99. *Murshidabad.*—The principal types of Murshidabad silk fabrics are—

Class A.—Fabrics made with ordinary looms, such as may be used for weaving cotton cloths also. Under this class come—

1st.—Plain fabrics, either bleached, unbleached or dyed.
2nd.—Striped fabrics.
3rd.—Checks.
4th.—Bordered fabrics.
5th.—Printed fabrics.
6th.—Banhus.

Class B.—Fabrics made with *naksha* loom for weaving figured silks.

Class C.—Embroidered and other hand-worked fabrics.

Class A (1st) —Plain fabrics are usually made with *khamru* silk and rarely with filature-made silk. *Matká* silk is also made use of for special purposes. Mirzapore (Jangipur) weavers usually obtain Maldah *khamru*, and sometimes very high-class native filature-reeled *Dháli* or Barapalu silk. The best fabrics are made of this latter kind of silk. The following silk fabrics fall under this class:—

(1) *Gown-pieces.*—The raw-silk used for gown-pieces is twisted and bleached and sometimes dyed before weaving. White gown-pieces are woven in four different styles—(*a*) plain, (*b*) twill or drilled (*terchi* or *át-páti*), (*c*) striped, and (*d*) checked. Coloured gown-pieces are usually made either plain or drill. The dimensions are usually 10 yards × 42 inches. Sometimes the width is made 44 inches, 45 inches, or even 54 inches. The price of gown-pieces varies from Rs. 12 to Rs. 40 per piece. An extra thick gown-piece, 10 yards × 42 inches, made out of filature-reeled Barapalu silk, is valued at Rs. 45 or even Rs. 50. The cheaper kinds are made of untwisted thread, and should be styled *corahs* rather than gown-pieces. The only difference between a *corah* and a gown-piece made of untwisted thread is, that for the latter bleached thread is used, while for the former unbleached thread, *i.e.*, raw silk as it comes from the *ghai*, is used.

The specimens of gown-pieces illustrated in the specimen sheets at the end of this chapter are—

1. An extra thick twill gown-piece, 12 yards × 54 inches (Rs. 50).
2. Thinner gown-piece, 10 yards × 40 inches (Rs. 28).
3. An extra thick plain gown-piece, 10 yards × 42 inches (Rs. 45).
4. Ordinary gown-piece of superior quality, made of *dhali* silk, 10 yards × 40 inches (Rs. 25).
5. *Dhali* gown-piece, somewhat inferior, 10 yards × 40 inches (Rs. 20).
6. *Lali* gown-piece, 10 yards × 40 inches, superior quality (Rs. 26).
7. Ditto, ditto, inferior quality, heavily starched (Rs. 14).
8. Plain striped gown-piece, 10 yards × 40 inches (Rs. 23).
9. Twilled and striped gown-piece, 10 yards × 40 inches (Rs. 34).
10. Twill gown-piece, *maurkanthi* colour, 10 yards × 40 inches (Rs. 35).
11. Plain gown-piece, red colour, 10 yards × 40 inches (Rs. 25).
12. Twill gown-piece, cheap quality, grey colour, 10 yards × 40 inches (Rs. 22).
13. Twill gown-piece, slightly superior quality (Rs. 28).
14. Plain grey gown-piece, 10 yards × 40 inches (Rs. 22).
15. Plain gown-piece, black, *i.e.*, deep indigo colour, 10 yards × 40 inches (Rs. 26).

Gown-pieces are in use among European ladies for making dresses and by Bengali gentlemen for making coats, *chapkans*, and *chogas*.

(2) *Corahs.*—These are the cheapest silk fabrics which form the staples of export to Europe, where they are used mainly for lining purposes. *Corahs* are generally woven 7 yards × 1 yard, and sold a rupee per square yard. They are made out of unbleached and untwisted thread, and they are bleached in the piece after they are woven. *Corahs* are also woven 10 yards × 42 inches like ordinary gown-pieces, and worn as *saris* by widows. Like gown-pieces *corahs* are valued by the number of warp threads (called *shánd*), 2,400 warp threads per yard making the best gown-pieces and *corahs*, while 1,200 or 1,000 warp threads per yard make the poorest gown-pieces and *corahs*. The price of *corahs* varies from 6 annas to Re. 1-8 per square yard. A sample of *corah* shown in the sample sheet (No. 16) which is cut out of a piece of 1,700 *shánd corah*, 7 yards × 1 yard, is valued at only Rs. 5-8 per piece. High-class *corahs* are used for making ladies' blouse-jackets and other garments usually after dyeing

(3) *Silk muslins* or *háwái* pieces are very fine fabrics made with filature-reeled *dhali* silk. *Háwái chadders, háwái dure* (No. 18 of illustration sheets) pieces, as well as plain *háwái* pieces or *malmals*, are illusrtated here (No. 17 of the illustration sheets). This last

was originally cut out of a 10 yards × 40 inches piece, valued at only Rs. 10. It is excellently adapted for trimming ladies' hats and for other similar purposes. Silk muslins are locally used by rich men for making shirts, coats, or *chapkans* which they wear in the hot weather, *háwái saris* being similarly used in the *zenana*. It is only highly skilled silk weavers who can turn out superior silk muslins. The best silk muslin weaver at present is not a Murshidabad, but a Mymensingh man. The weaver of Murshidabad who was able to weave as good silk muslin as this Mymensingh weaver, died about 10 years ago, and no one has been able as yet to exactly fill his place in this district.

(4) *Handkerchiefs*.—These are made either with twisted yarn or with raw-silk. Handkerchiefs are sometimes made with dark blue or red borders. A high-class Mirzapur handkerchief 2 feet × 2 feet costs a rupee. Poor *khám* handkerchiefs 18″ square may be had for 4 annas each.

(5) *Alwáns or thick chadders* are usually worn double by Bengali gentlemen of means. Each *chadder* is 3 yards long and 1⅓ or 1½ yards wide. They are as a rule twilled, and sometimes they are coloured. The price varies from Rs. 25 to Rs. 35 per pair. An ornamental bordered *alwán* first woven for Maharaja Sir Jotendra Mohan Tagore by Mrityunjay Sarkar of Mirzapur now sells for Rs. 50 a pair.

(6) Plain white *dhutis* and *jôrs* (*i.e.*, *dhutis* and *chadders* woven in the same piece, alternately) have a considerable sale throughout Bengal, as they are required for ceremonial purposes. The father of a bride or bridegroom wears a *jôr* at the marriage ceremony of his child. High-class priests also wear *jôrs*. *Jôrs* are worn at the *sradha* (funeral feast) ceremony also. Plain white *dhutis* are worn by rich widows when they go to see their friends. A *jôr* usually costs Rs. 16, and a *dhuti* Rs. 8 to Rs. 10. The length of a *dhuti* is 10 cubits and of a *jôr* 15 cubits, and the width 45 inches.

(7) *Mekhlas*.—These are a special kind of *corah* which are exported to Assam. There they are converted into women's skirts, sometimes after being embroidered with gold thread.

(8) *Mátkás*.—*Matka dhutis* and *saris* made in Murshidabad are much coarser than those made in Rajshahi. They are largely exported to the Mahratta country, but locally they are also worn by elderly men, by widows, and by the poor women of the villages where they are woven. They are made 4 to 8 yards long and 40 to 45 inches wide, and they can be had for Rs. 3 to Rs. 5 per piece. They are also woven into the *chadder* size (3 yards × 1½ yard), and in this state exported to Assam. Locally these *chadders* are worn dyed to a very limited extent.

(9) *Mátká* and *khamru* yarns are sometimes used mixed, *i.e.*, twisted khamru silk going to make the warp and the mátká silk going to make the weft, for weaving thick pieces suitable for making men's suits. These are sold for about Rs 2 a yard. The samples (Nos. 19 and 20) illustrate two styles of these mixed fabrics—one plain and the other twilled and striped (*i.e.* of *khejur-chhari* pattern).

(10) *Imitation Assam silks*.—These were introduced in this district by the writer of this Monograph, in connection with the famine operations of 1897. About 150 families of poor mátká-weavers came for relief, and the only kind of work they were capable of was coarse weaving. About Rs. 11,000 were spent for their relief, including cost of materials, and the fabrics they were made to weave realised by sale about Rs. 10,000. Messrs. Whiteway, Laidlaw & Co. patronised these silks largely, and they have since become very popular. About Rs. 50,000 worth of these silks are now exported annually from Berhampore, and the importance which this new industry has already achieved is locally a well-recognised fact, and it has given rise to a hope

that under a fostering care the silk-weaving industry of Bengal may be developed in other directions also. These imitation Assam silks, or Murshidabad Endies, as they are now called, are sold specially by one Berhampore firm (S. S. Bagchi & Co.), and the samples shown (No. 21 to No. 31) are taken from their pattern-book. The pieces are usually made 7 yards × 27 inches, as originally advised by Messrs. Whiteway, Laidlaw & Co., and they are sold for Rs. 6 or Rs. 7 per piece. They are just sufficient for making one ordinary suit of clothes. They are also woven double the width. Sample No. 26 (valued at Rs. 9) and sample No. 31 (valued at Rs. 14) are exceedingly pretty, and they show what Murshidabad weavers can do out of waste silk.

Class A (2nd)—*Striped fabrics.*—Gown-pieces with coloured stripes are made in two styles, called respectively *rekhis* and *dharis*. *Rekhis* are plain white or coloured gown-pieces (usually 10 yards × 40 inches) with some dark-coloured lines or double lines as per illustrations (Nos. 63 to 66). The ground of *rekhis* may be either plain (Nos. 63 to 65) or twill (No. 66, a to e). *Dharis* have broader stripes, usually of more than one colour. According to the colour of the widest stripe a *dhari* may be either (*a*) red, (*b*) yellow, (*c*) green, (*d*) purple, or (*e*) banesh (chocolate coloured). These five standard kinds of *dhari* are woven for the Arabian market, one of which is represented by specimen No. 62. The kind of *dhari* appreciated locally is not so highly coloured (*vide* specimen No. 61). Like *rekhis*, *dharis* are woven in 10 yards × 40 inches pieces, and are sold for Rs. 16 to Rs. 18 or Rs. 23 to Rs. 25 per piece; the heavily-starched, high-coloured pieces being sold cheaper, while the thick-woven, lighter-coloured pieces made for the local market are sold for the higher price.

Class A (3rd).—*Checks* are divided into five kinds of fabrics :—

(1) *Chárkhánás* or checks where the squares or oblongs are of diverse colour. These, like *rekhis* and *dharis*, are made in two styles—one suited to Arab taste, and the other suited to local taste. The former (called *chaukárás*) are more highly coloured and heavily starched, and are cheaper fabrics, sold for Rs. 18 to Rs. 19 per piece, while the latter are closer woven superior fabrics, sold for about Rs. 25 a piece. Two samples (Nos. 57 and 58) of the kind of *chaukárás* made for the Arabian market, and twelve of those *charkhánás* (Nos. 51 to 56) made for the local market are shown in the sample sheets for illustration. Fine flimsy checks of the latter style (No. 55) are woven in the Baluchar circle for the use of Jain ladies and Jain children of Baluchar and Azimgunge, who are habitually to be seen in *kurtás* and *pájámás* made of such cheap silk. They are made 40 inches wide and are sold for Re. 1-8 per yard. These fine and flimsy checks used to be made at Chandrakona and other villages in the Jahanabad subdivision of Hooghly, and the Baluchar weavers have simply taken over the Jahanabad industry.

(2) *Charkhánás* or checks, which consist of white ground and coloured square outlines, the squares being of various sizes as in the previous case. The lines are either double, triple, or single, and the ground is either plain or twill (*vide* samples Nos. 37 to 52). The dimensions and prices are the same as in the previous case, *i.e.*, they are usually made 10 yards × 40 inches, and priced Rs. 20 to Rs. 40 per piece.

(3) *Matrás.*—These are of a standard Arabic pattern, like *dharis*, *rekhis*, and *chaukarás*. They are striped like *dharis*, but all along the edges of the stripes are studded rows of little squares or oblongs. The dimensions are the same as in *dharis*, *rekhis* and *chaukarás*. Matrás exported to Arabia cost a rupee more than the other styles also made for the Arabian market.

(4) *Phulikát checks*—Illustrated by sample No. 68, are woven for the Rangoon market. The lines are white and the ground is either red, or yellow, or green, or purple, or banesh (chocolate), which are the five standard colours for the goods that are exported. Phulikát checks are considered suitable only for handkerchiefs. They are made a yard square, and 15 are woven together, which cost about Rs. 19.

(5) Check *matkás* (No. 67) are a very coarse class of fabrics woven for the Maharatta country. A check *matká sari* 8½ yards long and 45 inches wide may be had for Rs. 5 or Rs. 6. The trade with the Maharatta country in plain and check *matkás* is pretty extensive.

Class A (4th).—Bordered fabrics.—The demand for Murshidabad bordered *saris, dhotis, jórs, chelis,* and *matkás,* is very considerable. The upper middle classes of Bengal patronise these fabrics very largely, and *chelis* and *matkás* are in demand among the lower middle classes also. The price of a *sari* of two or three borders, varies from Rs. 10 to Rs. 18. White silk *saris* made out of *dhali* silk, with *dhákká táj pár* or border, of *kamlea*-orange colour, are considered very fashionable by Bengali ladies. A *sari* with spotted ground (No. 91*a*) has been recently produced by Mrityunjoy, which is sold at Rs. 30 a piece. This is the very best fabric produced in Murshidabad. But *tájpár, katkápár, padmapár,* and *bhomrapár saris* with plain white ground are the common styles in use. *Dháni katkápár, phitapár, ghunsipár,* and *churipár* are the common styles of border adopted for men's *dhutis.* The *sari* represented by sample No. 91 is a three-bordered *kalkápár sari.* Number 90 illustrates what is called "Dhakka" border. The borders of *dhutis* are made narrower, and there are never three but always two borders at the two edges. Number 84 illustrates a *kasipár dhuti.* Silk *saris* and *dhutis* when they have coloured grounds are called *chelis.* *Chelis* of very flimsy texture have a large sale. They are used for making ceremonial presents at various religious festivals. Parsis also use cheap *chelis* for making ceremonious presents in celebrating funeral rites. A seven-yard piece of *cheli* of this sort may be had for Re. 1-10 to Rs. 2, and when it is considered that the material used is pure silk, the worthlessness of the stuff can be very well imagined. A *cheli jór* (*i.e., dhuti* and *chadder*) of superior quality, such as is worn by a Bengali bridegroom of good family, may cost as much as Rs. 25.

Reyias have also coloured borders. They are sent to Assam, where they are worn by Assamese women to cover the upper part of their bodies, somewhat in the same way as *chadders* are worn. They are woven in the Baluchar centre. They are 4½ yards long and 22 inches wide, the two ends (*anchlás*) being ornamented with coloured borders. The gold embroidering of *reyias* is done after their arrival in Assam.

Handkerchiefs are sometimes woven with coloured borders.

Matká dhutis and *saris* are also made with black or red borders, the borders of *saris* being wider than those of *dhutis.*

Class A (5th).—Printed fabrics.—The art of printing *corahs* for making handkerchiefs, door-curtains, scarfs, and *namabalis* (or *chadders* containing religious texts) is almost extinct in Murshidabad. The industry has transferred itself to Serampore and Chandernagore, though silk pieces are taken to these places from Berhampore for the purpose. The dyers of Khagra are chiefly employed in dyeing yarns, but they still do printing to special order. Samples Nos. 71 (*a*) and (*b*) illustrate the defunct printed silk handkerchiefs of Murshidabad, and sample No. 72, a printed *namabali.* The price of these fabrics depends on the quality of *corah* used.

Class A (6th).—Bánhus or *bandannahs* (tie-and-dye silks) are dyed *corahs* or *matkás* with spots or rings, coloured or white. These spots and rings are made by tying strong knots at small distances, according to the required pattern and dyeing the pieces of *corah* or *matka.* The word '*bandhana*' in Sanskrit means tying, which is the origin of the term *bandannah.** The pieces after patient

* In his paper on "Art as Applied to the Weaving and Printing of Textile Fabrics," Sir Thomas Wardle in alluding to the tie-and-dye work, says:—"It is extensively practised in India, particularly in Jeypore and Ulwar. It was the precursor of printing in the silk handkerchief trade in Calcutta and Berhampore, and is a very remarkable means of producing designs in spots, round, oval or square, and plaids."

knotting are dyed and washed and dried, and the knots loosened. White spots or rings are formed at the points where the knots were made. When coloured spots or rings are desired, the strings with which the knots are made are first dyed in that particular colour before the tying of the knots. The colour of the strings is imprinted on the cloth at the points where the knots are made. Pieces with rings instead of spots are called *churis*. When the rings are small and close together they are called *matichurs*. Skirts and turbans are made of these materials, and there is a considerable trade with the North-Western Provinces and the Punjab in *bánhus* and *churis*. The price of a piece depends entirely on the quality of *corah* or *matká* used, about 8 annas per piece being added for the dyeing process. Sample No. 69 represents a *churi* and sample No. 70 a *bánhu* with square spots.

Class B.—Fabrics made with nakshá-loom—

1st.—Under this class we have first of all the Baluchar *butedar sari*. These *saris* with ornamental ground, ornamental border, ornamental corner figures (called *kunjas*), and a more highly ornamental end-piece or *ánchlá*, were at one time very highly prized by the upper middle class people of Bengal. Now the ladies of this class go in for the more costly fabrics of Benares. The ordinary Baluchar *butedar sari* is rather an ugly fabric to use for personal decoration (No. 92), but some are very neatly made and deserve encouragement (*e.g.*, No. 93). These *saris* are made 10 cubits long and 42 to 45 inches wide. The price varies according to quality from Rs. 10 to Rs. 50. For the cheaper articles untwisted and ill-sorted raw silk is used; the number of threads used for the warp is also less, the weft is loosely woven, the dyes used are fugitive, and the appearance is maintained by heavy starching, sugar being mixed with the starch used to add to the gloss. A cheap *Baluchar butedar sari* can be woven in a week, but a valuable one takes three four or months weaving. Sometimes these *saris* are made without *ánchlás*, but only with four *kalkas* or *kunjas* (conventional lotus buds) at the four corners. Such *saris* of the same size are somewhat cheaper (Rs. 8 to Rs. 40 instead of Rs. 10 to Rs. 50).

2nd.—*Rumals* (square shawls) and shawls with ornamental borders and corners, in imitation of Kashmir *rumals* and shawls, are occasionally made to order. Table-cloths (No. 94*a*) are also turned out from *nakshá*-looms. The ground is of twilled pattern and white, the ornaments either grey or more highly coloured. The shawls, are made 6 cubits long and 3 cubits wide, and the price asked is Rs. 40 or Rs. 50, there being no inferior articles of this class in demand. The high-class *saris*, *rumals*, shawls, and table-covers used to be woven until lately by only one man in the district, or rather the looms turning out these could have been set only by Dubraj, the weaving being done by others working under Dubraj's direction. Dubraj would not set looms for making these high-class fabrics for any one else. He used also to weave at one time shawls with religious texts in the place of the ground ornament, but he gave up this work in his old age, as the operation of weaving required that the cloth-beam should be below the navel, which is considered a sacrilege when one is dealing with a cloth containing religious texts.

3rd.—Scarfs and sashes (No. 94) were also woven by Dubraj to order. The width of these is always 1 foot, and the price varies with the length, a rupee being charged for every foot of length. The quality of silk (which is twill) is the same, and there is no variation made in the price. Dubraj's loom for weaving sashes has been acquired by the Rampur Boalia Sericultural School, and it is in working order and actually in use in this school. The products of Dubraj's looms are inferior only to the best products of Kashmir and Benares looms. The competition with Kashmir products would not affect the sale of these, as rich men who use Kashmir shawls and scarfs in the cold weather could use Dubraj's shawls and scarfs in warmer weather, as locally they are so used. But the competition with Benares gold-embroidered *saris*, shawls, etc., is too strong even for Dubraj's goods. A Hindu lady who can afford to wear a Benares *sari* will not look at even a high-class Baluchar *sari* on high days and holidays. One thing, however, should be mentioned in favour of these ornamental silks. They stand any amount of washing which Benares goods do not. It is too late, however, to think of reviving the industry of weaving ornamental silk fabrics, as the only man who could be used as a lever to uplift the industry is now dead. The Society for the Promotion of Indian Arts in London interested itself in the matter and raised some money also, but the local people were extremely apathetic and the scheme fell through. The only hope of reviving the art now rests on the fact that Dubraj's looms are still in existence.

Class C.—Embroidered and other hand-worked fabrics.—Embroidering on silk is chiefly done in rich Jain families and also in some Muhammadan houses for domestic purposes. The few professional embroiderers there are in the district live in City Murshidabad, and they come to Baluchar for embroidering *reyias* and *mekhlas* that are exported to Assam. A piece of embroidered *reyia* or *mekhla* costs Rs. 40 to Rs. 50. Foreign silks, satin, and velvet are usually chosen by Jain and Muhammudan ladies for their domestic work, in which they often exhibit great skill and taste. Hand-embroidered wearing apparel cannot be had in the district in shops or markets; and the fabric used being usually foreign, the art need only be mentioned here.

100. Knitting of silk socks was an industry of some note in Murshidabad in the days when there were English military officers in the district. The industry is now extinct. I sent an old Murshidabad silk sock to the Economic section of the Indian Museum a few years ago. I was told the industry was confined among some poor women of Berhampore in the palmy days of Murshidabad.

101. Having now given an account of the various classes of silk fabrics woven in Murshidabad, I will now simply quote the portions of the district monographs from the other districts dealing on this subject:—

102. The Hooghly monograph furnishes the following particulars regarding the silk fabrics manufactured in that district:—

"(1) *Swagaji pieces.*—These stand first in point of demand. They are made of a mixture of silk and *tasar* warp woven with cotton thread. They are made of various lengths from 10 to 38 yards, the breadth being 1½ yard. These are used in the Punjab in making skirts and jackets and wraps for women. They are made with red and white stripes on an orange ground. They are sold for Rs. 2-8 to Rs. 35 per piece.

(2) *Muskha.*—These are made of the same materials and are used for the same purposes as above. The length varies from 15 to 32 yards. The stripes are black and orange, and the price varies from Rs. 5 to Rs. 35.

(3) *Selai-Khata.*—Same as above, but fine black stripes on orange ground. The length varies from 15 to 30 yards and the breadth from ¾ inch to $\frac{3}{14}$ yards sold from Rs. 5 to Rs. 20 per piece.

(4) *Phularu.*—Same as above, but red *phuls* or flowers on yellow or white ground. Size varies from 12 yards by ½ yard to 18 yards by $\frac{11}{16}$ yard. These are made of silk and *tassar* used in the Punjab as *puggries* (head-dress) and *kummerbands*, sold from Rs. 2 to Rs. 4-8 per piece.

(5) *Jarda or sujasdi.*—These are made in red and white stripes on yellow ground. Size 10 yards by ½ yard, made of silk and *tassar* warp woven with cotton thread, sold at Re. 1 per piece.

Besides these, a variety called *sushi* in red and blue checks is occasionally manufactured to order. They measure 20 yards by 1¼ yard, and sell from Rs. 25 to Rs. 30 per piece."

103. In Burdwan "the silk is made into pieces with embroidered edges, and are used for *dhutis*, *saris*, *chadder*, *napkins*, *mooka* (turbans)."

104. In Birbhum "the products which generally consist of *dhutis*, *saris*, with printed and plain borders, pieces of 10 yards and 7 yards (*thâns*), and handkerchiefs, are sold locally and sometimes exported to other parts of the

Province through agents. *Thans* (pieces 10 yards or 7 yards) are sold at 12 annas to Re. 1-8 per yard; *dhutis* with ordinary borders at Rs. 6 to Rs. 10, *saris* at Rs. 8 to Rs. 15; handkerchiefs at Rs. 3 to Rs. 6 per dozen.

105. The various kinds of silk fabrics manufactured at Bankura and their prices are noted below :—

	Price. Rs. A.	Rs. A.
(1) *Fullam sari*, or cloth for females with patterns of flower on them	10 0 to	20 0
(2) *Dhuti*, or cloth for male	10 0 ,,	12 0
(3) *Thâns*, or pieces for making dresses with ...	1 8 ,,	1 12 per yard.
(4) Comforter	1 8 ,,	1 12 each.
(5) Handkerchief	0 12 each	
(6) Checks of silk	1 8 per yard."	

106. The Bogra monograph gives fuller information on this subject :—

"The kinds of silk fabrics manufactured in this district are very limited. The Tantis weave mostly *dhutis* and *chadders*. The other kinds of fabrics are handkerchiefs, *thans* or pieces for making coats, *chapkans*, *etc.*, and *alawans*.

"The things woven are all plain. No ornamentation can be worked in the body of the fabric. Only one weaver knows how to prepare ornamented borders. His name is Baul Tanti of Malatinagur. I have seen him weave Kalkapair *dhutis*. The Tantis do not dye the fabrics; all fabrics are sold white. Some *dhutis* are woven with their borders coloured. But the threads for these borders are generally brought from Calcutta. The Tantis do not know how to make fast dyes.

"Of the silk fabrics, we shall first take up *dhuties*. These are woven either with dyed or with plain borders. There is practically no difference in price between a *dhuti* with coloured border and one with plain border. *Garad dhuties* are preferred by Hindus for wearing when sitting at prayers or for worship. Men and widows use *dhuties* with plain borders, while married women use *dhuties* with coloured borders. None but Hindus wear *garad dhuties*.

"A dhuti is generally of the following dimensions :— 9½ cubits long × 2¼ cubits wide. The price varies from Rs. 9 to Rs. 12 per *dhuti*. The thread required for each *dhuti* will be about 6 chitaks.

	Rs.	A.	P.
"Price at the rate of Rs. 14 per seer	5	4	0
Cost of extra labour in preparing the thread for *dhutis* ...	0	9	0
	5	13	0
Price of a *dhuti*	11	0	0
Margin for the weaver	5	3	0

"A *dhuti* can be woven this way in eight days. But the weaver will require the labour of another man throughout—generally a member of his family.

"This will give a rough estimate of the profits of the weaver.

"*Chadder.*—This is a sheet required by men for wearing over the coat or other cover for the upper part of the body. The borders are plain. This is 6 cubits long × 3 cubits wide; price Rs. 6 to Rs. 9."

"*Thân* (required for making coats, *chapkans*, *chogas*, etc.). It is made generally 6 yards long and 1 yard wide. But longer or shorter pieces are made on order. The *thân* 6 yards long will be sold at Rs. 14 to Rs. 18 according to the quality.

"*Handkerchief.* Handkerchief 24 inches square sold at 10 annas to Re. 1. Handkerchiefs bigger than this are also woven."

"*Alawan* or *Terchi chadder 6 cubits × 3 cubits.*—From the manner of weaving this has a better look than plain sheets. The crossings of the warp and the weft show prominent lines inclined both to the length and breadth of the cloth. This form of sheets is believed to be more durable. Price Rs. 24 to Rs. 28 per piece."

107. In Maldah "silk *saris*, *dhuties*, handkerchiefs, sheets, and pieces of coating are manufactured. Fine silk *saris* and *dhuties*, 15 feet by 44 to 46 inches,

sell at from Rs. 10 to Rs. 15 per piece, and silk *thans* for coating sell at Rs. 20 to Rs. 25 per piece of 10 yards, the width being 44 inches. Silk sheets used as wrappers in winter, six to seven cubits in length, and $2\frac{3}{4}$ to 3 cubits in width sell at Rs. 25 to Rs. 28 per pair. Besides these *uranis* or *chadders* used in summer, made of fine threads, length 6 cubits and width 3 cubits, are also manufactured, the price per piece being Rs. 5 to Rs. 7.

"The following kinds of cloth are also made of silk or of mixed silk and cotton, the warp being of silk and the woof of cotton :—

	Rs.	A.		Rs.	A.	
"(1) Maldahi Gultishi Katar sells at ...	4	0	to	7	0	Per piece of 3 yards by 32 inches.
(2) Maldahi Udakatar	4	0	,,	7	0	
(3) Maldahi Belkhali Fuldar	9	0	,,	10	8	
(4) Chaki Mujlahar	9	0	,,	10	8	
(5) Sádá	8	0	,,	9	8	
(6 Nangfuli	9	0	,,	10	0	
(7) Fulam Senaja	10	0	,,	11	0	
(8) Kadumfuli (length 6 yards) ...	14	0	,,	16	0	
(9) Chand tara (ditto) ...	10	0	,,	13	0	
(10) Pattadâr Seraja	8	0	,,	10	0	
(11) Sârhor Serâjâ	8	0	,,	9	8	
(12) Bulbul chasma	9	0	,,	10	0	
(13) Mâldahi Kâtor Hiradana	6	0	,,	8	0	
(14) Mâldâhi Kâtar Kâlbali	6	0	,,	8	0	
(15) Masru Sells at	3	0	,,	6	0	(*a*) *Lalsahana.* (*b*) *Sikiar.* (*c*) *Qundlal.* (*d*) *Matichur.*
(16) Chanfulia	10	0	,,	11	0	
(17) Kashida	10	0	,,	11	0	

108. In Rajshahi only *matkás* of a superior quality (*matká* yarn being sometimes mixed with reeled silk yarn) are woven. *Matká* pieces (*tháns*) are well suited for making durable clothes. *Matká dhutis* and *saris* made in Rajshahi are also in requisition, chiefly in the Calcutta market.

109. The Rajshahi monograph speaks of *chasam* or tape waste (*frisson*) being utilised at Delhi for *kamarbands* (waist bands), *jhuls* for elephants, and for turbans. The *chasam* is exported to the North-Western Provinces and the Punjab as well as to Calcutta. "As regards the quantity of *chasam* produced," continues this monograph, "in comparison with silk, it was estimated that 11 villages bordering on the road of Natore from Boalia produced in a year 800 maunds of silk and 2,000 maunds of *chasam.*" The proportion between silk and waste is not, however, correctly put here. More waste is no doubt made by the native system of reeling, partly owing to the inferior cocoons used in the former and partly on account of rapid and careless handling A maund of *khamru* silk produces about 25 to 30 seers of waste, while a maund of filature silk produces only 11 to 20 seers of waste. Very little of the waste is utilised in the country, the greater portion being exported to Europe. In some districts borders of cotton *saris* and *dhutis* are made with dyed silk obtained from tape-waste. But the total quantity so used in the whole of Bengal must be very insignificant. Pierced cocoons, on the other hand, which are also a kind of waste, are mostly employed in the country for the *matká*-weaving industry.

110. Including *tassar* and *endi* weavers, there are over 43,000 silk-weavers in Bengal (*vide* Table A, Part III), representing about 9,000 families. There is not a Hindu family so humble that does not aspire to make a show of *chelis* and other indigenous silks on religious festivals. This demand is very large and very constant; and although the silks of one locality may get popular and of another locality may get cast into oblivion, silk-weavers, as a class, are well patronised and their earnings are higher than those of cultivators. The fact that during the last decade the number of silk-weavers has increased from 27,000 to 43,000, is also significant of the prosperity of the Province and the vitality of the Bengal silk industry.

CHAPTER X.

Disposal of Silk Fabrics.

111. No uniform plan exists for the disposal of silk fabrics in the different districts. Individual weavers going to *mahajans* (money-lenders), or merchants or shop-keepers, carrying their goods in their own hands, is the general rule. Occasionally one rich weaver secures goods from a number of weavers who look up to him as a sort of patriarch, and disposes of large quantities to rich merchants. A Berhampore merchant gets a requisition for 2,000 pieces of *corah*, for instance, from Calcutta or Bombay. He sends for Joykristo Mondal of Mirzapur and Batakristo Ranu of Islampur, and he gives them advances and they enter into contract with him. They have great influence with their fellow-caste-men, and they secure the pieces in a short time without much trouble. If the merchants have to deal with small weavers, they would lose a considerable portion of the advances they might make to them. Bisenchand Babu and Khetu Babu of Baluchar, who are both silk merchants and *mahajans*, buy up large quantities of silks from weavers direct.

112. The following account regarding the disposal of silk is given in the Howrah monograph:—

Howrah.

"Silk has no regular market in this district, as no silkcloth is woven here. It is taken to *hâts* or fairs, and sometimes to Ghatal and Calcutta for sale. The produce in thana Jagatballabpur is said to be taken mostly to Furfura in thana Krishnanagore, in the district of Hooghly, and is sold to the dealers of that place. Silk is also sold to the persons who trade in silk, and who give small advances to the cultivators of mulberry. Sometimes cocoons are sold in places in the neighbouring district of Midnapore, where there are silk filatures. The value of indigenous silk trade in this district may be roughly estimated at Rs. 12,500 during the year."

Hooghly.

113. The following information is furnished by the Hooghly report on the trade in silk yarns and silk fabrics:—

"The Tantis use the following materials in the manufacture of dress-pieces, etc.:—

(1) *Khaja Meju reshum* (silk of superior quality). Price from Rs. 11 to Rs. 13 per seer of 70 tolahs, purchased either direct from the Chasi Kaibartas of Khas Bar in Ghatal or from bunniah middlemen, who purchase from the Chasi Kaibartas.

(2) *Suddha Meyeri*, from Re. 1 to Re. 1-4 per seer less than above.

"They employ labourers for cleaning the thread at the rate of Re. 1 for each seer of good thread turned out. It is said to take from four to seven days for a man to turn out one seer. The thread when ready is called *Banak-resham*.

"After purchasing the silk they clean it by the process called *phirán*, *i.e.*, they take the thread from the spindle and gather it on to a *látai* or reel. About one to two chitaks weight of silk is lost in this process. The waste silk (*Phulki* or *kichar*) on being removed is said to have been formerly sold at from 8 to 10 annas per seer; there is no sale now. The thread is then made into *báda* or reels.

"Besides the weavers, there are a few families of Tantis at Udairajpur, Kalagachia, and Sudanganj, who deal in silk thread. They purchase the raw silk from Midnapore.

"The thread is sold by the Tantis in Calcutta at a profit of one and-a-half to two and-a-half annas per seer to Arracanese dealers.

"The trade is, however, inconsiderable.

"A kind of silk thread called *pakwan* or twisted thread was spun formerly, but has gone out of vogue.

"The looms used are the same as those which are used in turning out cotton pieces, and the process of weaving is similar. It is needless therefore to go into details on these points.

"All the silk fabrics manufactured are exported."

Burdwan.

114. Burdwan silks are sold preferably to dealers of native firms, who come round, as they give the best prices—Rs. 8 or Rs. 9 for a piece of *garad* silk 10 cubits long, and Rs. 7 or Rs. 8 for a piece of *tasar* silk 10 cubits long. In some cases the *mahajans* advance the money to the weavers to buy yarn from the dealers, and

then bring the silk when manufactured. For this they practically fix their own price, and leave the weavers only a living wage: hence the preference for dealing with the merchants. Very few bring their produce into Burdwan for sale, though a few do, and by thus avoiding the middlemen make better profits.

The majority of the Katwa silk goes to Calcutta, where it is sold or exported. Madrasi Mussalmans are very large consumers. They use long pieces, 21 feet by 3 feet, to make their turbans.

Birbhum.

115. With regard to Birbhum fabrics, the following account is furnished:—"Most part of the manufacture is exported from the district, a smaller portion being disposed of locally, and it is said that a small portion goes to Europe, where it can hardly compete with European-made articles as regards cost, although it is sometimes liked by the Europeans for its quality."

Bankura.

116. In Bankura "all the silk fabrics manufactured are sold locally at Bankura and Vishnupur. The fabrics turned out are said to be more lasting."

Bogra.

117. For Bogra we have the following account:—

"All the silk fabrics manufactured in this district are locally consumed. No exports are known. The weavers either make the cloths to order or take them to probable customers for sale. People also come to their houses and purchase the articles. The produce of this district is not sufficient to supply local demands. Traders in the bazar import silk fabrics from Calcutta or Murshidabad, and they find a market here. The reason for this is the want of a large stock in the district to choose from. The weavers do not produce silk fabrics in a sufficient quantity for sending them to the bazar traders. They cannot weave cloths of varied qualities and prices. Their fabrics are of the medium quality—neither very good nor very bad. So they cannot supply the demands of those who require cheap things or very fine things.

"Anyhow it is not possible that the weavers that now actually work should be able to supply the wants of the whole district; nor is it possible for the weavers to compete with the cheap foreign articles, and the result is that silk-weaving is gradually declining. The total price of silk fabrics woven in this district is estimated at Rs. 1,400 in the year."

Rajshahi.

118. The Rajshahi monograph has the following account regarding the disposal of the *matká* cloths woven in this district:—

"The cloth woven appears to be disposed of in three ways. The weaver either hands over the cloth to the person who advanced him the cost of the thread, whose order he is merely carrying out, or he sells on his own account, or lastly he sells to a *dalal*. This is the way most *matká* cloth is disposed of in the first instance. The great *dalal* of the district is Gokul Jugi of Kengachi, near Boalia. He buys from Dakra, where, including the immediately neighbouring villages, there are 23 looms, from Mirgunge, and from a few weavers he has at Kengachi."

Malda.

119. For Malda the following account has been furnished:—

"A very large proportion of the silk fabrics manufactured in the district is exported to Bombay, Calcutta, Joypur, Benares, and Mirzapur, by the *marwaris* and other money-lenders. There is also a small local demand for cloths made of mixed silk and cotton. There is no internal trade in silk. Silk goods are never sold at the local *háts* or periodical fairs. There are one or two shops in English Bazar town, where silk fabrics are sold. The two principal Benares firms who have establishments in Maldah for buying silks are those of Messrs. Dwarka Das, Raghunath Das and Messrs. Saligram Jagannath Das."

120. Table Q at the end of this Part gives some idea of the export of Bengal silks to the North-Western Provinces and Oudh, the Punjab, the Central Provinces, Rajputana, Sind, and other parts of India; by rail, over 10 lakhs of rupees' worth being exported in 1896-97 and over 20 lakhs of rupees' worth in 1897-98. From Table E it will be also seen that in 1896-97 over 11½ lakhs of rupees' worth of Bengal-manufactured silk was exported to foreign countries, and in 1897-98 about 9 lakhs of rupees' worth. This does not represent all the export of manufactured silk from the silk districts of Bengal. From Table R it will be seen that Calcutta received over 19 lakhs of Rupees worth of manufactured silk in 1896-97, and in 1897-98 nearly 16 lakhs of rupees' worth, by rail. The 11½ lakhs and 9 lakhs of rupees' worth of silk exported from Calcutta to foreign countries during those two years must be included in the 19 lakhs and 16 lakhs respectively; but Calcutta receives silks from Midnapore and other

districts by roads, canals, and rivers, which are not included in the 19 lakhs and 16 lakhs. Then there is some inter-district transaction also in Bengal, which is not included in the above figures, nor the local consumption in the silk districts themselves. The export of manufactured silk from the silk districts of Bengal by rail to Calcutta and to up-country is represented by about 33 lakhs of rupees, and the total exports, including inter-district and boat traffic, probably by about 40 lakhs of rupees. To this if we add what is consumed locally in the silk districts, the total product of Bengal silk-looms, must be estimated at, at least, 50 lakhs of rupees, *i e.*, at perhaps a higher figure than the product of raw silk which is exported to foreign countries. The raw silk exported by rail to up-country is worth about 15 lakhs of rupees per annum, and the 3,000 maunds of Bengal raw silk exported by steamer to Bombay, Madras, and Burma (*vide* Table G) are worth another 15 lakhs of rupees. These 30 lakhs of rupees' worth of Bengal silk is woven into fabrics outside Bengal, in other Provinces of India. The value of this silk would come to over 50 lakhs of rupees. Thus out of the silk spun in Bengal, the Indian silk-weaving industry benefits to the extent of over a crore of rupees per annum, while the foreign trade in Bengal raw silk brings to the country another 50 lakhs of rupees per annum. Tables H and J go further to confirm these statements.

121. Leaving out of question the broad channels into which Bengal silks find their way, we have already seen how each district disposes of its products. The information supplied on this point in most of the district monographs is very meagre and unreliable. That 27,000 weavers (*vide* Table A) are easily able to produce 50 lakhs of rupees' worth of silk can be seen from a little calculation. Of the 50 lakhs of rupees, about 12½ lakhs represent the wages of the weavers, including the profits of the middlemen, and the rest the cost of materials. The 12½ lakhs divided among 27,000 individuals give about Rs. 46 per annum to each individual, or Rs. 184 per family, *i.e.*, about Rs. 15 per month per family. As the profits of the middlemen, including money-lenders, are included in this calculation, the monthly wages estimated per family cannot be considered too high, and this estimate is, in fact, in accord with the statements in the district monographs regarding earnings of weavers. From another point of view we can substantiate this estimate. The Rs. 50,00,000 worth of silk fabrics represents about 4,800 maunds (*vide* Tables Q. and R.), and as in bleaching and unwinding, raw-silk loses a fourth of its weight, the 4,800 maunds of silk fabrics are equivalent to over 6,000 maunds of raw-silk, including *matká*, *tasar*, and *endi* silks. To this add the 3,000 maunds of raw and waste silks exported to the other Provinces by river, and another 3,000 maunds exported by steamer. This brings us to the total of about 12,000 maunds of raw and waste silk, as the quantity of indigenous silk utilized in Indian looms, which is equivalent to about 480,000 *kilos*. Now M. Rondot in his statistical work entitled *L'Industrie de la soie en France* (1894) gives 475,000 kilos of mulberry silk (indigenous) and 20,000 kilos of waste (indigenous) as the quantities consumed in Indian looms. Allowing 15,000 kilos as the total produce of raw and waste silk in the other Provinces, we get 480,000 kilos of Bengal silk consumed in Indian looms, *viz.*, the same quantity we have calculated out. Thus, while the estimate of 50 lakhs of rupees' worth of manufactured silk is borne out by the figures in the Administration Report, and in the Census Report of 1891, and the figures supplied by M. Rondot, the district monographs supply little clue as to where these 50 lakhs of rupees worth of silk are woven. It is possible, no doubt, to make an imaginary allotment of this amount according to the number of weavers in the different districts, but the result of such allotment would not be accurate by any means. As most of the district monographs give no real clue for tracing the total produce in different centres, the only feasible way, however, of doing this is to make the allotment, as suggested. The census figures of 1891, where positive, are, on the whole, reliable. Silk-weavers who are mainly cultivators or members of other trade or profession, have no doubt been returned as cultivators, &c. So that there were probably about 30,000 silk-weavers in Bengal in 1891 instead of 27,000, and the number seems to have materially augmented during the last ten years, as the condition of the silk industry since 1889 has been steadily improving.

The following table, therefore, gives a fairer estimate of produce in different localities than we can arrive by any other means, at present available.

Locality.	Number of weavers according to Census Report of 1891.	Value of silk woven.
1	2	3
		Rs.
Burdwan	994	1,80,000
Birbhum	609	1,00,000
Bankura	891	1,60,000
Midnapore	3,545	6,45,000
Hooghly	1,141	2,00,000
Howrah	100	18,000
24-Parganas	70	12,000
Nadia	98	18,000
Murshidabad	11,392	21,00,000
Rajshahi	2,312	4,00,000
Bogra	13	2,000
Dacca	55	10,000
Chittagong Division ...	52	10,000
Patna " ...	41	7,000
Bhagalpur	458	80,000
Malda	2,510	4,60,000
Sonthal Parganas ...	96	12,000
Cuttack	274	50,000
Balasore	87	10,000
Puri	221	40,000
Hazaribagh	6	1,000
Lohardaga	1	7,000
Manbhum	212	36,000
Singhbhum	358	64,000
Feudatary States	1,710	3,08,000
Total ...	27,286	50,00,000

122. As no distinction is made between mulberry, *tussar* and *endi* silk fabrics in the figures given in the Administration Report, the distinction is made in the above table in a conventional form. Figures with single lines only under them denote chiefly mulberry silk industry, figures with no lines under them denote mulberry silk industry exclusively, and figures with double lines under them denote either *tusser* or *endi* (chiefly *tussar*) silk industry. In other words, about 23,000 persons are employed in silk-weaving, about 2,500 persons in tusser-weaving, and about 1,800 persons in *endi*-weaving, and the respective values of the three classes of fabrics may be put down, in round figures, at 43 lakhs, 4 lakhs and 3 lakhs of rupees, per annum. The Census of 1901 gives us a still more hopeful view of the situation.

123. That the above estimate differs entirely from the estimates annually furnished by district officers may be judged from only one instance. Against 21 lakhs of rupees worth of silk fabrics, which I estimate as the annual production of Murshidabad, the district officer's estimate is only 2½ lakhs. The district monograph on this point has the following remarks :—

"No statistics are published, but from what I have been able to learn, I think that the annual value probably does not exceed Rs. 2,50,000. The district administration report of last year mentions Mirzapore alone as having turned out 6,052 pieces of cloth, valued at Rs. 45,396; this as against 6,895 pieces valued at Rs. 47,465 of the year before. The Statistical Reporter of May 1876 estimates the annual value at Rs. 6,00,000, but there is no doubt there has been a large decrease."

124. Such statements being based on vague guesses of police officers cannot be relied upon in the same way as the deductions from census figures and figures supplied by Railway and Steamer Companies can be relied upon. Let us see what quantities of silk found their way to Calcutta and to up-country in 1896-97 and 1897-98, as far as can be gathered from Steamer and Railway Companies' returns embodied in the Administration Report for 1897-98 (*vide* pages 203—210)—

	1896-97.		1897-98.	
1	2	3	4	5
	Mds.	Rs.	Mds.	Rs.
Silk piece-goods brought down to Calcutta by rivers.	300	2,92,200	726	7,08,576
Silk piece-goods brought down to Calcutta by rail	1,988	19,36,312	1,626	15,86,976
Total to Calcutta ...	2,288	22,28,512	2,352	22,95,552
Add silk piece-goods exported by rail from Bengal to North-Western Provinces and Oudh, Punjab, Central Provinces, etc., exclusive of what is exported from Calcutta (which may be assumed to be not indigenous).	486	4,73,364	1,359	13,26,120
Total quantity of Bengal silk ascertained to be exported.	2,774	27,01,876	3,711	36,21,672

125. To the above might also be added some of the 545 maunds, valued at Rs. 5,28,960, exported by rail in 1896-97, and of 788 maunds, valued at Rs. 6,94,640, exported by rail in 1897-98 from Calcutta to up-country. The table in page 210 of the Administration Report does not mention that the manufactured silk so exported by rail to up-country from Calcutta is indigenous; but it seems it is indigenous silk that is meant. Assuming, however, as I have assumed in the above table, that it is all foreign silk that goes from Calcutta to the North-Western Provinces and Oudh, Punjab, etc., and not taking into account any other route of transit to Calcutta and up-country (though there are such routes), not taking into account any inter-district trade and any local consumption, we have to account for over 36 lakhs of rupees worth of silk in 1897-98. As Murshidabad, according to the Census figures (Table A), contains about half the number of silk-weavers there are in Bengal, half the above quantity must have been derived from this district. That gives us at least 18 lakhs. Table J confirms this estimate as 4,135 maunds of silk piece goods exported from Bengal are worth nearly 50 lakhs of Rupees.

126. It will be seen that we have under-estimated the production of Bengal silk fabrics in the preceding paragraph, putting it down at Rs. 36,00,000. I have known weavers carrying bundles of silks with them by rail to Calcutta for sale before the Pujas. No account is taken of such personal luggage of passengers, and I know a large quantity of silk fabrics produced in Murshidabad find their way to Calcutta as 'railway parcel' or 'personal luggage.' If to this we add the inter-district trade and local consumption, we cannot be far wrong in putting the total production at 50 lakhs. The year 1896-97 being the famine year, there was a very considerable falling off in the silk trade of Bengal with the other provinces of India, and this is the reason for choosing the higher figure of the above table (Rs. 36,21,672) instead of the lower figure (Rs. 27,01,876) as the measure for the existing state of the silk-weaving industry of Bengal. The importance of the silk-weaving industry of Murshidabad and some other districts has therefore been vastly under-estimated, and I am of opinion that neither 6 lakhs nor 2½ lakhs of rupees represents by any means the present product of the Murshidabad looms; but,

as shown in the table given higher up, I believe Murshidabad produces more than 20 lakhs of rupees' worth of silk fabrics annually; and though the export trade in *corahs* has diminished of late years, from personal observation and enquiry I have ascertained that the silk-weaving industry of Murshidabad is looking up again, and there have been improvements in new and important directions within the last fifteen years. There is a larger internal trade now in superior fabrics, specially in the Jangipur circle, than there has been for many years past, and this may in fact be looked upon as an index of the general prosperity of this Province. The use of silk fabrics is considered even in Europe as a sure index of national prosperity, and the rise and fall of the silk trade is looked upon in the light of a social and political barometer. The famine of 1896-97 affected the use of silk fabrics most materially, but the prosperity that followed in the next year at once brought with it renewed use of silk goods. It should be also noted here that from personal enquiry from native merchants of Berhampore I have ascertained that if it had not been for the Plague, the trade both in Bengal raw silk and manufactured silk would have augmented far more rapidly within recent years. The decrease of trade with foreign countries has brought with it an increase of trade with the other provinces of India, and the general condition of the silk industry is, on the whole, more hopeful than it has been for many years past, and this fact is very clearly brought out by the census of 1901.

127. Referring to Table E, it will be seen that the countries to which Bengal silk fabrics are exported are:—(1) the United Kingdom of Great Britain and Ireland, (2) France, (3) Germany, (4) Austro-Hungaria, (5) Zanzibar, (6) Mauritius, (7) South America, (8) the United States, (9) Aden, (10) Arabia, (11) Ceylon, (12) China, (13) Persia, (14) the Straits Settlements, (15) Turkey in Asia, (16) Australia, and some other countries. The principal exporting agents are:—Messrs. Lyall, Marshall & Co., Messrs. Anderson, Wright & Co., Messrs. Walker, Goward & Co., Messrs. George Henderson & Co., Messrs. Graham & Co., Messrs. Irene Brun & Co., Messrs. Balmer, Lawrie & Co., Messrs. Blackwood, Blackwood & Co., Messrs. Buskin & Co., Messrs. A. Ashman & Co., Messrs. B. L. Sen & Co., Messrs. D. C. Roquitte & Co., Messrs. Shaw, Wallace & Co., Messrs. Kettlewell, Bullen & Co., Messrs. Tellery & Co., all of Calcutta.

128. The principal local merchants who buy for the foreign markets are the Bengal Silk Company, Messrs. Louis Payen & Co., Mr. M. Fergusson and Babu Shashi Bhushan Chowdhury of Berhampore, and Babu Radha Shyam Guin of Ghatal (Midnapore).

129. The costliest silk fabrics are used in Bengal. Some costly fabrics are exported to Assam also, but the quantity is insignificant. The fabrics used in Bengal are—*saris*, *dhutis*, *jôrs*, *Baluchar butedar saris*, *chelis*, *gown-pieces*, *háwái* goods, *rekhis*, *chárkhánas*, *scarfs*, *shawls*, and plain and bordered handkerchiefs. Individual weavers may be seen hawking them about in towns like Berhampore, Rajshahi, *Maldah*, and Midnapore, and sometimes carrying bundles of silk cloths down to Calcutta as personal luggage by train. Many such weavers come to Calcutta before the Puja time, in September and October, when there is always a brisk sale of silk *saris* in the Calcutta market. To Europe, *corahs*, printed handkerchiefs, and gown-pieces, also *tasars* and *baftas* (*tasar* mixed with cotton) are exported. To Rangoon are exported *phulikat* handkerchiefs and *banhus*. To the North-Western Provinces and the Punjab are sent *matichurs* or *churis* made out of *matkás* and *corahs*. To Arabia are exported *dharis*, *chaukaras*, and *matras*. *Chelis* go to most parts of India, also *corahs* for printing. *Matka dhutis* and *saris* (plain and check) go to all parts of India where there are Mahrattas.

CHAPTER XI.

THE NATIVE LOOM INDUSTRY—ITS INDUSTRIAL POSITION.

130. Enough has been said in the last chapter to demonstrate the importance and vitality of the Bengal silk-weaving industry at the present time and its growing importance. There is no doubt the industry has dwindled down into insignificance in certain localities, *e. g.*, in Hooghly, Nadia, Howrah, and Bogra; but it has made progress in others, *e.g.*, in Murshidabad, Bankura,

Burdwan, and Rajshahi. In Midnapore the industry is fairly extensive, but it is in a struggling condition, and the presence of a few enterprising *Marwari* and other up-country traders may alter the state of the loom-industry, which is at present far too much in the hands of a few rich men, specially if the cocoon-rearing industry of Midnapore can be saved by the Pasteur system.

131. The belief, however, that the English occupation of this country has been detrimental to the interest of arts and industries is so widespread, that a discussion of this question, so far as the silk-weaving industry is concerned, may not be out of place.

132. The silk industry, like the jute, or the tea, or the indigo industries, was developed from insignificant proportions by means of British capital and enterprise; and although this industry has held a lower position during the latter half of this century than it did during the earlier half, it is in a far better position now than it was in the eighteenth century, and in a better position still than it was in pre-British times. The "Reports and Letters concerning the Company's affairs in Bengal, 1661 to 1685," published by Mr. C. R. Wilson, gives a bird's-eye view of the commodities obtainable in Cossimbazar, Murshidabad, Hooghly, Patna, and Balasore, *i.e.*, in the principal marts of Bengal, Behar, and Orissa, in those days. Silk was quite a secondary article of trade in Bengal in those days in Cossimbazar and Murshidabad. It was recognised as an article of some importance in Patna. In Orissa and Hooghly it did not seem to have been known as an article of trade. With regard to Cossimbazar, the reports say:—

"The commodities chiefly vendible in this place are silver and gold. . . . . . Other commodities are vendible here, but not in great quantities, except *chauk* or *tinn*. Commodities procureable here are silk *taffaties*, long and short women's clouts of silk, about 14 *coveds* long, and several sorts of striped stuffs and striped girdles."

133. With regard to Murshidabad silk fabrics, the 'Reports' have the following note:—

"At Murshidabad, above three leagues from Cossimbazar, there are made several sorts of silver and gold girdles from 10 rupees to 60 rupees each, also fine *taffaties* from 9 to 12 rupees per piece, but none of those goods are near so fine or good as those that come from Persia."

134. In connection with the description about Patna and Benares merchandise, we have the following references to silk:—

"English cloth sold by the Plush yard, which is about ⅛ more than the English yard, so are *taffaties* and all other things measurable at Pattana. You may buy in the bazar anything by the yard, vending much by retail. All manner of Guzratt, Banara, Jehaunpore, etc., commodities are to be had here, as gold sashes, urney girdles, elatches, remerrys, etc.—all sold by weight, the 11 mace tola, and usually about Re. 1-15 to Rs. 2-1 per tola. . . At Benares 12 course from Pattana and Lachore, 16, theres white cloth fitt for Persia to be had called Umbertees and Comcomp, from Re. 1-8 to Rs. 3 per piece in which commodities are invested by Armenian and Mogull merchants at least ten hundred thousand rupees per annum, transported by land to Surat, and thence by shipping to Persia. Good profits are made of them from thence to Surat. There are better *taffaties* made at Pattana than Cossimbazar, which are sold from 9 to 10 annas the long yard, but no great quantities, but if followed a good quantitie might be procured."

135. Bernier, the celebrated traveller of the Seventeenth Century, no doubt, speaks in most glowing terms of the silk as of other industries of Bengal during that Century, but the number of workmen employed in the principal silk factory of Bengal is mentioned by him to be "seven or eight hundred" only, while a good many factories at the present time employ at least twice this number. The passage referring to the silk industry may be quoted here in full:—

"In regard to valuable commodities of a nature to attract foreign merchants, I am acquainted with no country where so great a variety is found. Besides the sugar I have spoken of, and which may be placed in the list of valuable commodities, there is in Bengal such a quantity of cotton and silks, that the kingdom may be called the common storehouse for those two kinds of merchandise, not of Hindustan or the Empire of the Great Mogol only, but of all the neighbouring kingdoms, and even of Europe. I have been sometimes amazed at the vast quantity of cotton cloths, of every sort, fine and coarse, white and coloured, which the Hollanders alone export to different places, especially to Japan and Europe. The English, the Portuguese, and the native merchants deal also in these articles to a considerable extent The same may be said of the silks and the silk stuffs of all sorts It is not possible to conceive the quantity drawn every year from Bengal for the supply of the whole of the Mogul Empire, as far as Lahore and Cabul, and generally of all those foreign nations to which the cotton cloths are sent. The silks are not certainly so fine as those of Persia, Syria,

Sayd, and Barut, but they are of a much lower price; and I know from indisputable authority that, if they were well selected and wrought with care, they might be manufactured into most beautiful stuffs. The Dutch have sometimes seven or eight hundred natives employed in their silk factory at Kassem-Bazar, where, in like manner, the English and other merchants employ a proportionate number."

136. Thus we get a glimpse of the silk trade of Bengal in the middle of the 17th century. It was not to be compared to the silk trade of Persia. It was poorer than the Benares silk trade, and the only market in Bengal in which silks comparable to Persian silk was to be obtained in any quantity was that of Patna. The *taffetas*, or coloured silks of Cossimbazar (*banhus*, printed handkerchiefs, *phulikats*, *dharis*, etc.), were to be had. But the industry had to be improved and developed before trade in these and other silk fabrics assumed any importance. And so we find as early as 1670 a factor "well skilled in silk" sent out from England to Cossimbazar. From this time forward for a whole century the Company was unremitting in their zeal to extend sericulture in all departments, until by 1776 "Bengal silk drove all competitors, except Italian and China silks, out of the English market." (*Geoghegan, page 5.*)

137. But the development up to this had come to a stage when the annual exportation reached 500,000 "small pounds," and this quantity included "all sorts of silk." What is the state of the industry now? In 1901-02 the exports to foreign countries alone were—

Of raw silk	727,651	lbs.
„ waste	1,165,754	lbs.
„ silk piece-goods, 1,180,833 yards-about ...	854,092	yards,

the total representing about 2,000,000 pounds, or about four times the annual quantity exported between 1776 to 1785. Then we must take into consideration the facilities now afforded by railway and steamer communications in Bengal silk (raw and manufactured) being exported to the other provinces of India. Tables H and J show that much larger quantities of raw and manufactured silk grown in Bengal, are used in India, than what are exported, and there is no evidence to show that any considerable quantities of Bengal silk were used in other parts of India in olden times, though Benares and Agra did use some, and there was some export even to Lahore and Cabul.

138. The Company developed the silk-weaving industry by establishing three weaving factories—one at Cossimbazar, one at Malda, and the third at Santipore. "Goods were manufactured, but from the country-reeled or Putney silk. All filature silk was exported raw." (*Geoghegan, page 14.*)

139. To what proportions the silk-weaving industry developed under the fostering care of the East India Company is not known. But from what Geoghegan says in the matter, it seems the industry attained to a greater prosperity than now in Maldah, but that the Murshidabad silk industry is in a more flourishing condition now than it was in the days of the East India Company. As all that Geoghegan says on the subject of silk manufacture is virtually contained in a single paragraph, it can be easily quoted here *in extenso* :—

"As to the extent of silk manufacture, I have not been able to obtain much information. We have seen that the Company manufactured silk-stuffs at three of its Residencies, but from country-wound silk. The stuffs seem to have been chiefly undyed piece-goods, known as *corahs* and *bandannas*. There was doubtless a good deal of silk made for home consumption also, but I have not found any figures to show either the exports or the total production for the period of the Company's trade. Buchanan gives an elaborate account of the silk manufacture in Maldah and the neighbourhood. The cloths made were almost all mixed, the warp being silk and the woof cotton. The warp was generally disposed in stripes, the woof being of one colour. The patterns did not display much taste. There were said to be about 11,000 looms in this region, but not one-half of them constantly employed. Buchanan estimates the value of the stuffs exported annually to the westward, to Murshidabad and Calcutta, at not less than 10 lakhs annually. The industry still exists about Maldah and English Bazar, but in a languishing condition. The aspect of the town of Old Maldah is that of the dreariest decay. Mr. Holwell, writing in 1759, mentions six kinds of cloth and raw-silk as being exported from Nator (in Rajshahi) both to Europe and to the markets of 'Bussora, Mocha, Jedda, Pegu, Acheen, and Malacca.' From the passage as quoted by Mr. Skrine (to whom I am indebted for the reference), it is not quite clear whether the cltohs were all of silk." (*Geoghegan*, page 24, paragraph 26, and footnote.")

140. With regard to Maldah also, it is not quite clear whether it is not the European side of the industry only that has decayed of late years. That the native silk-reeling industry, also mulberry-growing and cocoon-rearing industries have been steadily improving of late years, I have personally verified and I have also ascertained from native silk merchants of Maldah that they are exporting more silk fabrics from Maldah now than they ever did before. Mr. Morey of Baragharia Factory wrote to me a few years ago that he noticed extension of mulberry cultivation all over Maldah. Discussing this question with Mr. Batabyal, at that time Collector of Maldah, who had sent in a return showing shorter area for mulberry than in previous years, I saw that the general but erroneous impression that the silk industry was gradually dying out was the main reason for pessimistic reports and returns being submitted regarding acreage under mulberry and outturn of silk. Mr. Liotard in the "Memorandum on Silk in India (1883)" makes certain remarks, which represent the true position of the Maldah silk industry at the present time, and, I may add, the progress on the native side of the industry since 1883 has been continuous. "The native side of the industry, on the contrary," says Mr. Liotard following a report by Mr. R. Poreh, Collector of Malda, "is prospering in its agricultural aspects, and as regards the easy profits made by the natives, the mulberry silk industry must be considered as brisk, prosperous, and flourishing. The greater portion of the cocoons reared in the district is either bought by native manufacturers or are reeled by the rearers themselves, who most of them have one or two reels: the silk reeled by the natives and called *khangru* is partly bought by silk-piece manufacturers of Bombay, Benares, Delhi, Mirzapur, etc., and partly is used in home manufacture of *corahs*, *mosru*, and other kinds of cloth. These cloths are mostly exported to Calcutta, Bombay, Madras, Nagpore, Allahabad, Benares, and Delhi (the largest exports being to Calcutta and Bombay), and partly worn in the district."

141. From a study of Table A it will appear that the native side of the industry has a tendency to revive when the European side of the industry decays. But there is a limit to this, as will be explained later on. The revival of the silk weaving industry can be partly explained by the difficulty cocoon-rearers are now experiencing in obtaining good prices from European factories. The enhanced production of cocoons has thus resulted chiefly in an impetus being given to the native reeling and weaving industries.

142. The notion that the silk industry of Bengal is dying out is so deep-rooted that an official request from the Collector of Murshidabad to the late Maharani Surnomoyi of Cassimbazar to devote the Rs. 20,000 which she had promised in the year of her late Imperial Majesty's Jubilee (1887) to the founding of a silk-weaving school elicited the reply that the Maharani considered that the silk industry of Murshidabad had declined to such an extent that there was no hope of reviving the industry, and that therefore she was not willing to found a silk-weaving school. The establishment of a silk-weaving school in Murshidabad was definitely recommended in the report submitted by Mr. E. W. Collin, C.S., on the Arts and Industries of Bengal, after a personal enquiry into the condition of all the important industries of Bengal. That the silk-manufacturing industry of Bengal can be developed to something still better by systematic training and by proper organisation can be inferred from the fact of the recent development of the Bombay silk-manufacturing industry, though it depends for its raw product on Bengal and China. British interest lies entirely in the direction of developing the silk industries of Bengal, and Mr. Collin's suggestion is warranted not only by the actual vitality of the silk-industry of Bengal, but also by the decaying vitality of the British silk manufacturing industry, which is failing in competition with France, Italy, Switzerland, Germany, and even with Japan. The vitality of the Bengal industry is worth preserving and fostering in the interest even of the British silk industry.

143. Much as has been said of the decay of Bengal silk, it is doubtful if it has ever enjoyed such a healthy vitality in times past as it is now enjoying. We are on the threshold of the Pasteur system of sericulture being accepted by the peasantry of Bengal as the solution of their chief difficulty; we have traders from all the provinces of India coming to Bengal in increasing numbers both for silk piece-goods and for raw-silk and this raw-silk is utilised in the other provinces for manufacture of silk fabrics. Even the European side of the industry has

suffered only a comparative decay, and there is evidence of resuscitation of this branch of the industry in the direction of raw-silk, and waste (*vide* Table C).

144. "Concurrently with the decline in the raw-silk trade," says Mr. Liotard, "a considerable increase is apparent in the exports of waste-silk and piece-goods, thus :—

Official years.	Waste silk.	Piece-goods.	Goods of silk mixed with other materials.	Total value.
1	2	3	4	5
	Rs.	Rs.	Rs.	Rs.
1870-71 ...	Figures not available.	15,03,176	Figures not available.	15,03,176
1872-73 ...		18,60,248		18,60,248
1876-77 ...		22,26,985	9,326	22,36,311
1879-80 ...	5,30,476	21,78,937	1,04,738	28,14,151
1881-82 ...	8,34,213	20,57,722	1,55,282	30,47,217
1882-83 ...	10,04,361	25,19,997	2,43,890	37,68,248

These figures, coupled with those of raw silk, lead to the inference that the Indian silk production after falling till 1870—80 began in that year to assume a new aspect characterised by an increasing trade in waste silk, piece-goods, and goods of silk mixed with other materials. The export of piece goods, however, has fallen off of recent years.

145. It is not the decay of an old and prosperous industry that has to be mourned, but only a comparative decay in the export of silk piece-goods since the prosperity of 1887-88 (*vide* Table C), and it is a prosperity in the export trade lasting for 20 years (from 1870 to 1890) that may be only fondly looked back upon. But other provinces within the last 12 years have been taking more raw and manufactured silks from Bengal than they ever did before, and the comparative decay since 1887-88 in the export of manufactured silk from Bengal is therefore less than a study of the figures in table C alone would warrant one to suppose. Because during a period of 200 years of British transactions in Bengal silk fabrics, there was a boom for 20 years within recent times, it should not be inferred at once that the industry has hopelessly decayed. The memory of this boom in the export trade in silk is no doubt full of regrets to living men who saw it, and who have been also watching the decline for the last 15 years, but looked upon in a proper perspective the 20 years' boom, in one branch of the industry, would appear as a mere passing event which all trades may be expected to pass through. Barring these 20 years, the silk-manufacturing industry of Bengal has never enjoyed such a prosperous period as it enjoys now, and the prosperity is shared chiefly by those districts which have the largest number of silk-weavers in them, with the sole exception of Midnapore, where the decline is due chiefly to the decline in the cocoon-rearing industry caused by silkworm epidemics.

146. Having stated what I consider to be the true industrial position of the Bengal silk-weaving industry, I will now quote from the district monographs the remarks of the various local officers on this subject. They are nearly all pessimistic in tone and based on the groundless belief that the silk industry is decaying. One point noticed by most of them is of vital importance, viz., the harm done to the silk-weaving industry (as to other industries) by the indebtedness of the weavers to *mahajans*, who charge very heavy rates of interest on advances of money. If the silk-weavers could be relieved of this burden, the industry would be in a still more prosperous condition.

147. The Murshidabad monograph has the following lines bearing on the question of the industrial position of the silk industry as a whole and the silk-weaving industry in particular :—

"The method on which many of these rearers carry on their business is industrially a bad one. The filature-owners and their employés in many cases advance money to them and buy their cocoons at a price fixed according to the current rates in the silk market. Interest being charged, the rearers frequently get into financial difficulties. Those who work on their own capital are in a much more favourable position. As a class, rearers are a peaceful and quiet people, and litigation is almost unknown amongst them.

"There seems no doubt that the silk-weaving industry is on the decline. The importation of foreign stuffs has of course a great deal to do with this. Another reason lies in the lack of interprise displayed in disposing of native fabrics. Where there is an attempt at advertisement, it usually meets with great success. It would be a splendid thing for the trade if middle-class Bengalis with a small capital were to hawk round the silk products of Mirzapur and other places. At the time of the famine the sufferings of some of the weavers of this district were much alleviated by the efforts of a native gentleman, who advantageously disposed of their goods in Calcutta. It is a pity that more energy is not displayed in this direction. There is no doubt that as a class their condition is not prosperous, and that they are deeply involved in debt. They do not as a rule work for themselves, but for dealers who advance them material and pay them so much for their labour. Some of these dealers employ a very large number of weavers. I am told that in Kandi subdivision some weavers found the industry so little profitable that they have entirely given it up, and in many cases taken to agriculture. Others in the same subdivision have abandoned the weaving of silk for that of cotton. At present the price of cotton yarn is low and the demand for goods fairly great, so that industry is found to be more paying."

148. The Burdwan monograph has the following remarks:—

"There are no factories, but each man's loom is kept in a solid and respectable-looking house, considerably cleaner than most native huts ... It is rather hard to find any way of helping these people. Their machines are cheap and effective, and labour is cheap. A great deal of their misfortune is due to their own fault. They have run into debt, and thus either had to get yarn on credit from the merchant who took interest at the rate of a pice in the rupee and bought up the cloth manufactured at the end of the month, after deducting the price of yarn, or else they had to go to the *mahajan*, who charged interest at the rate of Rs. 2 per seer (*i.e.*, 15-16 rupees worth) of yarn, and then bought at his own price. If they could do cash business, they would be prosperous and contented. The other reason is, of course, European competition.

"There is probably nothing that will prevent the native putting his head in the money-lender's noose; but it is perhaps just possible that the industry might be saved from extinction by other means:—

(1) There might be a better supply of cocoons: it is possible to grow them in this district, as is shown at Kalna, but there the growth is only an auxiliary to agriculture. If this cultivation was extended and the cocoons sold directly to the weavers in the district, the initial cost would be lessened.

(2) The products might be advertised; many articles suited for ladies' garments could be made from this silk, and also cloths like Assam silk, though of better and more durable quality, could easily be purchased. If these were advertised and a better market obtained, it would help the weaver, who might then escape from the clutches of the money-lenders."

149. The Howrah monograph has the following lines bearing on this question:—

"No silk cloth nor any *tusser* is manufactured here. The trade in silk has considerably decreased, and is gradually dying out. At present the silk industry is carried on on a very small scale. The lower class of people who used to trade in it have taken to cultivation and other pursuits, as they find that the amount of labour spent gives no adequate return"

150. The following lines may be quoted from the Birbhum monograph:—

"In this district silk industry is carried on to some extent, and is in a somewhat declining condition, as the genuine silk manufactured in this country cannot compete with the adulterated silk manufactured in Japan."

151. The Bogra monograph has the following lines on this subject:—

"In the case of rearing worms, as well as in the cases of reeling and weaving, the industry has declined in this district owing to the want of demand, absence of encouragement, and lowering in prices due to competition. There was a time when there were one or more silk factories in this district conducted by Europeans. At that time every facility was offered to the grower of silk for cultivation and disposal of his articles. The factor would advance a lump-sum to a *paikar* or middleman for bringing up not less than a specified amount of cocoons.

"The *paikar* would then distribute portions of the advance money among the cultivators either for expenses of growing the plants or for purchase of leaves. The *paikar* would then take the produce from the cultivators and take his collection to the factory. These factories, therefore, encouraged the cultivation of worms, and took all the produce for exportation to other parts of India or to Europe.

"The silk factory of Nowdapara was situated on the western bank of the Karotoya river, about three miles away from Bogra town. This factory was abolished about 30 years ago. It is said that there was a factory at Kharna, which was abolished long before that, and another at Sajapur, which did not exist for a long time.

"The cultivators complain of inadequate prices obtained for the cocoons. This year they are selling cocoons at the rate of Rs. 20 per maund. But last year the price is said to have been as low as Rs. 13 or Rs. 14 per maund; so it is very difficult for a cultivator to make a handsome profit out of this industry.

"Of the cocoons grown in this district, only a very small portion is reeled here. Most of the produce is sent to the district of Rajshahi. People living near Bogra take these cocoons mostly to Tahirpur in the Rajshahi district, where they find a ready market. Cocoons are also taken to *hâts* in the Rajshahi district, which are close to this district. Some portion of the cocoons is purchased in these *hâts* by cultivators for breeding purposes. It also sometimes happens the traders or *beparis* come from Rajshahi and purchase and take away cocoons. Now and then cultivator, from that district also come for purchasing cocoons for breeding.

"The proportion of export to local consumption is estimated at 13 annas to 3 annas. But it should also be noted that a major portion of the silk thread reeled in this district, small as it is, is also sent to Rajshahi. The local reelers purchase the cocoons at the house of the cultivator, or it may so happen that the cultivator himself takes his produce to the reelers. In some of the *hâts* of this district a small quantity of cocoons can also be purchased.

"The number of persons actually employed in the weaving of *garad* is extremely small. There are not more than half a dozen skilful weavers in *garad* silk in this district, (excluding, of course, the other members of the family of a weaver who know something of the work and help him). Many Tantis have given up the occupation and have taken recourse either to cotton industry or to agriculture. The silk industry is not at all very paying, and it is not possible for a Tanti to maintain himself by silk-weaving alone.

"The processes of bleaching the threads, arranging them after bleaching, reeling, starching, warping, arranging the threads on the reels, forming the healds and fitting up the whole thing require a large amount of labour, and many of the above processes require the help of one, two or more additional hands. So silk-weaving is far from a profitable concern. The weaver has got to take recourse to agriculture or some such thing.

"The weavers of silk proper are Hindus. The silk industry imparts to them a certain importance, as they are the few representatives of workers in an art which was once the pride of India.

"Not a single weaver can be said to be well-to-do. The Tantis when they keep lands do not plough fields themselves, but servants do the field-work for them.

"Generally one family keeps a single loom; but there are instances of a family of weavers keeping two looms, but they are seldom worked together constantly. One loom is worked for preparing things urgently required, and the other for things that may be taken up at leisure.

"It will appear from the above that the silk industry in this district is of very limited extent. The industry has deplorably declined in all its branches. Some 30 years back, dealing in silk in some shape or other was a very easy way to fortune. Besides the growers of the worms, there was a class of middlemen who used to buy silk from the growers and dispose of them on a large scale in the *hâts* famous for trade in silk. Tahirpur, in the district of Rajshahi, was the most important place in this respect for the people of Bogra. Even now Tahirpur draws a major portion of the produce of this district in the shape of cocoons. There are many people now in this district who admit that their fathers and grandfathers grew rich by dealing in silk. Besides buying cocoons for sale, these middlemen also worked several furnaces each for reeling silks, and sold the thread.

"At a time growing of mulberry or rearing worms was considered the most lucrative employment for agriculturists.

"It is said that the decline of this trade has impoverished many people. The mulberry-fields bore very high rates of rent, for it is the common practice in this part of the country to leave the improvement of the land to the cultivator alone, while the zamindar comes in for his full share of the increased profits. In a village where good paddy-fields do not bring more than Re. 1-8 per bigha, a mulberry-field bears Rs. 4 as rent per bigha.

"Owing to the decline in the industry these mulberry-fields are lying waste, although the poor cultivator is paying very high rents for them. The zamindar will not allow him to surrender these raised fields alone. If he is to surrender at all, he should surrender the whole jote, which he cannot. So he is paying every year rents at a very high rate for fields which do not bring a pice into his pocket. So the decline in the industry is doubly detrimental to the interests of the cultivators.

"Several reasons are suggested for this decline, among which are—

(*i*) Want of encouragement by Government or factories, &c.
(*ii*) Falling off in the prices due to competition with imported articles.
(*iii*) The mulberry plant is said to be less thriving than before.
(*iv*) Diseases among worms. It is said that the worms do not thrive as before.
(*v*) Want of demand for cocoons and the difficulties of carriage.

"It is very difficult for a man to carry cocoons to distant places for sale. People who grow only a limited quantity cannot themselves carry their produce to the purchasers, nor is there any way of selling the produce at home, except to people who will pay a low price by deducting a commission for undertaking the sale.

"The new railway opened up to Bogra may remove this difficulty to a certain extent. But on the whole it is believed that the silk industry of the district will gradually die out if no encouragement be offered from outside."

152. The Maldah monograph may be also quoted fully on this subject, though I do not at all agree with the pessimistic view taken in this monograph of the condition of the industry :—

"Malda has, from a very ancient time, been famous for its silk industry. It is even now the largest silk-producing district in Bengal. About 70,000 maunds of cocoons are grown.

"It has been stated above that the silk-weaving industry is in a very decayed state. The best weavers of Shibganj, where the finest cloths are made, do not earn more than Rs. 8 to Rs. 12 a month. The Tantis were once a rich community. Owing to the importation of cheap foreign goods, the demand for indigenous silk fabrics has much decreased: imported goods are, however, less durable than country-made articles. If the best varieties of country-made fabrics could be sent to industrial exhibitions, which are now so numerous, it might help to revive this decaying industry. The backward state of the industry is due as much to ignorance on the part of purchasers regarding the quality of these fabrics, who generally prefer the gaudier articles of foreign manufacture, as to the want of organisation and enterprise on the part of the weavers, whose poverty prevents them from advertising their goods to any appreciable extent.

"No attempt has hitherto been made to give an impetus to the industry, and the weavers are too poor and illiterate to do it themselves. The weavers as a class are very poor. It is very seldom that they sell their manufactures to the consumers direct. They are entirely in the hands of the *mahajans* or money-lenders, who make advances to them for the purchase of thread and the support of their families. Frequently it is the *mahajans* who supply the thread, and the weavers get nothing but their wages. The wages for the manufacture of a piece of *sari* amount to about Rs. 2, which means that the weaver is paid at the rate of about 4 to 6 annas a day.

"The silk industry is thus entirely in the hands of the mahajans, who are generally Marwaris. So long as this state of things continues, it is hopeless to expect that the industry will flourish.

"A very large proportion of the silk fabrics manufactured in the district is exported to Bombay, Calcutta, Jeypur, Benares, and Mirzapur by the Marwaris and other money-lenders. There is also a small local demand for cloths made of mixed silk and cotton. There is no internal trade in silk. Silk goods are never sold at the local *háts* or periodical fairs. There are one or two shops in English Bazar Town, where silk fabrics are sold.

"The industry cannot possibly be improved, unless capital is invested for the purpose of advertising the goods widely and for creating a demand for them among the well-to-do people of the country and also for inducing the weavers to manufacture a large variety of new patterns of goods for which there is likely to be a demand in Europe, America, and other countries. It is well known that the silk fabrics made in Birbhum district are exported in considerable quantities to London, and find a ready market there. There is no reason why Malda-made cloth should not also find a foreign market, especially as Maldah grows the cocoons, which Birbhum purchases."

153. To this last point raised in this monograph, it may be answered, that Maldah silks are largely exported to foreign markets, far more than Birbhum silks. To another point mentioned in this monograph, I may say, there is a considerable internal trade in Maldah silk fabrics quietly carried on in the district. Every time I visited the villages of Maldah I noticed peripatetic weavers vending their silk cloths.

154. That the import of foreign silks into Bengal is materially affecting the indigenous industry is an opinion with which I entirely differ. The purposes for which the two kinds of silk are employed are different. Foreign silks as an article of luxury have been in use in India from very ancient times, and mention is made of *Chinángshuka* in Kalidas's *Sakuntala*, and in later writings, of Persian silk. But these were never to be employed on ceremonial occasions. A peculiar notion of purity is attached to indigenous silk fabrics by the whole Hindu population of India; and though the use of silk is enjoined and universally current in the celebration of certain rites, there is never a Hindu wedding or funeral in which the use of foreign silk is ever thought of. The amount of import into Bengal of silks of all kinds bears no comparison to the amount of export, and the tendency is not towards increase. Table M shows that during six recent years an average of only about Rs. 9,651 worth of raw silk has been imported into Bengal, while the export of raw silk from Bengal into other countries and into other Provinces of India is worth over a crore of rupees (*vide* Table H.) There is practically no import of waste silk into Bengal, while the export is valued at over 10 lakhs. About Rs. 25,000 of sewing silk, about 5 lakhs of rupees' worth of silk piece-goods, about 5 lakhs of rupees of piece-goods made of inferior fibre mixed with silk, and about Rs. 9,000 worth of ribbons and other silk goods are now imported annually into Bengal from foreign countries, or a total of less than 11 lakhs. Against this we have 50 lakhs' worth of Bengal Silk Fabrics only, most of which

is woven to meet the requirements of this country. Table K gives figures for import for the whole of India, which no doubt shows some tendency towards increase during the last 30 years, but not more than is warranted by the consideration of increase of population and of prosperity. Besides such articles as sewing silk, ribbons, etc., are imported into India almost exclusively for the European and Eurasian population. The wardrobe of an ordinary Hindu or Muhammadan may have no cotton or woollen fabrics produced in Indian looms; it may not have any foreign silks, but it is very rarely without some Indian silks. It is also well recognised that Bengal silks last for many years, and if carefully used, they last for two or three generations, while foreign silks are never lasting. That Bengal produces 50 lakhs of rupees' worth of fabrics and imports only 11 lakhs of rupees' worth of silks of all sorts is in itself a strong proof of the native vitality and stability of the Bengal silk industry.

155. There is another point of very considerable importance which has a direct connection with the increased use of indigenous silk fabrics in India. The spread of English education has resulted in a very peculiar degree in a widely spread sentiment of patriotism, and the use of indigenous articles that are of real intrinsic merit is spreading very rapidly among the educated classes. The development in the manufacture of high-class silks has been quite phenomenal in the Mirzapur centre of the Murshidabad industry within recent years.

156. It may be mentioned here that the value of Bengal raw silk in foreign-markets has depreciated to about half of what it was 20 years ago. This depreciation rather than any material diminution of produce has resulted in considerable strain, chiefly in the condition of the foreign trade with Europe. The depreciation in the value of Bengal raw-silk in European market has resulted in no appreciable change in the selling price of cocoons or of *khamru* silk, and the strain which is felt by European exporters is hardly shared by native cocoon-rearers, silk-spinners, or silk-weavers, who do not depend mainly on the condition of the European markets for the sale of their respective produce. The European silk factor may buy cocoons for Rs. 30 a maund and lose money by doing so, while the *khamru* spinner may pay Rs. 32 for the same cocoons and pay higher wages to his workers, and sell his poor silk for Rs. 14 a seer, while the superior European filature-reeled silk scarcely fetches a higher price. The native competition is keen, and in some localities, as in Maldah, more than equal. This competition is injurious to the European trade, but so far it has been conducive to the prosperity of the industry as a whole; but should European silk factors ever retire from the field altogether, the harm that will be effected to the Bengal silk industry will be incalculable. Bogra and Midnapur are now suffering keenly owing to the withdrawal, entire in the one case and partial in the other, of European enterprise. Native merchants (chiefly Marwari money-lenders) try to take all the good out of an industry, and ultimately leave it in a wretched condition. There is always money-lending at high rates of interest associated with native enterprise, and in the absence of European rivalry this money-lending saps the foundation of any industry.

157. I would conclude this chapter by a quotation from the "Hand-book of Sericulture":—

"*Import of silk into India*.—The import of foreign silk thread into India has declined considerably of recent years, while the transhipment of Bengal silk thread into other parts of India has developed with rapid bounds during the same period. The figures given below will show to what insignificant proportions the import trade in foreign silk thread has been reduced within recent year:—

Year.			Quantity.	Value.
			Seers.	Rs.
1885-86	...	...	53,000	1,97,000
1886-87	...	...	18,000	81,000
1887-88	...	...	17,000	89,000
1888-89	...	...	6,500	30,000
1889-90	...	...	6,300	28,000

The import of silk into India consists chiefly in piece-goods. The total import of silk thread and silk pieces for four years since 1889 has been—

				Rs.
In 1889-90	...	...	...	2,84,51,590
" 1890-91	...	...	...	2,50,14,800
" 1891-92	...	...	...	3,01,46,980
" 1892-93	...	...	...	2,81,76,510

"From what has been said, it can be clearly inferred that India buys two or three crore of rupees' worth of foreign silk. This is the least hopeful feature of the Indian silk trade. If India bought two or three crores of rupees' worth of English silk, she could have consoled herself with the thought that it was a price paid for loyalty to England. But nearly the whole of this import is from continental countries and not from England. England on her part has been showing anxiety of late for utilising more of the Indian raw material. The condition of the English silk trade, again, has become most deplorable. England now imports annually about 24 crores of rupees' worth of silk from other countries, while she exports only three crores of rupees' worth. For England to buy 17 to 18 crores of rupees' worth of silk-pieces manufactured in France, Germany, Switzerland and Italy is not to her advantage. England has not always used foreign silks in such large quantities. For the last 30 years the import of foreign silks into England has steadily increased, while the export of English silks into other countries has steadily declined. The more silk thread she imports and the less of piece-goods and the more piece-goods she exports, the better it is for her. But the course of the English silk trade has gone on exactly in the reverse order for the last 30 years. It is pretty nearly certain that England will be unable to compete successfully with other European countries in the silk trade. English labourers are not satisfied with the wages of even Rs. 60 per month. Italian and French labourers are quite as skilful as English labourers in weaving silk, but they receive about Rs. 30 to Rs. 40 per month. The labour strikes we constantly hear of from England are most intense in the case of silk factories. The foremost silk-weaving establishments in England (viz., those of Messrs. Lister and Company) sometimes find it difficult to work more than four days in the week. A few years ago Messrs. Lister and Company used to export about fifty lakhs of rupees' worth (£30,000) of velvet per annum to America alone. The American export of velvet of this Company has gone down to about six lakhs of rupees' (£3,600) worth per annum. There seems to be only one means now by which England can combat successfully with the continental silk trade, viz., by transferring the centres of competition from Manchester, Manningham, and Leek to Baluchar, Mirzapur, Benares, Amritsar, and Srinagar. Such a policy alone can restore the commercial supremacy which England enjoyed in the days of the East India Company. The interests of England and India are identical in regard to the silk trade. Indian silk-weavers are artizans of no mean order. Skilled Indian labour guided by English enterprise can produce silks of European excellence and finish. Indian weavers work on the monthly wages of Rs. 5 or Rs. 6 only."

158. A visit to the Economic section of the Indian Museum, where silks of very superior quality manufactured in Europe out of Kashmir silk, since the above remarks were published, are prominently displayed, would amply satisfy any one of the cogency of these remarks.

CHAPTER XII.

Statistical Tables.

A few explanatory notes bringing out the special information which is desired to be conveyed in each case by the following tables are given below:—

Table A.—The population of Bengal which depend on the silk industry.—This Table, compiled from the census figures of 1901 and 1891, shows that the silk-weaving industry of Bengal has made considerable strides during the last decade. The number of silk weavers including silk dyers and sellers of silk cloths, increased from 27,301 in 1891 to 43,836 in 1901. This table, however, also shows a very serious falling off in the number of mulberry growers, silk-worm rearers and cocoon-gatherers, the numbers for 1891 and 1901 being respectively 92,318 and 55,256. It does not, however, appear very clear, how the number of spinners could have remained about the same, *i.e.*, 19,904 in 1901 as against 19,238 in 1891, and how the number of weavers has increased so largely, if there has been an actual falling off in the number of cocoon rearers and mulberry growers. In page 32, paragraph 69, it has been shown, how the silk industry of India, which is virtually the silk industry of Bengal, declined from 1875 to 1885, but that since then there has been a steady improvement for the last 16 years. The improvement in the export trade in raw silk which is a fact, and the improvement in the silk-weaving industry, cannot be accounted for by the figures for silkworm-rearers and cocoon-gatherers as given in the census tables for 1901. A very considerable proportion of cocoon rearers must have been returned as cultivators pure and simple. I am inclined to put the number of mulberry growers, cocoon-rearers and sellers, including "partially agriculturist" and "dependants" at even a higher figure than 92,318, which was the figure for 1891, and estimate the total population of Bengal which depends wholly or partly on the silk industry at 160,000 instead of 118,169, the corresponding figure for 1891 being 138,857.

Table B.—Relative importance of the different branches of the Bengal silk industry.—This Table has been based on the census figures for 1891. I do not think the silk-rearing industry has declined to that extent at any rate within the last ten years to which the census tables for 1901 would lead us to suppose it has. The figures for 1891 also are very low in some cases for cocoon-rearers. Palamau, Manbhum and Singhbhum which have "Nil" against them under this heading, must have thousands of Tusser-rearing Sonthals and others living in them, as will appear from the district monographs which will be quoted later on. The tendency to class cocoon-rearers as pure cultivators was only more exaggerated during the last census. The Tusser and Endi rearing industries are far more extensive than this Table would lead one to infer, and the mulberry silk industry also has been understated in the departments both of rearing and weaving.

Table C.—Export of raw silk, waste and silk piece goods from India to foreign countries during the last twenty years.—This Table shows improvement in the export of raw silk and waste, but a considerable decline in the export of piece goods. It is compiled from the Annual Report of the Bengal Chamber of Commerce for 1901 and the Annual Statement of the Director-General of Statistics for 1902. The figures must be considered reliable. But it should not be inferred from these that the silk-weaving industry of Bengal has been declining of late years. There is no doubt a great decline in the export of Corahs and other cheap silks to foreign countries, but the use of indigenous silks has been increasing by leaps and bounds during recent years in India itself. This improvement has more than compensated for the decline in the export trade in Indian silks to other countries.

Table D.—More detailed view of export of silk from India by sea.—This Table, compiled from the Annual Statement of the Director-General of Statistics for 1902, shows the present strength of the export trade in the different branches of the silk industry, the total value coming up to about seventy lakhs of rupees.

Tablo E.—Countries to which Bengal silk (raw and manufactured) is exported. This table has been compiled from the Bengal Administration Report for 1900-1901. It shows how England, France, Australia and Arabia including Turkey in Asia are the greatest patrons of the manufactured silks of this Province, while France, England, Italy and Turkey in Asia are the greatest patrons of the Bengal raw silk.

Table F.—Relative importance of English, French and Nakuda trade in Bengal silk fabrics.—This Table has been compiled from the Bengal Adminstration Reports and from the Annual Report of the Bengal Chamber of Commerce. It shows how Bengal silk has been losing the patronage of France of late years, also the greater stability of the English and Arabian markets as the natural outlets for Bengal silk fabrics.

Table G.—Exports of raw silk (including cocoons) from Calcutta.—This table gives in a succinct form the relative importance of different foreign and Indian markets over sea for the Bengal raw silk.

Table H.—Export of raw silk from different parts of India by rail and river.—This table shows how the indigenous raw silk in circulation in the country is about 32,000 maunds against 16,000 maunds of foreign raw silk, and nearly 27,000 maunds out of 32,000 maunds represent what goes out from Bengal filatures and indigenous gháis. The value of 32,000 maunds of raw silk, about 12,000 maunds of which is 'waste', is about one crore and twelve lakhs of rupees. As the value of the raw silk exported to foreign countries is about fifty lakhs (*vide* Table D), the value of what is utilised in the other Provinces of India is about seventy lakhs of rupees, producing cloth to the value of at least a crore of rupees.

Table J.—Export of silk piece goods from different parts of India by rail and river.—This table shows how the indigenous silk fabrics of India in circulation in the country is more than double in quantity of foreign silks. The value of 7,000 maunds of silk fabrics is over fifty lakhs of rupees. Of this ten or eleven lakhs (*vide* Table D) only represent foreign export. Of the 6,925 maunds of indigenous silks, Bengal sends out 4,135 maunds, and calculating the price of one maund of manufactured silk at Rs. 800, the value of the export from Bengal looms comes to over 33 lakhs of rupees, of which twenty-five lakhs represent the export to other Provinces and eight lakhs over sea.

Table K.—Imports of silk into India from foreign countries during thirty years.

Table L.—More detailed view of imports of foreign silk into India.

Table M.—Import of foreign silk into Bengal.—These three tables being studied together show that Bengal uses comparatively little of foreign silks, either raw or manufactured.

Table N.—Import of raw silk into different parts of India by rail and river.—This table shows how Bombay and the Punjab are the most prominent importers of foreign raw silk for manufacturing purposes, while the Central Provinces and Madras as the chief places next to Bengal where the indigenous raw silk is used for manufacturing purposes. It also shows how twice as much Indian raw silk is used in the country as foreign raw silk.

Table O.—Import of silk piece goods into different parts of India by rail and river.—This table shows how Calcutta is the principal emporium of Indian silks, while the Punjab, the United Provinces and Bombay also patronise Indian silk fabrics to a considerable extent.

Table P.—Imports of raw silk (including cocoons) from the differents district of Bengal into Calcutta.—This table compiled from the Bengal Admnistration Report gives some idea of the produce of silk in different districts of Bengal. It does not take into consideration the raw silk that goes to the other provinces of India, nor what is used in the Bengal looms, nor does it give a fair idea even of the relative production of different districts. Malda comes out at a great disadvantage in this table as the silk filatures of Malda send a good deal of their produce to the central factory of Rajshahi by country boats ,&c., to be there tested and packed up before despatch to Calcutta.

Table Q.—External Railway Traffic of Bengal in silk.

Table R.—Internal Railway Traffic of Bengal in silk.—These two tables have been considered at length in pages 55 and 56 of this Monograph.

Table S.—Relative importance of export and import of Bengal silk.—This table brings out the importance of the export trade in Bengal silk and the insignificance of the import trade in foreign silks.

Table T.—World's Production of silk.

Table V.—World's Importations of silk.

Table W—World's Exportations of silk.

Table X.—Consumption of mulberry raw silk in different countries.

Table Y.—Consumption of spun silk in different countries.

Table Z.—Total consumption of silk yarn in different countries.—

These tables, taken from M. Natalis Rondot's work *L'Industrie de la soie en France* (1894), explain themselves, and they show the position occupied by India (*i.e.*, by Bengal chiefly) as a producer and user of silk among the many silk producing countries of the world.

Table A.

The population of Bengal which depend on the Silk industry.

Serial number.	Name of Districts.	Silk worm rearers, cocoon gatherers and Mulberry growers.		Silk spinners and filature staff.		Silk weavers, dyers, sellers, &c.		Total population depending on silk industry.		Remarks.
		1901.	1891.	1901.	1891.	1901.	1891.	1901.	1891.	
1	Burdwan	...	4	...	5	367	994	367	1,003	The number of cocoon-rearer including "partially agriculturists" and "dependents" could not have declined so very much within the last decade, while the filature industry scarcely shows any deterioration and the weaving industry shows considerable amelioration. The figures for cocoon-rearers are evidently too low, and these must have been generally classed as cultivators, in most districts. There being only 16 cocoon-rearers including dependents in Midnapore, for instance, is on the very face of it, absurd.
2	Birbhum	390	8,524	1,046	40	1,309	609	2,745	9,173	
3	Bankura	418	878	...	1,300	2,683	891	3,101	3,169	
4	Midnapore	16	3,624	...	225	12,634	3,545	2,650	7,394	
5	Hooghly	...	83	...	4	1,294	1,141	1,294	1,228	
6	Howrah	2	13	...	...	14	100	16	113	
	Total for Burdwan Division ...	826	13,226	1,046	1,574	8,301	7,280	10,173	22,080	
7	24-Parganas	...	5	24	...	1	...	25	5	
8	Calcutta	...	...	150	...	256	74	406	74	
9	Nadia	26	7	11	...	85	98	122	105	
10	Murshidabad	10,761	31,698	15,441	12,052	15,413	11,392	41,615	55,142	
11	Jessore	...	...	...	...	22	...	22	...	
12	Khulna	...	...	...	...	...	...	...	...	
	Total for Presidency Division	10,787	31,710	15,626	12,052	15,777	11,564	42,190	55,326	
	Carried over ...	...	...	...	...	...	...	...	...	

TABLE A—*concluded.*

Serial number.	NAME OF DISTRICTS.	Silk worm rearers, cocoon gatherers and Mulberry growers. 1901.	1891.	Silk spinners and filature staff. 1901.	1891.	Silk weavers, dyers, sellers, &c. 1901.	1891.	Total population depending on silk. 1901.	1891.	REMARKS.
	Brought forward ...	...	...	...	...	...	...	...	...	
13	Rajshahi ...	7,435	8,793	1,344	3,107	6,583	2,312	15,362	14,212	The figure for female silkworm-rearers and cocoon-gathers actually entered in Table XV of the Census Report for 1901, for the District of Rajshahi is 28,825. This is probably a clerical error, and I have assumed 2,825 to be the right figure. The additional 26,000 persons thus thrown in by a clerical error vitiates the whole table as it stands in the Census Report and shows up the silk industry of the whole Province as having improved somewhat during the the last decade (which however is a fact). There is no reason why in Rajshahi alone there should be such a disproportionate rise in the number of females employed in cocoon-rearing, the number of males entered against the 28,825 females being only 1,608.
14	Dinajpur ...	13	19	...	...	...	...	13	19	
15	Jalpaiguri ...	...	...	...	...	...	1	...	1	
16	Darjeeling ...	...	...	...	...	1	...	1	...	
17	Rangpur ...	...	...	...	...	...	...	...	...	
18	Bogra ...	...	1	...	87	7	13	7	101	
19	Pabna ...	10	...	1	...	1	...	12	...	
	Total for Rajshahi Division ...	7,458	8,813	1,345	3,194	6,592	2,326	15,395	14,333	
20	Dacca ...	...	...	...	1	4	55	4	56	
21	Mymensingh ...	...	...	...	...	...	...	...	...	
22	Faridpur ...	...	...	...	...	...	...	...	...	
23	Backergunge ...	...	...	...	...	5	...	5	...	
	Total for Dacca Division ...	...	...	...	1	9	55	9	56	
24	Tippera ...	...	...	...	...	...	20	...	20	
25	Noakhali ...	...	...	...	...	...	5	...	5	
26	Chittagong ...	...	...	...	...	6	37	6	37	
27	Chittagong Hill Tracts ...	...	...	...	...	...	...	...	...	
	Total for Chittagong Hill Division.	...	...	...	...	6	62	6	62	
28	Patna ...	...	...	...	...	7	3	7	3	
29	Gaya ...	...	...	2	4	...	33	2	37	
30	Shahabad ...	...	...	...	...	3	...	3	...	
31	Saran ...	...	...	...	...	1	5	1	5	
32	Champaran ...	...	...	...	...	4	...	4	...	
33	Muzaffarpur ...	...	...	...	...	...	...	...	...	
34	Darbhanga ...	...	...	...	...	10	...	10	...	
	Total for Patna Division ...	...	...	2	4	25	41	27	45	
35	Monghyr ...	...	38	...	...	25	...	25	38	
36	Bhagalpur ...	...	...	...	...	825	458	825	458	
37	Purneah ...	...	...	...	...	3	...	3	...	
38	Maldah ...	35,893	38,433	1,4[illegible]	1,953	6,116	2,510	43,477	42,896	There are at least 2,000 tusser silk worm rearers in the district of Santal Parganas, and the census figures for this district are certainly wrong.
39	Sonthal Parganas ...	31	30	...	35	79	96	115	161	
	Total for Bhagalpur Division	35,924	38,501	1,473	1,988	7,048	3,064	44,445	43,553	
40	Cuttack ...	1	...	...	...	1,233	274	1,234	274	
41	Balasore ...	...	...	...	13	112	87	112	100	
42	Angul ...	...	1	...	...	...	...	...	1	
43	Puri ...	...	8	...	53	366	221	366	282	
	Total for Orissa Division ...	1	9	...	66	1,711	582	1,712	657	
44	Hazaribagh ...	...	...	...	2	325	6	325	6	
45	Ranchi or Lohardaga ...	110	...	...	15	85	41	195	56	
46	Palamau ...	...	...	412	...	13	...	425	...	
47	Manbhum ...	...	...	...	179	89	212	89	391	The district monograph from Palamau estimates 400 to 500 families as being dependent on tusser silk-rearing in that district. The district monograph from Singbhum says "In the Kolhan Government estate the average number of cultivators of cocoons is about 4,000 annually."
48	Singhbhum ...	...	...	...	...	48	358	48	358	
	Total for Chota Nagpur Division.	110	...	412	196	560	617	1,082	813	
49	Kuch Behar ...	3	6	...	...	2	...	5	6	
50	Tributary States Orissa ...	40	53	...	16	2,974	1,641	3,014	1,857	
51	Ditto Chota Nagpur ...	107	...	...	...	4	69	111	69	
52	Hill Tippera ...	...	...	...	...	...	...	...	...	
53	Sikkim ...	...	...	...	...	...	...	...	...	
	Total for Feudatory States ...	150	59	...	163	2,980	1,710	3,130	1,932	
54	Cities ...	...	...	...	...	827	...	827	...	
	Total for whole Bengal ...	55,256	92,318	19,904	19,238	43,836	27,301	188,169	138,857	

TABLE B.

Relative importance of the different branches of the Bengal silk industry.

(Table based on the Census figures for 1891.)*

Division	District	Mulberry grows.	Silkworm Rearers and Cocoon-gatherers.			Silk-carders and Spinners.			Silk-weavers and Dealers.			Silk Braid and Ribbon-makers and Sellers.			Total.			Grand Total.
			Silk.	Tusser.	Endi.	Silk.	Tusser.	Endi.	Silk.	Tusser.	Endi.	Silk.	Tusser.	Endi.	Silk.	Tusser.	Endi.	
1		2	3	4	5	6	7	8	9	10	11	12	13	14	15	16	17	18
Burdwan.	Burdwan	Nil	4	Nil	Nil	5	Nil	Nil	346	648	Nil	Nil	Nil	Nil	355	648	Nil	1,003
	Birbhum	2,249	6,000	275	Nil	30	10	Nil	500	109	Nil	Nil	Nil	Nil	8,779	394	Nil	9,173
	Bankura	308	670	Nil	Nil	1,300	Nil	Nil	891	Nil	Nil	Nil	Nil	Nil	3,169	Nil	Nil	3,169
	Midnapore	2,866	700	58	Nil	200	25	Nil	3,500	45	Nil	Nil	Nil	Nil	7,266	128	Nil	7,394
	Hooghly	Nil	83	Nil	Nil	4	Nil	Nil	1,141	Nil	Nil	Nil	Nil	Nil	1,228	Nil	Nil	1,228
	Howrah	1	12	Nil	Nil	Nil	Nil	Nil	100	Nil	Nil	Nil	Nil	Nil	113	Nil	Nil	113
Presidency.	24-Parganas (including Calcutta).	Nil	5	Nil	Nil	Nil	Nil	Nil	70	Nil	Nil	4	Nil	Nil	79	Nil	Nil	79
	Nadia	Nil	7	Nil	Nil	Nil	Nil	Nil	98	Nil	Nil	Nil	Nil	Nil	105	Nil	Nil	105
	Murshidabad	10	31,688	Nil	Nil	12,052	Nil	Nil	11,392	Nil	Nil	Nil	Nil	Nil	55,142	Nil	Ni	55,142
	Jessore	Nil	Nil	Nil	Nil	Nil	Nil	Nil	Nil	Nil	Nil	Nil	Nil	Nil	Nil	Nil	Nil	Nil
	Khulna	Nil	Nil	Nil	Nil	Nil	Nil	Nil	Nil	Nil	Nil	Nil	Nil	Nil	Nil	Nil	Nil	Nil
Rajshahi.	Rajshahi	70	8,723	Nil	Nil	3,107	Nil	Nil	2,312	Nil	Nil	Nil	Nil	Nil	14,212	Nil	Nil	14,212
	Dinajpur	Nil	Nil	Nil	19	Nil	Nil	Nil	Nil	Nil	Nil	Nil	Nil	Nil	Nil	Nil	19	19
	Jalpaiguri	Nil	Nil	Nil	Nil	Nil	Nil	Nil	Nil	Nil	1	Nil	Nil	Nil	Nil	Nil	1	1
	Darjeeling	Nil	Nil	Nil	Nil	Nil	Nil	Nil	Nil	Nil	Nil	Nil	Nil	Nil	Nil	Nil	Nil	Nil
	Rangpur	Nil	Nil	Nil	Nil	Nil	Nil	Nil	Nil	Nil	Nil	Nil	Nil	Nil	Nil	Nil	Nil	Nil
	Bogra	Nil	1	Nil	Nil	40	Nil	47	13	Nil	Nil	Nil	Nil	Nil	54	Nil	47	101
	Pabna	Nil	Nil	Nil	Nil	Nil	Nil	Nil	Nil	Nil	Nil	Nil	Nil	Nil	Nil	Nil	Nil	Nil
Dacca.	Dacca	Nil	Nil	Nil	Nil	1	Nil	Nil	55	Nil	Nil	Nil	Nil	Nil	56	Nil	Nil	56
	Mymensingh	Nil	Nil	Nil	Nil	Nil	Nil	Nil	Nil	Nil	Nil	Nil	Nil	Nil	Nil	Nil	Nil	Nil
	Faridpur	Nil	Nil	Nil	Nil	Nil	Nil	Nil	Nil	Nil	Nil	Nil	Nil	Nil	Nil	Nil	Nil	Nil
	Backergunge	Nil	Nil	Nil	Nil	Nil	Nil	Nil	Nil	Nil	Nil	Nil	Nil	Nil	Nil	Nil	Nil	Nil
Chittagong.	Tippera	Nil	Nil	Nil	Nil	Nil	Nil	Nil	Nil	Nil	20	Nil	Nil	Nil	Nil	Nil	20	20
	Noakhali	Nil	Nil	Nil	Nil	Nil	Nil	Nil	Nil	Nil	5	Nil	Nil	Nil	Nil	Nil	5	5
	Chittagong	Nil	Nil	Nil	Nil	Nil	Nil	Nil	Nil	Nil	37	Nil	Nil	Nil	Nil	Nil	37	37
	South Lushai Hills ...	Nil	Nil	Nil	Nil	Nil	Nil	Nil	Nil	Nil	Nil	Nil	Nil	Nil	Nil	Nil	Nil	Nil
Patna.	Patna	Nil	Nil	Nil	Nil	Nil	Nil	Nil	Nil	3	Nil	Nil	Nil	Nil	Nil	3	Nil	3
	Gaya	Nil	Nil	Nil	Nil	Nil	4	Nil	Nil	33	Nil	Nil	Nil	Nil	Nil	37	Nil	37
	Shahabad	Nil	Nil	Nil	Nil	Nil	Nil	Nil	Nil	Nil	Nil	Nil	Nil	Nil	Nil	Nil	Nil	Nil
	Saran	Nil	Nil	Nil	Nil	Nil	Nil	Nil	Nil	5	Nil	Nil	Nil	Nil	Nil	5	Nil	5
	Champaran	Nil	Nil	Nil	Nil	Nil	Nil	Nil	Nil	Nil	Nil	Nil	Nil	Nil	Nil	Nil	Nil	Nil
	Musaffarpur	Nil	Nil	Nil	Nil	Nil	Nil	Nil	Nil	Nil	Nil	Nil	Nil	Nil	Nil	Nil	Nil	Nil
	Darbhanga	Nil	Nil	Nil	Nil	Nil	Nil	Nil	Nil	Nil	Nil	Nil	Nil	Nil	Nil	Nil	Nil	Nil
Bhagalpur.	Monghyr	Nil	...	38	Nil	Nil	Nil	Nil	Nil	Nil	Nil	Nil	Nil	Nil	Nil	38	Nil	38
	Bhagalpur	Nil	...	Nil	Nil	Nil	Nil	Nil	Nil	458	Nil	Nil	Nil	Nil	Nil	458	Nil	458
	Purnea	Nil	...	Nil	Nil	Nil	Nil	Nil	Nil	Nil	Nil	Nil	Nil	Nil	Nil	Nil	Nil	Nil
	Malda	6,500	31,933	Nil	Nil	1,953	Nil	Nil	2,510	Nil	Nil	Nil	Nil	Nil	42,896	Nil	Nil	42,896
	Sonthal Parganas ...	Nil	...	30	Nil	Nil	35	Nil	Nil	96	Nil	Nil	Nil	Nil	Nil	161	Nil	161
Orissa.	Cuttack	Nil	Nil	Nil	Nil	Nil	Nil	Nil	Nil	274	Nil	Nil	Nil	Nil	Nil	274	Nil	274
	Balasore	Nil	Nil	Nil	Nil	Nil	13	Nil	Nil	87	Nil	Nil	Nil	Nil	Nil	100	Nil	106
	Angul and Khondmals	Nil	Nil	1	Nil	Nil	Nil	Nil	Nil	Nil	Nil	Nil	Nil	Nil	Nil	1	Nil	1
	Puri	Nil	Nil	8	Nil	Nil	53	Nil	Nil	221	Nil	Nil	Nil	Nil	Nil	282	Nil	282
Chota Nagpur.	Hazaribagh	Nil	Nil	Nil	Nil	Nil	2	Nil	Nil	6	Nil	Nil	Nil	Nil	Nil	8	Nil	8
	Lohardaga	Nil	Nil	Nil	Nil	Nil	15	Nil	Nil	41	Nil	Nil	Nil	Nil	Nil	56	Nil	56
	Palamau	Nil	Nil	Nil	Nil	Nil	Nil	Nil	Nil	Nil	Nil	Nil	Nil	Nil	Nil	Nil	Nil	Nil
	Manbhum	Nil	Nil	Nil	Nil	Nil	179	Nil	Nil	212	Nil	Nil	Nil	Nil	Nil	391	Nil	391
	Singhbhum	Nil	Nil	Nil	Nil	Nil	Nil	Nil	Nil	358	Nil	Nil	Nil	Nil	Nil	358	Nil	358
Feudatory States		Nil	Nil	Nil	59	Nil	Nil	163	Nil	Nil	1,710	Nil	Nil	Nil	Nil	Nil	1,932	1,932
Total ...		12,004	79,826	410	78	18,632	336	210	23,928	2,596	1,773	4	Nil	Nil	1,33,454	3,342	2,061	1,38,857

* The Census figures for the silk industry for 1901 appearing to me more unreliable than those of 1891 I have based this table on the Census figures for 1891.

N. G. M.

Table C.

Export of raw-silk, "waste" and silk piece-goods from India to foreign countries during the last twenty years.

Year.			Raw silk.	Waste.	Silk piece-goods.
			lbs.	lbs.	yds.
1881-82	...	...	340,750	748,693	2,126,635
1882-83	...	...	501,576	834,405	2,589,217
1883-84	...	...	673,360	885,395	2,781,128
1884-85	...	...	531,205	950,983	3,467,308
1885-86	...	...	358,071	1,023,807	3,728,213
1886-87	...	...	449,515	1,020,595	3,161,179
1887-88	...	...	453,568	998,235	3,352,528
1888-89	...	...	433,473	1,313,874	2,807,203
1889-90	...	...	559,342	1,233,494	2,330,360
1890-91	...	...	502,603	1,112,313	2,002,959
1891-92	...	...	187,055	1,012,254	1,728,969
1892-93	...	...	655,338	1,087,500	1,768,165
1893-94	...	...	613,330	1,080,684	2,129,815
1894-95	...	...	510,800	793,892	1,343,652
1895-96	...	...	707,683	1,072,452	1,528,225
1896-97	...	...	595,433	898,713	1,427,611
1897-98	...	...	622,587	1,037,701	1,180,813
1898-99	...	...	512,830	1,046,541	1,261,300
1899-1900	...	...	722,286	1,217,432	1,217,332
1900-1901	...	...	559,776	1,030,523	1,175,924
1901-1902	...	...	727,651	1,165,754	854,092

Table D.

More detailed view of export of Silk from India by Sea.

	1897-98.	1898-99.	1899-1900.	1900-1901.	1901-1902.	Average export of five years.
Raw silk	lbs. 622,587 Rs. 45,18,203	lbs. 512,830 Rs. 39,06,821	lbs. 722,286 Rs. 61,49,898	lbs. 559,776 Rs. 43,02,707	lbs. 727,651 Rs. 57,53,220	lbs. 629,026 Rs. 49,26,170
Chasam or waste ...	lbs. 1,037,701 Rs. 6,27,196	lbs. 1,046,541 Rs. 6,70,071	lbs. 1,217,432 Rs. 8,36,208	lbs. 1,030,523 Rs. 8,09,619	lbs. 1,165,754 Rs. 8,49,948	lbs. 1,099,590 Rs. 7,58,788
Cocoons	lbs. 1,742 Rs. 3,105	lbs. 4,780 Rs. 2,240	... ...	lbs. 13,976 Rs. 9,731	lbs. 42,356 Rs. 31,041	lbs. 15,713 Rs. 11,529
Silk piece-goods ...	Yds. 1,180,833 Rs. 10,88,623	Yds. 1,261,300 Rs. 11,65,888	Yds. 1,217,332 Rs. 11,39,272	Yds. 1,175,924 Rs. 10,96,770	Yds. 854,092 Rs. 8,90,540	Yds. 1,137,896 Rs. 10,76,220
Mixed silk piece-goods	Yds. 161,058 Rs. 154,735	Yds. 95,202 Rs. 1,13,462	Yds. 221,333 Rs. 1,46,536	Yds. 152,367 Rs. 1,56,197	Yds. 196,072 Rs. 1,61,507	Yds. 165,206 Rs. 1,46,489
Sewing thread	lbs. 2,888 Rs. 16,458	lbs. 17 Rs. 700	lbs. 150 Rs. 750	lbs 175 Rs. 630	lbs. 257 Rs. 2,022	lbs. 729 Rs. 4,112
Other sorts	lbs. 117 Rs. 593	lbs. 100 Rs. 1,840	lbs. 2,201 Rs. 2,460	lbs. 60 Rs. 850	lbs. 81 Rs. 616	lbs. 912 Rs. 1,272

Total value ... Rs. 69,24,580

Table E

Countries to which Bengal Silk (raw and manufactured) is exported.

	Raw.					Manufactured.			
	1896-97.	1897-98.	1898-99.	1899-1900.	19 0-1901.	1896-97.	1897-98	1898-99.	1899-1900.
1	2	3	4	5	6	7	8	9	10
						Rs.	Rs.	Rs.	Rs.
United Kingdom	lbs. 416,713 Rs. 18,21,341	lbs. 753,080 Rs. 26,91,299	lbs. 553,994 Rs. 15,63,540	lbs. 691,642 Rs. 28,22,527	lbs. 433,553 Rs. 14,81,067	6,20,569	6,02,285	6,24,981	6,69,499
France	lbs. 735,347 Rs. 28,54,117	lbs. 531,133 Rs. 20,79,155	lbs. 664,698 Rs. 25,76,764	lbs. 848,491 Rs. 35,28,578	lbs. 772,680 Rs. 32,05,684	3,39,616	1,21,655	1,01,633	1,55,634
Germany	......	......	......	......	......	1,500	......	150	970
Austria-Hungary	......	......	......	......	......	186	......	......	......
Italy	lbs. 35,368 Rs. 2 54,800	lbs. 23,833 Rs. 1,59,655	lbs. 31,494 Rs. 25,45,800	lbs. 36,720 Rs. 3,32,194	lbs. 18,113 Rs. 1,44,440	......	......	......	......
Zanzibar	......	......	......	......	......	1,000	......	......	......
Mauritius	......	......	......	......	lbs. 40 Rs. 120	7,210	9,434	8,600	2,010
America	......	......	lbs. 149 Rs. 1,080	lbs. 7,003 Rs. 56,024	lbs. 1,490 Rs. 11,920	24,973	10,399	3,547	3,243
Aden	......	......	......	......	......	......	2,031	4,317	1,383
Arabia	......	......	......	......	......	38,282	26,103	1,388	44,296
Ceylon	......	lbs. 2,687 Rs. 17,280	......	lbs. 845 Rs. 6,210	......	296	797	4,236	5,089
China	......	......	......	......	......	2,045	7,212	3,312	29
Persia	......	......	......	......	......	2,575	1,387	......	400
Straits Settlements	......	......	......	......	......	12,752	8,211	13,990	11,583
Turkey in Asia	lbs. 4,393 Rs. 15,704	lbs. 6,468 Rs. 24,449	lbs. 1,663 Rs. 7,755	lbs. 5,143 Rs. 17,790	lbs. 4,231 Rs. 18,464	21,292	15,699	11,145	13,041
Australia	lbs. 966 Rs. 4,752	lbs. 1,222 Rs. 5,436	......	......	lbs. 41 Rs. 100	19,987	42,372	59,051	88,014
Other Countries	......	......	lbs. 26 Rs. 146	lbs. 1,820 Rs. 12,170	......	58,177	52,206	22,477	10,922
Total quantity ... Total value ...	lbs. 1,192,777 Rs. 49,50,709	1,318,423 49,77,274	1,262,014 43,95,085	1,591,364 67,75,493	1,229,948 48,61,795	11,50,460	8,99,791	8,58,827	10,06,113

Table F

Relative importance of English, French, and Nakoda trade in Bengal silk fabrics.

Year.	To United Kingdom of Great Britain and Ireland.	To France.	To Arabia and Turkey in Asia.
1	2	3	4
	Yds.	Yds.	Yds.
1878-79 ...	882,337	426,882	134,649
1879-80 ...	1,074,479	687,437	131,272
1880-81 ...	858,024	861,300	138,853
1881-82 ...	740,961	978,446	127,716
1882-83 ...	1,611,720	624,389	105,250
1883-84 ...	1,368,481	1,003,285	82,925
1884-85 ...	2,080,018	1,045,781	13,589
1885-86 ...	2,480,425	924,036	130,218
1886-87 ...	2,236,986	618,521	109,180
1887-88 ...	2,764,234	601,590	25,937
1888-89 ...	1,907,995	710,901	72,996
1889-90 ...	1,430,859	723,776	72,534
1890-91 ...	1,448,010	392,336	51,526
1891-92 ...	1,084,310	412,184	87,141
1892-93 ...	1,667,775	295,228	94,533
1893-94 ...	1,526,165	339,166	95,205
1894-95 ...	780,240	291,538	111,466
1895-96 ...	792,126	359,051	245,439
1896-97 ...	720,595	345,469	206,829
1897-98 ...	735,191	125,033	128,653
1898-99 ...	773,390	116,173	102,811
1899-1900 ...	810,581	160,787	70,820
1900-1901 ..	665,315	174,715	97,193

TABLE G

Exports of Raw Silk (including cocoons) from Calcutta.

	1896-97.	1897-98.	1898-99.	1899-1900.
	Mds.	Mds.	Mds.	Mds.
To United Kingdom ...	5,064	9,152	6,733	8,406
,, Other Foreign ports ...	9,432	6,871	8,925	10,934
,, Madras	2,706	1,206	...	...
,, Other ports in Madras ...	126	118	93	71
,, Bombay	622	1,048	3	4
,, Other Indian ports ...	156	157	170	14
,, Burma	153	134	212	212
Total ...	18,259	18,686	16,971	20,248

TABLE H

Export of Raw Silk from different parts of India by rail and river during recent years.

	1897-98	1898-99.	1899-1900.	1900-1901.	1901-1902.	AVERAGE.
(1) FOREIGN.	Mds.	Mds.	Mds.	Mds.	Mds.	Mds.
British Provinces (excluding chief sea-ports)	194	50	72	73	119	
Native States	...	2	2	...	2	
Chief sea ports—						
Bombay	15,478	17,900	13,027	11,558	16,979	
Karachi	900	972	1,219	1,028	2,639	
Other ports	85	9	85	42	77	
Total ...	16,057	18,933	14,406	12,701	19,810	16,502
(2) INDIAN.						
British Provinces (excluding chief sea-ports)						
Bengal	23,825	23,579	24,089	18,150	24,212	
Other Provinces ...	1,123	946	2,388	1,778	4,414	
Total ...	24,948	24,525	26,477	19,928	28,626	
Native States—						
Mysore	2,903	2,566	3,136	4,099	5,149	
Other States	75	i	397	93	...	
Chief sea-ports—						
Calcutta	1,808	2,401	1,164	1,582	2,109	
Bombay	751	388	1,918	563	305	
Karachi	605	3[illegible]3	728	4[illegible]5	329	
Madras ports	1,035	800	596	150	88	
Total ...	32,125	30,984	34,406	26,670	36,606	32,158

TABLE J

Export of Silk Piece-goods from different parts of India by rail and river during recent years.

	1897-98.	1898-99.	1899-1900.	1900-1901	1901-1902.	AVERAGE.
(1) FOREIGN.	Mds.	Mds.	Mds.	Mds.	Mds.	Mds.
British Provinces (excluding chief sea-ports).	71	169	25	68	4	
Native States	...	30	...	...	...	
Chief sea-ports —						
Bombay	1,827	3,781	2,406	1,356	2,056	
Karachi	1,024	427	453	1,273	668	
Other ports	52	481	194	38	53	
Total ...	3,448	4,888	3,078	2,735	2.781	3,386 (Foreign).
(2) INDIAN.						
British Provinces (excluding chief sea-ports)—						
Assam	490	364	385	318	458	
Bengal	4,058	3,140	2,403	5,102	2,600	3,460 } Bengal.
Bombay	795	688	562	417	848	
Other Provinces ...	496	220	466	722	193	
Native States	89	63	19	3	18	
Chief sea-ports—						
Calcutta	724	518	346	311	1,479	675 } Bengal.
Bombay	665	913	801	782	1,279	
Other ports	195	211	374	788	420	
Total ...	7,512	6,117	5,356	8,443	7,385	6,925 (Indigenous).

TABLE K

Imports of Silk into India from foreign countries.

YEAR.	Yarn.	Piece-goods.	Silk mixed with other materials.
1	2	3	4
	Lbs.	Yards.	Yards.
1870-71 ...	2,328,854	4,053,411	The figures for this column for 1870—75 are included in the previous column.
1871-72 ...	1,799,723	4,775,023	
1872-73 ...	1,933,565	5,010,532	
1873-74 ...	2,284,836	5,469,168	
1874-75 ...	2,469,372	7,266,159	
1875-76 ...	2,468,274	770,283	345,279
1876-77 ...	1,463,057	5,075,749	270,577
1877-78 ...	2,106,765	7,080,711	1,248,005
1878-79 ...	1,813,999	7,350,804	1,535,965
1879-80 ...	2,002,050	7,467,815	1,035,643
1880-81 ...	2,511,802	11,628,163	1,945,922
1881-82 ...	1,663,653	10,397,147	1,404,417
1882-83 ...	2,385,940	8,518,119	1,153,142
1883-84 ...	2,210,781	9,627,673	922,388
1884-85 ...	1,814,242	10,221,778	1,858,399
1885-86 ...	1,724,477	8,999,359	2,174,429
1886-87 ...	1,730,000	10,541,862	2,626,011
1887-88 ...	2,595,635	11,760,401	3,970,372
1888-89 ...	2,038,529	10,952,732	4,223,332
1889-90 ...	2,360,058	11,426,168	3,978,949
1890-91 ...	2,405,721	10,032,619	1,997,677
1891-92 ...	2,698,391	11,790,744	3,146,107
1892-93 ...	2,289,293	12,558,447	2,844,631
1893-94 ...	2,943,705	13,356,429	3,062,298
1894-95 ...	2,493,614	9,955,154	3,932,772
1895-96 ...	3,023,825	13,269,424	5,051,282
1896-97 ...	2,285,818	10,065,569	5,693,313
1897-98 ...	2,049,608	10,185,716	4,012,052
1898-99 ...	2,250,866	12,271,372	4,935,684
1899-1900 ...	1,694,848	8,212,032	3,633,536
1900-1901 ...	2,535,377	17,416,313	3,256,349
1901-1902 ...	2,128,483	12,625,280	4,847,000

Table L

More detailed view of imports of foreign Silk into India.

	1897-98.	1898-99.	1899-1900.	1900-1901.	1901-1902.	Average of five years.
Raw Silk	lbs. 2,049,608	lbs. 2,250,866	lbs. 1,694,848	lbs. 2,535,377	lbs. 2,128,483	lbs. 2,131,836
	Rs. 66,97,717	Rs. 79,76,569	Rs. 57,60,853	Rs. 1,01,69,402	Rs. 80,96,200	Rs. 77,40,154
Silk piece-goods ...	Yds. 10,185,716	Yds. 12,271,372	Yds. 8,212,032	Yds. 17,416,313	Yds. 12,625,280	Yds. 12,142,143
	Rs. 76,48,256	Rs. 89,24,006	Rs. 65,93,753	Rs. 1,17,36,372	Rs. 86,78,441	Rs. 87,16,265
Goods of Silk mixed with other materials	Yds. 4,012,052	Yds. 4,935,684	Yds. 3,633,536	Yds. 3,256,349	Yds. 4,847,000	Yds. 4,135,524
	Rs. 30,78,568	Rs. 34,14,673	Rs. 27,43,642	Rs. 26,15,611	Rs. 36,13,740	Rs. 30,93,247
Sewing thread ...	lbs. 4,826	lbs. 6,346	lbs. 2,481	lbs. 1,652	lbs. 1,490	lbs. 3,359
	Rs. 32,690	Rs. 41,101	Rs. 18,179	Rs. 12,892	Rs. 11,126	Rs. 23,197
Other sorts	lbs. 285,109	lbs. 395,059	lbs. 476,489	lbs. 581,299	lbs. 802,579	lbs. 508,105
	Rs. 7,33,089	Rs. 12,38,154	Rs. 19,42,736	Rs. 22,92,733	Rs. 25,43,702	Rs. 17,50,082

Table M

Import of foreign Silk into Bengal.

Year.	Raw silk		Silk piece-goods (pure and mixed).		Other silk goods.	
	lbs.	Rs.	Yards.	Rs.	lbs.	Rs.
1895-96 ...	1,611	8,846	1,016,881	12,26,671	1,597	16,018
1896-97 ...	1,124	2,917	1,709,122	13,96,224	9,407	48,556
1897-98 ...	3,950	6,956	903,587	7,42,778	6,830	35,237
1898-99 ...	1,663	6,976	1,414,537	10,07,275	6,677	40,805
1899-1900 ...	5,957	9,255	1,393,549	11,26,619	3,806	19,658
1900-1901 ...	15,494	22,955	905,627	8,33,087	3,838	11,304
Average consumption of foreign silk in Bengal.	4,966	9,651	1,223,883	1,054,276	5,359	28,596

Table N

Import of Raw Silk into different parts of India by rail and river.

	1897-98.	1898-99.	1899-1900.	1900-1901.	1901-1902.	Remarks.
(1) Foreign.	Mds.	Mds.	Mds.	Mds.	Mds.	
British Provinces (excluding chief sea-ports)—						
Punjab	6,185	6,418	4,005	6,182	8,749	
Bombay	8,823	11,580	9,555	5,511	10,068	
Other Provinces	1,460	879	746	861	670	
Native States	15	27	75	116	258	
Chief sea-ports	174	29	24	31	71	
Total ...	16,657	18,933	14,405	12,701	19,816	
(2) Indian.						
British Provinces (excluding chief sea-ports)—						
Bengal	834	1,201	1,440	1,224	1,337	
Punjab	756	1,058	2,438	671	488	
Central Provinces ...	2,190	2,126	2,414	3,794	2,959	
Madras	1,043	843	601	208	135	
Other Provinces	1,768	879	808	555	1,017	
Natives States	73	79	79	43	81	
Chief sea-ports—						
Calcutta	21,745	21,217	21,704	14,629	21,839	
Bombay	765	963	1,816	1,361	3,579	
Karachi	2	4	81	15	...	
Madras ports	2,949	2,648	3,025	4,175	5,171	
Total ...	32,125	30,984	34,406	26,670	36,606	

TABLE O

Import of Silk piece-goods into different parts of India by rail and river.

	1897-98.	1898-99.	1899-1900.	1900-1901.	1901-1902.	REMARKS.
(1) FOREIGN.	Mds.	Mds.	Mds.	Mds.	Mds.	
British Provinces (excluding chief sea-ports)—	3,307	2,706	2,910	2,644	2,704	
Native States	80	1,949	153	76	68	
Chief sea-ports	61	173	15	15	9	
Total ...	3,448	4,828	3,078	2,735	2,781	
(2) INDIAN.						
British Provinces (excluding chief sea-ports)—						
Bengal	236	261	445	158	185	
United Provinces of Agra and Oudh	1,026	845	609	869	1,909	
Punjab	1,391	1,765	1,592	1,725	1,979	
Other Provinces	286	448	305	1,191	475	
Native States	140	80	24	77	147	
Chief sea-ports—						
Calcutta	3,200	1,925	1,704	3,696	1,635	
Bombay	787	673	584	680	936	
Other ports	446	120	93	47	119	
Total ...	7,512	6,117	5,356	8,443	7,385	

TABLE P

Imports of Raw silk (including cocoons) from the different districts of Bengal into Calcutta.

	1896-97.	1897-98.	1898-99.	1899-1900.
	Mds.	Mds.	Mds.	Mds.
From—				
Midnapore	2,141	2,191	1,118	1,127
Birbhum	886	1,265	745	1,053
Bankura, Burdwan, Hooghly, Howrah, 24-Parganas	113	487	493	135
Murshidabad	7,913	9,750	13,227	13,764
Nadia	997	1,051	1,426	841
Jessore	15	Nil	...	...
Rajshahi	3.351	4,290	3,805	4,049
Bogra	Nil	64	...	...
Maldah	1,088	455	150	242
Total mulberry silk ...	16,504	19,553	20,964	21,211
From—				
Gaya	28	9	?	?
Singhbhum	1,281	1,508	4	7
Manbhum	17	Nil	247	102
Balasore	...	...	...	...
Total of *tusser* ...	1,326	1,743	?	?
From—				
Assam (chiefly *endi*) ...	95	448	?	?
Other Provinces of India ...	77	11	?	?
Total of all raw silks imported into Calcutta	18,002	21,755	21,512	21,854

Table Q

External Railway Traffic of Bengal in Silk.

	Imports into Bengal from N.-W. P., Oudh, Punjab, C. P., &c.						Exports from Bengal to N.-W. P., Oudh, Punjab, C. P., &c.					
	Total.		To Calcutta.		To other places.		Total.		From Calcutta.		From other places	
	Quantity.	Value.	Quantity.	Value.	Quantity.	Value.	Quantity.	Value.	Quantity.	Value.	Quantity.	Value.
1	2	3	4	5	6	7	8	9	10	11	12	13
	Mds.	Rs.	Mds.	Rs.	Mds.	Rs.	Mds.	Rs.	Mds.	Rs.	Mds.	Rs.
Raw silk (including cocoons), 1896-97.	181	60,706	79	27,006	102	33,700	2,336	11,91,664	989	5,06,041	1,347	6,85,623
Raw-silk (including cocoons), 1897-98.	30	11,439	12	4,639	18	6,800	3,615	18,33,525	1,078	5,42,752	2,537	12,90,773
Manufactured silk (Indian), 1896-97.	82	55,466	75	50,036	7	5,430	1,031	10,02,324	545	5,28,960	486	4,73,364
Manufactured silk (Indian), 1897-98.	73	49,108	58	38,352	15	10,756	2,147	20,20,760	788	6,94,640	1,359	13,26,120

Table R

Internal Railway Traffic of Bengal in Silk.

	Down Traffic.						Up Traffic.					
	Total down traffic.		Down Calcutta traffic.		Down traffic to places other than Calcutta.		Total up traffic.		Up traffic from Calcutta.		Up traffic from places other than Calcutta.	
	Quantity.	Value.	Quantity.	Value.	Quantity.	Value.	Quantity.	Value.	Quantity.	Value.	Quantity.	Value.
1	2	3	4	5	6	7	8	9	10	11	12	13
	Mds.	Rs.	Mds.	Rs.	Mds.	Rs.	Mds.	Rs.	Mds.	Rs.	Mds.	Rs.
Raw silk (including cocoons), 1896-97.	21,008	1,06,97,632	12,919	65,80,331	8,089	41,17,301	860	4,37,740	384	1,95,456	476	2,42,284
Raw-silk (including cocoons), 1897-98.	21,776	1,10,83,284	14,325	72,90,725	7,451	37,92,559	1,472	7,14,91,248	469	2,38,721	1,003	5,10,527
Manufactured silk (Indian), 1896-97.	1,991	19,39,234	1,988	19,36,312	3	2,922	32	31,168	25	24,350	7	6,818
Manufactured silk (Indian), 1897-98.	1,632	15,92,832	1,626	15,86,976	6	5,856	206	2,01,056	174	1,69,824	32	31,232

Table S

Relative importance of Export and Import of Bengal Silk.

Year.	Raw Silk.				Manufactured Silk.			
	Import.		Export.		Import.		Export.	
	Maunds.	Value. Rs.	Maunds.	Value. Rs.	Maunds.	Value. Rs.	Maunds	Value. Rs.
1898-99 ...	150	48,201	3,734	18,99,461	53	30,397	1,963	18,88,253
1899-1900 ...	875	3,71,872	3,021	15,22,256	31	20,731	1,235	11 99,281

TABLE T

World's Production of Silk.

Country.	Silk.	Waste.	Total production.
1	2	3	4
	Kilogrammes.	Kilogrammes.	Kilogrammes.
China	10,500,000	8,500,000	19,000,000
Japan	3,900,000	3,200,000	71,000,000
Indo-China	950,000	750,000	1,700,000
India	625,000	550,000	1,175,000
Central Asia	1,040,000	865,000	1,905,000
Asiatic Turkey	700,000	650,000	1,350,000
Turkey in Europe	160,000	50,000	210,000
Balkan States	30,000	15,000	45,000
Greece	35,000	20,000	55,000
Austro-Hungary	2,65,000	220,000	485,000
Italy	4,200,000	3,600,000	7,800,000
France	720,000	600,000	1,320,000
Spain and Portugal	80,000	50,000	130,000
Switzerland	30,000	50,000	80,000
Germany	Nil	5,000	5,000
Great Britain	Nil	30,000	30,000
Morocco	5,000	5,000	10,000
United States and Canada ...	5,000	50,000	55,000
Mexico	1,000	Nil	1,000
Total ...	23,246,000	19,210,000	42,456,000

TABLE V

World's Importations of Silk.

Country.	Silk.	Waste.	Total importation.
1	2	3	4
	Kilogrammes.	Kilogrammes.	Kilogrammes.
China	Nil.	Nil.	Nil
Japan	10,000	2,000	12,000
Indo-China	175,000	...	175,000
India	600,000	600,000	1,200,000
Central Asia	40,000	...	40,000
Russia in Europe	450,000	200,000	650,000
Arabia	12,000	...	12,000
Turkey in Asia	200,000	...	200,000
Turkey in Europe	2,000	...	2,000
Balkan States	6,000	...	6,000
Austro-Hungary	500 000	540,000	1,040,000
Italy	1,400,000	765,000	2,165,000
France	5,310,000	6,590,000	11,900,000
Spain and Portugal	125,000	...	125,000
Switzerland	2,175,000	1,300,000	3.475,000
Germany	2,390,000	900,000	3,290,000
Belgium	75,000	...	75,000
Great Britain	1,140,000	3,290,000	4,430,000
Egypt	170,000	...	170,000
Tunis and Tripoli	75,000	...	75,000
Algeria	30,000	...	30,000
Morocco	65,000	...	65,000
United States and Canada ...	2,650,000	630,000	3,280,000
Mexico	10,000	...	10,000
Australia	...	140,000	140,000
Total ...	17,610,000	14,957,000	32,567,000

Table W.

World's Exportations of silk.

Country.	Silk.	Waste.	Total exportation.
1	2	3	4
	Kilogrammes.	Kilogrammes.	Kilogrammes.
China	4,750,000	3,780,000	8,530,000
Japan	2,840,000	1,800,000	4,640,000
Indo-China	75,000	120,000	195,000
India	160,000	600,000	760,000
Central Asia	125,000	630,000	755,000
Turkey in Asia	620,000	550,000	1,170,000
Turkey in Europe	135,000	20,000	155,000
Balkan States	10,000	...	10,000
Greece	22,000	...	22,000
Austria and Hungary	415,000	385,000	80,000
Italy	5,200,000	1,670,000	6,870,000
France	2,430,000	1,900,000	4,330,000
Spain and Portugal	50,000	40,000	90,000
Switzerland	740,000	700,000	1,440,000
Germany	490,000	550,000	1,040,000
Belgium	20,000	...	20,000
Great Britain	105,000	435,000	540,000
Egypt	4,000	...	4,000
Total ...	18,191,000	13,180,000	31,371,000

Table X.

Consumption of mulberry raw-silk in different countries.

Country.	Home-made.	Foreign.	Total consumption.
1	2	3	4
	Kilos.	Kilos.	Kilos.
China	5,750,000	......	5,750,000
Japan	1,150,000	10,000	1,160,000
Indo-China	1,000,000	175,000	1,175,000
India	475,000	625,000	1,100,000
Central Asia	850,000	......	850,000
Russia in Europe	......	450,000	450,000
The Levant	115,000	400,000	515,000
Austria and Hungary	100,000	360,000	460,000
Italy	150,000	250,000	400,000
France	650,000	2,950,000	3,600,000
Spain and Portugal	40,000	120,000	160,000
Switzerland	......	140,000	1,400,000
Germany	......	1,900,000	1,900,000
Great Britain	......	900,000	900,000
United States and Canada ...	......	2,650,000	2,650,000
Mexico	......	10,000	10,000
Egypt, Tunis, Algeria, and Morocco ...	......	250,000	250,000
Total ...	10,280,000	12,450,000	22,730,000

Table Y.

Consumption of spun-silk in different countries.

Country.	Home-spun.	Foreign.	Total consumption.
1	2	3	4
	Kilos.	Kilos.	Kilos.
China	1,500,000	......	1,500,000
Japan	400,000	......	400,000
Indo-China	200,000	......	200,000
India	20,000	200,000	220,000
Central Asia	215,000	......	215,000
Russia in Europe	......	100,000	100,000
The Levant	20,000	......	20,000
Austria and Hungary	100,000	130,000	230,000
Italy	200,000	30,000	230,000
France	1,100,000	500,000	1,600,000
Spain and Portugal	......	40,000	40,000
Switzerland	125,000	......	125,000
Germany	250,000	950,000	1,200,000
Great Britain	550,000	......	550,000
United States and Canada ...	'190,000	10,000	200,000
Mexico	......	5,000	5,000
Egypt, Tunis, Algeria, and Morocco ...	......	90,000	90,000
Australia	......	50,000	50,000
Total ...	4,870,000	2,105,000	6,975,000

Table Z.

Total consumption of silk yarn in different countries.

Country.	Consumption.
1	2
	Kilos.
China	7,250,000
Japan	1,560,000
Indo-China	1,375,000
India	1,320,000
Central Asia	1,065,000
Russia in Europe	550,000
The Levant	535,000
Austria and Hungary	690,000
Italy	630,000
France	5,200,000
Spain and Portugal	200,000
Switzerland	1,525,000
Germany	3,100,000
Great Britain	1,450,000
United States and Canada	2,850,000
Mexico	15,000
Egypt, Tunis, Algeria, and Morocco ...	340,000
Australia	50,000
Total ...	29,705,000

PART IV.

SILK-WEAVING AND DYEING.

CHAPTER XIII.

BLEACHING.

159. The art of bleaching silk is a very ancient one, and it is mentioned in the Institutes of Manu (*c. f. Koushikábikayo-rushaih*=Silk and shawl are to be bleached with urine and water). The ancient method, though recognised by *dhobis*, is not practised by weavers in bleaching yarn. Whatever the yarn used for weaving, European filature-reeled silk or *khamru*, twisted or untwisted, or *matká* thread (which is always twisted thread), bleaching usually precedes weaving. In the case of *corahs*, however, bleaching follows weaving, the meaning of the word '*corah*' itself being 'unbleached.' The colour of the raw Bengal silk, both of European and native manufactures, is yellow, that is, like that of the cocoons out of which it is made. This, however, is not a permanent colour, and it has to be removed by bleaching it white before it is dyed. The silk of the annual *Barapalu* cocoons is usually white, but this also has to be subjected to the bleaching process before it can be dyed. In bleaching a seer of silk—(*a*) one pow ($\frac{1}{2}$ lb.) of *sají* (crude carbonate of soda) is powdered and mixed up with $2\frac{1}{2}$ seers of hot water, and the liquid strained through the same piece of cloth for a number of times, or (*b*) half-a-seer of ashes obtained by burning plantain leaves only is mixed up with $2\frac{1}{2}$ seers of hot water, and the liquid strained as before, or (*c*) half-a-pow of *sají* and one pow of the ashes are mixed with the water and then strained as before. A piece of cloth is spread over a basket, and the water to which the powdered *sají*, or ashes, or a mixture of the two, has been added is poured on to the cloth and gathered in a vessel underneath. This liquid is again poured into the basket and strained a second time. The straining is repeated until the liquid looks like oil. This liquid or lye is mixed with about half-a-maund of water and boiled. Into this boiling water the seer of silk is introduced, out of which it is taken when the bleaching is done and washed in a tank of clean water. After the silk is dry it will be found on weighing that it has lost about a quarter of its weight by the bleaching operation. If a piece of white (or undyed) silk weighs 21 tolas, it should be inferred that $21+7=28$ tolas of unbleached silk thread have been used in weaving it.

160. Weavers usually do their own bleaching and even their own dyeing, but *corahs* are bleached by *dhobis* or professional washermen, and there are professional bleachers in Murshidabad as there are professional dyers. Men are the chief operators, but they are sometimes assisted by women. There are probably not more than a hundred professional silk-bleachers in the district of Murshidabad. They earn about six or eight annas per diem; but as the washing of *corahs* is a fluctuating business, the professional bleachers cannot be said to be very well off. They live chiefly at Khagra, Saidabad, and Kunjaghata, where the principal dyeing establishments of Murshidabad are situated. The process of bleaching is done somewhat differently in Bankura and Bogra, and the following extracts on the subject will show how the work is done in those two districts. The Bankura monograph has the following lines on this subject:—

"The first process that the native-reeled silk undergoes in the hands of the weaver is winding all silks of different degrees of fineness on different *latais*. The second process is that of bleaching; for this silk is boiled for an hour in water mixed with the ashes of *sál* leaves. It is then washed and dried and again rolled on a *latai*. A sort of gum, prepared by boiling parched paddy in water, is then applied. The warp and woof are then prepared, the former consisting of two strands and the latter of four strands of thread. After the warp and the woof are prepared, they are separately dyed."

161. The Bogra monograph has the following lines on this subject:—

" *Bleaching.*—For this purpose the 8-shaped skein of twisted thread is taken away from the *khatia*.

"The skein is then tied at the two extremities by two strings passing through the two loops. These knots serve the purpose of keeping the turns of the thread from being entangled with each other.

"A solution is then prepared of soap water, water in which *ritha* fruits had been steeped and ashes of plantain leaves. No definite proportions are given for the ingredients of the solution, as they are all things that can be used singly for the purpose of ordinary washing.

"This solution is then boiled and the skein of threads steeped in it, held by the string in the extremities. The skein is stirred now and then with the strings. When the requisite amount of whiteness is acquired, the skein is taken off, thoroughly washed with pure water and then dried.

"The next process is that of arranging the washed thread called *paikara*.

"Two flat pieces of split bamboo are inserted through the two loops in the skein, and the strings are untied and taken off. Then the two bamboo pieces are gently pulled apart, so as to give a moderate tension to the thread. The turns of the thread are then arranged one by one on the bamboo pieces so as to allow reeling. The thread is then reeled off into *latais*.

"Then the thread is starched with rice gruel or a similar substance obtained by boiling *khai* (fried paddy) in water. When the thread is still wet, it is reeled once. When dry the reeling is repeated, which process removes the superfluous starch, as the thread is allowed to pass between the thumb and forefinger of the left hand. The thread is now ready for the next process of warping locally called *tåná-hátáná* or *taná-párná*."

CHAPTER XIV.

Dyeing and Printing.

162. Dyeing is done either in the thread or in the piece. In both cases bleaching (of the thread or of pieces of cloth), and in most cases mordanting, precedes dyeing. The following seventeen colours are recognised in Bengal:—(1) Indigo, (2) black, (3) blue, (4) grey or light blue, (5) red, (6) light red or *ánárdáná* (*i.e.*, pomegranate-seed colour), (7) yellow, (8) orange, (9) green, (10) purple, (11) *banesh* (*i.e.*, chocolate), (12) *pitambari*, (13) *sonali*, (14) *hiramankanthi*, (15) *mayurkanthi*, (16) *dhupchháyá*, and (17) *áshmáni*. Of these, black and blue colours are not recognised in Murshidabad, Maldah, and Rajshahi. The last five colours are in each case the effect of the combination of two colours—one employed for the warp and the other for the woof. *Pitambari* (*i.e.*, appropriate to Siva) colour, for instance, is produced by red warp and orange weft; *sonali* (golden) colour, by green warp and orange weft; *hiramankanthi* (parrot-necked) colour, by green warp and red weft; *mayurkanthi* (*i.e.*, peacock-neck) colour, by red warp and green weft; *dhupchháyá* (*i.e.*, light and shadow) colour, by red warp and blue weft, and *ashmani* (*i.e.*, sky) colour, by blue warp and red weft. Silks of such combined colours are known as shot-silks.

163. *Mordanting.*—As a rule, bleached silk needs mordanting before a dye can be permanently fixed into it. To mordant a seer of bleached silk, 10 tolas of alum is used. This quantity of alum is mixed up with about 10 seers of water and boiled. The silk is put into the alum water when it is still hot, and turned about in the solution for half-an-hour to get the fibre mordanted evenly. It is then wrung out and put in the dye in a moist state. This preparatory mordanting is not required for dyeing silk with lac, anatto, and indigo.

159. *Indigo and grey.*—Ten tolas (4 ounces) of indigo is used for having the indigo vat ready for one dip. Six such dips in six days would make the colour of the silk almost black, and one dip makes it grey. The number of dips depends on the kind of colour wanted. Silk which has been dipped in six vats is regarded in Murshidabad as black; while in Bankura and Bogra, the art of dyeing silk with a true black dye, seems to be known. To the indigo vat

is added some lime, some ashes obtained by burning indigo-refuse, and some powdered seed of chákandá (*Cassia tora*). When these are not used, the colour in the silk is not permanent. The quantities are regulated by the appearance of the liquor in the vat and not by the weights, handfuls, of these substances being thrown into the vat and the whole stirred. The froth or scum which rises on the top should be blue, but underneath the froth on the surface the liquor should look green. These appearances indicate that the indigo has properly dissolved. These substances (ashes, lime, and cassia tora seed) are not put in the indigo-vat when it is intended to get only a fugitive dye. In weaving figured fabrics silk weft dyed in fugitive indigo is used, when white ornamentation on white ground is ultimately desired. The blue colour helps the weaver to weave in the pattern neatly and properly, as he can see the work better if the figures are of a different colour from the ground. Such cloths get gradually bleached white by washing. To dye silk grey the bleached silk is put in the indigo-vat, wrung out, and dried. If the silk is to be dyed a deeper shade, the dry silk already dyed grey, as described, is again put in an indigo vat. The operation is repeated six times (60 tolas of indigo being thus used up) if the colour wanted is very deep, almost black. Of all the dye-stuffs used in Bengal, indigo is the most expensive, though in the silk districts, where indigo is generally produced, there is a great deal of illicit traffic in this dye, unknown or undetected by indigo factors from whose factories the article is robbed and sold cheap in shops. Weavers in Murshidabad pay only about 8 annas for every 10 tolas of indigo, or about Rs. 4 per seer, at which price they could not always get the article in the wholesale market. To dye silk grey, only 10 tolas of indigo are needed for each seer of silk, and it costs Re. 1 per seer inclusive of labour. If the silk is dyed black by six dips, the cost comes to Rs. 4 per seer.

165. *Black.*—The Bogra monograph gives the following recipe for producing black colour in silk:—

"The following things are kept steeped in water for two days, viz., *haritaki* (Terminalia chebula), *amlaki* (Imblica officinalis), *bahera* (Terminalia bellerica), and *bhela* (Anacardium indica). Then the thread to be dyed is kept steeped in this water with the other ingredients for, say, five days. After that the fruits are thrown away and the silk thread boiled with the solution. *Haritaki* and *amlaki* are two well known fruits. *Boira* or *bohera* is fruit sold by *baniyas* in the bazar. The fourth ingredient (*bhela*) is the thing used by washermen for marking cloths. No definite proportion was given for the ingredients to be used."

166. In Bankura black dye is obtained from "*haritaki*, iron filings, and ferrous sulphate in small proportion." In the Sonthal Parganas tusser yarn is dyed black by first bleaching it in lye, then putting it in a mixture of water to which powdered myrabolams and *bahera* have been added, boiling the yarn in this mixture, and finally burying it for a night in black tank earth. It is taken out in the morning and washed.

167. *Blue.*—Two or three dips in the indigo-vat are employed for producing 'blue' colour in Murshidabad. In Bankura "blue is made of indigo, *haritaki*, soap, and a few other ingredients."

168. *Red and light red.*—To get the exact shade of red on silk is considered by native weavers a very difficult art. The reason for this is two-fold—*first*, native weavers do not weigh their dye-stuffs, etc., nor keep exact time by the clock, nor measure the temperature of liquids with thermometers, but do everything by guess-work; *secondly*, lac and lodh (*Symplocos racemosa*) dust are both substances which are more or less adulterated, and it is impossible to get exact results simply by weighing, while a hydrometer is not in use. The weavers depend on experience to get the exact shade of red. The lac is first made into a coarse powder with a quern. It is then placed on some vessel, some water added to it, and it is rubbed with the palm of hand against the vessel. While this rubbing goes on, *saji* is dusted over it. For each seer of lac $1\frac{1}{4}$ to $1\frac{1}{2}$ *tola* of *saji* is used. Two to three times the quantity of raw silk to be dyed is the proportion of lac used. After the rubbing of the lac and the *saji* is over, the paste is transferred to a piece of cloth spread inside a basket. The basket is placed on three pieces of bamboo over a trough (*gamla*). Water is then poured over the paste in the basket, and the solution of the dye gathered in the trough below. About 30 seers of water is used, when a seer of silk has to be dyed, for

getting all the colour of the paste into the trough. The boiling of the liquid so obtained, goes on for about three hours. When the boiling is going on lodh dust is sprinkled over the liquid. The quantity of lodh used is the same as the quantity of *saji* that has been already used for making the paste. To ascertain when the 'bowl' of liquid is exactly ready, the following test is used:—A drop of the boiling liquid is dropped into a vessel of plain water. If it sinks to the bottom of the vessel in the form of a ring, the 'bowl' is ready. If it does not sink in this neat manner, but disperses in the water, it should be inferred that it requires more *saji* to make it right. A solution of *saji* has then to be added until the boiling liquid satisfies the test. If the drop of the liquid appears too dark (blackish), a little more lodh dust is dusted to make the 'bowl' right. When the 'bowl' is ready, the *gamla* is taken down from the fire and kept covered up for a day. Next day it is again put on the fire, and as soon as boiling takes place, bleached (but not mordanted) silk is put in the liquid and stirred. When this stirring of the silk in the boiling liquid is going on, tamarind water is added to it. The tamarind used for this purpose should not be quite fresh from the tree nor very old. It should be a few months old. For a seer of silk a seer of tamarind in seed is used. When the proper shade of colour has been obtained, a chitak of alum is put in the liquid, the silk stirred for a moment longer, taken out, wrung, and dried. If alum is not used, the dyed silk requires to be 'lodhed' before the dye is permanently fixed. To 'lodh' a seer of the dyed silk half a powa ($\frac{1}{4}$lb.) of turmeric is made into a paste and mixed up with half a powa of lodh dust, and the mixture boiled in about 15 seers of water. The dyed silk is put in this liquor and taken out, when the dyeing will be quite finished. If there is too much water in the 'bowl', the colour obtained is pink. To get a seer of bleached silk dyed red at a dyeing establishment costs Rs. 2-8.

169. In Bogra "the silk to be coloured red is first mordanted in a boiling solution of alum. The lac is powdered and kept steeped in water for one day. Then the powder, as far as possible, is thrown away and the solution boiled. Then the silk is steeped in the solution." The black and red dyes obtained in Bogra are not quite fast, and Bogra weavers sometimes obtain coloured silk thread from the Calcutta market.

170. The Bankura monograph says:—"Red is made of lac dye. The lac is finely powdered. It is then boiled with tamarind, alum, and *khar*" (*i.e.*, crude sodium carbonate).

171. In Burdwan "resin from the banyan and ashad (*peepul*) trees is used" for obtaining red dye in silk. "The resin is rubbed with water in an earthen vessel, and then the thread with alum and the bark of the *lodh* plant is put in." By resin of the banyan and peepul trees, is no doubt meant, lac.

172. *Yellow.*—Four seers of sawdust of jack wood (*Artocarpus integrifolia*) and one seer of *bakash* (*Adhatoda vasica*) leaves are boiled together in half a maund of water. The liquor is strained off and a seer of bleached and mordanted silk put in it, stirred well, taken out, wrung, and dried. This process is repeated three times more, when the yellow colour will be permanently fixed in the silk. The four seers of sawdust cost two annas. To make the liquor four times and get the silk dyed yellow, costs, therefore, about one rupee per seer.

173. In Burdwan "bazar turmeric is used for obtaining a yellow dye."

Orange.—The following account of this dye is taken bodily from the "Hand-book of Sericulture":—

"Of all the dye-stuffs used in Bengal for dyeing silk, *kamela* dust is considered the best. This substance is found as a granular deposit on the fruits of a small tree called Abir or Patsindure (*Mallotus philippinensis*). This tree is found in most Indian forests. The dust can be gathered in abundance in the forests of Dehra-Dun, Manbhum, Singhbhum, Jalpaiguri, and of Central India. In Murshidabad, however, it is difficult to procure this article for dyeing silk, and its use is therefore extremely limited. Weavers cannot get unadulterated *kamela* dust even by paying 25 or 26 rupees for a maund. Brickdust and sand are the substances used for adulterating *kamela* dust. If the weavers are to secure pure *kamela* dust, they should propagate the trees at Mirzapur, Baluchar, Khagra, Islampur-chak, and Bashwa-Bishnupur, which are the principal centres of silk-weaving in Murshidabad. The trees being small, they fruit within four or five years after they are planted. The fruits or capsules ripen in February to April. When they ripen they burst, and that is the proper time for collecting them. The fruits are like bar (*Ficus indica*) fruits. The *kamela* dust is analogous to the dust that is seen on *bar* fruits. When the fruits are not sufficiently ripe, the *kamela* dust is greenish in colour. In this state the proportion of dyeing material obtained from the dust is smaller. If the fruits, on the other hand, are allowed to get too ripe, the dust gets detached from the fruits and carried away with wind. It is important therefore to gather the fruits at the right time. When they are gathered at the proper time the dust contains over 75 per cent. of dyeing material. In gathering the dust Sonthals place the fruits on a string *charpoy* (bedstead) and spread a cloth underneath. The fruits are rubbed against the strings of the *charpoy*, and the dust comes showering down on the cloth. Anatto trees are commonly grown by weavers close to their houses. The *kamela* dust gives a permanent colour, while the colour obtained from anatto is not altogether so. That it is very important to propagate the pat-sindure tree in Murshidabad is therefore self-evident. The propagation of trees is not such hard work as the cultivation of agricultural crops, and one or two high-caste men can easily earn their livelihood by propagating trees yielding dye-stuffs in Murshidabad. There is no better or faster dye than what is obtained from *kamela* dust, and its introduction into the European market is also within the range of probability.

"*The preparation of the dye.*—Orange colouring matter is obtained not only from *kamela* dust, but also from the dust of *bar* fruits, but the latter yields a much poorer dye. In the Sonthal Parganas, Manbhum, and the neighbouring districts, an orange (almost red) dye is obtained from the roots and barks at the base of the trunk of the tree called *Cheli* (*Cæsaria tomentosa*). The *kamela* dust is sometimes used mixed up with *bar* dust or *cheli* wood. The mixture yields a deeper orange. *Anatto* and *bakam* (*Caesalpina sappan*) wood are also sometimes used mixed up with *kamela* dust. Those mixtures also yield a deeper orange Used by itself, the boiled liquor imparts a straw colour to silk. In Murshidabad the *kamela* dye is prepared in this way—One powa (=½ lb.) to one powa and-a-half of *saji* and a similar quantity of *lodh* dust are boiled together with about ten seers of water. The liquor is strained out and again boiled. One powa of *kamela* dust, mixed up with half a tola of *colza* oil, is put in the boiling liquor, half the quantity being put in first and the remaining quantity afterwards. A seer of bleached and mordanted silk is then introduced into the boiling liquor and well stirred until the dyeing is finished. The use of *bakam* wood in conjunction with *kamela* dust to get a deeper colour is also in vogue in Murshidabad.

"Cost of dyeing silk orange with *kamela* dust—

	Rs.	A.	P.
(1) Mordanting a seer of bleached silk with alum ...	0	2	0
(2) Price of one powa of *kamela* dust	0	4	0
(3) Do. half-a-powa of *bakam* wood dust	0	0	6
(4) Fuel for making the liquor	0	1	6
(5) One powa of *saji*	0	0	6
(6) Ditto *lodh*	0	0	6
(7) Labour	0	2	0
Total cost of dyeing a seer of silk orange with *kamela* dust	0	11	0

"*Anatto orange.*—One-half powa of *anatto* seed (price three annas) is boiled with 15 seers of water. Half a powa of *saji* is powdered and got previously ready mixed up with water and strained. When the *anatto* liquor is boiling, this *saji* water is poured into it, and the boiling continued for a few minutes more. Another way of preparing the liquor is to put the *saji* water in the plain water, tie the *anatto* seed in a piece of cloth, suspend it in the water, and get the boiling done afterwards. This saves the straining of the liquor before it is boiled again. In either case the raw silk (that is, silk which has not been bleached or mordanted) is put in the boiling liquor, got evenly dyed by stirring, washed in clean water afterwards, and got dried. To dye a seer of silk orange with *anatto*, costs less than eight annas. The *anatto* orange is not so fast as the *kamela* orange, that is, it fades gradually in time and by washing. The colour obtained by the use of *anatto* is brighter, and *anatto* is also cheaper and more readily available than *kamela* dust. The use of *anatto* is, therefore, much more common in Murshidabad and other districts than that of *kamela*.

174. The Bankura monograph has this short notice on *jarad* or orange colour in silk:—"*Jarad* is made of *kamela* powder, *khar* (crude sodium carbonate), and alum."

175. The following accounts of green, purple, and *banesh* dyes are taken from the "Handbook of Sericulture":—

"*Green.*—Neither in Murshidabad nor in any other part of Bengal is the art of producing a fast green dye commonly known to weavers. The shawl-makers of Kashmir can produce a fast green dye. How they do it, and if the dye is applicable to silk, are not known. Silk is dyed green in Murshidabad in the following way:—One seer of *bakash*

(*Adhatoda vasica*) leaf and five seers of jack-wood saw-dust are boiled together in water, strained, and a seer of bleached and mordanted silk dyed yellow by stirring in the manner already described. The silk is then put in a 'spent' indigo vat, when it becomes green. By 'spent indigo vat' is meant a vat which has been already used for dyeing silk blue, and in which there is very little blue-colouring matter left. If 10 tolas of indigo are bought for 8 annas, it may be assumed that 2 annas' worth of indigo still remains in the vat after it has been used for dyeing silk blue.

"Cost of dyeing silk green—

	Rs.	A.	P.
For bleaching	0	3	0
" mordanting	0	2	0
(*Bakash* leaf costs nothing, as it is found in abundance everywhere.)			
Five seers of jack-wood saw-dust	0	2	6
Fuel for making the liquor	0	1	6
Indigo left in the 'spent vat'	0	2	0
Labour	0	6	0
Total cost of dyeing a seer of silk green ...	1	1	0

"*Fast green.*—Have one seer of bleached silk mordanted with half a seer of powdered alum mixed with eight seers of water, and kept over night soaked in this mixture. In the morning the silk is to be wrung nearly dry and shaken up. The same evening that the silk is soaked in alum water a seer of dry *sephálíká* (*Nyctanthes arbortristis*) flower-buds is to be kept soaked in 10 or 12 seers of water,—also over night. The water with the flower-buds is to be boiled in the morning, and the liquor afterwards strained out into another vessel by means of a cloth. Into this hot *sephalika* liquor is to be plunged the mordanted silk while it is still moist, and kept stirred so that all parts of the silk may be evenly dyed. When the liquor gets somewhat cold, the silk is to be wrung out and shaken up. The remains of the flower-buds on the cloth are then to be put into the liquor and boiled again for about half an hour, and the liquor strained out once more as before with the help of the cloth. The silk is to be put again into this liquor and kept inside it for an hour, occasionally stirred as before. For facility of stirring, the skeins are tied with a tape and plunged in the liquor. After an hour's soaking in the liquor, the silk is be taken out and wrung nearly dry and shaken up.

"Next day have 12 seers of cold water in a *gamla* and mix with it two tolas of aniline green, which is sold in the bazar as European green. Have the silk while still moist plunged into this green water and stirred in it until the desired shade of green is obtained. This green will be found to be permanent.

"*Purple.*—Bleached and mordanted silk is first dyed red in the lac liquor, and then put in the indigo vat. A small quantity of lac is used that the silk may be dyed light red. The cost of dyeing silk light red is Re. 1-8 for a seer. The subsequent dyeing in the indigo vat costs another rupee. The total cost of dyeing silk purple is therefore Rs. 2-8 per seer.

"*Chocolate* (*banesh*).—*Banesh* is black with a shade of red. To obtain this colour the silk is first dyed deep red in the lac liquor, and it is then dipped once in the indigo vat. It costs Rs. 2-8 to get a seer of bleached silk dyed deep red. The subsequent blueing costs 12 annas; that is, the total cost of dyeing silk *banesh* is Rs. 3-4 per seer.

176. *Weight of dyed silk.*—It has been said, a seer of raw-silk is reduced in weight to 12 chitaks after it has been bleached. These 12 chitaks of bleached silk weigh about 12½ chitaks after it has been dyed. When silk is dyed green 12 chitaks enhance to 12½ chitaks in all other seasons except during the rainy season, when the enhancement in weight is half a chitak more. Silk is naturally highly hygroscopic in character. This hygroscopicity increases when it is dyed green. Twelve chitaks of bleached silk weigh 13½ to 14 chitaks after it has been dyed deep blue.

177. *Secrecy.*—Most of the monographs speak of the reticence on the part of the weavers in giving information about silk-dyeing. They also speak of the use of European chemical dyes being very common. In Birbhum "colour is not generally used in dyeing *saris.*" This is all the information on this subject obtained from this district. In Rajshahi "there is no silk-dyer."

178. *European dyes.*—The use of aniline dyes, which is so very much easier than that of country dyes, is bound to extend. All aniline dyes are not equally fugitive. They are all more or less fugitive when they are exposed to sunlight for any length of time; and the encouragement of the native dyes which are

permanent is very necessary. But if aniline dyes must be used, those that can stand alkaline washing should be alone used. The Rampur Boalia Sericultural School has instituted some experiments in this direction, and so far the Maypole Soap (obtainable of Messrs. Whiteaway, Laidlaw and Company) seems to have given very showy results. A short account of the experiments conducted in this school may be of interest, as the shades of colour obtained were very beautiful.

179. The soap washes and dyes the silk at one operation. Soaps of the following colours are made:—pink, cream, mauve, heliotrope, light blue, canary, fawn, orange, cardinal, aloe pink, salmon pink, scarlet, cerise, terra-cotta, nut-brown, crimson, maroon, navy blue, and black. A cake of soap is dissolved in half a gallon of boiling water in an enamel-lined vessel. The soap dissolves in the boiling water in about a minute. When all the soap has dissolved the thread or fabric is put in the bath and kept stirred, in a simmering, but not in a boiling state, for a quarter of an hour, when the vessel is taken down altogether from the fire and left to cool. When thoroughly cold the yarn or the fabric is rinsed in cold water, a little starch being used if the fabric is needed to be stiff. In that case after wringing and drying, the fabric is ironed. If the colour obtained is not sufficiently deep, a second operation may be necessary.

180. In Hooghly aniline dyes are in common use for dyeing silk. The following lines occur in the report from that district on this subject:—

"The colours used are—Red, green, orange, and violet. The dyes are not fast. For red, magenta is used. Aniline dyes are used for green. Orange or yellow is made of *latkan* seeds and *kamala* dust (see Mr. N. G. Mukerji's "Hand-Book of Sericulture," section 222), and sometimes from aniline dyes. Aniline dyes are also used for producing violet."

181. *Printing.*—Dyeing and printing pieces of *corah* is a decaying industry for Murshidabad. Whether country dyes or European aniline dyes (magenta, etc.) are used, the dyeing liquor—of a thicker consistency than that used for dyeing yarn—is mixed up with a quantity of cotton wool when printing has to be done. Wooden blocks with religious texts or conventional designs carved on them are used for taking up the dyeing material from the cotton-wool pad, and the piece of silk being spread out properly on a wooden platform, the imprinting of the design is done on the piece. Where mordanting is necessary the piece is mordanted beforehand with alum.

182. *Bandanna dyeing.*—There is a special process of dyeing pieces of *corah*, called *Bandanna* dyeing or *Bánhu* dyeing. To make a piece of *bánhu* knots are put on a piece of silk at regular intervals with cotton threads. Thousands of knots are sometimes put on a piece before it is plunged in alum and in the dyeing vat. It is then washed in clean water, and the knots are taken out, when it is seen the knotted spots remain white, while the ground becomes dyed. The knots being put at regular intervals, the presence of the spots does not look bad, but the slight effect is produced with such enormous labour that it is hardly worth producing. *Bánhus*, in fact, are made only out of cheap *corahs* and *mátkas*. The spots are sometimes made coloured by plunging a white spotted *bánhu* in a coloured vat, when the spots take one colour, while the ground becomes altered in colour. Another process of dyeing silks in the piece is called "momin" or waxing. A *momin* piece is produced with drops of melted wax being arranged in regular figures in those spots which are meant to remain without colour. After this the piece is plunged in the dyeing vat, and the wax afterwards removed. If the white spots are required to be coloured, the piece is afterwards put in another vat, when the spots take the colour of this vat, while the ground becomes altered in colour by the mixture of two colours. Thus, if the waxed piece is put in the yellow dyeing vat, and after removing the wax, if it is put in the indigo vat, the spots originally waxed take blue, while the ground is coloured green. Pieces of silk are sometimes dyed with the help of stiff clay exactly in the same way as they are dyed with the help of wax, little pellets and strings of clay being used for drawing the figures on the piece before it is mordanted and dyed. The practice also prevails of protecting portions of a piece by tying them with straps of leather or of strong cloth, plunging the piece in a dye vat, then protecting the dye portions, and dyeing those protected in the former operation in a different colour. In making *bánhus*, knots are sometimes put with freshly coloured pieces of cotton thread,

when, after the piece is dyed and the knots taken out, little rings are formed all over the piece of the colour of the cotton thread used for knotting.

183. *Dyers.*—Dyeing is usually done by the weavers themselves, but where, as in Murshidabad, silk-weaving is done on an extensive scale, there is more division of labour; and as there are special twisters of yarn, so are there special dyers' establishments. These are miniature factories, employing eight or ten men each, in brick-built houses, containing a number of vats embedded in the floor, and also a number of brass and copper pans. There are probably between twenty and thirty such factories in the district of Murshidabad. The men who work in them are chiefly *Tantis* and *Kaibartas.* They are moderately prosperous, their wages amounting to about four annas a day. Baluchar, Khagra, Mirzapur, and Islampur may be regarded as the chief centres of the industry. Radha Krishna Khan and Mohesh Chundra Mandal of Khagra, with Bhagbat Bhushan Dara of Kunjaghata are the principal dyers of the district.

184. A diagram sheet at the end of this Monograph (No. 98 to 115) illustrates the silk-dyeing industry of Murshidabad.

CHAPTER XV.

Processes preparatory to weaving.

185. The process of unwinding skeins of raw silk and gathering them into *latais* of shorter skeins of thread of even thickness and without break has been already described. The raw silk thus gathered into *latais* is sometimes employed for warping without any further processes being gone through, as in weaving *corahs.* The process of twisting has been also described. The twisted thread gathered into *latais* is employed for warping in the case of *pakwan* or superior fabrics. The processes of bleaching and dyeing have been also described. Bleached and unbleached thread, dyed and undyed thread, twisted and untwisted thread, are employed in producing different classes of fabrics. The warp may be bleached and dyed, or the thread used in the warp may have been bleached and dyed before warping takes place.

186. *Warping.*—The next process to be described therefore is warping. Four posts (A, B, C, and D) are planted in the ground as shown in the figure (Fig. 10). They are so planted that the width B to C may allow a man to move

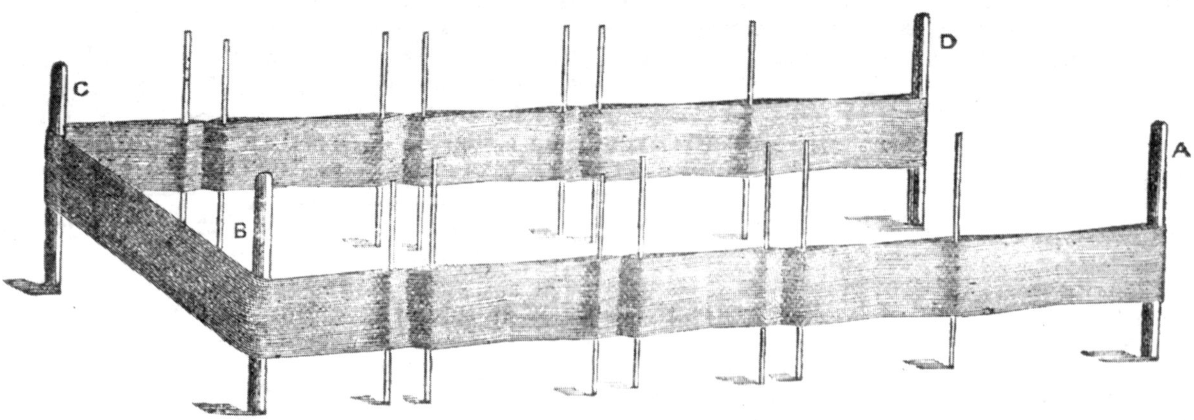

Fig. 10.—Warping.

about freely in the space enclosed within the four posts. The distances A B and C D are so measured out that the total of A B, B C, and C D may be equal to the required length of the pieces to be woven at one setting of the loom. If, for instance, the loom is set for weaving five 10-yard gown-pieces, the warp has to be made 50 yards long, and the four posts are set at a distance of 24 yards lengthwise and two yards breadthwise. *Kathis* or bamboo *laths*, 3½ feet long and ½ inch in width, are then planted, singly or in pairs, about 8 feet apart from post to post, except from A to D. The yarn (twisted or raw silk) is then taken in two *charkies* of more compact and of stronger make than the *charkies* used for unwinding skeins of raw silk. One of these is represented in the figure (Fig. 11). Each *charki* is provided with a handle called *hulki* (*a*), ending in a

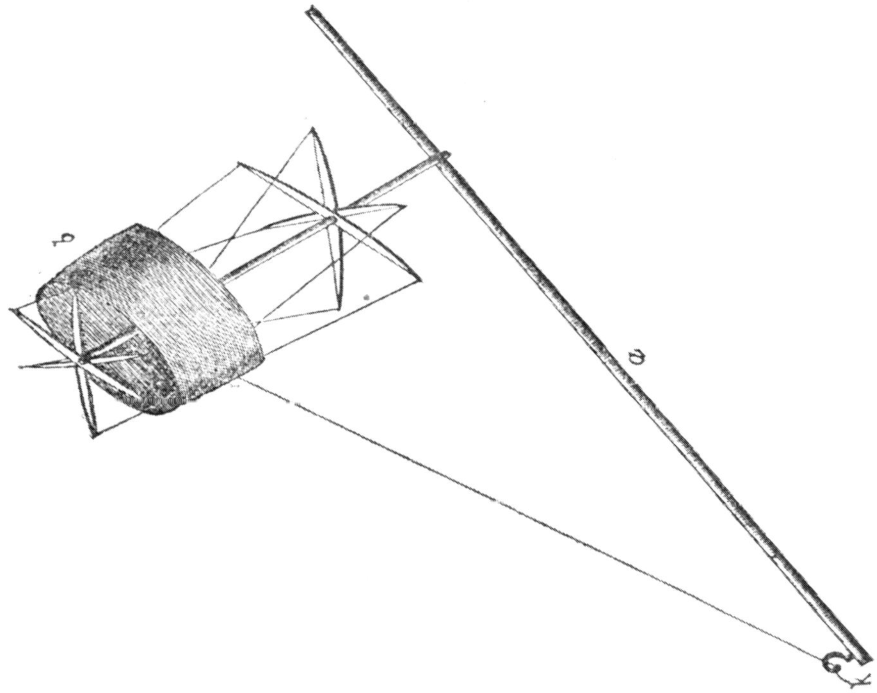

Fig. 11.—Charki and Hulki used for warping.

glass or metallic loop or ring. The threads pass out from the two *charkies* through the two loops, and are laid on alternate sides of the *kathis* and posts. Both *charkies* are used simultaneously by the same person who holds one in each hand. The threads of both *charkies* are first knotted together, and the operator begins by putting the united thread round the post at A. He then walks on in the direction of B, laying the threads of the two *charkies* alternately on both sides of the *kathis* and posts. How the two threads (A and B) are alternately laid from the two *charkies*, from A to B and B to C and C to D, is diagramatically represented in section in the following figure (fig. 12.)—

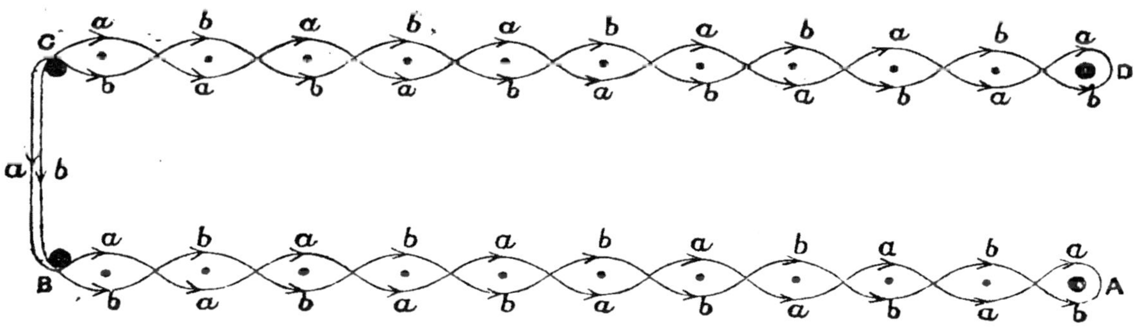

Fig. 12.—Diagramatic representation of warping.

As the operator moves on with the *charkies*, the threads are drawn out without any effort. As he approaches each post or *kathi* he passes one thread by the right of it and the other by the left, in such a manner that the two threads may intersect between two *kathis* or a post and a *kathi*. The operator proceeds in this manner up to D, no intersections being made at or between B and C, the thread simply passing round them. The same process is repeated when the operator comes back from D to A, laying two more threads above the first two. This goes on till the requisite number of '*shana*' is obtained, whether 1,200, 1,800, 2,000, or 2,400 double (and sometimes quadruple or eight-fold) threads in the yard of width. If the cloth is to be one yard in width and of first quality, 2,400 double threads are laid one above another before the warp is ready. The set of intersections between a pair of *kathis* is called *jalá*. The *kathis* are removed when the warping is completed and tapes inserted in their places. These keep the two sets of thread from the two *charkses* quite separate during the processes of bleachng and dyeing if the warp is bleached and dyed before it is introduced into the loom. If no bleaching or dyeing is done at this stage, but the warp removed to where the loom is, slender bamboo rods (called *joás* or *joá-kathis*) are introduced at once instead of tapes, where the posts and the *kathis* are. The *joá-kathis* are also introduced into the warp after the warp has been bleached or dyed, the tapes being removed and bamboo *laths* inserted in their places.

187. The warp with *joás* inserted in them is rolled up and brought to where the loom is. One extremity of the warp is then attached to the yarn-beam or off-beam (*bb*) of the loom by a series of knots, and the whole warp with the *joás* is wound round this beam (fig. 13)—

Figure 13.—Improved loom used in the Rajshahi Sericultural School, showing the yarn-beam.

188. Then begins the next operation, which is called *shana-parana, i.e.*, passing the warp through the reed. This is a work of great patience, and this is the reason for weavers objecting to weave one or two pieces only. When they are sure of being able to dispose of eight or ten pieces of any fabric, they go in for setting the loom, though the weaving of the eight or ten pieces may take them two or three months. This accounts for silk-weavers needing to spend a good deal of money in advance. If ten gown-pieces have to be woven, silk for the warp for all the ten pieces must be bought at once, and it means an outlay of over Rs. 100. When a weaver gets an order to weave one or two pieces of some fabric and receives half the price in advance, say Rs. 20, he is still unable to begin work. He looks out for possible buyers of other six or eight pieces, and he needs an advance of another Rs. 80 or Rs. 100 before he can begin his work. This is how silk-weavers get entangled with *mahajans*. The *mahajan* assures the weaver he will buy the remaining pieces at cost price, and he advances the requisite amount of money at a high rate of interest. The weaver may succeed in selling the remaining pieces at a profit to outsiders; but if he fails, he sells them to his *mahajan* at cost price, and out of the profits of sale of the one or two pieces for which he had received order, he has to pay the *mahajan* interest on the loan.

189. The process of inserting the threads of the warp through the reed and attaching them to the cloth-beam or near beam, is thus described in the Bogra monograph:—

"A *jalá* or crossing is brought near the extreme rod. Then the operator introduces a needle through an interval in the reed, and the second operator, sitting on the other side of the reed where the whole yarn is, encloses the needle by two or more threads (ordinarily three) by a temporary loop. Then the first operator pulls this loop out into the other side of the reed by means of the needle. The number of threads to be introduced through each interval depends upon the width of the cloth to be woven, the total number of threads in the warp, and the number of interstices in the reed employed. But this number cannot be less than two. Having introduced, say, the first three threads through the first interval in the portion of the reed selected, they are drawn out a little. Then the next three threads are introduced in the same manner through the second interval, and so on.

"This proceeds on to some distance in the reed, say one inch. Then a slender bamboo rod (*c*) is placed above the threads in the first half inch and below the threads in the second half. The ends of these two sets of threads are brought together and knotted in a single knot; so as to leave the rod between the knot and the reed.

"Then another inch of the reed is worked in the same manner, and the threads knotted beyond the rod (*c*) as before. Thus when the end of the warp is reached, the newly-introduced rod (*c*) is held in position and cannot get off in a direction parallel to the warp threads (see fig. 14).

"The warp is now ready for the process of forming healds."

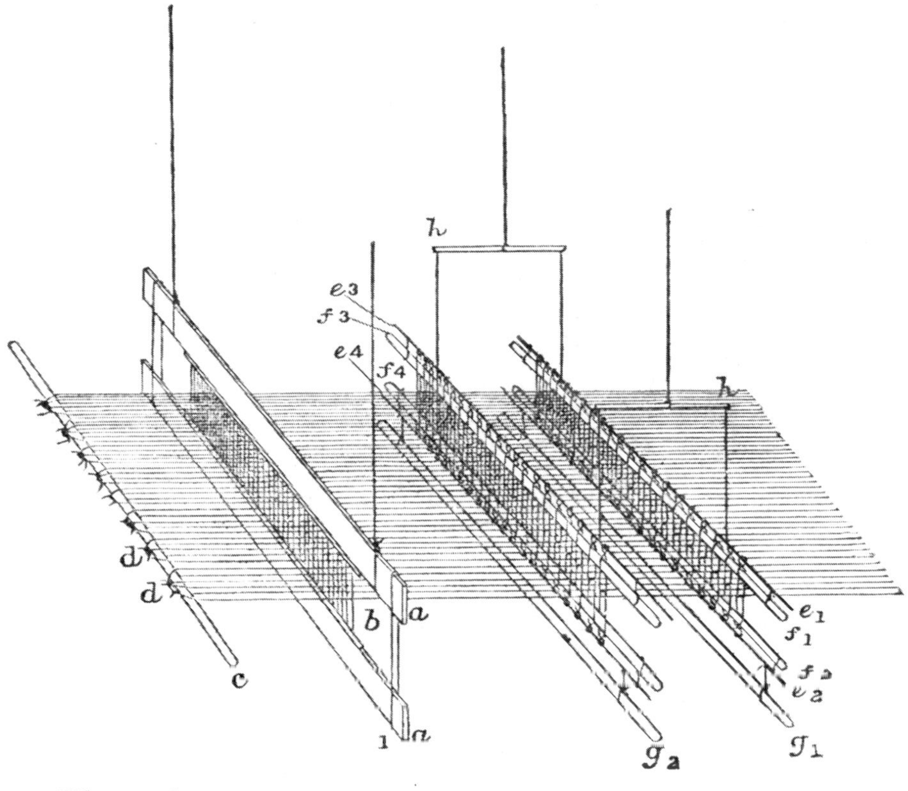

Fig. 14.—Arrangement of reed and healds.

Explanation of the figure.

a, a—*Dapti* or frame enclosing the reed.
b *Shánά* or reed.
c Yarn-beam.
d d Knots on the sets of warp threads.
e_1, e_2, e_3, e_4—Slender rods over the shafts of the healds called *moori*.
f_1, f_2, f_3, f_4—Shafts of the healds called *baw*.
g_1, g_2—Bamboo rods tied with the shafts of the healds and connected with the treadles.*
h, h—Two *náchants*, or heald suspenders.

190. *Forming of healds.*—The next operation, viz., forming of healds (or *bawparána*), is also fully described in the Bogra monograph, and this monograph may be again quoted here:—

"For forming each set of healds four round rods are required, viz., two of the thickness of the little finger and two others much less thick, and all of them a little longer than the width of the warp.

* (The treadles are not shown in this figure).

"The thicker rods are called *baws* and the thinner ones *mooris*.

"One of the *jalás* or intersections being brought to a convenient position, the two rods (or *joas* corresponding to this are removed, after putting in their places two pieces of thin split bamboo, about 2 inches wide.

"Then one of the thinner rods, intended for the healds, is placed over the warp, and an instrument called *fandi* is placed close to it, also above the warp. This *fandi* consists of a rectangular piece of thin split bamboo about 1⅜th inch in width, with one of the ends rounded off, which contains a hole. A thick cotton thread is passed through the hole and tied with the *fandi*. The thread is tied at the other extremity with the apex of a small, hollow, metallic cone.

"A thick silk thread from a *charki* is then introduced between the upper and lower sets of threads in the warp, and drawn out to the other side, where the *fandi* has been placed

"The extremity of this thick thread is tied by a slip-knot with the slender rod mentioned above.

"The operator then picks up a loop from this thread by his forefinger between the first and the second thread in the upper set. This loop then passes round the *fandi*, and is knotted on to the slender rod cose to the *fandi*, by turning the end of the loop twice, so as to form a second loop through which the slender rod (called *moori*) is made to pass.

"When the next loop is picked up between the second and the third warp thread, any slackness in the first loop and the corresponding knot round the *moori* is removed. The same process is repeated with the second loop, and so on to the end. The *fandi* is meant for regulating the length of each loop which is formed round it. The *fandi* is moved onward as the work proceeds, and in the end the string tied to the *fandi* will be found to have passed through all the loops.

"Then one of the thicker rods (*baws*) which have all conical ends, fitting exactly into the hollow cone. is taken up and one end of it is pressed into that hollow cone. The string of the *fanai* being pulled at the other end draws the cone and with it the *baw* shaft, so that in the end the shaft occupies the position of the string, having passed through all the loops.

"The *moori* is thin tied with this *baw* shaft at several places (see fig. 14). After this the whole thing is turned upside down, and the *jalá* or intersection moved beyond the set of loops formed. Thus the set of threads that have been dealt with before are again on the surface Then another *moori* is taken up and loops formed with the *fandi* in the same manner as before, with this exception that the new loops formed enclose each thread as well as the one string of the loop that is already round it. Then the *baw* shaft is introduced as before and tied with the new *moori*.

"This completes half the process of forming the healds. The remaining set of threads is dealt with in a simlar manner to complete the process.

"Fig. 14 shows the sets of healds when completed: e^1, e^2 are the *mooris*, and f^1 and f^2 the corresponding *baw* shafts.

"Now the wholething is ready for fitting up in the loom."

191. The description of *setting the loom* is also fully given in the Bogra monograph. Though the Bogra loom is ruder in construction than the Murshidabad looms, a full description of it is a good introduction to the explanation of more complicated forms. The Bogra loom consists of the following parts (Fig. 15.): —

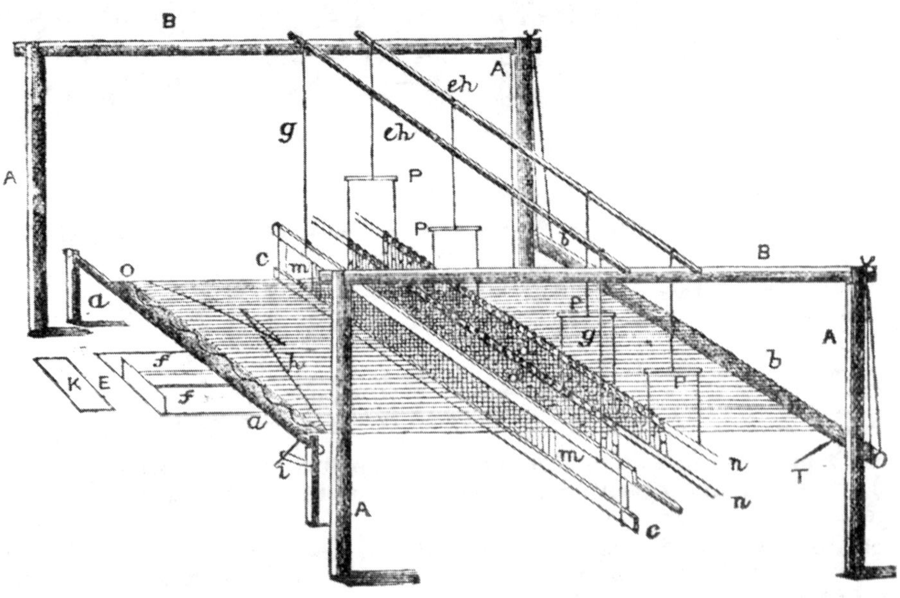

Fig. 15.—The Bogra silk-loom.

"Four stout posts of wood (A) or bamboo are planted in the ground, forming a rectangle.

"Two parallel bars called *sabdhars* (B) are attached to the tops of these posts, each joining a front and a back post.

"There is a pit (E) dug in front of the place where the operator is to sit (K). On either side of this pit, and near the two front posts, are planted two short posts which support the cloth beam, locally called *kola-narod* (*a*), and allow it to turn.

"The yarn-beam, also called *narod* (*b*), is suspended from the tops of the two back posts by strings passing round it which allow it to turn.

"The cloth beam is provided with a cross peg called *moran* (*i*), at the right hand end. The end of this peg is tied, from time to time, by a string with the post that is near, so as to keep the cloth beam in position.

"The yarn-beam has two similar holes at right angles to one another, also in the right-hand end.

"A rod called *khil* (T) fits in one of these holes, and rests with the other extremity on the ground.

"The yarn-beam can be prevented from turning by means of this rod, and can be kept in any position by varying its length.

"The warp had been wound round the yarn-beam after taking it out. The beam, with the warp, is now brought in, and the former is placed in its position.

"Then the reed or *sana* (*m*) is fitted on to the *dapti* (*c*).

"The *dapti* consists of two stout pieces of palm-wood nearly equal to the beams in length, about 4 inches wide and little less than an inch in thickness.

"The edges of these bars are nearly rounded off.

"One of these bars is placed below the reed parallel to the cloth beam with the narrow face uppermost.

"The other bar of palm-wood is then placed in a similar position above the *sana*. The *sana* now fits in into two grooves in the bars, one below the upper one and the other above the lower one. The two bars are then joined by means of iron rods passing through holes in their extremities. The bars are then tied with one another at either end. The whole thing is now termed *dapti*.

"This *dapti* is suspended by two strings from a moveable cross rod, which is supported on the two *sabdhars*, and is called *chalna* (*ch*).

"The warp is kept at a tension by tying the extreme rod in it with the cloth beam, by means of a string or strings in such a manner that the rod is at some distance from the beam.

"The shafts of the healds are then suspended from a rod (also called *chalna*) supported on the two *sabdhars* in the following way—

"Two or more *nachnis* (P) are hung down from the rod so as to rest about a foot higher than the upper shafts of the healds. A *nachni* consists simply of a piece of bamboo rod of the thickness of a pencil, suspended from above by a string tied to its centre, and provided with two other strings, tied with its extremities, which hang down. One of these two strings is tied with the front shaft of healds and the other string is tied with the back shaft while the *nachni* is suspended from another *chalna* resting on the *sabdhars*.

"Thus when one shaft of healds is pulled down, the *nachni*, acting as a lever, pulls up the shaft of the other set of healds.

"Below the lower shaft (*baw*) and *moori* of each set of healds is tied a bamboo pole (see fig. 14, *g* , *g*). These two poles are tied by strings with the two treadles, locally called *ghoras* (*f*), (one with the right *ghora* and the other with the left one).

"In an arrangement for weaving plain cloths with plain borders, only two treadles are necessary.

"The treadles are put in the pit in front of the operator. The operator sits on a wooden plank (K) and lowers his feet into the pit, this arrangement dispensing with the use of a chair and diminishing the height of the apparatus considerably. The whole thing is now ready for the process of weaving.

"When ornamental borders are to be woven with the cloth, a few more sets of healds are formed at the two borders suspended by similar *nachnis*, and an additional number of treadles corresponding with these are fitted up, the operator working them all by the feet. Only one artist knows the preparation of ornamented borders in this district. The process is complicated and difficult to learn.

"In weaving *terchhi* (twill) sheets, four sets of healds are made instead of two. There are, therefore, four treadles. In such cloths the successive crossings of the threads of the warp and of the weft form rather prominent lines at an angle with the length of the cloth.

"These cloths are very rarely woven. They are never woven except on order. Only two weavers in the district know how to weave *terchhi* sheets."

192. *Charging of Spools*.—Having got the warp placed in the loom, the weft is got ready for introduction into shuttles. This is done by untwisted threads (but dyed or undyed, raw or bleached, as the case may be) from two *latáis* being gathered into spools, which are small pieces of bamboo tubes of a size just fitting into shuttles. Spool after spool is taken and attached to the narrow end of the axle (fig. 16, A), of a spinning wheel. As the handle H is turned the axle A rotates very rapidly as also the spool connected with it. The threads (*f* and *f*) from the two *latáis* or *charkies*, placed on the pivots c and c_1 [one

charki only (C) being shown in the figure, as planted on the pivot c_1] come out freely and get wound round the spool as a single thread F. When a sufficient number of spools have been charged (with threads of different colours if necessary), the operator is ready to begin weaving. He takes up a shuttle (fig. 17) which is made of steel, and puts a spool inside it in the manner shown in the figure, and the weaving proceeds as shown in fig. 13.

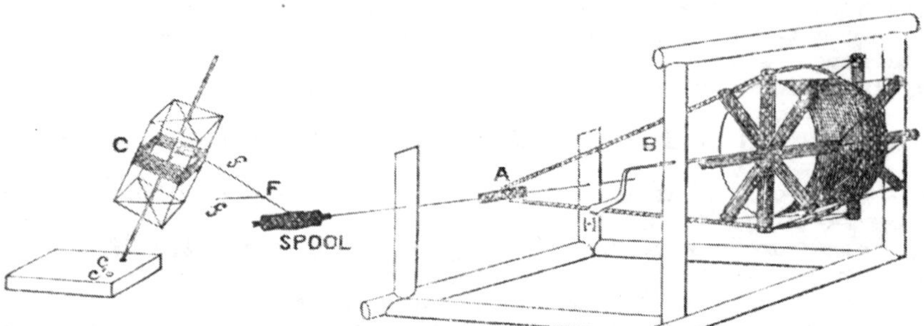

Fig. 16.—Charging of spools.

Fig. 17.—Maku or shuttle.

CHAPTER XVI.

Weaving.

193. There is nothing special about the methods ordinarily employed in silk-weaving, and the same looms are employed in some districts for weaving both cotton and silk fabrics, the looms employed in silk-weaving being indistinguishable from those employed in cotton-weaving. There are, of course, as many varieties of looms as there are patterns of weaving. The more complexity there is in the pattern, the greater is the number of healds. The more complex figured patterns cannot be woven with looms fitted with healds only, but by special arrangements of harness-cords and loops to be described in the next chapter.

194. The ordinary loom for weaving *dhutis*, *corahs*, and plain gown-pieces (not twill) used in the different silk districts, differs in no essential respect one from another. An improved loom used in the Rampur Boalia Sericultural School (fig. 13) and the ordinary country loom of Bogra (fig. 15) have been already illustrated in the previous chapter. These may be said to be the most refined and the crudest silk-looms respectively used for weaving *corahs* and gown-pieces in Bengal. In principle they are identical in construction. Instead of sitting on a stool, bench or chair, the ordinary weaver sits on the floor, his legs hanging down a rectangular hole dug out or built round in the floor. The table-like arrangement of the Rampur Boalia School is nicer and more convenient, but it is not so steady or substantial, while the reed being suspended with wooden shafts instead of strings makes this part of the Rampur Boalia arrangement more satisfactory. The pulleys (PPPP) of the Rampur Boalia loom, which work the healds, are also an improvement over the corresponding *nachanis* of the Bogra loom. The flys-huttle has been also successfully employed in this school. This simple mechanical arrangement makes the working of the shuttle easier and swifter.

195. We give here also the sketch of a Murshidabad loom and one of the Malda loom. Representing similar parts by the same figures, it will be seen how they correspond almost exactly with each other and with the other two looms illustrated in the previous chapter. The differences that occur are only in the manner in which strings are suspended or posts propped up or supported, and so on. A general description of the Murshidabad

and Malda looms (set as illustrated in the two figures—figs. 18 and 19) for weaving *saris* may be given here, and also a general description of the process of weaving.

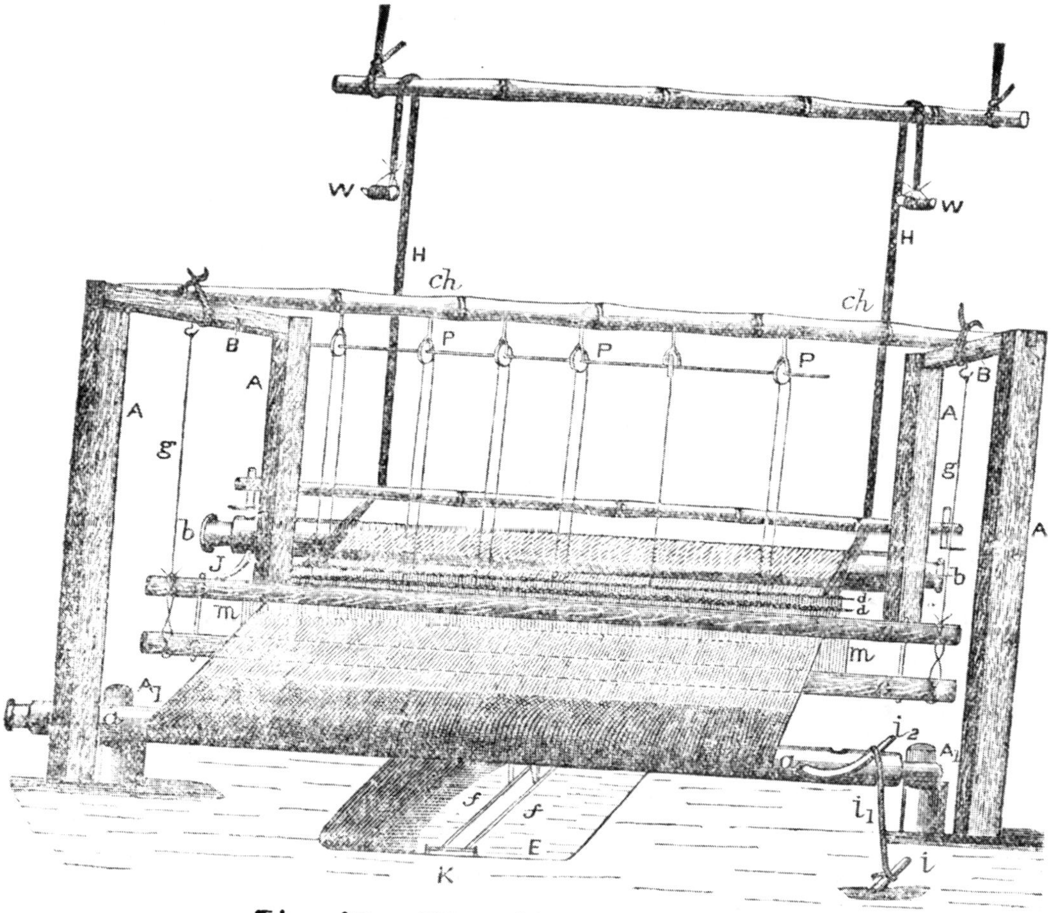

Fig. 18.—The Maldah loom.

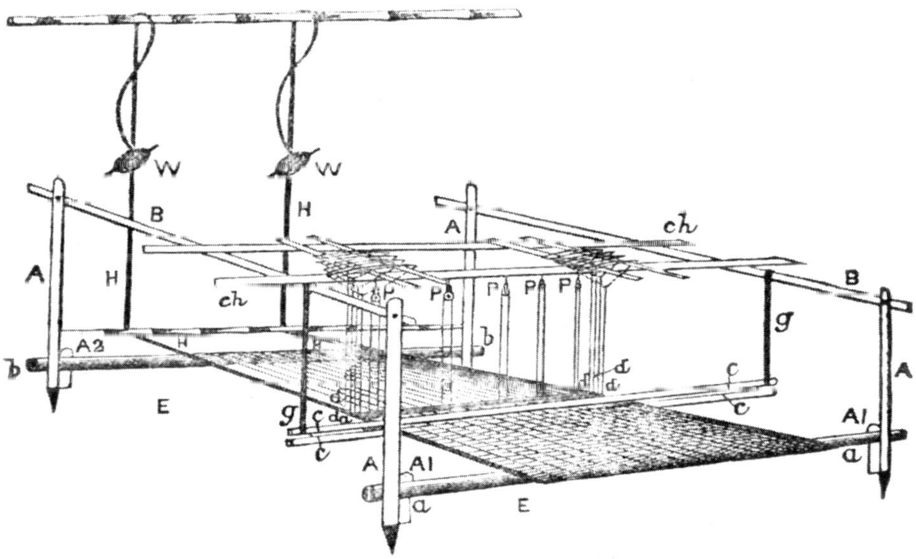

Fig. 19.—The Murshidabad loom.

196. The whole framework is rectangular—about 6 feet long and 4 feet wide, and it consists of the following parts :—

(1) AAAA are four *khunties* or upright posts, a yard high, fixed in the ground at the four corners of the loom.

(2) A_1A_1 are two *kol-khunties* or support-posts, each about nine inches high, placed just in front of the *khunties* nearest to the operator. These are the pivots for the cloth beam.

(3) aa is the *kol-naroj* or *kol-narod* (cloth beam) which rests on the *kol-khunties.*

(4) i is *biskarmar-khunti*, which is an iron hook rigidly fixed to the ground. This is not shown in the figure illustrating the Murshidabad loom. At this point is the Art-god, *Bishvakarmá* (*lit.*, the Architect of the Universe) worshipped by the weaver with great ceremony once a year, and daily he bows down before this hook when commencing the day's work. To it is tied the handle of the cloth beam (i_2) that the warp may remain stretched, and that the cloth beam may not roll.

(5) BB are the two *bahus* or shafts placed lengthwise on the four *khunties*, on which are placed loosely the *chalá-bajus* or *thhelá-bajus* (ch. ch.), *i.e.*, moving battens.

(6) From the *bahus* are suspended two strings, to which the *dakti* or the reed frame (cc) is suspended. From the *chalá-bajus* resting on the *bahus* are suspended wooden *pulleys* or *nachnies*, or both wooden *pulleys* and *nachnies*, to which the *baws* or healds are attached.

(7) The *dakti* or *dapti* (cc), reed-frame, which consists of two battens, between the grooves of which lies the reed or *sháná*, are made of the common reed (*shar-kati*). There are 1,000, 1,200, 1,500, 1,800, 2,000, 2,200, or 2,400 dents in the *sháná*, and a *sháná* with a larger number of dents is put in the *dakti* when a close web is required to be woven. As the cloth is woven, the *dakti* is further and further removed along with the *chalá-bajus*, until the weaver finds it inconvenient to reach the 'shed.' To the yarn-beam (bb) is fixed an iron lever (J), which is worked to loosen the warp. This is not shown in the Murshidabad loom. The bamboo handle (i_2) of the cloth beam is then worked to roll up the cloth that has been woven, the lever reattached to the *biskarmár khunti*, and the weaving is continued, the *dakti* and the *chálá-bajus* being at the same time brought closer to the operator.

(8) The *bahir-naraj* (bb), called also *bahir-narod* (warp or yarn-beam), is suspended by means of ropes or supported on two small posts, one of which (A_2) is shown in the figure illustrating the Murshidabad loom. The figure illustrating the Bogra loom (fig. 15) shows how the yarn-beam is suspended from the off-posts by means of ropes, while also resting against the off-posts.

(9) The *baws* or healds (dd) have to be adjusted every time the loom is set. A *baw* consists of a slender stick (*shir*), and a thicker stick (*dangi*) at the top, arranged side by side, and a thicker stick (*dangi*), a slender stick (*shir*), and a batten of wood (*juthas*) at the bottom. Between these two sets of sticks a cord is arranged in loops crossed in the middle, where the particular threads of the warp meant for this particular heald are made to lie. In other words, the cord of the heald is made to pass successively through the proper threads, the cord being fastened at each passage through the warp to the top or the bottom sticks.

(10) The *páshá-naris* or treadles (ff) are attached to the healds at their bottom, with ropes crossing each other as they go up. They are not shown in the Murshidabad loom. These treadles are simply bamboo sticks resting on one end on a fulcrum (*garkhilé*), which in its turn is fixed on two wooden pivots called (*garkhas*). Between the free ends of the treadles are planted a number of upright bamboo sticks called *barkatis* which keep the treadles from interfering with one another. It requires a good deal of practice to work the healds properly.

The toes of the weaver alone are used in this operation. As one heald is lowered some of the threads of the warp are lowered and a shed or space is formed between the web already woven and the two series of warp threads so divided. Along this space the shuttle is passed, say, from right to left. Then the *dakti* is used for pressing the thread (or the double thread) laid by the shuttle. Another treadle is then pressed, another set of warp threads goes down, and the shuttle is passed through the 'shed' now formed, the other way, *i.e.*, from left to right. In plain weaving two treadles are thus alternately worked, and the shuttle passed from left to right and right to left along the 'shed' formed each time while the *dakti* helps to press the web close. When coloured checks are woven, the warp is made of different coloured threads, and the weft is also laid with shuttles, more than one, containing threads of different colours. The weaver knows which treadle to press to bring down a thread of a certain colour. When the border is ornamental two or four healds are worked for the border only.

(11) The *kátáni* or *kánt dhanuk* (fig. 20) is a bow-shaped stick made with

Fig. 20.—The Katani.

two pieces of bamboo, with an iron pin at each end. This helps to keep the warp stretched breadthwise when the weaving is going on. Two or three of these are generally used within one cubit of the web. The pins are fixed to the borders or 'salvages.' One *katani* is shown *in situ* in the Bogra loom (fig. 15).

197. As the weaving goes on, the web is rolled in from time to time in cloth beam, the *joa-kathies* taken out from the warp as each approaches the furthest heald, and when one piece (5 yards, 7 yards, or 10 yards, as the case may be) has been woven, an inch of warp is left without weft and the weaving of the next piece commenced. When a portion of the second piece has been woven, the first piece may be unrolled from the cloth beam, if necessary, and disposed of. When the weaving of a piece is finished, it is cut out and stretched in the manner shown in the figure (fig. 21) and a blunt knife, called *shipi*, which

Fig. 21.—Sizing the cloth.

is almost as long as it is broad, is worked breadthwise to and fro on the top or reverse side of the piece. This is done to make the cloth more homogenous and look thicker. A thin paste made with parched rice (*khai*) is then put on the same side of the piece and worked in with the *shipi* to give a 'sizing' to the fabric. The addition of sugar to the size impart a greater gloss to the fabric, but it is a vicious practice. The sugar spoils the fibres, and a fabric sized with sugar gets spotted, being stored for any length of time in the rainy season. Sizing is also practised to make some of the stuffs heavier. Weavers themselves are opposed to weighting, as the local sale of all silks is invariably conducted on three principles, viz , (1) by actual count of the threads used in the warp; (2) by the length and width of the stuff; (3) by the regularity and other excellence of the web. Dealers in Calcutta, however, go mainly by weight. An unsized piece of *chaukara*, for instance, 10 yards long and 42 inches wide, weighs (if the piece is a 2,000 *shâná* piece) about 10 ounces. The Calcutta dealers, however, want that the 2,000 *shâná-chaukará* pieces should uniformly weigh 12½ ounces per piece. An inferior piece weighing 7 ounces only may by sizing be made to weigh 12½ ounces, for the benefit not of the weaver, but of the dealer or merchant, who trades with other countries or other parts of India, where they judge a piece of silk by its touch and look.

198. The Burdwan monograph states that 1,000 cubits of wrap are warpped round the yarn-beam at a time, and that it takes 3 to 3½ months to turn this amount into cloth. The Burdwan silk-weaver must have very good business to be able to weave 10 cubits a day uninterruptedly for 100 days. It is not impossible work, but it is heavy work, and it is only when weavers have very good business that they work at such high pressure, but probably 100 cubits was only meant and not 1,000 cubits, as 100 cubits of warp is considered the right quantity to put in at a time in the district of Murshidabad, which is the recognised centre for silk-weaving.

199. The Malda monograph speaks of superior cloths being of 2,500 to 3,000 *shánás*. The ordinary Murshidabad maximum is 2,400. But probably some Malda weavers can weave closer webs.

200. In weaving *matkás* the same system is followed, but the number of dents in the reed used for weaving *matkás* is smaller.

201. In weaving *corahs which are* exported in thousands, more wholesale methods of weaving are employed. Warp for 10 or 12 pieces is first introduced; afterwards by knotting to the last piece more warp is put in. Two warp threads are passed through each reed-space and one through each *baw*-space. The shuttle lays four warp-threads at each stroke. Inclusive of the cost of setting the loom, it costs one rupee per piece to weave *corahs* which are of the standard dimensions, *i.e.* 7 yds. × 1 yd. It takes a weaver 2 days to weave a piece of *corah*. With the fly-shuttle loom introduced by Messrs. Shaw, Wallace & Co., viz. with Messrs. Hattersley's Domestic Loom one weaver can finish one piece of *corah* per day.

CHAPTER XVII.

Special processes of Weaving.

201. No attempt has been made in any of the district monographs to describe those processes of weaving which result in highly complex webs. Mrityunjay Sirkar, who was the cleverest plain silk-weaver of Murshidabad, was asked at one time by the writer of this Monograph if he could construct looms for weaving ornamental fabrics like those made by Dubraj. After many efforts he succeeded in reproducing the border of Dubraj's shawls and table-covers without the corner ornaments. It is by a special arrangement of healds for the borders that he produced his plain shawl with a wide ornamental border, an article which is now highly valued in the Berhampore market. He also succeeded in producing a *sari* with ornamental ground (sample 91*a*). Mrityunjay was familiar with the *naksha* loom of Baluchar, but it is of such complicated mechanism that he failed to understand and reproduce it. There is now no one in the district since Dubraj's death who understands the mechanism of those looms (fig. 22) which are still in use in the Baluchar circle for producing figured fabrics. When any of these looms would get out of order Dubraj was sent for to set it right, but he reserved the neatest patterns for himself. The looms for turning out these patterns are in possession of Dubraj's son, who is represented in fig. 22*a* weaving a piece of figured *sari*, in a loom left by his father.

202. It seems from the wording of some of the district monographs that figured silks are woven elsewhere also. The Bankura monograph, for instance, speaks of a Fullam *sari*, or cloth for females with patterns of flower on them, "as being sold for 10 to 20 rupees a piece." These are probably something like the *Baluchar butedar saris*. Then there is in the Malda monograph mention made of the "Maldahi Belkhali Fuldar," the "Fullam *seárjá*," the "*Kadamfuli*," and the *chándtara saris*, valued at Rs. 9 to Rs. 16, which are probably figured. A different system of weaving figured patterns is also alluded to in the Midnapore monograph, in connection with the *Tasar*-weaving industry. An arrangement for raising and lowering some of the threads of the warp in regular succession, of introducing coloured thread with spools only instead of shuttles, and thus bringing out coarse patterns of flowers (something in the Punjab *Phulkari* style), is recognised in cotton-weaving also. *Gulbáhár* cotton *saris*, however, cannot be compared in complexity of web or richness of design even to the ordinary *Baluchár butedar sari*. I will quote here my description of the *nakshá* loom, given in the article on the Silk Industry of Murshidabad, which appeared in the *Journal of Indian Art* (*No. 38*), which will help to illustrate Figs. 22 and 22*a*, which have been reproduced from photographs of two of these complicated looms :—

"The arrangement of the loom used for making *Baluchar butedars*, shawls, and scarfs is somewhat different. The cloth beam is placed on two pillars or platforms, the weaver sitting on a plank resting on the same pillar alongside the cloth beam, his legs going between, and his feet working the treadles, which are fixed in the floor at one end in the same manner as the treadles are fixed in the pit in the case of the ordinary loom. The warp-beam is also placed on the floor, being slightly elevated with two pivots. Thus the warp runs up in a slant from the warp-beam to the cloth beam, instead of horizontally, as in the case of the ordinary loom. The use of four healds where two only is essentially necessary, has been already mentioned. The essential peculiarity of the *naksha*-loom consists in the presence of the *shirak*, or a large number of strong twines running across and above the warp just beyond the healds. Each of these twines is attached below to a certain number of threads in the warp by means of long loops of strong cotton suspended vertically from the twines and allowing one, two, or more warp threads to pass through each, according to the figure intended to be brought out. Above the twines are attached two *nakshas* or sets of harness-cords, which the draw-boy, sitting beyond the twines on an elevated platform, manipulates, thus bringing up each time a number of twines, which in their turn raise by means of the loops the required threads of the warp. To make the 'sheds' on this side the reed distinct, two *nanglis* or plough-shaped wooden wedges suspended from the ceiling with ropes are thrust in by the weaver among the twines. He then passes the little sticks called *shirkis* (not 'spools' put in shuttles) charged with coloured weft threads through the 'sheds,' along the whole width of the piece, corresponding to the different *buts* or figures. When the coloured threads for the *buts* have been *once* passed, the *nanglis* are withdrawn while the reed is pressed home to the web, the treadles worked, and the shuttle passed *once* to lay one thread of the ground weft. The reed is again worked, and then the 'draw-boy' manipulates the cords of the *nakshas* which govern the elevation of the warp for the two borders only. The *nanglis* are again thrust in to bring the two sheds on the two sides (for the borders) distinctly up, and then the two sticks with coloured threads meant for the two borders are passed through the sheds *once*. Another weft-thread for the ground is then put in with the shuttle. These three sets of operations go on throughout the weaving. As a rule there are two *nakshas* for the borders, two for the *buts*, two for the *anchla* or the ornamental end piece, and one for the beginning and finishing up. The 'draw-boy' manipulates a 'harness cord' for the *buts* and the weaver puts in a thread for the *buts*. At the next operation, viz., the putting in of a weft-thread for the ground, the 'draw-boy' does nothing; then the "draw-boy' manipulates a harness-cord for the border, while the weaver puts in a thread for the border. At the next operation again the 'draw-boy' does nothing, while the weaver passes the shuttle to put in another weft thread for the ground. At each operation, therefore, time is spent by the weaver not only in his own manipulations, but also in watching those of the boy. For richer designs as many as 14 *nakshas* are sometimes employed. It is easy therefore to imagine how a piece five yards long and 42 inches wide can take as much as six months for a weaver and his boy to weave, beginning at the adjusting of the loom and ending in the completion of the first piece, for even in the case of the figured patterns 5, 10, and sometimes 20 pieces are turned out before a readjustment of the loom is allowed.

203. An ordinary loom costs Rs. 4 to Rs. 10, while a *naksha* loom costs Rs. 30 to Rs. 40.

204. Figure 22 illustrates a *naksha* loom that has been set up at the Rampur Boalia Sericultural School by one of Dubraj's workmen. It is not so complicated as the looms which produce *saris* with ornamental ground (Fig. 22*a*) Figure 22 illustrates the weaving of a shawl with a wide ornamental border, and

Fig. 22*a* of a *sári* with ornamental ground, border, *kunja* or corner figures and *anchla* or ornamental end piece.

Govt. School of Art. Cal.

FIG. 25 THE NAKSHA LOOM OF BALUCHAR.

Lith: by G. M. Ruckm.   Govnt. School of Art. Cal.

FIG. 22a NAKSHA LOOM OF MURSHIDABAD (MORE COMPLICATED.)

PART V.

INFERIOR SILKS.

CHAPTER XVIII.

THE TASAR SILK INDUSTRY.

Introductory.—There are several classes of cocoons, spun by wild or semi-wild silk-worms of different species, which go by the generic name of *tasar* or *tusser*. Those recognised in commerce are according to the quality of the silk they yield—(1) the Yamamai cocoon of Japan (Antheria Yamamai), (2) the China *tasar* (Antheria Pernyi), (3) the Muga cocoon of Assam (Antheria Assama), and (4) the Bengal *tasar* (Antheria mylitta). Cocoons, such as the Attacus atlas and the Actias selene, which are not utilized in commerce, are known as *Bharuas* in Manbhum.

206. Of these, the Bengal *tasar* cocoon has the greatest length of fibre, though the fibre is inferior to that of the other three classes of *tasar* mentioned and it is also more difficult to reel.

207. The Yamamai cocoon is so highly prized in Japan that by law capital punishment may be awarded to any person exporting seed-cocoons or eggs of this insect. Though some attempts have been made at the introduction of this insect (which feeds on the oak) into Europe, the attempts have not met with any practical success, and Yamamai *tasar* silk, which is almost as good as mulberry silk, is still made only in Japan.

208. The China *tasar* cocoon is smaller than the Bengal *tasar* cocoon. The average length of fibre is 550 metres, as compared with 700 metres which the average length of fibre on the Bengal *tasar* and the European mulberry cocoon, and with 250 metres which is the average length of fibre on a Bengal mulberry cocoon. In reeling a China *tasar* cocoon an average of about 300 millegrammes of 'waste' are obtained, while in reeling a Bengal *tasar* cocoon, an average of about 720 millegrammes of 'waste' are obtained. The proportion of reelable silk in fresh *tasar* cocoons of Bengal is about 8 per cent., while it is about 5 per cent. in the case of fresh China *tasar* cocoons. The Bengal *tasar* cocoon has a few other advantages over the China *tasar* cocoon. The tenacity of the '*bave*' (*i.e.*, the double fibre as it comes out of the mouth of the silk-worm) is 28½ grammes, as compared to 18 grammes which is the tenacity of the *bave* of the China *tasar*. The elasticity of the *bave* is 21½ per cent., as compared to 19 per cent. which is the elasticity of the *bave* of the China *tasar*. The Bengal *tasar* also loses less of its weight in bleaching; China *tasar* losing as much as 21 per cent., while Bengal *tasar* loses only 11 per cent. The Bengal *tasar* is, however, more difficult to bleach and dye than the China *tasar*. The Bengal *tasar* is reared by Sonthals, Kols and other aboriginal tribes of Bengal who live in warm localities, where the oak on which the China *tasar* feeds cannot be propagated. In the cold, regions of Bengal where the oak is to be found (*i.e.*, in the Darjeeling district), wages are nearly four times larger than it is in those places where Sonthals and other aboriginal tribes live.

209. The rearing of the *tasar* silk-worm requires an amount of patience and skill which without the aid of heredity it is difficult to attain. The introduction of the China *tasar* rearing industry in the Darjeeling hills, which seems to be in contemplation, is likely to be attended with peculiar difficulties, and the success of the enterprise is extremely doubtful. In connection with the contemplated introduction of the China *tasar* by the Forest Department, I may here quote the opinion of Mr. Otto Anz, a distinguished *tasar* expert, contained in a letter, dated Yino-hiapu, China, dated the 9th November 1897, addressed to Her Majesty's Consul at Newchwang :—

"I further venture to remark that it would be a pity in my opinion to abandon the native *tasar* silk of India, as my study of these have shown that they possess qualities specially adapting them for important requirements of the silk industry; I hope to be able to prove this in the course of next year. But while recommending to further, nay, to greatly increase, the culture of Indian *tasar* (Antheria mylitta), on an improved basis, I am entitled strongly to support Mr. Wardle's suggestions to introduce into India the culture of Antheria Pernyi too. The silk of the latter has other properties which for other requirements give a value superior to that of Antheria mylitta, and from a point of view, considering the economic value of both kinds for India as a whole, I should think that it would not be wise to neglect it now; or as the one of two silks, the oak silk is not indigenous in India, to import its culture to the benefit of the cool and hilly regions, while the culture of *tasar*, mylitta, would, if based on better principles, largely benefit the poorer classes of the people in the tropic parts of India."

210. So the Bengal *tasar*, though it has been greatly ousted by the China *tasar* in the European market, has a future before it, if full advantage is taken of its capabilities. It seems strange that the cocoons should be gathered in the jungles of Singhbhum, Manbhum, Sonthal Parganas, and even of Assam, and brought down to the filatures of Murshidabad for reeling. The *tasar* silk reeling and weaving industries must be estranged from the mulberry silk-reeling and weaving industries, and the former devoloped on their own lines. There should be no difficulty in establishing *tasar* factories in *tasar* growing districts, where labour and fuel (both coal and wood) are abundant and cheap.

211. The industries (those of rearing, reeling and weaving) exist in the same original condition in those districts, in which the mulberry silk-rearing, reeling and weaving industries existed in other parts of Bengal before these were developed by British enterprise and capital. The climate of these districts is also more congenial to Europeans than the climate of Lower Bengal. A *tasar*-reeling and weaving company organised on European principles, and working in the *tasar*-growing districts is likely to have a very prosperous career before it.

212. It will be best to deal with the *tasar* silk industry district by district.

Murshidabad.—It has been already said *tasar* cocoons are reeled in European filatures in the district of Murshidabad, but they are imported from distant places. *Tasar*-reeling is done chiefly at the Bajarpara (opposite Berhampore) and Narayanpur Factories.

213. *Hooghly*.—The following extracts from the Hooghly monograph refer to the *tasar* industry of the Jahanabad subdivision of that district:—

"*Weaving of tasar and mixed fabrics*.—Fabrics made of *tasar* and of a mixture of *tasar* and cotton are manufactured in several scattered villages in thana Goghat, but chiefly in Shambazar, Badanganj, Kristoganj, Bettiah, Kayapata, Phubi, Hajipur, Moheshgeria. Kirtichandrapur, Debkhanda and Gosainbazar.

"I have not been able, owing to the villages being scattered over a large area to ascertain the number of people engaged in this business. The figures supplied by the police appeared to me to be altogether unreliable. The number, however, may be roughly taken to be between 300 and 350.

"The fabrics manufactured by these people are *tasar saries* for women and *jors* (or suits of *dhuti* and *chudder*) for men, beside dress-pieces made of a mixture of *tasar* and cotton. These fabrics are sold in local markets or at Ghatal and other centres.

"*Tasar*-weaving is in vogue in several villages in thana Goghat and notably in the villages in Badanganj outpost. The area included in Badanganj outpost is contiguous to those parts of Bankura and Midnapore where there is an important *tasar* industry. The industry appears to have extended to this subdivision from Bishunpur, Ghatal, and Garhbeta. The chief centre is Shambazar.

"The fabrics manufactured are such as are in local demand, and consist chiefly of *saries* or *dhutis*.

"The people engaged in this industry belong for the most part to the Tanti caste and to a more limited extent to the castes of Kamar, Kumar, Jelias, Goalas, Chandals, and Bagdis.

"The fabrics are purchased by mahajans or wholesale dealers who make advances to the weavers, and are sold by them at the *hâts* or markets at Ramjibanpur in Midnapore, at the Howrah *hât*, and at the local bazars.

"*Tasar-spinning*.—*Tasar*-spinning is confined to Sripur, Madhubati, Bairi, Hajipur, Kirtichandrapur, Borjo, Gosainbazar, Shambazar, and Baburampur in thana Goghat. These spinners are included amongst the *tasar* weavers mentioned above.

"The *tasar* thread is spun from cocoons imported from Manbhum and Singhbhum. The fabrics are made either of pure *tasar* thread or of *tasar* mixed with cotton thread. The *tasar*-spinning is done entirely by women and gives occupation to most of the widows of the weaving classes.

"The following are the different kinds of cocoons used in spinning:—

(1) *Dàba* (superior) at Rs. 10 per 1,280. | (2) *Bàgui* (medium) at Rs. 9 per 1,280.
(3) *Jadui* (inferior) at Rs. 7 per 1,280.

"*Tasar* thread is bought at Rs. 7 to Rs. 8 per seer of 70 tolahs direct from the manufacturers of Sultanpur in Ghatal, and also to a more limited extent, from Manikhat, Raipur, Salepur, &c., in Jahanabad.

"*Tasar saries* and *dhotis* made of *tasar* are made in the following sizes:—

Saries.	*Dhotis.*
5 yards by 1 yard 9 inches.	5 yards by 1 yard 9 inches.
3 ,, by 2 feet 7 ,,	

"Besides these pure *tasar* suitings are made to order measuring 10 yards by 1 yard for the use of *Bhadraloks.* These are sold for Rs. 11 per piece and are made in one quality only, called *chausuti, i.e.*, two threads warp and two threads woof. The texture is very strong.

"The *saries* which have a red or black border and the *dhutis* are made in two qualities:—

(1) *Chausuti, i.e.*, two threads warp and two threads woof.
(2) *Der-suti, i.e.*, one thread warp and two threads woof.

"The first quality of *saries* is sold at from Rs. 6 to Rs. 6-8 per piece and of *dhutis* at about Rs. 7 per piece, the second quality being sold at Re. 1 less per piece.

"*Kethe cloth.*—A worse kind of *tasar* called *kethe* is made at Badanganj. Only about ten families of weavers are engaged in this manufacture. The fabric is made of pierced *tasar* cocoons and is purchased by dealers from Calcutta and Orissa. It resembles in appearance the well-known Assam silk.

"*Garbha suti.*—A mixed fabric called *Garbha suti* is sometimes made to order. It consist of a mixture of cotton and *tasar*. The size usually made is 10 yards by 1 yard. The material is suitable for suitings and is sold at Rs. 8 per piece.

"The industry is in a decidedly prosperous condition. In fact it has to some extent taken the place of the old cotton industry. Owing to the depression in the cotton trade, the cotton weavers have taken to *tasar* manufacture, the looms being entirely adapted for the purpose.

"The time of the year when the fabrics are in the greater demand is the marriage season in spring. The business is slackest during the rains. The cloths are worn during festive occasions and in the performance of religious ceremonies. Borderless *tasar* cloths are largely used by widows, an idea of sanctity being associated with silk and *tasar*. During the rains the *tasar* weavers betake themselves to cotton weaving."

214. *Burdwan.*—In the district of Burdwan *tasar* spinning and weaving are carried on in the Sadar and Katwa subdivisions. In the Sadar subdivision they are carried on in the following places:—

	Families.
In Galsi thana—	
At Khanpara by about	29
At Uttarpara by about	42
At Halbazar by about	26
At Jagatpur by about	29
At Kota by about	60
In Satgachia thana—	
At Memari by about	7
At Radhakantapur by about	30
At Tantigar by about	6
Total ...	228

Thus in the Sadar Division about 228 families are dependent on the *tasar* industry: they are all *Tantis* by caste.

215. In the Katwa subdivision, thanks to the efforts of Radhicananda Ray of Amdanga, an officer in the employ of a former Nawab Nazim, *tasar* cocoon-rearing, silk-spinning and weaving are carried on in the following villages:—

"Bagdigi, Goalkanigi, Madhatpur, Musthul, Amdanga, Ghoranash, Panchberia, Jagadlanandapur, Chandul, Sribati, Multi, and Maygachi.

"Employment is given to about 500 families.

"Various castes take part in the growing and spinning, but the weavers are Tantis of the Navasak caste, which is only inferior to Brahmins, Baidyas, and Kayasthas.

"No cocoons from which *resam* or *garad* might be manufactured are grown in this subdivision or imported: all importations are in the form of yarn.

"Cocoons for *tasar* silk manufacture are grown at Kalna along the banks of the river. Cocoons are imported from various places, of which Chaibassa in Singhbhum is the most favoured. Sonamuki in Bankura, Huusongoon in Cuttack, and some places in the Sonthal Parganas also send cocoons. These are imported by Uriya merchants and also by traders from Rajgram, Bankura, and elsewhere: at Katwa there are a few merchants who import.

The cocoons are of various classes, viz.—

(1) *Daba*, the best quality, comes exclusively from Chaibassa in Singhbhum; one *kahan* makes two seers of yarn. Its price is Rs. 10-8 to Rs. 12-8 for 1 *kahan* =1,280 cocoons.

(2) *Bagai*, which also comes from Singhbhum, produces 1¼ to 1½ seers of yarn per *kahan*, and its price is Rs. 7-12 to Rs. 9 per *kakan*.

(3) The *mugo*, which comes from Hazaribagh, produces 1¼ to 1⅜ seers of yarn per *kahan*, and its price is Rs. 7 to Rs. 8-8 per *kahan*.

(4) *Jaidui* or winter cocoons is a quality imported from various places in the cold weather: it produces only 12 to 13 chitaks of yarn per *kahan*, and is sold at Rs. 3 to Rs. 5 per *kahan*.

"Yarn for *tasar* manufacture is prepared in the following way:—

If the cocoons are not dead, they are hung in a cloth over boiling water until they become so. After being dried in the sun, they are placed in a vessel containing water, cattle-urine, and potash or *saji* water (the former being preferred at Katwa, the latter in the Sadar) and boiled for about an hour. As they become soft they are taken out and peeled by the finger and placed in a stone vessel. The spinning is done by the women of the family, while the males weave or engage in other occupations. The spinner takes hold of the cocoon and pinches it and draws out the clue. The thread is wound on to a bamboo frame (*latai*) which is held in the right hand. The cocoons are kept on the left side of the spinner, and as the thread passes over the right thigh, it is twisted with the left hand before it passes on the *latai*. The women manage to weave about two seers of yarn a month, and they sell the best quality yarn for Rs. 12½ to Rs. 14 a seer. As the price at which they purchased the cocoons of the best sort was Rs. 10-8 to Rs. 12-8, their average monthly earnings are rather under Rs. 2. One anna a day is about the rate of wages prevalent."

216. *Midnapore.*—In Midnapore *tasar* cocoons are found in the jungles of Gogooi, Mooga, Sildha, and Ramgaon. The jungle mahals to the western side of the district generally and the jungles of Mourbhanj, and Dhalbhum produce these cocoons in abundance. They are imported from these places, and they gradually find their way into the villages of Anandapore in thana Keshpore and Kesiari in thana Narayangarh, where weavers live.

217. The following account is furnished in the district monograph regarding the present industrial position of the *tasar*-weaving industry in these two villages:—

"These villages are wholly inhabited by weavers who prepare various sorts of *dhutie saries*, and *thâns* from the silk, and after local sale send out the surplus to Calcutta for sale there. At one time the weavers of Anandapore and Kesiari made their fortune by preparing *tasar* cloth, but for about 20 years the industry is on the decline, owing to want of purchasers for their cloths and owing to the influx of machine-made European silk cloths of all sorts, which being superior in make and comparatively cheaper in price, the people like them and do not care to buy cloths made by native weavers in the native method, and the best weavers complain that they can hardly make Rs. 10 a month for their livelihood."

218. The following description is also furnished in the same monograph of the rearing and manufacturing processes in vogue in this district:—

"One or two wild cocoons are found upon trees known as *ashna* (*Terminalia tomentosa*). These are plucked from the trees in the months of *Assin* and *Kartic*, and are kept inside a small pot made of green leaves and kept tied to a small twig of the tree full of leaves, and in the course of a month the caterpillar* comes out of the cocoon, and another caterpillar† is soon found there. Whence it comes no one can say, and after both these had grown well for about a month‡, they give out eggs. When some hundreds of worms are produced at this time, small twigs containing green leaves are put upon these little worms, and they go on feeding upon these new leaves, and gradually numbers get attached to these newly-cut twigs. At this time the little worms with the newly-cut twigs are removed to different parts of the trees as also to other trees having large quantities of leaves. In this way all the little worms produced from the original cocoons are removed to numbers of branches and trees, and they gradually grow to the size of big caterpillars and form cocoons. In the course of three months—October and September are favourite months for putting in young worms upon trees, and in January they ripe and are collected by the dealers and taken to different markets. The seed-cocoons are always found in jungles.

* Female moth is meant. † Male moth is meant.

‡ This is a mistake, eggs being laid by the female the very next day.

They are never reared at home. Every year during the rainy season the jungly people, who live inside the jungle, go out in search of seed-cocoons, and each person collects about 20 to 30 such cocoons, from which they prepare the seedlings, which they plant upon different trees, and in the course of three months, they get their supply of *tasar* cocoons in abundance.

"The different kinds of *tasar* in this district are—

1. Jorai	...	Are ready in September (*Assin*) and commenced in June
2. Fooki	...	
3. Ampetia	...	
4. Bagrui	...	Generally the best kinds, all gathered in *Pous*. Largest of all.
5. Joora	...	
6. Doba	...	
7. Moogdal	...	

"*Ashna*, *sâl*, and plum trees are the best plants for growing *tasar* cocoons.

"The hardest kind of cocoon that does not get hollowed by pressure is the best kind of *tasar*. The cocoons are either reddish, yellowish, or blackish in colour. The colour does not affect the material—if the cocoons are the hardest in kind—the softer kinds known as *jorai*, *fooki*, and *ampetia* are the worst kinds of *tasar*.

"The cocoons are boiled in water mixed with alkaline matter or Fuller's earth. The upper covering gives a sort of coarse silk called *locha*, which is first taken out in a separate *latai* (spindle). Then the softer and better kind of silk comes out, and this is taken in a separate *latai* (spindle). The *tasar* cocoons are never sold by weight. They are sold by *pons* or 80 in number, and are valued according to the quantity of silk that is produced from the 80 cocoons. The best kinds of cocoons produce 5 *tolas* of silk from 1 *pon* or 80 cocoons, and the worst kinds produce 2½ to 3 *tolas* of silk; the cocoons are sold at the rate of Rs. 10 to Rs. 12 per *kahan* of *20 pons* (80 × 20 = 1,600) in number for the best ones that produce 5 *tolas* of silk per each *pon* or 80 cocoons, and Rs. 5 or Rs. 6 per each *kahan* that produce 2½ to 3 *tolas* of silk for every 80 cocoons.

"The hardest kind of silk known as *locha*, produced from the upper covering of the cocoons are made into a sort of coarse cloth known as *kethia*, and is used for various purposes amongst the people of the country.

"Caterpillars (*sic*) coming out of the cocoons do not spoil the silk so much as when a hole is made inside a cocoon by small red ants; so the cocoons require a great deal of protection from ants.

"During the rainy days and in cold weather the *tasar* silk remains in good form, and when woven during these months, nice cloth is prepared from *tasar* silk, while during the hot months better kind of *tasar* cloth cannot be turned out.

"*Tasar* cocoons are at once put in boiled water, immediately after they are collected from the trees. This procedure only kills the insect inside the cocoons and protects the cocoon from being spoiled by the caterpillars (*sic*) coming out, and before the silk is reeled, the cocoons have again to be boiled in water mixed with Fuller's earth or some sort of alkaline matter prepared from vegetable ashes of all kinds; the silk is reeled off. While the cocoons are yet damp and softened by the boiling water, 5 to 10 cocoons are at a time taken to reeling in accordance with the requirements of the weaver who prepares the cloth either thick or thin.

"*Winding and warping.*—This work is done by the women, who prepare a sort of paste from fried *dhan* (*khai*), and after putting two or three and sometimes four *latais* of raw silk loosely upon the floor, and then the ends of the skeins of raw silk is attached to another *latai* which is held by the right hand, and the threads transferred to the right-hand *latai* by keeping it turning by the right hand, while the threads are made to pass between the thumb and the index-finger of the left hand. The paste made of parched *dhan* is at times taken in very small quantities between the thumb and the index-finger of the left hand, while the right hand *latai* is being turned. After this process the silk is again kept soaked in cold water and passed a second or a third time through the thumb and the index-finger before it is ready for weaving, and the best weavers say that if the silk is prepared by a passing through the thumb and the index-finger nine times, then it will produce really fine cloth. The clue is sometimes lost during the process. To get back the same and to join the ends together, some skill is necessary, and an unskilled person is sure to make the thread thick and uneven in many places if he is not well-skilled in this art.

"*Looms.*—The native looms are of one and the same kind, except the ones used in preparing flowery or figured cloths. The process of making flowery and figured cloths are well understood by experts in the work. For outsiders it is a difficult process, and cannot be understood by a mere description of the same by persons who are ignorant in the art of weaving; and although my informant gave me some idea of it, yet I could not exactly follow him, and I do not think that any layman will be able to understand the same without a proper drawing of the loom. All I can say is that experts, who prepare figured and flowery cloths have to work both with their hands and legs, instead of by their hands alone.*"

Bleaching and dyeing.—*Tasar* silk is hardly bleached with soap or alkaline matters. If necessary, the silk is only put in warm water for a few seconds and then washed in cold water. The weavers say that if the silk or cloths are put in boiling water for a long time

* This is incorrect. Hands and feet have both to be employed in ordinary weaving. The reference here is evidently to the *Naksha-loom* as I have stated in paragraph 202.

or any alkaline matter is mixed with the boiling water, the silk loses not only its gloss, but also its weight, and the cloth gets spoiled. So the best process used in washing is a little soap with cold water only.

"In this district the following dyes are generally used in preparing *tasar* cloths:—(1) Red and high red, (2) yellow, (3) green, and (4) purple, besides mixtures of coloured *tasar* silk in preparing (5) *maurkanthi* and (6) *pitambari* cloths. The red is prepared from lac and a sort of bark called *lodh chal* by boiling both the substances, and while boiling a small quantity of *Fuller's earth* is sprinkled over the boiling water. The exact quantity of each material cannot be stated by the weavers, but the red colour is obtained from a particular caste of people known as *nooris*.

"Yellow is prepared from a sort of earth obtained in many places in Midnapore. It resembles something like yellow ochre, and can be obtained in large quantities near deep wells and beneath laterite blocks. This earth is mixed in water and a small quantity of *lodh chal* put in and boiled and afterwards strained through a piece of cloth. Turmeric and wood of jack-fruit trees are also used in the preparation of this colour.

"No fast green can be prepared by the weaver: it is prepared from turmeric and indigo, and though boiled with a little of alum, and the cloth dried three times to make the colour fast, yet it fades away very soon.

"Purple is prepared from the barks of *peepul* trees, boiled with alum and mixed with indigo. This colour is much faster than green.

"The *maurkanthi* cloth is prepared from a mixture, two sorts of coloured silk—one for the warp and the other for the weft. Generally the red prepared from lac is used for the warp and the green for the weft.

"*Pitambari* cloth is prepared by the use of red silk for the warp and yellow for the weft.

"*Export and import of tasar silk and silk cloth.*—Nobody can exactly say the quantity of the *tasar* silk that is manufactured in this district, but, roughly estimating, I think the export of cloth will be worth Rs. 40,000 to Rs. 50,000 with a manufacture of yarn prepared from the cocoons, worth Rs. 3,000 a year."

219. *Birbhum.*—The Birbhum monograph has the following account of the *tasar* silk industry of that district:—

"Besides silk as described above, *tasar* or wild silk industry is followed in many villages of the district, important of which are Karidhu, Kalipur, and Tantipara. Some 200 or 300 families have taken up this business. It is principally centred in the western part of the district and at Illambazar. The cocoons are brought in from the western jungles, where they are either reared by the aboriginal or semi-aboriginal tribes or gathered from the forest trees. They are reeled off and woven in the villages.

"The quantity of cocoons gathered or reared in this district is not found sufficient to meet the demand of the quantity of *tasar* manufactured in the district. The manufacturers, therefore, get their supply from Manbhum and other districts in the vicinity, from which they manufacture *tasar* cloth into *dhutis*, *saries*, and *thâns* of 10 yards. They are also coloured as per demand. *Dhutis* sell at Rs. 3 to Rs. 6; *saries* sell at Rs. 4 to Rs 8; but *thâns* of ordinary *tasar* sell at Rs. 7-8 to Rs. 10 and of *pakwan* thread at Rs. 12 to Rs. 18. These cloths are sold locally and exported to other parts of Bengal.

"The industry is carried on by 200 or 300 families in this district in about 20 or 25 villages belonging to the same caste as the silk manufacturers belong. In social and industrial position, the *tasar* manufacturers are exactly the same as of silk manufacturers. They come from the same caste, and it is found that the same man has taken up both the industries in his hand."

220. *Bankura.*—The *tasar* silk industry is in a fairly prosperous condition in the district of Bankura. The *kethés* or coarse cloths, made out of thread spun from pierced cocoons (answering to *matka* cloths), made in this district are well known, though the district monograph does not happen to mention this cloth. A piece of *kethé* sufficient for a complete suit of clothes can be had for Rs. 4 or Rs. 5. The whole of the account given of the *tasar* industry in the district monograph is quoted below:—

"The eggs of the silk-worm are gathered and put on the leaves of *asan*, *sal*, *hartaki* and *sidha* trees in the jungle. The eggs are hatched on the leaves, and the worms feed upon the leaves. In due time the cocoons are formed, and they are gathered by cutting the small branches from which they are suspended. The cocoons are sold at Rs. 5 to Rs. 9 a *kahan* (=16×80). The cocoons are purchased wholesale by substantial merchants, such as Kedar Nath Kundu and Faquir Chandra Dutta, of Rajagram, and retailed to the weavers. The principal centres of industry in *tasar* silk are Birsinghpur, Gopinathpur, and Sonamukhi. The manufacturers are all of the *Tanti* caste, who generally prepare the silk themselves from the cocoons. The cocoons are at first boiled in water mixed with wood ashes. They are then washed and cooled. Five cocoons are then taken at a time, and the silk from them is wound by a woman on a *latai*. The silk thus obtained is gummed and otherwise prepared for weaving as in the case of domesticated silk.

"The *tasar* silk is generally coloured violet and red with aniline dyes The yellow colour on *tasar* silk is made from turmeric and komala powder.

"The various kinds of *tasar* fabrics manufactured in this district and their prices are noted below :—

	Price.				
	Rs. A.		Rs. A.	
(1) *Sari* or cloth for women	3 0	to	8 0	
(2) *Dhuti* or cloth for men	2 0	to	5 0	
(3) *Thân* or long pieces for making dress ...	0 12	to	1 0	per yard.
(4) *Bafta* or a species of mixed cotton and *tasar* fabric	0 8	to	0 10	"

"The major portion of the *tasar* silk produced in this district is sold locally. A few brokers come annually to Birsinghpur from Jessore and other districts, and take away a considerable quantity of *tasar* fabric from the weavers for sale in those districts."

221. *Bhagalpur.*—As a cheap fabric, the *bafta* of Bhagalpur, is far more widely known and appreciated than the *kethe* of Bankura, and though the Bhagalpur *tasar* and *bafta* industries are perhaps not in such a flourishing condition as they were a few years ago, they are still of considerable importance. The following description of these industries has been supplied by Mr. L. C. Adami, C.S. :—

"Silk fabrics take a very important place among the manufactures of the district of Bhagalpur. From enquiry it has been shown that in the Sadar subdivision alone is the industry carried on, and even there to no very great extent.

The chief woven silk fabric is *tasar* silk cloth. About two thousand weavers gain a livelihood by its manufacture—Tantis, Golas and Momins, the two former classes being Hindus and the latter Musalman. Most of them are poor and live in Champanagar, Nathnagar, Rampur, Kelahavi, Kutubganj, Khangarpur, Lodipur, Poorami, Mustafferpur, Radhanagar and Dariapur. All these places lie round Bhagalpur.

The cocoons have to be imported from the Sonthal Parganas, Hazaribagh and Manbhum They are sold at Nathnagar at rates varying from 80 to 250 to the rupee according to quality. Pierced cocoons, the fibres of which are broken, are sold at from 100 to 400 to the rupee.

To yield a *tola* of *tasar* silk 15 to 20 cocoons are necessary, and eight to ten *tolas* of *tasar* silk will bring in about a rupee.

The preparation of the silk is as follows :—

The cocoons are first exposed to the heat of the sun, and then steamed in an earthen vessel and dried. The combination of heat and moisture makes the fibres loose and easy to reel. The silk is next wound off the cocoons by means of an instrument called *pulias*.

The loom used in this district consists of five parts :—

(1) The *Chaph* (warpbeam), a piece of timber measuring about 6′ long 2½″ broad and 2½″ high. Round this the warp threads are wound before the weaving commences.

(2) *Baisurs* (healds), pieces of split bamboos fastened together with thread so as to form a trend of comb. The healds separate the different sets of warp threads. Just below the *baisurs* there are two corresponding *paisurs* made of wood and measuring about 5′ × 2″ × ½″. They are connected by rope links of a triangular shape. The two links are worked in turn by the legs. The *baisurs* hang from ropes fastened to a bamboo frame above. The *paisurs* to which they are fastened keep them moving up and down.

(3) The *tanu*, consisting of two pieces of timber, 6′ × 3″ × ¾″. Between these there is a framework of three reeds, like a comb, and through this the warp threads pass. This presses the weft thread when the loom is working.

(4) *Kapurhini* (shuttle with spools) which introduces the weft thread through the warp thread horizontally.

(5) *Nanda.*—An octagonal piece of wood about 6 feet in length round which the woven fabric is rolled.

Bafta is another sort of fabric manufactured in the same villages. It differs from *tasar* in that the warp is all *tasar* and the woof cotton. Pieces of 6, 10 and 12 yards are made and dyed by the weavers. In one month a weaver can make three pieces of 12 yards each.

Tasar as well as *bafta* is used for *dhutis*, *saris*, coats, overcoats, *chapkans*, *pakris* and wrappers.

The rates at which this silk is sold vary. It is taken by the piece and not by the yard, and the size and quality of a piece makes a difference.

A piece of *tasar* ten yards long to be used for a *sari* or *dhuti* will cost from Rs. 7 to Rs. 10. For coats, pieces measuring 10 to 15 yards are sold for from Rs. 5 to Rs. 15.

A piece of *bafta*—*danzi sarh*—measuring 11 yards will bring from Rs. 3 to Rs. 5 for the making of clothes. For *pakris* seven yards are sold at from Re. 1-8 to Rs. 3. A piece of twelve yards for a coat will cost as much as Rs. 10.

Bafta for wrappers (*dhosa*) will bring from Rs. 5-8 to Rs. 12 for pieces of seven yards, Rs. 3 to Rs. 3-8 for six yards, and Rs. 2 to Rs. 2-4 for five and-a-half yards.

For colouring matter the Bhagalpur weavers depend almost entirely on English dyes. The chief native dyes used are flowers of *kusum*, *sufali*, and *palas*, *haldi* (turmeric), *kusis* (sulphate of iron), *rasuras* (a yellow powder) and indigo.

The English dyes have only to be mixed with water and also give a more brilliant colour than native dyes, and therefore are preferred.

In many cases two native dyes are mixed to form a third colour. The favourite mixture is *khaki*, made up of *haldi* and *kusis*.

Very often one colour is used for the warp and another for the weft, for instance, in the so-called peacock-coloured pieces, where the warp is red and the weft green.

The trade in *tasar* is gradually diminishing, though Bhagalpur used to be famous for it, and in time it seems it will die altogether, and imported cloth alone will be used.

It is a great pity, but the hand-loom cannot compete with machinery."

222. *Sonthal Parganas.*—In the Sonthal Parganas *tasar* cocoons are reared throughout the district, for exportation chiefly to Murshidabad. There is some *tasar*-weaving also in the subdivision of Godda, and the following description of the industry has been compiled out of the monograph furnished by the Subdivisional Officer of Godda. With the exception of some of the vernacular terms used, the description of *tasar* weaving and its subsidiary processes will be found to be almost identical with the description of silk weaving, though the appliances used for *tasar*-weaving are of a ruder description:—

The main class who carry on the industry are a class of people called Patwas. They are really residents of the Gaya district, but a few of them have come and settled in the northern part of the subdivision, and have taken up their hereditary occupation as *tasar* weavers. They appear to be the only class of people who manufacture silk cloth. Paharias, Sonthals, Bhuiyas and Khetoris also assist them in preparing the materials, but these classes take no active participation in the manufacture itself. Their work is again referred to later on.

The Patwas number only 40 in number and live all together in one village, called Mal Bhagaya just outside on the borders of the Government estate (Damin-i-koh). This class of people are found nowhere else in this subdivision. They also go in for some cultivation as an additional source of income.

Their social position is that of simple weavers and their industry is that of *tasar* silk manufacturers. They make the cloths and sell them in the local markets, occasionally disposing of their cloths in the hills.

The following are some of the names of the cloths they make with a short description of their size and use :—

Dhuti.—The *dhuti* is a waist cloth made for males. They measure about 4 yards × 1 yard and are sold according to their texture. Coarse quality Rs. 2 per piece ; a piece consists of 4 yards × 1 yard. Superior quality Rs. 5 per piece. They are sometimes coloured yellow and red. They are used at the time of marriages and on festive occasions.

Sari.—The *sari* is a chief cloth worn by women. It measures 6 yards × 1 yard. The pieces are sold according to their quality. Coarse quality at Rs. 3 per piece, and the superior quality at Rs. 7. They are of various kinds, white, yellow, red, purple, according to the demand. Sometimes they are made with coloured broad borders. These *saris* are also used by various classes at the time of marriages.

Gamcha.—The *gamcha* is a towel, worn by children round their bodies. They are made in pieces, measuring 2½ yards × 1 yard.

The coarse kind cost about Re. 1, and the superior quality Rs. 2 per piece.

The cloth is also made into one continuous piece called *thân*, measuring 8 yards × 1 yard, and costs Rs. 8. The various colours used are made from various dyes, some of which the weavers purchase, others of which they make themselves in their homes.

The red dye is purchased from local *banias* who bring it from elsewhere for sale. The materials for the dye (yellow) is also procured from the local *banias*.

It is said that they procure a kind of flower called *komla* which grows in the jungles.* They bring this flower home and dry it and powder it. The powder or dust the weavers purchase from them taking it home and making a yellow dye. They put this dust into an earthen vessel boiling it for about an hour till it begins to simmer and bubble up, then, taking it off, they put the thread into it, and let it remain for some time; when the colour has soaked well into it they take them out and allow them to dry.

The other colours are purchased from the shops.

Process of manufacture.—The following class of people, viz., Paharias, Sonthals, Khetoris rear the *tasar* worms on the *Asan* trees, either on the hills or plains.

There are four kinds of cocoons (*koa*).

1. *Sarihan.*—No. 1.
2. *Langa.*—Produces less thread than No. 1.
3. *Munga.*—The best, bigger than (1) and (2).
4. *Phuka.*—Sold to Jogi or Bhairagi caste, who make a kind of thread with them for jalis (nets); they are used also for purposes of making beads.

The process for cultivation is as follows :—

They take the seed of the *munga* for breeding purposes and enclose them in a covering of *Asan* leaves called (*thonga*). Then they keep these for two days in their houses ; when

* It is the dry capsule or fruit (not flower) of the Mallotus Philippinensis that is meant. A granular dust is found on these fruits which yields the valuable dye *Kamela* or *Kamala-gunri*. See the description of the preparation of this dye in paragraph 173.

the worm forms, they suspend it on to the twigs of the *Asan* trees. The worms (*pilu*) of their own accord leave the (*thonga*) and spread about the tree making the cocoons (*koa*).

The men live close by and protect them from the kites and crows. This takes place in the month of *Asin*, *i.e.*, towards the end of September and beginning of October.

Three months after (*i.e.*, in the month of *Augrahan*), when the cocoons are ready, they take them down from the Asan trees. This process is called (*koa kata*). They cut it with a knife (*hasua*). The worms make the cocoons on the twigs. After taking them down they dry them on the ground for two days. When the cocoons are first taken down from the trees they are raw and of various colours, white, blackish, yellow (ujla, kala, and peila). The colours do not affect the quality of the threads; when dried they are brought to the nearest market (*hatia*) for sale, and are sold at various prices.

The *sarihan* is sold for three *pons* (80 cocoons = 1 *pon*) per rupee, to Patwas; *longa*, five *pons* per rupee; *munga*, two *pons* per rupee, *phuka*, eight *pons* per rupee.

The prices sometimes go up owing to the number of marriages.

Then the cocoons sell as follow:—

Sarihan for two *pons* per rupee.
Longa ,, three *pons* per rupee.
Munga ,, one and a-half *pons* per rupee.
Phuka ,, four to five *pons* per rupee.

The patwas or weaving class then bring them to their own houses and boil them in hot water (*bhapana*); they place about 80 to 100 at a time in a large earthen vessel (*haria*). This process is called (*koa sejkana.*)

In order to prepare them quickly and make them clean, they use (*saji-matti*) a kind of local soap and mix them (*ghoma*).

They keep the cocoons steeped for about eight hours, then they take them out from the *haria* and wash them in clean water and put them on the top of cowdung ashes (*chaie*). This process is called (*koa sukana*). It is done for the purpose of absorbing the water. If they remain very wet, the thread is very liable to break when used. They then take one cocoon in the left hand, and with the right hand they slightly rub it in order to remove the rough coating over the shell (*tusar phuriyana*) and to get out the *khani* or *tasar*.

After this is done they commence the process for manufacturing the thread itself.

After the rubbing process is first gone through, the thread comes out of the cocoon.

They then take five different kinds of *khai* from five separate kinds of cocoons and place them in a small earthen pot (*atari*).

The five threads are called *taga*. This process (called *koa katna*) is chiefly done by women, and in their private quarters. In the figure a man (No. 1, in fig. 23) is represented as spinning thread out of five cocoons.

FIG. 23 TUSSER WEAVING IN SANTAL PARAGONAS.

The woman sits down on a low four-legged stool (*machia*); the *machia* is made with four wooden legs, the seat being interwoven with sabai grass strings, with her legs stretched, and she rubs the *khais* on her left thigh, and one end of it is attached on to the reel (*latai*) which she holds in her right hand, and she keeps turning in her hand winding the thread into the *latai*.

Five gundas (*i.e.*, 20 cocoons) yield one *anti* of thread. Its weight is about 1½ *bhoris* (*tolas*). It takes about 18 *antis* of *tasar* twist (*taga*) to prepare a piece of cloth 5 yards × 27 inches in length and width.

Then comes the preparation of the thread for the purpose of making the cloth.

The preliminary process called *khewa katna* has been described above.

Now they take the *antis* from the *latai* and put them on to the *charki* one on each side. (*Vide* sketch No. 2 of fig. 24.)

Then they attach them on to the *latai* and commence to reel. This process is called *sarki karna*. They then take this single thread (*sarki*) and place it in rice starch (*mar*) to make it stiff. This process is called *patwari mukhanwe*. After this they put it on one side of the *charki*, and twist it again on the reel or *latai*. This process is called *patwari ubbarna*.

The *lata* is then placed in the sun to dry. The thread is then taken off and placed under a stone, and well pressed. This process is called *sarki chapna*.

The thread is then put into a wet cloth in order to moisten it slightly. This is called *dohari mehde*. Threads (*sarki*) are again put on each side of the *charki* and twisted on the reel (*latai*). This is called *dohari ubbarna*.

Warping process or Naritana process. Two *latais* are taken, one in the right hand and the other in the left, and the threads are attached on to the *killa* post (*vide* fig. 23).

The person then passes the *latai* in his right hand on the right side of *mukban* or lath, and the *latai* in the left hand is passed to the left side of the *mukban* and so on, forming a kind of figure (8) right round. The person keeps the whole time on the outside of the sticks; when he comes round to the next post a change occurs, the threads being kept on either side without being crossed, *i.e.*, they do not intersect or form the figure (8). They run parallel from the second to the third post, as explained in fig. 10 and 12.

Then the threads are passed on to the fourth post forming again the figure (8), *i.e.*, they are crossed. The above process is called *naritana*. In this way they complete *naritana* process according to the size of the cloth they desire.

When a number of threads have been taken round, the person then with some silk ties the intersecting threads so as to prevent their being mixed or confused with other threads. The posts are then uprooted, except the first and last. This process is called *naritana*.

The person then takes two *sarsis* (pieces of bamboo about 3 feet in length, half an inch in width). They cut the thread off with a knife in two places at one of the end posts, and attach it on a *sarai*, placing the other sarai over the thread. This process is called *bhanya laptana*, and wrap it in order to form the heald.

The reed or *sana* is shown in fig. 24 (No. 4). It is a sort of a comb consisting of teeth made out of the outer covering of columns of the common *sar* grass usually found on *dearh* land.

The teeth are just far enough to admit of the passage of the thread. The interval between the teeth (gewa) varies according to the quality of the cloth.

They also differ in fineness as well as in length. The reed used in the Sonthal Parganas contains 752 teeth, and is 3 feet 9 inches in length. The teeth (*gewa*) are about 3 inches in length. The reed costs about 4 annas each. It is made by Rusbania or Odna Godna caste (Muhammadan sect) in the district of Gaya.

The frame enclosing the reed—It consists of two long flat wooden bars, each about 5 feet in length, 2 inches in width, and having a groove along one of the edges and a hole near each end, and passing breadthwise through it. The reed is placed between these two bars (*vide* No. 5 of fig. 24 and No. 21 fig. 25) and tied by string at the end, which passes through the hole. (Vernacular name of the bars is *bhanri*.) The two bars are pinned together by wooden pegs (*kanale*) which pass through the holes at two ends.

To insert the reed, the two pins are taken out, and the upper bar is lifted up, and the bottom edge of the reed is set to rest in the groove in the lower bar. The upper bar is again brought down, so that its groove fits on to the upper edge of the reed, and the two bars are again pinned within The reed is thus supported with its length horizontal and its breadth vertical. When this is done it is supported from the centre bar (chalan). The centre bars (chalans) are placed parallel and tied together and are placed across the two side arm bars (*bahu*). These bars are used for the purpose of suspending the *lachni*. The other (*chalan*) is used for suspending the reed frame.

Lachnis are made of bamboo, and each is about 4 feet 7 inches in length, and is attached to one of the bars (*chalans*) by string—*vide* figure 25.

The reed frame is suspended by strings from the cross rod.

Description of loom.—There are four posts usually made of bamboos, and these posts are fixed into the ground, so as to form a rectangle. They are about 3½ feet in length and 1½ inches in diameter. The posts are usually placed about 3 feet apart vertically. They are cylindrical. The two front posts are almost of the same length to the rear posts.

The yarn beam is tied loosely to the rear posts.—*vide* No. 7, of fig. 25.

The cloth beam, however, rests on two posts, about 1 foot in length and 2 inches in diameter. These posts are driven in close to the two front posts on the inner side, and have their tops cut in the form of a ledge, shaped somewhat like the letter V; on this the cloth beam rests. These posts are called "biskarna."

The yarn beam (*chapti*) is a square bar, about 5 feet 4 inches in length. The faces are 2 inches wide. Along the inner face runs a groove ($\frac{1}{2}$ inch × $\frac{1}{2}$ inch) which is called *pakri*). This groove runs along the face of the beam. At the left end of the beam at about 5 inches from its end there are two holes (*ched*). They are bored right through two opposite faces of the beam, and similarly two other holes on the other two faces at right angles to the others—*vide* No. 8, of fig. 24.

The cloth beam (*narad*) is very similar to the yarn beam, except that it is cylindrical, *vide* No. 9, fig. 24.

The yarn beam is made of *sâl* wood, and the cloth beam is made either out of the *sâl* tree wood or palm wood. The warp is kept in a state of tension by the beams being rolled round and then fixed in position, each by means of rods which pass through the holes above-described till they touch the ground at right angles. The rods are made of ordinary bamboo, and are about 2 feet in length. The rod passing through the holes in the yarn beam is called the *dunta*, the other which passes through the cloth beam is called the *tuncho*.

The posts support two bars, which are tied on by string to them. These are called *bahus* (No. 10, fig. 25). Across the centre of these two bars is placed two cross rods of bamboo (chalans) (No. 20, fig. 25). These two cross rods are tied together by means of string with their flat faces sticking to one another. One of these rods (chalan) is used for the purpose of suspending the (*lachni*) which will be described hereafter, and the other for suspending the reed frame.

The loom is enclosed in a frame which has been described.

The arrangement for working is rather a complicated one, and not easy to describe; however, the arrangement must be so adjusted that it can be pulled up and down, alternately the one shaft rising as the other falls.

The device is as follows:—

From one of the *chalans* is suspended three or four *lachnis*, No. 11, fig. 25. They are made out of pieces of bamboo, about 6 inches in length, with a hole through the centre. A thin round bamboo rod, about 3 feet in length (No. 19, fig. 25), passes through these holes. This bamboo rod is suspended from one of the two *chalans* or cross rods. These *lachnis* are placed at right angles to the bamboo rod which passes through the centre.

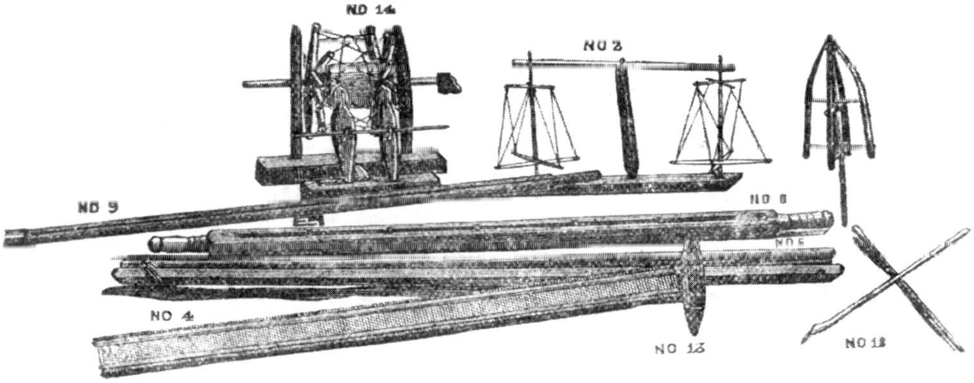

Fig. 24.—Implements for tusser-weaving in the Sonthal Parganas.

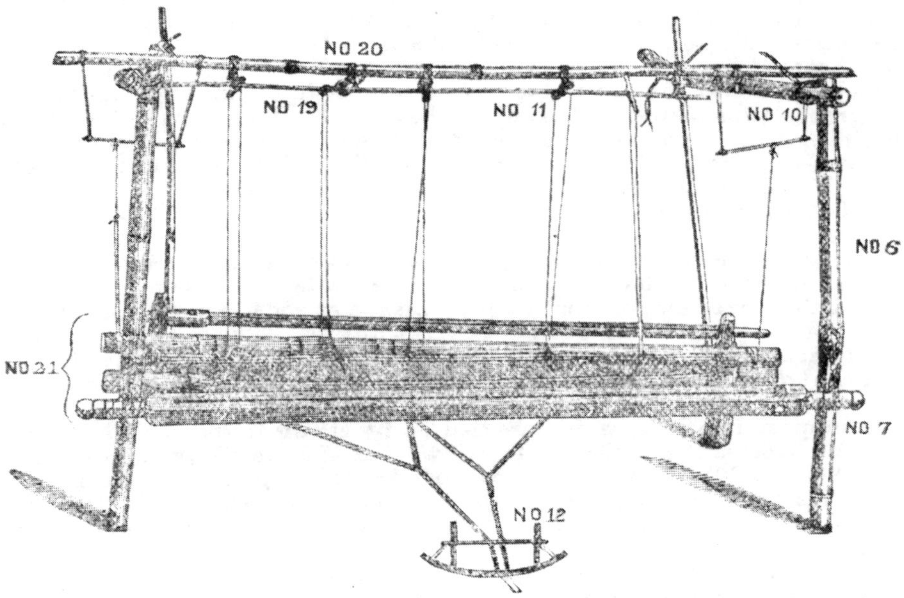

No. 25.—The tusser-weaving loom of the Sonthal Parganas.

The *lachnis* thus lie parallel to the warp. At each end of these (*lachnis*) are attached strings which are connected to the *kanda* and *sik*, corresponding to *sir* and *dangi* of the Murshidabad silk loom. The *kanda* is a thin bamboo rod, about 4 feet in length. The *sik* is similar but a thinner rod. Both are suspended from the *lachnis*. Just below these two thin bamboo rods, another bamboo rod, somewhat thicker, is attached, which is called *pustawan* corresponding to *juthas* of the Murshidabad loom.

The *pustawan* has two holes at the ends, passing right through them. There is a stout string about the thickness of the small finger which passes through them, and is attached to the *kanda* and *sik* on the other side. There are four holes in the *pustawan*, about an equal distance from each other. Through the two inner ones are attached strings which are joined, and this forms the treadle—*vide* No. 12, Fig. 25.

The two upper rods (*kanda* and *sik*) are intended to secure the upper *baw* and the lower to secure the lower *ba*.

The weaver by pressing one treadle pulls down the shaft of healds attached to it. This, in turn, pulls down the *lachni*, and consequently raises the back ends, which drop with them the other shaft of healds. The pressure of the other treadle pulls down the second shaft of healds, and draws up the first, and so on.

The shuttle (No. 13 of Fig. 24) is about 8 to 9 inches in length, and 1½ inches in width, and ½ inch in depth. It is made of cast-iron, and is shaped like a sculling boat. At either end is fixed a piece of wood, 2½ inches in length, shaped like a cone. They are called *mangi*. In the centre is a rectangular hollow, measuring 4 inches × 1½ inches × ½ inch.

In the centre of the hollow is a round small hole (bir); in one of the ends of the hollow is a small hole, and in the other end wall, exactly opposite, is a slit or notch. Those are to receive the spool pins, one end of which is inserted in the hole, and the other fits into the notch, and these secured by a small peg (pakhhir) which is passed through a hole drilled across the notch from one side of the shuttle. It is made out of the spital of the worm (mussi). The shuttles are made by local blacksmiths who belong to the Moreya caste. The spool consists of a length of the silk thread wound in an iron pin. The thread is wound on to a hollow tube first, which is placed on to the iron pin.

The tube is made out of a kind of reed called *nol nurkat*. The iron pin is called *teri*, and the hollow tube *chuchi*.

There is another instrument called the *churka* (No. 14 of Fig. 24 and No. 18 of Fig. 26). It is used for the purpose of winding the thread on to the *chuchi* or hollow tube described above. The hollow tube is placed on to a thin round iron rod or pin. The thread is wrapped round the *churkha*; one end of the thread is attached on to the hollow tube (*churkha*). The person then turns the handle, which sets the wheel in motion, and thus the thread is wound on the hollow tube.

Before weaving proper starts, four processes are gone through.

S. D. O.

Lith. by N. L. Halder. Govt. School of Art. Cal.

FIG. 26 WEAVING AND CHARGING OF SPOOLS.

The first process is warping or *naritana*, already described.

The second is called *sana*. The weaver passes the threads one by one through this *sana* (reed), and attaches one end of the threads on to a bar by means of a stick. The stick (joa) fits into a groove of the bar which is called the (*narad*).

The third process is called *chapti charana*, which consists in attaching the threads on to the *narad* and *chapti*.

The fourth process is the tying of the *baws*, which is done by some thick brown thread. Each thread is tied with this thick brown thread into loops.

Then the *kandas* and *siks*, which have been described above, pass through these loops, and are attached on to the *lachnis* above. Similarly, the lower threads are tied on to the *kanda* and *sik* to the *pustawan* below.

The fifth process is the weaving proper, which is as follows:—

Weaving proper.—The weaver takes his seat in front of the cloth beam, facing the loom.

On the left-hand side of the weaver, within easy reach of him, a supply of spools are kept in an earthen pot (*huroli*) or in a bamboo basket (*mowni*). On his right there is a small vessel containing oil. The oil is used for the *sana* (reed) and for the shuttle as well as the tube.

The weaver then starts his work. He sits on the ground with his legs in a hole (*khad*), as in Fig. 26. The weaver starts pressing one of the treadles with his left foot raising the shafts of the healds, and lowering the other, thus making a gap between the upper and lower threads of the warp, and throwing the intersection against the cloth-beam. The weaver throws the shuttle through the gap with the spool of thread, holding the loose end of thread on the left of the warp (*vide* Fig. 26).

After this is done, the weaver pulls the reed towards him. He then presses the other treadle, making a fresh gap, and proceeds in the same way, with this difference, that the shuttle is passed from right to left. After they have woven about 6 inches of cloth, they put an instrument called a *punni*—*vide* No. 18, fig. 24, which is intended for the purpose of keeping the cloth of a uniform width.

The *punni* consists of two bamboo rods, about 2 feet 6 inches in length, and string is attached on to the two ends. The other two ends contain a fine iron spike or needle made of iron and tied round with string.

When the weaver finds he cannot reach the gap beyond, the pegs are removed from the beams, and the cloth is wound round the cloth beam, and the pegs again adjusted. It takes the weaver only two days for weaving; and in four days' time he will make a piece of cloth 5 yards long and 27 inches wide.

223. The above description of weaving tusser cloth can be very well understood on a reference to the description of silk-weaving in Bogra and Murshidabad. Though *tasar*—weaving is done chiefly in the Godda Sub-division of this district, it is also done by stray weavers living towards the Birbhum side of the Dumka sub-division.

224. ***Hazaribagh.***—No *tasar* cloth is manufactured in the district of Hazaribagh, but *tasar* cocoons are grown, and reeling of the cocoons is also done on a

small scale. The following account has been furnished in the local monograph :—

" There is no silk industry in this district properly so called. *Tasar* cocoons are cultivated to some extent in the jungles on *asan* trees by lower-class people, such as Bhuians, Bhoktas, Sonthals and others. A very small portion of the cocoons is unreeled by a class of people called Patwaris, inhabiting the thanas of Gomia and Kasmar, whence the thread is exported to Azimgur, and sold to the *mahajans* at the rate of Rs. 360 per maund. No silk cloth is woven in this district.

"Almost all the cocoons produced in this district are exported and sold at the rate of Rs. 10 to Rs. 30 per *khari* (a *khari* varies according to local custom, and is equal to 1,300 and sometimes to 2,200 cocoons). The cocoons are taken to Purulia, Katras and Giridih and sold to the *mahajans*. The silk thread which is exported to Azimgur is sold at the rate of Rs. 8 per seer."

225. *Ranchi.*—In Ranchi also no *tasar* cloth is woven, nor is any spinning done; but about a thousand persons earn their livelihood by rearing *tasar* cocoons. The following account of this industry has been furnished by the district officer :—

" Silk-growing is not a profitable occupation in the district of Ranchi ; with the increase in cultivation, it is gradually dying out.

Its production is confined only to a small area of the district. It is reared within the jurisdiction of the police-stations of Tamar, Torpa, Palkote and within some selected areas of the pargana Biru.

There are two kinds of *tasar* cocoons, viz., (1) jungle-bred cocoons ; (2) domesticated cocoons. The latter class are more largely met with than the former.

The jungle cocoons are larger than the domesticated ones, and give much more silk. When the worms are on the trees they are carefully watched by the growers and protected from birds and insects. Cocoons are collected in considerable quantities from the jungle, and eggs are hatched either in the growers' houses or in huts erected for the purpose in jungles.

"There are two harvests or breeding seasons in the year, first of which begins in June and ends in August, while the second begins in September and ends in November. The mode of breeding followed in the district is this :—

When the moths emerge from the cocoons kept for seed, the females are exposed or left to form their connexions whether with the males emerging from the same batch of cocoons or with jungle moths. Impregnation having taken place, the eggs which are immediately laid are collected in baskets or tufts of grass. When in about 8 or 10 days the worms begin to emerge, they are placed on *asan* or *sâl* trees as they devour the foliage of their first location, till finally in about 50 days they spin their cocoons upon the trees. These cocoons, when ready, are picked from the trees, packed in nets and slung to the roof. Twelve days later, they are taken down, the wood extracted, and they are stored.

" The cocoons in their wild state feed upon the following trees—*sâl, kusumb, deota, sida kokire, khowa.* The quality of the cocoon depends not only upon the species of the tree, but upon the soil on which the tree grows.

" The rearing of *tasar* cocoons is not confined to any particular class. The following tribes are found employed in this work—Cheras, Kherwars, Mundas, Uraons, Bhuians, Chamars, Dosadhs, Ghasies. All these tribes are not found exclusively to engage in this work. They are found to rear silk-worms in order to supplement their income from other sources, chiefly agriculture. It is difficult to give an idea of the number of people engaged in silk-rearing industry. It is believed that the actual number would not exceed 1,000.

" Cocoons are sold and counted by *khari*, which contains more than 1,100 or 1,200 cocoons. The cultivators generally receive advances from *mahajans*, chiefly *banias*. When the cocoons are ready, the creditor collects his dues, and the remainder is sold by the producer either to the *mahajans* or to the *hâts*, at prices varying from Rs. 5, Rs. 6 and Rs. 7 per *khari*. Cocoons are exported to Purulia, Birbhum, Mirzapur, Gaya and Patna.

The production of *tasar* cocoons is gradually diminishing. The falling-off is ascribed to (1) increase of cultivation, (2) greater demand for agricultural labour and higher wages, making the production of cocoons a less profitable employment. Collection of cocoons is no longer profitable. There is, it seems, no prospect of improvement of this branch of industry in the near future."

226. *Palamau.*—In this district also there is no manufacture, but cocoon farming for the manufacture of *tasar*, is carried on to a certain extent and as this is a branch of the industry, the following facts may be of interest:—

" Cocoons are farmed chiefly by Cheros, Mallahs, Bhuians and Dosadhs, numbering from 400 to 500 families. With the exception of the Cheros who have a certain position these castes belong to the lower orders of the Hindu community. The process is as follows :—

In the second fortnight of *Kartic* a number of cocoons, generally about 100, are placed in a bag made of paddy straw and kept in a closed room, where they can get neither heat nor light. In the beginning of *Adra Nachhatra* in *Asarh* (about the beginning of July) the cocoons are taken out of the bag, strung on a rope and exposed to the cold. In from two to four days the moth emerges from the cocoons. The males, which are of a reddish colour, are called *phursa*, the female, which is yellow, being called *kir*. They are mated in pairs and kept from morning till about 4 P.M., when they are separated. The females are then fastened together in pairs, their wings being fastened with their fibres, to prevent them from flying. The pairs are gently shaken and placed in a basket, where they lay their eggs. The laying of eggs is generally finished by 7 P.M. In the morning the eggs are gently rubbed with the wings of the moths, the object being to keep them carefully cleaned. In the evening the eggs are put in small cloth bags and exposed to cold during the night, being kept in a dark room during the day. The eggs are hatched by the eighth morning. The young silk-worms are then taken, still in the bags, to *asan* trees. Small cups are then made of leaves of the *bar* tree, in which the silk-worms are deposited. The cups are then closed and fastened to leaves of the *asan* tree, about three or four feet from the ground. The cups are most carefully made with the object of protecting the silk-worms from heat and rain. From now for 30 days the breeders follow a curious custom, the reason of which I am unable to ascertain. They observe the strictest abstinence, not drinking any wine, nor eating meat, onions, garlic, tamarind or turmeric. They will not shave nor allow any women to touch them, and sleep only on mats.

Three days after the cups have been fastened, they are opened again. About one-third of the young worms are generally found dead; the rest are allowed their freedom on *asan* trees. On the evening of the third day they become torpid, and after remaining 24 hours in this state, cast their skins (*kenchur*). They again become torpid in the evening of the fifth day, and after 48 hours in this state, again cast their skin. The process is repeated in six days, the period of torpidity on this occasion being 60 hours. The three stages are called *ekjari*, *dojari*, and *tejari*. The period of 20 days from the time when the worms were first shut up in the leaf cups is called *bisouri*. In another day cocoons will be found all over the trees. By the 15th of *Katric* the cocoons are again collected; a sufficient quantity is left for breeding the next year, the rest being sold to *mahajans*.

The rate is from Rs. 6 to Rs. 10 per lot of 1,200. This lot is called *khari* or *hajar* (*lit.* 1,000) on the same principle, I suppose, as a "baker's dozen."

The *jibanias*, as the breeders are called locally, pay the owners of the *asan* trees Rs.4-8 per sickle, viz., 8 annas as *khutkar* and 4 annas as *patkar*—*khutkar* and *patkar* being a royalty on branches and twigs and leaves, respectively. The rent is calculated, not according to the number of trees occupied, but according to the number of sickles employed; in another word, the number of labourers.

There is no particular centre of the industry, but it flourishes most in Tuppas, Koto, Pundag, Imli, Talleya and Goawal."

227. *Singhbhum.*—There are only a few *Tanti* (*tasar*-weavers) in the Political State of Seraikela in this district. The cocoons are reeled by hand by the weavers themselves and the thread gathered on to *latais*, the cloth being woven in the ordinary loom. The cloths are of yellow colour and are made to measure 5 yards by 44 inches, *i.e.*, the size of *dhuti* or *sari*. The price of one of these is from Rs. 3 to Rs. 4. They are exported to Dacca and other parts of Lower Bengal, and are not much used locally. The trade in these *saries* and *dhutis* is not a very large one. The growing of *tasar* cocoons, which is an industry of considerable importance, may be thus described in the words of the Deputy Magistrate, Mr. P. Meerza :—

"The cultivation of *tasar* cocoons is not peculiar to any particular class of people, but members of most of the different tribes of the place engage in it in addition to their ordinary agricultural pursuits. The people who employ themselves in this work are mainly Hos and Santals, but Dharwas, Gonds, Bhuiyas, Gours or Gowalas, and Kharias also carry on the business. The other occupations of all the above-mentioned classes are chiefly agricultural.

It being as likely as not that people engaged in *tasar* work one year give it up entirely the next, it is almost impossible to form any correct ideas as to the numbers engaged in the trade. In the Kolhan Government estate the average number of cultivators of cocoons is about 4,000 annually. *

The *tasar* silk-worm is reared from eggs hatched artificially in sheds erected by the cultivators for the purpose, near the jungles or in their houses.

Three sorts of cocoons are known in the district; the *naria*, *bagai*, and *dabha*. The two former are obtained from the jungle parent moth the moths laying their eggs in August. The *dabha* cocoons are reared wholly in captivity and are ready for sale in September, the silk derived from them commanding the highest prices.

The process of rearing in some of its stages requires great care on the part of the cultivators. The *naria* and *bagai* cocoons are sought by the cultivators in July and August, being found in the jungles on *sál* trees. They are brought home by the cultivators, and hung up in their houses till the moth forms. The moths are then paired off and placed in small baskets, where they lay their eggs after a few days. The eggs are taken from the above-mentioned baskets and rubbed with ashes, turmeric, and some jungle roots called *raun*, which latter the natives of the place use for fermenting their rice-bear called *haria*. After being rubbed as above, the eggs are placed between leaves sewn together and hung up in the

* The Census tables for silk give no idea of the number of people engaged in Tusser rearing in this and other districts. The return both in 1891 and in 1901 is usually blank (*vide* Table A Part III).

houses. The worms are hatched in from six to nine days, the length of time depending on the strength of the *raun*. They are first discovered by their eating holes in the leaves containing them. The cultivators take the young worms and place them on small *asan* trees, where they are left for a fortnight or so to grow. On their becoming bigger they are placed on larger *asan* trees and left to themselves to form cocoons, which, as a rule, commence to be ready for collection in September. During the earlier stage a little rain is beneficial to the worm, but fatal when the worm grows higher and commences to form its cocoon. The *dabhu* cocoons are the home cocoons, a few being kept each year by the cultivators for the next year's cultivation. They are reared and brought up in the same way as the *naria* and *bagai*, and originally came from one of these two kinds, having derived their present superiority over the *narai* and *bagai* from the fact of their having been tended and kept by the people for several years.

Naria and *bagai* cocoons are never now kept for a future crop of silk-worms.

Besides the above three kinds of cocoons, there is one more known among the natives as the *moorg* or *moonga*. This latter is very rarely found, its peculiarity being that instead of being found hanging from a twig by a circular stem, as is usual, it is formed between two or three leaves. Although it goes by a distinct name, the *moonga* in reality belongs to one of the three classes mentioned, coming from one of their worms and the thread being the same in quality and quantity as of those of the kind to which it belongs.

The good or bad results of a *tasar* crop depend entirely on the weather. As has been said before, rain is beneficial to the worm in its earlier stage, though the reverse later on. Heavy winds also affect them by blowing the worms off the trees, they being unable to find their way back again

Cocoons form in September, October, and November, when they are collected and sold off, being purchased by *mahajans* and *banias* in large quantities, the rates varying, according to market competition and the state of the crop, from Rs. 8 to Rs. 12 a *kahan*, or 1,280 cocoons.

In a good season one cultivator might get between two or three *kahans*, and as in the Government estates of the district he would pay only one rupee for the privilege of being allowed to cultivate *tasar*, this would mean a sensible profit; the time taken up in the whole business, that is to say, from the commencement of the rearing to time of collecting, being about three months and other expenses nominal.

Good crops, however, are uncommon; such great care being necessary and the worms being so easily affected by the weather, that very often several cultivators in the same place have been known to reap absolutely nothing.

The purchasers steam their cocoons after purchase. The method of steaming here is very simple in its arrangement; a perforated chatty with cocoons in it being placed over a chatty of water, which is kept boiling. The cocoons are thus steamed for a short time, till the worm inside dies. They are then dried in the sun, packed up in bags, and sent off to Bankura and other places."

228. *Manbhum.*—The *tasar* weaving industry of Manbhum is of considerable importance, and the following account has been compiled out of the report written by Babu Prasanna Kumar Dass Gupta, Deputy Magistrate. The diagrams illustrating the *tasar* weaving industry of Sonthal Parganas will serve to explain this description also :—

" *Raw material.*—Manbhum is one of the few districts in Bengal in which the silk-worm is reared. The worm is of the *tasar* species. The industry has, however, declined during the last ten years, as jungle has year after year been cleared. Now the weavers of the district depend for the supply of cocoons chiefly on the neighbouring district of Singhbhum, where the industry is carried on, on a large scale by the Kols. Chaibassa is an important cocoon mart from which cocoons are exported in large quantities, not only to this district, but to distance places more largely since the opening of the Bengal-Nagpur Railway. The facility of exportation afforded by the railway has raised the price of cocoons from Rs. 8 to Rs. 10 per *kahan* (1,280) within the last decade; and in consequence the price of silk goods has risen, which has again led to reduced sale. Silk-worms are reared in the thanas Barabazar, Manbazar, and Chandil, chiefly by the Sonthals, and to a small extent by the Kurmis, on jungle trees locally known as *sál* and *asan* and on plum (*kul*) trees. There is no special cultivation for the purpose. Worms are put on here and there on the trees scattered over the jungle like lac-worms. Seeds have to be moved from tree to tree (grafted on as it were) without which cocoons do not grow properly. This process is locally known as *chala*. The period of rearing is from *Sraban* to *Kartic*. An early crop is gathered in *Bhadra*, which is poor in quality* and the cocoons are mostly 'pierced' *i.e.*, pierced through by the worms, and yield a small quantity of bad thread. Those gathered in *Kartic* are good cocoons. The price of cocoons varies from Rs. 4 to Rs. 10 per *kahan* (1,280) according to quality.

Classes of weavers and their social position.—The weavers in the district are *Tantis* who belong to the class known as *Nabasakhs* of the Hindu caste system which includes the *kamars* (blacksmiths), *kumars* (potters), *sankharis* (makers of bangles of conch shell)—all artizans. A Brahmin would drink water touched by them and would accept personal service from them. In Lower Bengal a *Tanti* will not do menial service, but here the poor *Tantis*

* What is intended is evidently this. The cocoons of the first crop being the next generation to the few wild cocoons gathered from jungles, give very healthy result, and are therefore entirely used for seed. But moths cutting out of seed-cocoons spoil them for the purpose of reeling. *Ketha* cloth is made out of *tasar* thread spun out of pierced cocoons. The description of *tasar* silk-worm rearing contained in the Handbook of Sericulture should be consulted

do it. In these days of education the *Tantis* of this district, who are generally illiterate, occupy a much inferior position in society to that of their brethren in Lower Bengal.

Industrial position.—So far as the silk industry is concerned, the *Tantis* of the district are skilful weavers, and rank perhaps next to none in the country except in the matter of dyeing. They cannot make good fast colours as the people of Murshidabad can. Their looms turn out fine and strong textures of various qualities (*vide* samples Nos. 73 to 79). With more capital and improved method of work it would really be a rich industry.

Number of weavers.—According to the last census returns, *Tantis* number 12,911. The industry is confined to only two places in the district—Raghunathpur, a municipal town (about 3 miles from the Adra station on the Bengal-Nagpur Railway), and Singbazar (a village about 4 miles from Purulia) on the Purulia-Bankura road. In Raghunathpur there are about 100 families and in Singbazar about 20. Thus the number of *Tantis* who actually engage in the trade is not perhaps more than 500.

Processes.—The processes are all very simple and of the most primitive character. I arrange them in their order:—

(*a*) Reeling cocoons are boiled for about half an hour in *saji* (crude carbonate of soda) water, and then spread on a piece of cloth under which some ash is spread to enable the excess moisture to dry out; but the cocoons are never exposed to the sun for that purpose. The cocoons, as the local *Tantis* say, must be half moist when they are reeled, or the fibres do not come off easily. After boiling and drying begins the actual process of reeling with the help of an instrument called *latai* or *natai*, to which the ends of four fibres (of four cocoons) are fastened, and the winding of the *natai* makes the cocoons give up the thread. Four cocoons are worked at once for two reasons—(1) to economise labour, and (2) to give the thread the requisite strength. Silk obtained from the upper surface of cocoons is waste silk under which is the good fibre yielding a continuous thread. Waste silk is locally known as *latha*, which is cheap, being sold at 2 seers per rupee, while the price of good silk thread is Rs. 8 to Rs. 9 a seer. Silk thread is rarely exported from the district; what is made is used by local weavers. Reeling is specially the women's province. Women of the family engage in it in their spare hours. They are said to work hard for about three hours from early dawn, and for another three hours after the mid-day meal. One woman takes 15 to 16 days in drawing out a seer of thread. One *kahan* (1,280) of cocoons yields about a seer of thread. A woman gets a rupee for reeling a *kahan* of cocoons, *i.e.*, a seer of thread.

(*b*) Next to reeling is the spreading of threads of the requisite length for the texture to be woven side by side supported on two vertical posts to which the ends of the threads are tied. Some strips of bamboo are made to pass through the lines of threads laterally so that they may not entangle. This process is known as *parani* (warping).

(*c*) Then comes brushing with rice-water. The brush or *kuchi* is made of the grass locally known as *khas khas*.

(*d*) The product is then taken to the loom and folded round a wooden roller in the loom, one end being tied above round another wooden roller. The lines of threads are made to pass through a comb-like instrument called *sana*, each line being thus separated from the other.

(*e*) A spinning wheel is used in order to fold round some sticks (spools) the thread which is to be used in making the warp; this is known as *nuli*, and is placed inside a socket called *maku* (shuttle), which the weaver passes constantly from one end of the woof to the other laterally; this is the actual weaving.

(*f*) *Dyeing*—As I have already stated, the district is deficient in the art of dyeing; ordinary imported dyes are used. But a kind of fast yellow is obtained from the dust over the skin of a kind of jungle fruit known as *kamalaguri*.

Labour.—I have already referred to the labour necessary for the reeling of thread. The other processes require the services of one man for 30 days to turn out a texture of 20 yards. The man's wages are 5 to 6 annas a day. The cost of 20 yards of texture (of the best kind) may be calculated thus:—

		Rs.
(*a*)	Price of two *kahans* of cocoons yielding two seers of thread ...	16
(*b*)	Labour for reeling	2
(*c*)	Ditto weaving, &c.	10
	Total ...	28

The cost per yard is therefore Re. 1-6. There are cheaper stuffs at prices varying from 8 annas to Re. 1 per yard.

Centres.—Raghunathpur is the only important place in this district in regard to silk industry.

Disposal of product.—A portion of the product is sold in local markets and a portion is exported to Calcutta and Dacca by traders from those places. The weavers of this district are not enterprising speculators, and do not know how to carry their own goods to distant places themselves, and very few of them carry on an external trade. I believe there are not more than three or four men who send their goods out of the district.

Weaver's plant and tools.—I described in detail the plant and tools of the weaver in my monograph on cotton industry, submitted with No. 1708R., of 20th March 1897. That portion of the monograph may be regarded as a part of this as well.

Conclusion.—Want of capital and enterprise seems to be the chief cause of the decline in the trade. Exportation of cocoons has, as I have stated, largely enhanced the price of silk goods and led to reduced sale. No protective measure is of course possible; but the *Tantis* of Raghunathpur may with advantage be helped with capital, and the formation of joint-stock companies may be encouraged by advances. This may help in keeping up a useful and rich industry of the district and add to its material prosperity."

229. The appliances used by the tusser weaver are:—

(A) *Charka* or the spinning wheel. Only one person is necessary to work this tool.

(B) The *natai*, the reel and (C) the *charki* which is only a broader *natai* (with a larger circumference). These are sometimes worked together. The man is engaged in transferring ready-made yarn from the *charki* to the *natai*. The *natai* is a simple instrument made of a few strips of bamboo or wood, the upper ends of which meet at a point and the lower are supported on a wooden or bamboo circular base through which an axle (of bamboo strip) passes to the top, which serves the purpose of a handle by which the instrument is turned for rolling up thread. The *charki* consists of two arched pieces of bamboo strips crossing one another and forming four arches on four sides. The circumference must be the same as that of a skein of the tusser yarn, so that the latter may exactly fit on to it. The instrument moves on an axle which may be loosely posted on the ground, as the thread is rolled up on the *natai* to which one end of the twist is fastened before the operation commences.

For (*nari-tana*) *making the warp* (D) certain bamboo sticks about two cubits long are posted on the ground about three cubits apart. Each post is composed of two sticks meeting at the bottom with the upper ends about two cubits apart, thus forming a triangle with the vertex on the ground. A man goes from the first to the last post and back again with two reels on his hands briskly arranging the threads in two layers on two sides of the posts. For the sake of convenience, when the texture is very long the range is shortened by arranging the posts on parallel lines, leaving a passage for the movements of the workman. The number of posts varies according to the length of the texture. *Bithuri kara*, or arranging the lines of threads is only a continuation of the above process. The posts are taken up, and the warp (with the sticks through) is made to occupy a horizontal position. Each line of thread is carefully arranged one after another and the breadth of the texture is obtained. A man brushes the warp after it has been drenched with boiled rice-water (*mar*). The brush or *kushi* consists of a bamboo or a wooden handle attached to a brush made of *khas khas* (*Andropogon Muricata*).

(E) *The tant or the weaving loom.*—The warp is first attached to the loom. There is a pit just below the centre of the lower end of the loom, where the weaver keeps his feet and draws and relaxes thereby the *paisars* by pressing on the wooden knob affixed to two strings suspended from the *paisars*. The arrangement contains the moving principle of the loom. It is known as *as tant garah* (the hollow of the loom).

(F) The *naraj* is a circular-shaped wooden bar to which one end of the texture is fastened by means of a thin stick which is made to pass through the texture over one line and below the next, and is affixed to the *naraj* on a hollow cut on its surface. This stick is known as *bindui*. It is round the *naraj* that the texture is gradually rolled up as the weaving proceeds by winding it by a handle, and thus drawing the texture towards the weaver. The *naraj* is supported on two posts about half cubit high fixed vertically on the ground.

(G) The *tana* consists of two pieces of timber suspended from the roof. There is a comb of reed known as *sana* between these two pieces of timber. The *sana* keeps each line of thread of the warp apart. The *tana* is pulled towards the weaver each time as the *maku* (shuttle) made to pass and repass over and below the two layers of thread in the warp in alternation. The process tightens the woven part of the texture by pressing it towards the *naraj* and giving each line of the warp its proper position.

(H) The *baisars* and the *paisars* form together one apparatus in the loom, the object of which is to keep apart the two layers of thread and also the lines of thread; the *baisars* are two comb-like substances made of two sticks, each with stout threads laterally arranged between them, so as to give them a comb-like appearance; the *baisars* are two sticks below the warp suspended from the *paisars* by strings; the *paisars* have again two strings suspended from them with two wooden balls at their ends. Each of these balls is pressed between two toes of the weaver's each foot, and the action raises and depresses the *paisars* and the *baisars* which enables the shuttle containing the thread of which the woof is made to pass and repass over or below a layer of thread of the warp. The rising and the depression of the apparatus in alternation separate the two layers of threads of the warp and leaves a passage for the shuttle to be passed by the weaver's hand.

(I) *Panikkata.*—It consists of two wooden or bamboo sticks placed across each other with two nails at the ends to keep the texture straight. It is moved forward as the weaving proceeds.

(J) *Atrams.*—These are plain bamboo sticks placed across the warp over some lines of thread below others just to keep the texture tight and preventing the lines of thread from mixing up.

(K) *Bandurkati.*—It is a small stick dividing the lines of thread into two parts, perhaps for convenience sake.

(L) *Siru*—It is the tied-up ends of the collected threads, and is kept lying on the ground or fastened somewhere on the roof.

(M) There is a rope tied to two pegs. The rope is gradually drawn towards the weaver as weaving proceeds and the woven texture is rolled up on the *naraj*.

(N) *Tangnaka.*—The beam supported on two vertical posts from which *tana, sana baisars, paisars* are supported by means of ropes passing through sockets (made of wood) or wheels (like punkha-wheels) to enable the parts named to be raised or depressed alternately: the *tagna* is sometimes suspended from a permanent beam of the house, so that the whole apparatus may be removed out of doors and worked there with the assistance of two vertical posts fixed on the ground to support the *tangna*.

(O) The *maku* or the shuttle. This is a handy iron or wooden frame with an iron rod in the middle to which is affixed the tube with the yarn at whicht he woof is made rolled round it.

The loom described above is that used by the Jolahs. The Tantis' loom is slightly different. There the upper end of the texture is rolled up round a second *naraj* just beyond the *baisars* and, as weaving proceeds, it is moved round giving up the necessary portion of the warp which again (as soon as woven) is rolled up on the first *naraj*. This economises space and keeps the texture tight at both ends.

230. *Gaya.*—The *tasar* weaving industry of Gaya is also of considerable importance, though cocoons are no longer reared in this district. It will be refreshing to read the following somewhat hopeful monograph furnished by Mr. L. S. S. O'Malley, C.S., when so many of the district monographs look upon the silk-weaving industry as a decayed or a dying industry.

" *Extent of the Industry.*—The silk industry is carried on to a very small extent in the Gaya district, being confined to a few particular localities named below :—

(1) In the Sadar Division—
In Buniadganj, Manpur and Gayawalbigha, all within the limits of the Gaya Municipality, and at Chakand, some five miles north of Gaya.
(2) In the Nawada subdivision—
At Kadirganj and Akbarpur.
(3) In the Aurangabad subdivision—
At Daudnagar.

The silk cocoon itself is not produced in this district now. Some ten years ago the silk-worm was reared to some extent in the jungly country south of Sherghati, close to the Palamau border, where *asan* trees, which were once cultivated for the purpose, are still found, but latterly the cocoons have been imported from the Hazaribagh and Palamau districts.

Importance of the industry.—Owing to this limited extent of the industry, the total amount of production is necessarily equally small.

In the villages of Buniadganj and Manpur there are about two hundred and fifty looms: one loom turns out a good piece in three days, and a piece of inferior silk in two or one and-a-half days. If we take two days as the average time, it will be seen that these two villages produce one hundred and twenty-five pieces a day, or to make a rough estimate, allowing for the slack season of suspended labour, 30,000 pieces in the year, for in the Gaya district silk-weaving is essentially one which is liable to slack periods, and in which continuous and consistent labour throughout the year is not prevalent.

The highest value of these pieces is Rs. 8, the lowest price obtained for *bafta* (mixed *tasar* and cotton) is 10 or 12 annas. As a matter of fact, pieces of the best silk are not usually woven, and are generally made only for special orders. On the average, pieces, the value of which ranges from Re. 1 to Rs. 5, are common. If we take the average as Rs. 2-8 per piece, the annual outturn may be roughly estimated at Rs. 75,000 annually. The outturn for Kadirganj and Akbarpur is estimated at 6,000 yards, valued at Rs. 5,000 for the year just past; that of 1897-98 at 6,800 yards, valued at Rs. 5,100, so that Rs. 5,000 may be taken under present conditions as the average value of the products for the year; this silk, however, is extremely coarse and of poor quality. The report for this year from this subdivision on the subject of the total supply of silk fabrics has not yet been submitted: for 1897-98 it was 200 *thâns* or pieces, each of eight yards, calculated to be worth Rs. 600, allowing Rs. 3 per yard.

It is difficult to make anything but a rough calculation of the amount and value of the cloth woven in Gayawalbigha, where there are only five families of weavers, and at Chakand, where there are 14 families. Perhaps Rs. 500 might be taken as the maximum value of the products of these two places. The total annual outturn of the district might be valued at a rough estimate at Rs. 81,100.

Present condition of the industry.—The present state, however, of the industry cannot be regarded as bad, or its prospects as gloomy. The value of the outturn for 1890-91 (to take a period of some considerable duration, in order to facilitate a comprehensive view) was valued at about Rs. 18,000 at Gaya and at Nawada at Rs. 7,500, *i.e.*, for the whole district, at Rs. 25,500 in all. The year before the total outturn was estimated at only Rs. 22,000, so that in the last decade the industry may be said to have made very great strides. At that time the centres of silk-weaving were the same as now, but at Daudnagar the *patwas* were reduced to such a low pitch, and the silk industry had so far declined, that the Subdivisional Officer at Aurangabad made no reference to it in his report. The *patwas* there had taken to weaving only cotton, and many of them had had recourse to ordinary labour to eke their living.

At Buniadganj and Manpur there were nearly 200 families of *patwas*, but silk-weaving was in the hands of only 40 families, employing about 170 hands. Most of the *patwas* had given up silk for the weaving of cotton cloth, and many families were obliged during the off season to work as labourers.

At the present time, out of nearly 300 families, about 100 work on silk and *bafta* regularly, and the proportion of those who have to work as ordinary labourers has largely decreased.

In Kadirganj and Akbarpur there were only about 30 families working in silk ten years ago, where there are now about 60 families weaving. In recent years there has been a great advance in the amount produced here. They produced—

				Rs.
In 1895-96, 3,000 yards worth	...	...	...	1,500
In 1896-97, 3,100 „ „	...	...	...	1,550
In 1897-98, 6,800 „ „	...	...	...	5,100
In 1898-99, 6,000 „ „	...	...	...	5,000

the last year showing a slight decrease, which may not be permanent.

The quality of the silk woven here has lately improved, as may be seen by a comparison of the values of the years 1897-98 and of 1896-97. At the same time it must be admitted that in spite of this recent improvement, the industry has declined since 1890-91, when the outturn was valued at Rs. 7,500. At Daudnagar, where the industry has recovered something of its old vitality, we find that the outturn for 1895-96 was estimated at 202 pieces of 8 yards each, the value per piece being between Rs. 2-8 and Rs. 3. The total value of 1,616 yards was estimated at about Rs. 600.

In 1896-97, it fell to 800 yards, valued at about Rs. 300, but this was probably due to the prevailing scarcity, as in 1897-98 the supply rose again to 1,600 yards at Rs. 600.

At present it is reported that fifteen families carry on the industry, which is admitted to be flourishing in comparison with past years.

Future Prospects.—The silk produced by the *patwas* in the Gaya district is generally of a coarse description. The silk produced is *tasar*, the cocoon from which it is woven being the *antheræa paphia*: much of it is remarkable neither for durability nor beauty. The class rich enough to buy it is necessarily rather small, and generally able to purchase a better kind of silk cloth, such as that of Murshidabad, which greater cheapness of carriage puts upon the market at a reduced rate; such competition naturally tells against the home-made stuffs. The result is that the cloth woven tends to deteriorate in quality; the best kinds are now rarely woven, and the quantity of *bafta* (or mixed *tasar* and cotton) increases.

The weavers also complain that they can only produce slowly and in small quantities, while their want of capital prevents their being able to tide over a bad year, so that in a way they may be said to live from hand to mouth. At the same time, however, there appears to be no reasonable grounds for apprehension, at least for some time, that this industry will decline. The town of Gaya supplies a market for their goods: it is to Gaya and to the vicinity of Nawada that all the silk woven in the Nawada subdivision is sent; coarse as is the material made at Chakand, it has a sale in Gaya, while the *patwas* of Gayawalbigha weave good *dhotis*, which are bought by Gayawals and those connected with them.

The cloth of the Daudnagar weavers likewise obtains a local sale, which does not extend beyond the district, but they produce practically no pure silk cloth, but only *bafta*.

The cloth woven at Buniadganj and Manpur is sold at their doors in Gaya town, though this village differs very largely from the other centres of the industry, as it exports largely to Azimgarh, and has *banias* who export to many parts of India. The best cloth is sold in Gaya itself, though this is not of any high merit; the ordinary cloth is generally sent away. Gaya itself offers a good market, owing to the great number of pilgrims who are glad to take away a piece of the silk made here.

For the most part *thâns* or pieces are woven for *angas*, *chapkans*, *kurtas*, and also *saris* and *chudders*. The weavers themselves are proud of the fact that the Manpuri silk is used for *murdaris* in which to wind the dead, and that these are exported all over India.

The weavers, their social and industrial condition.—The families of the weavers (*patwas*) themselves on the whole manage to earn a competence by weaving alone, in spite of the evils of intermittent labour, for the busy season, beginning in December, after the best crop of cocoons, lasts for four months, in which nearly half of the total outturn is produced, and the rest of the year is more or less a slack time for work.

Most of them have only one loom, but some have as many as four or five. In the villages of Buniadganj and Manpur, out of the 100 families of regular weavers, no less than 14 families are assessed for income-tax from Rs. 10 to Rs. 20, sums which represent an income of Rs. 500 to Rs. 1,000. The maximum daily wage of a family with four or five looms is Rs. 4. But in the last two years the number of these more prosperous families has decreased from 18 to 14, in itself probably an economical advantage, caused by the levelling up of wages. The ordinary *patwa* gets only two annas a day. The great merit of the industry is that it gives employment to men, women and children; the first weave, the second spin, and the third set the warp. Labourers are not employed by the *patwas* at all.

A man who weaves *bafta* will work three yards at the most a day, and gets four annas per yard, or else works about two and-a-half yards of coarse *tasar* for eight annas per yard. The price, in fact, of the cloth naturally varies according to its quality from four annas to two rupees; but of this best cloth only one and-a-half yards at the utmost can be woven in the day. A woman gets five Gorakhpuri pice for a day's spinning, *i.e.*, for one *chitak* of spun silk. For waste silk, they get one rupee for six seers; formerly the rate used to be two rupees per seer.

The small profit derived from this is compensated for by the small expense of materials, as even a loom with all its parts only costs about Rs. 2-4, and the Daudnagar weavers are reported to pay one rupee only for their set of instruments (*patata, narad, rach, chopta charkhi*). These instruments are all made by local carpenters and last for 25 years, the *karigah* being said to last even longer.

Besides this main source of profit, a small quantity of surplus silk is made up for children's charms, which are sold in the village, and not exported like the pieces. This is made in a very rough-and-ready fashion, the only instruments necessary being a wooden *reel* and an *ankusá*, or iron hook with a ring which goes round the toe.

The cocoons (*kowa*) are all imported from Palamau, and also from Hazaribagh. The rate is eight rupees for a *kárhi* (further east called a *kahan*), *i. e.*, an aggregate of 1,346 cocoons.

In Buniadganj there is a monopoly in the hands of two brokers who act as middlemen; they get a commission of one per cent. on the sales from their principals in Palamau.

The *patwas* resident in the villages of Buniadganj and Manpur do not appear to be natives of this part of the country; their own account is that the village was founded by Raja Man Singh and named after him. They were brought here by him 'from the direction of the Rohtas hills,' and their dialect lends colour to the idea that they came from Central India. Moreover, out of the twelve *banias* who deal in silk, no less than eight are not natives of the place, but come from Mobarakpur in Azimgarh district. The practice is for them to come here for nine or ten months in the year and superintend the manufacture; they find wages and work cheaper here, though the finer qualities of silk are not manufactured here for them, but in Azimgarh. They only take woven pieces and not spun silk, and are the means by which these cloths are sent over other parts of India.

The process of manufacture, beginning with the raw material, the cocoon, and ending in the finished fabric, may be divided into the following stages:—

(1) The preparation of the cocoon.
(2) Spinning.
(3) Warping.
(4) Weaving.

The preparation of the cocoon.—The first step in this evolution is indispensable for the purpose of extracting silk from the cocoon. For this purpose, the number of cocoons required for use are put into *gharas;* in these some *sajjimitti* is placed, and then water is poured in, the object of the former being to soften the water.

This is then boiled for three hours; after this the vessel is taken from the fire, and, when sufficiently cool, the cocoons are taken out: the chrysalis (*pilu*) inside is dead, and the outer husk of silk has been softened sufficiently to enable the spinner to manipulate it. It only remains to clean it. In order to effect this, the cocoons are placed in baskets, and cold water poured over them, by the percolation of which the cocoon is properly cleaned and ready for spinning.

Spinning.—This is done entirely by women. The spinster sits down with a spindle in her right hand, and two pots by her left side, in one of which she has put as many cocoons as there are to be filaments in the thread of silk which she spins, while the other is filled with water. Generally she spins from four cocoons simultaneously, the strand being composed of four filaments.

She first draws out a thread with her thumb and index finger and spins off waste silk upon a separate spindle kept for this purpose. This waste silk (*pheti*) is sent to Calcutta to be worked up by more expert weavers, as here the weavers are not skilled enough to deal with it. When it has been spun off, she draws out a filament of the *tasar* silk proper from each cocoon after first wetting the cocoon itself, her left leg just above the knee, and her winding reel, which is generally called *natai* (though the word *charkhi* is also used). This is done in order to get a hold upon the silk, and attach it to the *natai*, when she begins to spin. This is a cone-shaped reel, which revolves round a spindle. The framework of this cone consists of four pieces of bamboo set at an equal distance from each other, and with a base of four slips of bamboo set diagonally. When ready to work, the spinster lays the four filaments already attached to the *natai* across her wetted leg, and moves her left hand backwards and forwards, so as to twist them into one strand, while her left hand is busy turning the *natai*, which receives and winds the thread.

This spinning requires an extremely delicate hand and light touch, not only for twisting the silk, but also for joining, when one or more of the filaments break; this seems to be done without any effort: as a matter of fact, this technical skill is only acquired by learning to spin in early childhood; not unfrequently a spinster spins from as many as twelve cocoons. This is the maximum number of filaments used, and this thicker thread is only employed when the best cloth has to be produced; the minimum appears to be four cocoons.

An ordinary spinster will spin from as many as eighty or ninety cocoons in the day, producing one *kanama* or chitak of silk; she receives five Gorakhpuri pice for her day's work, but it is doubtful if this means very continuous labour.

After the silk has been spun on the *natai*, it is left to dry. When it is dry and glossy, it is taken off and made into small "knots" or skeins about three inches long, called *kharchi;* the silks in these are subsequently joined together in larger skeins, and put once more on to *natais* for the purpose of setting the warp.

Warping: setting the warp.—The process of setting the warp is, for practical purposes, uniform, though where the length of the warp is small, slight modifications are introduced. For the larger warps, pairs of sticks (*sar*) are fastened in the ground at equal distances, in two parallel straight lines; the number of pairs varies according to length: at the end of each line a large post is fixed, and close to each of these is a smaller post.

As a general rule the women of the family perform this work, and they walk outside the lines holding in each hand a *natai*, on which the silk is wound: the reel revolves and pay out silk as they walk, and the two lines are passed between each pair of sticks (*sar*) in opposite directions. The result is that at each pair of sticks (*sar*) the threads interlace, and the threads at this point of intersection are kept separate, the thread of one *natai* passing from right to left, and that of the other from left to right. Where the warp to be set is smaller, the process is somewhat different. In this case there are also two parallel lines with two stout posts, about 2 feet high, but at one end there is another post standing a foot or so beyond the lines and at an equal distance from each.

Taking a length of, say, twenty to thirty feet, there will be four *sars* altogether in each parallel line, but these are of different character, as they are not sticks or posts fastened in the ground: the two middle *sars* consist in each case of a solid base of dried *mitti* (clay) broad enough at the bottom to stand firmly. In this there are four bamboo splints about 2½ feet high; the two *sars* which flank these on either side have only two splints of bamboo fastened in this base.

The reel also is different: it is long and straight, consisting of two parts, one the iron axle, *kunda*, about 1½ feet long, which is held in the hand, and the other the wooden reel, about 6 inches long, on which the silk is wound, and which revolves, and pays out the silk.

In this case the operator walks up and down, on one side of, and not round, the posts. In this case also she has two reels, which she passes in and out of two of the bamboo splints of the central *sars*, and through those of their next.

In each case, the crossing of the thread helps to keep them distinct and separate.

When all the thread has been set upon these *sars*, the thread on the post at the end of the two lines is cut, and the thread removed; it is then made up into a big hank called *lunrhi*, and afterwards set upon the loom.

This process obtains in the case of cotton no less than silk, but with silk the process employed of wetting and brushing with a preparation of mustard oil is not resorted to. The silk is naturally so smooth and glossy as to preclude any necessity of smoothing and brushing out irregularities. However, before transferring the warp to the loom, it is stretched and spread horizontally at a height of 3½ feet from the ground; the upper and lower sets of thread are quite distinct and separate; they only interlace at each end, where there are three bamboos at the crossing of the threads; except at the ends, the threads lie smoothly and evenly.

The warp is suspended in mid-air by means of the support of a trestle-shaped stand (*dogra*); the end bamboo keeping the threads crossed is called *danrhi*, the next two *cheurh*; the stand itself is secured by a rope, fastened to a peg in the ground, which is tight enough to keep the warp straight and firm, till it is transferred to the loom.

Weaving proper.—The loom itself is worked by one *patwa*, who sits with the loom before him, and with his legs in a small pit, in which are placed the treadles (*paunri*), with which he works the loom. His method of weaving is as follows:—

In front of him stretches the warp, with its upper and lower layers of threads: separated between them he slides his shuttle (*kaparbinni*): this is a canoe-shaped iron instrument hollowed to contain the needle (*tiri*), on which the silk thread is wound, and on which the tube (*chuchchi*) revolves, the whole being called *nari*; the latter is kept in its place by a small peg made of a big sort of feather (*pakhnari*), and pays out thread as it revolves inside the shuttle, which is pushed into and slides between the two sets of threads.

When it has passed through, the *patwa* pulls forward a wooden frame (*hatha*) suspended from a bamboo bar above his head.

This *hatha* consists of three parts: the upper, a heavy bar, the lower, a light bit of bamboo, while between them is a comb of fine reeds, keeping apart the threads of the warp, each of which is set between two of these reeds, and separated thereby from the next.

This *sana* (as it is called in Gaya, besides a variant word *rachh*) hangs from an upper bamboo (*parkha*), from which the *nachni* are also suspended.

At the same time the *patwa* works his treadles with the feet, the result of which is to move the healds (*bai*), and thereby alternately raise and depress each set of threads of the warp; they are connected with the *nachni* already mentioned, a small lever about 6 inches long, so called because its movements, which correspond to the working of the treadles, suggest the motions of dancing.

It must not be forgotten that behind these treadles are two sets of reeds (*ban*) separating the two sets of thread, and that the intersection of the threads not yet worked upon by the weaver is still preserved.

The *patwa* is not only busy with the weaving of fresh cloth, but he is obliged, at the same time, to secure the web already woven: this he does by means of two elastic bows, consisting of two arches (*kanti*), connected by strings: these strings are pushed along the bow to tighten it; by this means he regulates their tension, and adjusts their lengths exactly to the width of the cloth. At the end of each arm is a pin, which is fastened at either side of the cloth, and keeps them in their places.

The cloth itself is fastened to a roller immediately in front of the weaver (*chanpal*), which is also used for winding up the cloth when woven. This is supported by two short posts about 1½ feet high (*khunta*); it rests upon the left-hand one (*banuaria*), and passes through the right-hand one, which in shape recalls a tongue, and is consequently called *jibhela*. The portion of the warp which has still to be woven is tied up by a piece of wood (*dansa*), which is itself supported by pillars, or rather wooden posts; there is no loose end to it, but it ends off just as the cloth will when woven: it is kept tight by a string which is brought back close to the weaver's left hand, and which enables him to tighten or relax the warp as necessary. From the above account it will be easily gathered that the means of ornamentation of the cloth can be readily supplied by charging the shuttle with the different coloured silks required; in this way the cloth may be shot with various coloured threads, and bars of different colours may be introduced into the plain background of the silk.

This is the method also in which the *bafta* (mixed *tasar* and cotton) is introduced. The warp is composed entirely of silk, and the shuttle introduces the woof of *sut* (cotton).

Where, as is generally the case, the piece is left in the natural colour, nothing remains, when it has been woven and removed from the loom, but to stiffen it with a preparation of rice water (*manrh*).

If bright colours are considered desirable, it is handed over to the dyer. It is noticeable that in this district the cheap English aniline dyes are not used for silk, as they always are now-a-days for cotton. Native dyes, carmine and yellow by preference, are exclusively employed, but this is a subject which does not legitimately belong to the province of silk-weaving proper."

231. *Patna.*—In the Bihar subdivision of the district of Patna, potia or *tasar* silk cloth is manufactured to a certain extent. The extent and nature of the industry are detailed in the following extract from the district monograph:—

"*Potia* is silk cloth as manufactured by Bihar weavers. The process is as follow:—

Tasar cocoons are imported into the Bihar subdivision from the Bhagalpur and Hazaribagh districts by Beni Shah and Jhanda Shah, of Alinagore, in Bihar town, who sell them to other dealers. Cocoons are purchased in batches of 325 *gandas*, called locally *hari*. The price varies from Rs. 5 to Rs. 8 per *hari*.

Cocoons should be hard. Soft cocoons are of little value, their price being fixed according to their quality.

Spinning.—A class of Hindus called *patwas* purchase the cocoons and boil them in earthen pots in a solution of crude carbonate of soda, *saji*, for about two hours. After this as soon as cool, they are washed in cold water and are then kept under shade so that they may remain damp. They are then taken, one by one, and strand of thread is drawn out of the cocoon, with thumb and index finger of the right hand, and attached to a spindle, on which it is wrapped by the revolutions of the spindle. From this the thread is afterwards transferred to a *latami* (pyramidal bobbin made of bamboo *lathies*). About $1\frac{1}{4}$ or $1\frac{1}{2}$ *chitaks* of thread are wound in the *latami* in a day. Each *latami* contains thread of about 20 cocoons. This is removed and made into a bundle, which is called *auti*. The bundles are then dried and stored for use in receptacles so that vermin may not injure them. The price of thread varies from Rs. 8 to Rs. 10 per seer of 80 *tolas* weight. The quality of the thread is determined by its fineness or otherwise.

Pierced cocoons are also spun by the above process and are utilised for textile purposes. The thread of pierced cocoons is comparatively thicker and is used as woof (*bharni*) at the time of weaving. This thread is also made into a coarse kind of cloth called *potia*. Coarse *tasar* cloth is sometimes made in Bihar and sells for Rs. 6 per piece of 10 yards.

Steaming.—An earthen pot containing boiling water is kept on an oven, and another pot with small holes bored below it, and containing a number of cocoons, is placed over it, and is kept there for steaming for about half an hour. This steaming kills the chrysalis within. The cocoons are then taken out and dried for purposes of reeling, which can now be easily done.

The wage of the person who does the reeling is generally Re. 1 per seer of thread. One *hari*, *i.e.* 325 *gandas* of cocoons, is said to yield a seer of *tasar* thread.

Winding and weaving.—Before warping, the weavers soak the bundles of thread in a mixture of rice flour and water. Each seer of thread is wetted in half a seer of flour mixed with five seers of water. When coloured *tasar* cloth is required, the thread is coloured before being wetted with the above mixture. When the skeins are saturated they are loosened and wound in a thin bamboo wheel called *charkhi*. The end of the skein is then attached to a *latai*, and the thread is transferred to the *latai* by keeping it turning with the right hand, while the thread is made to pass between the thumb and index finger of the left hand. After making the thread into convenient bundles and skeins, they are ready for warping

Warping.—The warping is commenced by placing the skeins again round the *charkhis*. Two at a time are held in both hands and laid alternately against the two side of the bamboo *lathi*, called *sirai*, which are supported by *kilas* or pegs on both sides. The warps are made from 10 to 100 yards long, according to the capital of the weavers. During warping, bamboo *lathis* are placed at convenient distances to keep the thread separate, and also to help at the time of weaving flowers or checks on the cloth. Bleaching is done on the warp.

Setting of loom.—When warping is finished, the loom is set and the warp is tied to it and is wrapped round the warp beam, called *chapti*, at one end; the other end is fixed to the cloth beam, called *nardi*. As the weaving proceeds, the cloth is wrapped round the beam, and the warp is set free from time to time from the other beam.

Weaving.—The skeins of weft thread are transferred to a little piece of reed, called *nari* or *chuchhi*, and are placed in shuttles called *dhirkies*. The weavers of Bihar work single-handed. Introducing the spools, using of the loom, &c., are done by one man. The looms and the working of them are similar to those used in weaving cotton cloth.

One man can weave about 2½ yards of cloth in a day. For weaving a *thân* of 10 yards long the weaver gets Re. 1 as wages.

Coloured *dhutis* and *saris* are also manufactured in Bihar, and are used by bridegrooms and brides at time of marriages. The colours liked best by the people are yellow and red. The *thâns* or pieces of 10 yards length are usually of the natural colour of *tasar*.

Thâns in pieces of 10 yards length are seldom sent to other parts of the country for sale, as they generally obtain ready sale in Bihar.

No reliable statistics can be obtained about the actual outturn, as looms do not work the whole year in weaving *tasar* cloth. Cotton cloth and cloth of a mixture of cotton and silk are also woven during the greater part of the year. There are approximately 200 looms in the Bihar subdivision. The estimated outturn of each loom, according to the weaver, is 30 *thâns* a year. *Tasar* cloth made in Bihar is sold to *mahajans*, who visit the villages periodically. These people take the cloth to Calcutta and elsewhere. *Tasar* cloth is also sold to residents of Bihar. The weavers allege that they do not keep any account.

The price of a *than* or piece of *tasar* cloth varies from Rs. 4 to Rs. 9.

The following persons are reported to be local experts in the making of *tasar* cloth :—

Sukul Patwa, of Nipura.	Gopal Patwa, of Alinagore.
Chamari Patwa, of Silas.	Kirti Patwa, of ditto.

While *tasar* cloth is made by Tantwas, a few Jolahas also make very fine muslins, in imitation of Dacca muslin, in Assanagore within Bihar town. The *tani* of this cloth is of cotton thread and the *bhurni* (woof) is of *tasar* silk. The process is similar to that followed in the making of *tasar* cloth. The weavers also make flowers of different patterns on the muslin. This is done while the cloth is on the loom.

The Tantwas who make *tasar* cloth are Hindus, and Jolahas are Muhammadans : the former consider themselves higher socially than Jolahas, and they are also better off than them. Jolahas, who have been successful in business and have means, are usually ashamed to call themselves Jolahas and use the word "Sheikh" before their names. The number of Tantwas and Jolahas is not known."

232. *Balasore.*—The following short account of the industry has been furnished from Balasore:—

"SILK industry is not carried on on an extensive scale in this district. Among important industries it has no place. Of its various branches the only kind of silk manufactured here is *tasar* silk The article manufactured is not of a superior quality. The industry, such as it is, is carried on by some 200 persons altogether in the whole district. By far the greater number of these people live in the northern part of the district, in the villages of Patpur and Kaibonia; the rest are inhabitants of the village of Purusanda, within the Bhadrak subdivision. The manufacturers of the northern part are not confined to any particular caste. They are real natives of the soil, and a Brahmin is as much at liberty in this part of the country to engage himself in the manufacture of *tasar* silk as a Kapudia, a Bania, a Raju, a Jola, or a man of any other caste. This manufacture is not, however, their sole occupation. They follow their respective avocations, and consider the industry as only a supplementary means of augmenting their limited income. They perform the same religious rites and are governed by the same social customs as are obligatory upon those of their castes who have no concern with this particular industry. Such is, however, not the case with those men who dwell within the jurisdiction of the Bhadrak subdivision. They are known as Bengali *Tantis* (weavers), and not original natives of the soil, from whom, however, they are at present hardly distinguishable, inasmuch as having migrated from Bengal and settled down in this district years ago, they now speak the language of the country of their adoption, and have, more or less, accommodated themselves to the conditions of their environs They number only about 50 men, all told, but silk manufacture is their sole occupation. A man is excommunicated for ploughing land with his own hand.

Among both these classes of men, the rearing of silk-worms or cocoons does not form any part in the process of manufacture. They purchase cocoons from the Sonthals and the Bhumijes of the Garjat (Mourbhanj and Keonjhar) at the rate of about 200 per rupee, then boil them in hot water, reel them and gradually draw out all thread out of them. Afterwards they knead the thread with a paste of boiled potatoes, dye them, weave them by using ordinary looms, and thus manufacture cloths both for males and females. The article thus manufactured, after meeting the demand of the local consumers, mostly Hindus, who have to use such cloths for the various religious ordinances, goes to the merchants of the towns of Balasore and Cuttack and at Mahmed Nagar, Patna, within the Jellasore thana. Silk thread is not sold. It has been roughly calculated that altogether cloths to the value of Rs. 5,000 are sold by the manufacturers of this district annually. The local name of the cloth is *katia*.

It has been already mentioned that silk-worms and cocoons are reared by the Sonthals and Bhumijes of Mourbhanj and Keonjhar. The worms are black in colour and feed upon the leaves of *asan* trees. The months intervening between the end of the rainy season and the beginning of the cold weather are chosen for the rearing of cocoons. Hundreds of men are engaged in this pursuit. Each man takes charge of 100 insects and places them on the leaves of the *asan* trees, himself living in a temporary hut hard by, on one meal a day and strictly on vegetable diet. He believes that the least diviation from this practice would cause death among the insects or induce them either to fly away or refuse to feed upon the leaves. He watches the insects anxiously every day, and finds them gradually weaving the cocoons within which they would at last shut themselves. As soon as the cocoons are completely formed, the man puts them in hot water and kills the insects within, for otherwise, they would cut their way out through the shells and spoil them, for pierced cocoons are not purchased by the manufacturers of *tasar* cloth in this district."

233. *Puri.*—In Puri *tasar* silk weaving is confined only to a few families in the subdivision of Khurda. The following description of the industry has been furnished by the Subdivisional Officer of Khurda :—

"The only kind of silk industry in the subdivision consists of *tasar* cloths, and the only castes who weave them are the Gouria Patras and the Asani Patras.

The Gouria Patras consist of 16 families with a population of only 32, and the Asani Patras consist of 25 families with a population of 60. The social position of the two weaving classes noted above ranks just above that of the Uriya Tantis, who stand 24th in the general social scale of the Hindus, comprising of 68 castes.

Subjoined is a description of the process of weaving. *Matha boulpata, panchi*, and *kantia* are the different kinds of silk fabrics prepared within the subdivision.

The Patras sell their cloths to consumers of neighbouring villages and hâts and to *beparis* or traders at their house and their neighbouring hâts, which are chiefly the following :—

Names of Hâts.

In Khurda.	Elsewhere.
Lingipur.	Pargana Lembai, zilla Puri, Sadar subdivision—
Sarkantar.	Ghororia.
Bhaliabari.	Atharbhaga.
Narangar.	In Banki, district Cuttack—
Chhangiri.	Tulisipur.
Tangy.	Charchika.
Bengi Tangy.	Kalapathar.
Banpur Bazar.	In killa Ranpur—
	Ranpur.

The *tasar* cloths made in this subdivision are chiefly consumed locally, and are only partially taken by *beparis* or traders to neighbouring places in the Puri Sadar subdivision, the Cuttack district, killas Ranpur, Nayagarh, Narsingpur, Daspalla, and Tigiria.

The Patras like all the middle classes of Orissa also partially cultivate lands.

The Patras or the weaving class procure the raw silk from killa Keonjhar. They boil the raw silk with hot water, which process separates the silk (or *tasar*) from the husk or the covers protecting the silk within it.

After the silk is separated from the husk it is dyed* and made into bundles, and the process of *kanda*, or the preparation of the thread for the use of the weaver, follows.

The use of *areta* and *sana charki* is required for the preparation of the *kanda*.

The *areta* consists of a wooden base, both ends of which are fixed to two sticks. To these two sticks at the top is fixed another stick. A heavy block of wood in the shape of a globe is attached to the horizontal stick, at the top of which also a bundle is attached. The globe revolves when the handle is turned round. There is a piece of iron splinter called *takuri* which is attached to the globe and revolves with it. *Sana charki* is composed of a small stick, 12 or 15 inches long, thrust into a hole of a circular piece of stone, which serves as the base, and from the top of this main stick four or five other slender pieces diverge out inclined in an acute angle to the main stick. Some threads are twisted round this instrument, and of this a single thread is attached to the *takuri*. One end of the *takuri* is thrust into a piece of tube. The bundles of silk are presented to the machine, the bundle is worked out, the *takuri* and *areta* whirl in opposite directions, and the silk is spun into thread. The threads are first twisted round the *sana charki* and then all round the tube. This completes the process of *kanda*.

The thread is moistened with *chuda* or flattened rice water. Half the quantity of the thread is kept wet for the weaver's shuttle, while the other half is twisted round the *nati*.

The weavers fix into the ground (in a rectangular form according to dimensions of the piece of cloth) four pieces of wood, each 6 inches long, and keeping the threads in the *ukuni* take the shuttle in one hand and *ukuni* in the other and then twist the threads all round the aforesaid pieces of wood. This part of the work is called *lundicora*.

Construction of baw.—It is composed of two pieces of well polished, round and split bamboos, attached to each other by means of firm strings. Both on and below this machine threads are fastened and meshes are formed of them. This is the chief instrument of weaving.

A piece of bamboo stick is thrust into one end of the *lundi*, and this stick is fastened at its middle point with a firm string which again is fastened tight to a pole fixed on the ground at a distance. Now another piece of stick is thrust into the other end of the

* The weavers procure European chemical powders, and with them they dye the *tasar* threads before they are used for weaving purposes. Formerly the weavers used to dye the same with dyes prepared by themselves.

lundi and two pieces of strings are tied at both the ends of the stick, and these strings are again tied to two *ghoras*. The *ghora* is a pair of splinters of bamboos fastened crosswise. The strings mentioned above are tied just at the point of intersection of the two splinters which the *ghora* consists of. These two cross-pieces are attached tight to two other sticks fixed firmly to the ground. Now the *lundi* is stretched quite tight, and the weaver separates the several threads and makes them quite apart from each other and here and there thrusts some other bamboo splinters into the *lundi*. These bamboo splinters are called *tiaricathi*. Now, if the single threads are found to be torn, then the weaver joins them. Then the threads are cleaned by means of a brush called *kancha*, which is made of a kind of grass. The brush is wetted with rice gruel before it works. This process is called *tasan* in preparation of the thread for weaving.

Now the *lundi* thread is taken into the loom. Here the *lundi* is called *punian*. By certain contrivances, one set of threads are laid in one direction and another in the opposite, so that when the weaver by means of his legs sets in motion some part of the loom, where the *lundi* has been fixed, the threads are entwined round across each other, and thus make a fabric. Along with this fabrication goes on the process of *varani*, *i.e.*, the *kanda* is kept in a small canoe-shaped instrument called *nali*, which is very skillfully and rapidly made to pass across the abovementioned threads breadthwise. This completes the process of weaving."

231. As the diagrams illustrating the description of the tasar weaving industry of Sonthal Parganas serve also to illustrate the descriptions of the same industry in the districts of Bihar and Chota Nagpur, so also would one set of illustrations (figures 27 and 28) serve to illustrate the industry for all the districts of Orissa. The resemblances between the different silk-weaving appliances used all over Bengal are indeed quite obvious, though the Bengal Bihar and Orissa types are quite distinct, and the vernacular names also differ somewhat for the three provinces, though some of the names such as *baw* and *maku* are pretty universal.

Fig. 27.—Tasar reeling and weaving appliances of Jajpur (Cuttack.)

Bengal type.

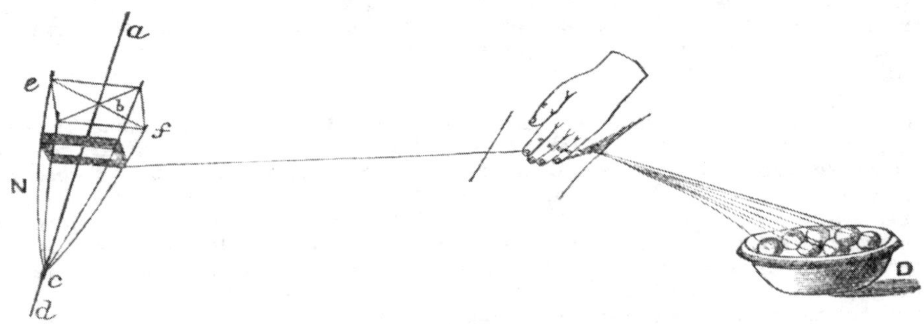

(*a*) Reeling of Tasar cocoons.

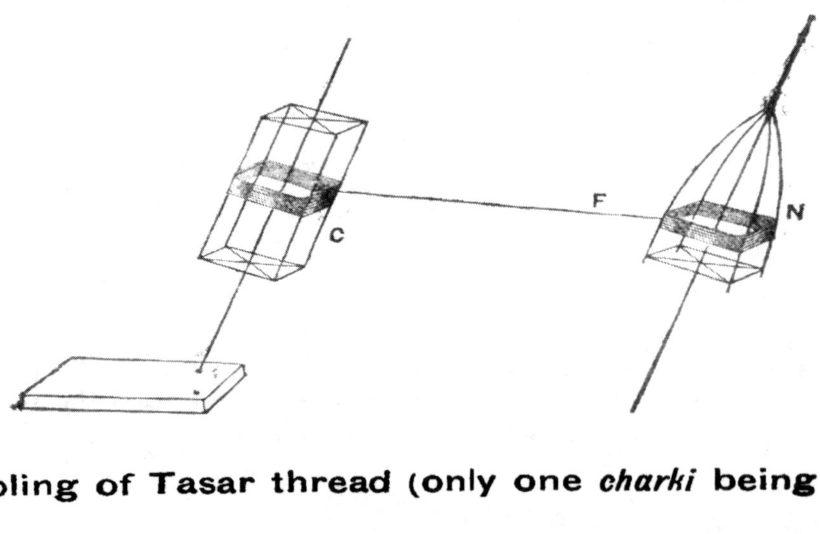

(*b*) Doubling of Tasar thread (only one *charki* being shown).

(*c*) **Warping of Tasar.**

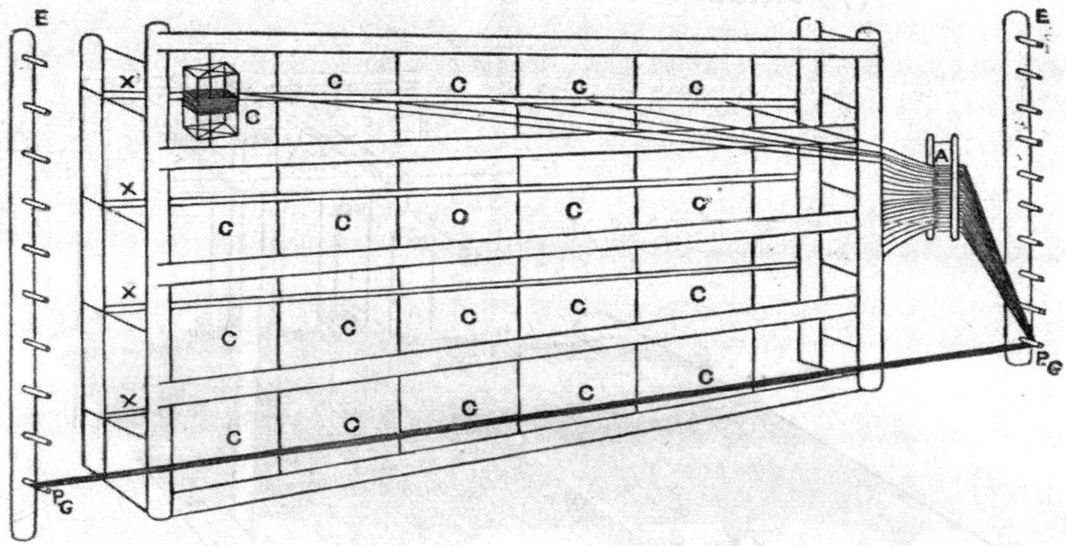

(*d*) **Another process of warping.**

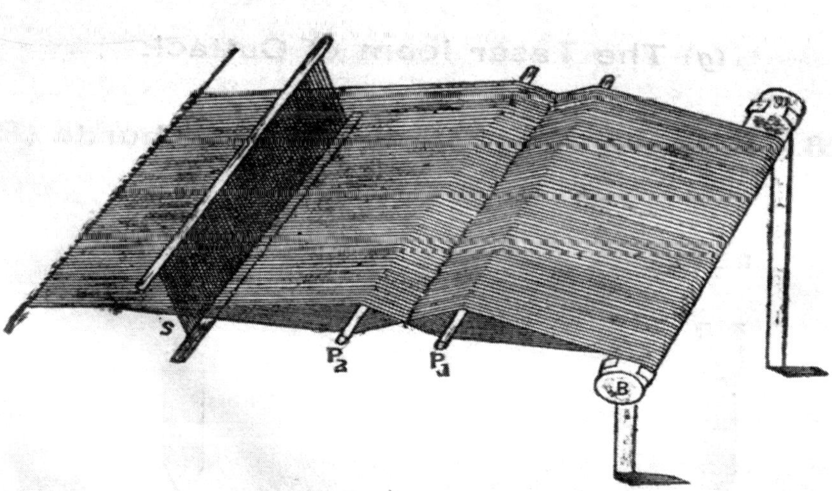

(*e*) Setting the reed.

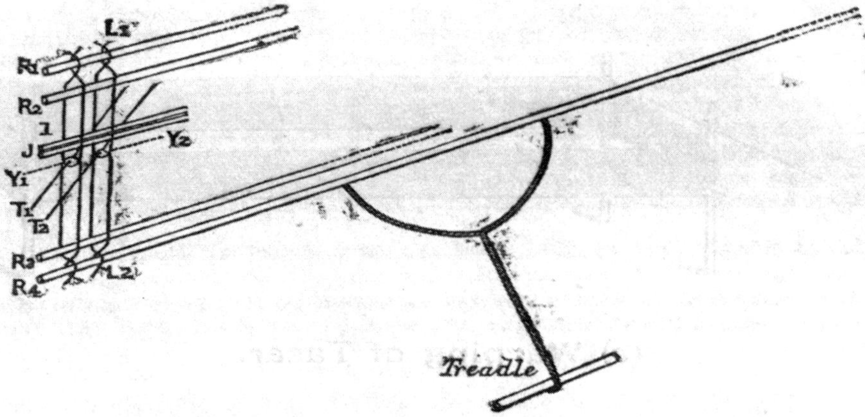

(*f*) Attachment of heald to treadle.

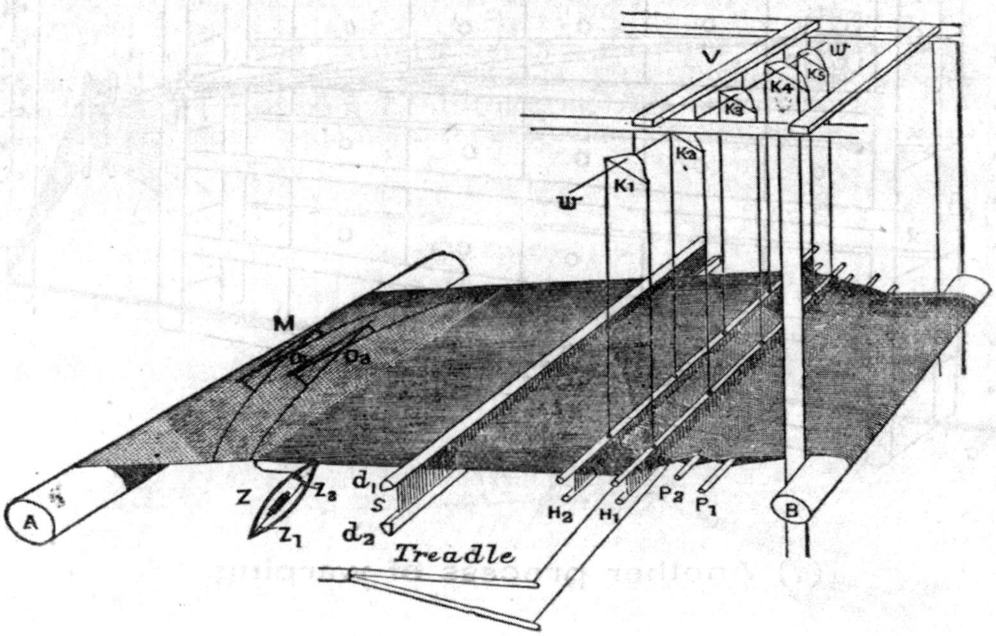

(*g*) The Tasar loom of Cuttack.

Fig. 28.—Tasar-weaving appliances of Khurda (Puri).

Orissa type.

Cloth-beam (*Pauza*).

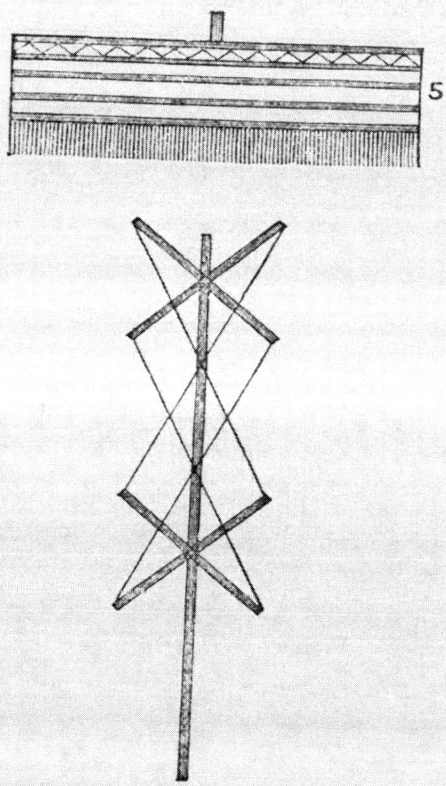

Comb (*Talow*) and *Charki*.

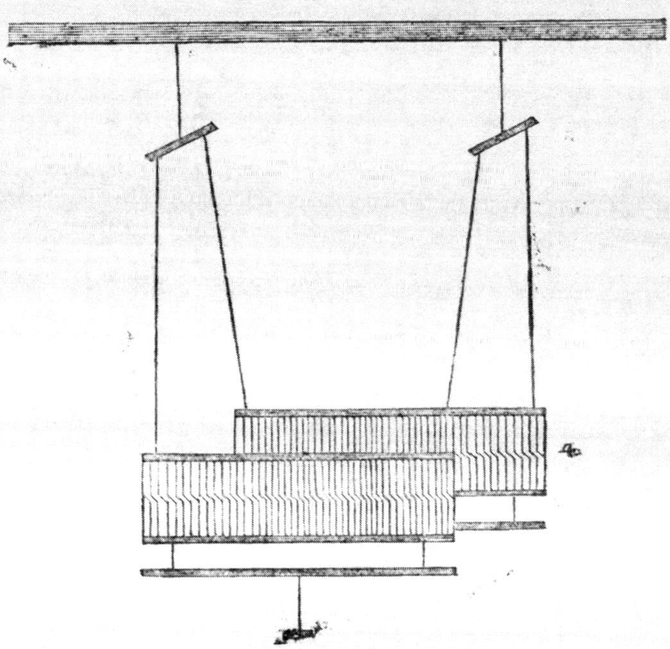

Healds (*Baw*).

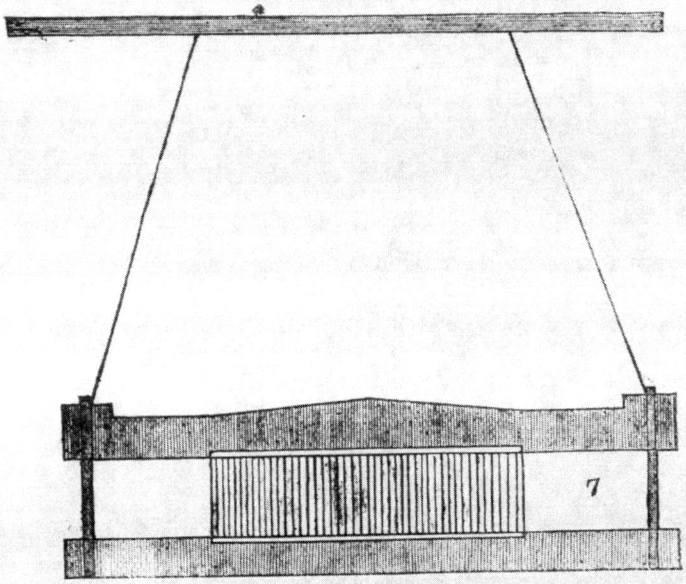

Reed (*Shana*).

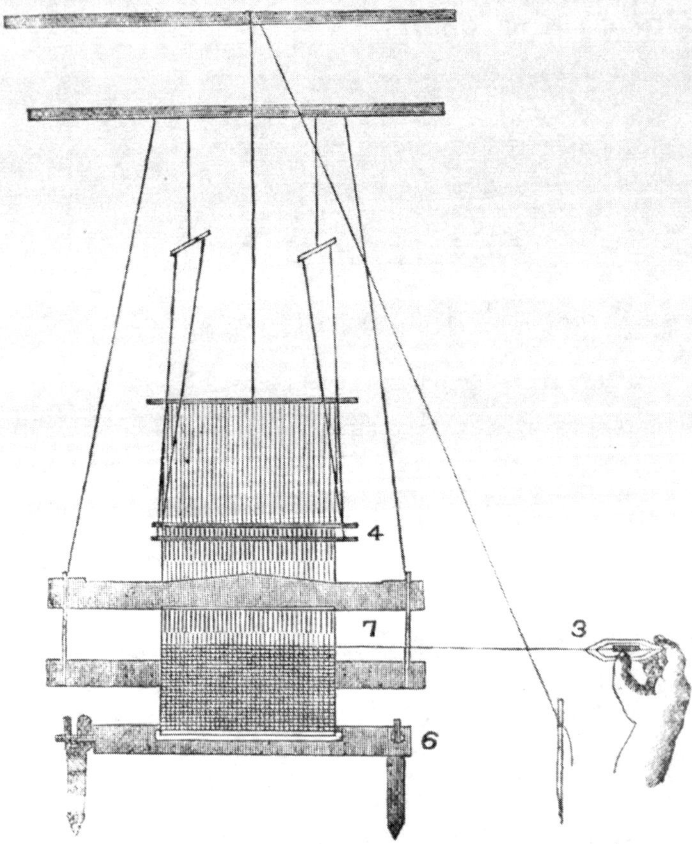

1. Spinning wheel (*areta*).
2. Spool (*takuri*).
3. Shuttle (*maku*).
4. Healds (*baw*).
5. Comb (*talow*).
6. Cloth-beam (*pauza*).
7. Reed (*sháná*).

The Tasar loom of Puri.

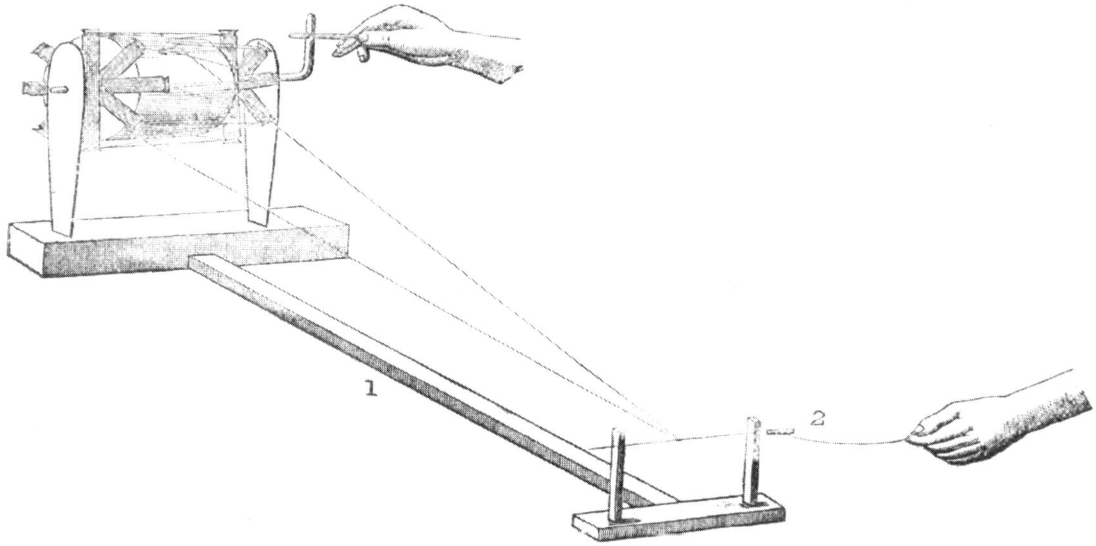

Spinning wheel (*areta*).

235. *Cuttack.*—The following fully illustrated and interesting report on the *tasar* silk-weaving industry which is carried on only in the village of Gopalpur (thana Dharamsala, Jajpur subdivision) in this district, has been furnished by Babu Braja Durlabha Hajara, Subdivisional Officer of Jajpur :—

"(*i*) *The classes who carry on the industry.*—Only *tasar* silk industry is carried on on a very small scale, at the village of Gopalpur, which lies partly in pargana Olas and partly in killa Madhupur, thana Dharamsala, by a class of weavers who are called *Bangali Tantis* (or *Tantis, i.e.*, weavers, of Bengal). The weavers are so called as they are not of Uriya origin. They have settled here from time of which no accurate account is available. Their ancestors came to Orissa from Burdwan or Chandrakona in Midnapore on pilgrimage, and for some reason or other settled here. There has been addition to their number from time to time owing to people coming to Orissa on a similar object, and ultimately settling to live with their brethren of the same stock. They have formed a class by themselves, and are not socially connected with any class of Uriyas.

(*ii*) *Their number.*—There are about 200 houses or families of these weavers at the village. Almost every family owns a loom, and carries on the industry independently by the labour of its own members, including that of females and girls, who have parts assigned to them as hereinafter described.

(*iii*) *Their social and industrial position.*—As stated above, these weavers form a class by themselves. Their socal intercourses are confined to their own circle. They may be said to belong to the middle class in position. Other people do not have anything to do with them except in the dealings of their proper profession. These weavers weave *tasar* as well as cotton cloth. They do not engage in any other industry or business or hold or cultivate any lands. Somehow they have kept on their industry and get on in life with the earnings from it. By this I do not mean to say that they are poor or in stringent circumstances. Indeed, some of them are well off and have money enough to carry on a small money-lending business in their own humble circle, as everyone who can save anything does at almost every rural village.

(*iv*) *The processes they follow.*—The process that these weavers follow is as simple as the scale of their business is small. They maintain no extensive filature or possess any intricate or improved form of machinery, or own any forests to rear cocoons. They use only *tasar* cocoons, which they purchase from those who rear them in the jungles of Keonjhar, Mourbhanj and other places.

Rearing cocoons.—The account that these weavers give of how cocoons are reared is somewhat interesting and is, therefore, given below in brief, although I have personally made no enquiry.

The *bihan* (or seed) cocoons are purchased at 10 to 12 *gandas* (*ganda*=4 in number) by a class of men called *Bhunuyas* and *Sahars.* These men get the *bihan* to their house in the month of Sravan (August), and keep them in earthen pots, which are kept covered during the day. The man who goes to rear cocoons must observe strict and religious cleanliness. He must have only *atap* rice for his meal, *i.e.*, observe *habishya* and will not see his wife during the time he is engaged in the business. The pot in which the parent worms are placed, is kept in a clean room, and is uncovered at night, when they are said to be joined by worms of the opposite sex who find their own to the place, and thus they lay eggs, each laying about 1⅓ *pons* (1 *pon*=80 in number). The eggs are collected in the morning, wrapped in a piece of clean cloth, and placed in the same pot with the parent worms. This goes on for about a week, during which all the parent worms die, leaving their eggs. After this the eggs are taken out and spread on a piece of clean cloth and fanned. They grow in about 15 days, and are then put on *asan* and *dha* trees, on the leaves of which they make cocoons.

(*b*) *Collecting and selling cocoons.*—These cocoons are collected about the month of *Paus* and *Magha* (December and January), and sold either at the place where they are reared or at the market. They are also taken to the houses of the weavers for sale. Cocoons are sometimes sold raw as they are taken down from the tree, or after being boiled and killed, for if they are kept raw for many days the worms will pierce out through them. The bigger cocoons sell at 3 *pons*, and the smaller ones at 6 *pons* to the rupee (*pon*=80 in number).

The raw cocoons are cheaper by 10 to 15 *gandas* to the rupee than the killed ones. The weavers purchase either kind; but they generally purchase the raw ones for the sake of cheapness.

(*c*) *Killing worms by boiling.*—It is, however, with great reluctance and pang of the heart that they boil and kill the cocoons. This part of the work is left to the females. It is almost with tears in their eyes that these weavers of Gopalpur complain that as a consequence of this cruel and sinful business (of killing the worms) their women lose their husbands, and have to live the miserable life of widows from their very youth. The simmering of the cocoons in the boiling pot is interpreted to be the plaintive utterances of the worms appealing to "Siva, Siva." The weavers also say that those who are engaged in killing coccons are in time stricken with some sort of loathsome skin disease, which, when aggravated, brings on their end. They could not, however, show me anyone who was so suffering. Those families that are comparatively better off, do not, on account of this belief, by their own hand do that part of the work which consists in killing cocoons. They hire labour for this from among their own class; and such men or women, as have no domestic ties, are readily available for the purpose, and the charge is about 3 annas for boiling one *kuhan* (16 *pons*) of cocoons.

And this is how the worms are killed: a large *handi*, with pure water in it, is, placed on a fire. The cocoons are put in another, the mouth of which is covered by a piece of cloth tied to it. The latter is then placed on the former, upside down, mouth to mouth, so as to allow the hot steam from the boiling water to pass through the covering cloth into the upper pot to kill the worms. The worms when they feel the heat are said to make a noise and when this ceases, the killing business is done, and the cocoons are kept away after cooling.

(*d*) *Preparing the cocoons for filature by a second boiling.*—After this the cocoons are prepared for drawing out the thread from them. This is done by boiling the killed cocoons a second time in water which has been passed through ashes obtained by burning the leaves and bark of plantain trees; about half-a-seer (a pound) of the ashes is taken and put into an earthen pot, with a hole at the bottom on which has been spread some cocoanut husk, or similar substance, to prevent the ashes from passing out. Then about 1¼ seer (2½ pounds) of water is poured on the ashes. The water drops through the ashes, and the hole at the bottom and is collected in another pan on the top of which the perforated pot is placed. This water is then poured into an *atika* (cooking pot) and 1 *pon* (80 in number) of killed cocoons is put into the water and boiled. The above-mentioned quantity of water (1¼ seer is generally sufficient for one *pon* of cocoons. Sometimes, however, the quantity is insufficient for the number, and more water (water which of course has been passed through ashes as described above) has to be added till the cocoons are soft enough for reeling. This part of the work is done usually at night, by the females.

(*e*) *Separating waste silk.*—In the morning after they have cooled, the cocoons are taken out one by one, and the loose and coarse fibres that adhere to them are separated by the females with their hand. This waste *tasar*, it will not be out of place to note here, is not used by the weavers of Gopalpur, but they keep it apart for sale. The *Patras* take it for making pendants and strings attached to ornaments. This waste silk is locally called *arua tasar* and is sold at about two pice per *chatak* (*i.e.*, 5 *tolas*). A rupee worth of cocoons gives about 2½ *chataks* of *arua tasar* and 3 *chataks* of good *tasar* fit for weaving.

(*f*) *Reeling or khia katai.*—After the waste *tasar* has been separated, the cocoons are ready for reeling or *khia katai* (drawing out thread). This part of the work is done by the females and little girls. Figure 27(*a*) illustrates how this is done. Seven or sometimes 8 cocoons are taken at a time. The end of the thread is taken out of each, and they are all joined together and tied to a *nata* made of bamboo sticks (N in figure 27) This is called the *katuni nata* after the purpose for which it is used. It is altogether about 2 feet long; about 8 inches from *a* to *b* one foot from *b* to *c*, and 5 inches from *c* to *d*. The diameter of the lower part of the frame, *e* to *f*, is about 6 inches. The woman holds this in her right hand, and puts the cocoons in a pan (*d*) to her left. She takes off her cloth to a little above the knee, and the threads pass over the uncovered part of her thigh. She goes on twisting, with a light pressure of her left hand, the 7 or 8 threads coming out of the cocoons and passing between her hand and thigh, and revolving the *nata* with her right hand to wind the single thread on it. And thus the reeling goes on drawing out the threads, twisting them into one, and winding them on the *nata*, all simultaneously. Particular care is not taken to join the ends of threads when one lot of cocoons is exhausted, and another taken up or when they happen to break. An attempt is made at first to join them by the pressure of the hand, but if that fails, the ends are joined by knots. The thread is taken out of the *katuni nata* when one skein is drawn. About 24 cocoons yield one skein, and it takes about three hours to draw this quantity. One rupee worth or 6 *pons* of cocoons yield about 3 *chataks* of good *tasar*, the price of which is Re. 1-8.

This part of the work is sometimes done by hired labour, and the cost of it is 10 pice for drawing from Re. 1 worth of cocoons. This would show that about 60 hours' labour fetches only 10 pice.

(*g*) *Khandi bhanga.*—The next process is called *khandi bhanga, i.e.*, dividing the skeins obtained from the *katuni nata* into two, and to enlarge the short skeins. This is required to allow the hand to be put into the skein more conveniently to apply paste to the thread. The skein obtained from the *katuni nata* is put on a *charki* called the *pa-charki*, the girth of which is equal to that of the *katuni nata*. The shape of the *charki* is different from that of the *nata*, as will appear from the illustration, and the ribs of it are of string instead of bamboo sticks. The *charki* is loosely fixed to a hole in a block of wood, and the thread is unwound as it is wound on a *nata* of larger girth (called the *bulani nata*, marked N in the illustration) which is revolved by the right hand, while the thread passes between the thumb and the index finger of the left hand at F (*vide* figure 27*b*.)

(*g*) *Colouring the thread.*—After this process the threads are coloured, if required. The method of colouring is not at all elaborate. The skeins are simply dipped in water in which, while warm, colour powders are dissolved. Orange and red colours are chiefly used. The powders used are of European manufacture purchased from the bazar. Some use also a decoction of *natkan* seeds. The colour produced is not fast.

(*h*) *Basáni.*—The next process is called *basáni*. The skein is taken from the *bulani nata*. Paste (made from boiled rice) is applied to it with the hand, and the skein is put on another *charki* of the same girth as the *bulani nata*. From this the thread is wound on another *nata* called the *basáni nata* by a process exactly similar to that of *khandi bhanga*. Two *charkis* are sometimes used when the *Tanti* is able enough to manage, two skeins being thus collected on the *nata* at the same time. By this process the excess paste gets off from the thread, and the threads are freed and separated from each other, as they got confused in the application of the paste. Oil is applied to the ribs of the *nata* to prevent the pasted thread from getting attached to them, and the girth of the *basáni nata* is a little larger than that of the *bulani nata*, as the skein taken from the *basáni nata* becomes shorter when it dries up. This work—*basáni*—must be done early in the morning, *i.e.*, before the sun's heat can render the pasted thread too stiff for working. When the thread has been rolled on the *basáni nata*, the *nata* with the thread on it is exposed to dry in the sun. At evening the skeins are taken off the *nata* (little water being applied to the thread on the ribs of it to moisten the paste in order to be easily taken off), wrapped in a piece of wet cloth and exposed to the dew of night to procure softness.

(*i*) *Kaken bulá.*—The next process is to transfer the skeins again to the *bulani nata* through the *pa-charki*. This is done to have the skeins on a *nata* as well as to finally separate the threads should any have got attached to each other on account of the paste.

(*j*) *Warping or nundi-making and dhala-making.*—The threads are now ready for warping. This consists of two distinct processes (1) laying the threads sufficient in number for the required breadth of the cloth to the required length, and (2) rolling this thread on the warp-beam. There are two methods of laying the threads to the required length and thickness. These methods are not really different; but one is an improvement on the other. The two methods are illustrated by figures 27(*c*) and (*d*), respectively. The method illustrated by figure 27*d* is gradually replacing the other, though the latter is more common, being simple and less expensive. After the *káken bulá*, the last described process, the skeins are put on *charkis*. This *charki* C is of the same size and shape as the *pá-charki*, with this difference, that there is attached to its handle a rod with a ring, at the end through which the thread passes in order that it may not get out of the line. Two such *charkis* are generally used at the same time. Two rows of bamboo *láthis* are planted on the ground at an open place—which is generally selected under the shade of trees—at sufficient distances so as to give the desired length. A man (women also do it sometimes) takes two *charkis*, one in each hand, on which skeins have been put as stated above. The outer ends of the two threads are taken out through the iron ring and tied to one of the *láthis* and the man, with the two *charkis* in his hands, walks along the *láthis*, the *charkis* turn and the threads are unwound as he walks, and the threads are laid along the *lathis* as shown in the illustration (figure 27*c*).

The method illustrated by figure 27*d* is only somewhat more complex. Twenty *charkis* being used at once, instead of two, and a small reed—called *halachanguri* (A in Fig. 27*d*) being used, instead of a ring to guide the thread. This reed has as many dentations as there are *charkis*, through which the threads are passed. The *charkis* are not held in the hands, but loosely planted on rows on a frame of bamboo sticks. In the illustration only one *charki* is shown so planted. Nineteen more are similarly planted at the places marked C. Instead of *láthis* fixed to the ground, there are two posts (E. E. in the illustration) on either side with 8 to 10 pegs on each. Behind the frame on which the *charkis* are planted, there is another row of horizontal bars (X in the fig. 27*d*) passing one behind each row of *charkis*. The outer end of the thread is taken out of each *charki* and passed over the bar behind it, and the twenty ends are passed on through each dentation of the *haláchanguri*. The ends are then tied to one of the pegs (see P.G. in Fig. 27), and the man holding the *haláchanguri* walks in front of the (frame, which is called the *charki ará* to and fro, and as he walks all the *charkis* turn at once, the threads are unwound and laid lengthwise along the pegs. The weavers say they have introduced this *charki ará*) from Bengal. The advantages of this frame over the other method are (1) that it can be worked inside the house, as on account of the pegs much space is not required: and (2) that twenty instead of two *charkis* are unwound at the same time, and thus one-tenth of the time is required.*

The *nundi* (as the length of the threads so laid is called) is generally made long enough for 10 pieces of cloth, and is about 2,400 threads thick—the number required for a cloth of ordinary width (2¼ cubits).

The next process is called *dhála* or warping proper. The ends of the threads are passed two and two through each indentation (*paniá*) of a long reed called the *saná* (S. in figure 27*e*) with the help of the pointed end of a porcupine quill. The ends that are thus passed are secured with a string to a beam and rolled on it (B of figure 27*e*). This beam is supported and turned on two posts fixed to the ground. When the whole length has been nearly rolled up, the threads of the warp are crossed with the help of two rods (P_1, P_2), called *páchánis*. Each alternate thread is taken up one by one with the finger and one bar passed through it. The other bar is similarly introduced, the threads crossing in the middle, *i.e.*, the thread which passes above one of the rods, passes *below* the other. This is called *jua*-making, an intricate arrangement, which gives much trouble, and an error in which spoils the whole warping, and to which the Bengali word *jua chor* (a cheat) owes its derivation. This *jua*-making is a preparation for the *baw* or healds in the loom.

(*k*) ***Weaving.***—The warp is now ready for the loom. The warp-beam is placed on short posts and makes the off-beam of the loom (B in figure 27*g*). The ***páchánis*** are replaced by thinner rods which are called ***chalanis***. The reed is pushed off to the end of the thread. The upper threads are taken one by one and passed between two short cotton threads (L_1, L_2 figure 27*f*), each of which is doubled, the ends of one downwards and those of the other upwards; the former ends are fastened and tied to two rods below the warp, (R_3 R_4), and the latter are similarly tied to rods (R_1, R_2). The warp threads (T_1, T. 2) can play through the heald eyes (Y_1, Y_2). Similar eyes are made by similarly doubled threads arranged in parallel sets, fastened and tied to the rods, above and below. Two more rods are placed between the doubled threads. These rods serve to keep the threads in position. The upper warp-threads thus pass through one heddle or heald. The lower threads similarly are passed through another heddle. Two heddles are required, and they appear on the warp as shown in the figure 27*g* (H_1 and H_2). The threads which pass above the off-*chalani* (P_1), are held by the off-heddle, and those which pass below it by the other heddle. Five strings are then tied to the upper edge of each heddle at corresponding points. The free ends of these threads of one heddle are tied to as many cocks (K_1, K_2, K_3, K_4, K_5), which are hung from a cross-beam overhead (V). The strings from the other heddle are tied to the other ends of the cocks. These cocks turn on a rod (W) passing through holes in them, as one heddle mounts, and the other goes down. This is effected by working a treadle, (Q), which is attached to each heddle by strings as shown in figure .

The free end of the warp is now tied to the cloth beam A. The weaver sits near it at M, works the treadle, so that while one heddle goes down, the other mounts, making an opening between the warp-threads as shown in the illustration through which he shoots the shuttle, which is charged with the weft-thread. The shuttle is shot first, say from the right-hand side. The next time when the shuttle has come to the left-hand side, the other treadle is worked so that the heddle which mounted first, goes down, and that which went down, mounts, *i.e.*, the lower threads come up and the upper go down, making a similar opening between. The shuttle is now shot back to the right-hand side, and thus the weaving goes on. Z is the shuttle in the illustration. Before the cloth is woven, thick pieces of wood (called *daktes*) are fixed to either edge, top, and bottom, of the reed or *sana*. So some weft-threads are given, the reed is pushed towards the cloth beam to press the weft-threads closer. Two bows, called *kantunis*, are pinned to the woven part to prevent the warp from collecting. (The bows are marked O_1, O_2, in the figure.) As the woven cloth is wound on the beam A, the warp beam (B) unrolls and sets free the thread at the off-end.

The maku and the nali or the shuttle and the spool.—I must now say something about the shuttle. It is a thing made of buffalo horn (I speak of the thing that the Gopalpur weavers use; others use iron things also) of an elongated egg-shape, the two sides enclosing an open space. These are procured from Anandapur in Keonjhar. There is a needle lengthwise at one end inside (Z_1) and another (Z_2) crosswise joined to the side at the other end. The weft-thread is rolled on small reeds (*nalis* or spools) from *chakis* with the help of a wheel called the *arat*. Two threads are ordinarily rolled on one *nali* by planting two *chakris* on a block of wood and turning the handle of the wheel. The threads are not twisted, sometimes threads are taken. Several such spools are kept ready with the thread wound on them. One of these is put into the shuttle at a time being fixed on the lengthwise needle; and the outer end of the thread is passed below the crossing-needle, so that it unwinds from the spool as the shuttle is shot. The thread, which is wound on the needle, does not pass through any of the processes subsequent to the *katuni* described above. If it has to be coloured, that is done when the skeins are taken out of the *katuni nata*. Paste is not applied to the weft-thread.

* This kind of warping frame with spools is supplied with fly-shuttle looms by Mr. P. N. De of Chinsurah.

The method of weaving described above is no special method of weaving *tasar*. Cotton cloth is woven in the same loom. The loom that these Bengalis use differs somewhat in construction from the loom that weavers of other classes use, but that is not on account of weaving *tasar*. Different classes of weavers in this country have differently constructed looms, which probably shows that they have come here from different places.

(*v*) *The manner in which the products are disposed of.*—The *tasar* cloth and these weavers of Gopalpur turn out is of a coarse and inferior quality. The bulk of the products is taken away by people coming from Madras, Berhampore and other places in South India. These people come to the village, advance money to the weavers and take away the fabrics when they are produced. They are said to take about Rs. 12,000 worth of *tasar* cloth in the year. The weavers also sell about Rs. 500 worth at the Cuttack market.

One pair of *tasar* cloths of ordinary size is sold for about Rs. 5-8. It would take a man about 10 days if he has to finish a cloth from killing the cocoons to taking it out of the loom. About 18 *pons* or Rs. 3 worth of cocoons are required for one pair of cloths. The colouring costs about 4 pice, the rice-paste two pice, and fuel two pice per pair. The materials thus altogether cost Rs. 3-2. The weaver's net profit comes out to be Re. 1-14 per pair, the proceeds of ten days' labour, *i.e.*, 3 annas per day. As females and children take part in the work, the average daily earnings of a man may be estimated roughly at 4 annas per day.

A pair of ordinary *tasar* cloths weighs about 13 *chataks*. Allowing for the weight of the paste applied to the threads, the net weight of the *tasar* would be about 9 *chataks* or 45 *tolas*.

Besides cloth, the *Tantis* sell skeins of *tasar* thread also, which are used in the borders or *pars* of cotton cloth by the weavers of Balipatna. The thread is sold at about 11 *tolas* per rupee.

(*vi*) *Influence of imports.*—The industry does not appear to have ever been affected by imports. From the account given by the weavers, the industry appears to have remained stationary so far. Only in the present year, they complain that their *mahajans* from the south have not yet made their appearance, although they have left behind an advance to the extent of five to seven hundred rupees."

236. In Dhenkanal Tributary State which is under the management of the Deputy Commissioner of Angul, about a hundred persons rear *tasar* cocoons.

"They are Hadies and Kostias by caste. The Hadies (Mehernters) are drummers, and Kostias are weavers of cotton cloth by profession.

Process of rearing cocoons.—In January and February the people collect wild cocoons for seed from *shorea robusta* (sâl), *terminalia bellerica* (bahara) and *terminalia tomentosa* (asan) trees, or they buy the wild cocoons at two to three cocoons per pice from the collectors of the cocoons, and at one cocoon per pice from the traders (middlemen). For three to four months, from February to June, they preserve the seed cocoons by tying them in rows with strings and hanging them over the fencing of huts in front of their houses. In June or July, when heavy showers fall, they remove the cocoons to other huts near jungles and at some distance from homes and hang them as before. During the nine days of their removal, the worms come out of the cocoons, with the wings on both sides of their bodies like a butterfly and with appearances quite unlike that when they shut themselves within the cocoons. The wings of the male worms are of violet colour and those of the females are yellow. On the tenth day of their coming out, the male and female worms join, and after nine days of their joining the female worms beget each about six to eight hundred eggs, which are white, flat and as small as mustard seeds. After joining, the male worms are thrown away and the female worms are put in baskets wherein they produce eggs. During nine days after birth, the people brush the eggs off the wings of the mother worms, and then keep them in small bags of *asan* leaves, each leaf-bag holding a handful of eggs. After nine days since birth, the bags containing a handful of eggs as well as worms fresh from eggs (during these nine days some worms come out of the eggs) are hung on the twigs of *asan* saplings. During 45 days since removal to *asan* saplings, the eggs produce worms which grow to their full size, and complete the cocoons, which are removed from the trees and are sold at three to five hundred per rupee for manufacture of *tasar* cloth. After the bags holding eggs are put on *asan* saplings the eggs by and by produce worms which eat the *asan* leaves and grow as big as round plantain fruits when they begin to make cocoons. The full size of the worm is 5 inches long and 3 inches in girth. The worms appear black for eight days just after birth and white for the next eight days, and then green for the days until they shut themselves in their nests (cocoons). During the progress of the preparation of the cocoons, the size of the worm is gradually reduced to the size of an onion, so as to be easily contained within a cocoon. While within the cocoon, the worm appears in violet colour, and is said that the male worm is of a violet colour and the female of a yellow colour, while within the cocoons. The male worm, with the wings of a violet colour, and the female, with yellow wings, get out of the cocoons. The male cocoon is white and small and the female cocoon yellow and large.

Process of the manufacture of tasar cloth.—The reared cocoons, just after their removal from the trees, are stored on a platform under which a fire is made, so as to affect the cocoons by heat. Consequently, the worms within the cocoons die of excessive intolerable heat and the cocoons become then useful; because the worms, if left alive within the cocoons, cut holes or outlets in the body of the cocoons and get out of them. Consequently, the cocoons become utterly useless for manufacture of cloths. The stuff is then soaked one day in pure hot water or hot water boiled with ashes of husks of *kalai* (birhi), ashes of *til* (rasi) twigs or those of *castor* trees. Six or four cocoons are placed at equal distances in one row and six or four ends of six or four fine threads of the cocoons are mixed together into one which is drawn and folded up until the whole stuff of the cocoons is entirely exhausted. With these threads which may be doubled or tripled, as the case may be, the *Patras* (a class of people) weave *tasar* cloth. The better the cloth the greater the folding of thread. As for instance, *chowtari* cloth is the best, having twelve folded threads lengthwise and the same breadthwise. It sells at Rs. 7-8 to Rs 11 for a cloth of 16 cubits long and 2¼ to 2½ cubits broad. *Titari* cloth, twelve folded thread, lengthwise and eight folded threads breadthwise, It sells at Rs. 5,8 to Rs. 8 for a cloth of the aforesaid dimension.

The cocoons are reared in the following places of this State, viz :—

Basuloi, Manikmara, Kulai, Brahmanbedia, Kualo, Kolda, Barjhara of Parjang Biso.
Gurh Palasuni, Jarada, Dasipur, Birhibolai, Bhejia, Pangaitra, Asanbahali and Khoirmunda, of Palasuni Biso.
Koi, Dhulpasi, Rahani, Birasal, and Marnabil of Sourika Biso.
Rekula of Jenadesh Biso.
Kalang of Chhadesh Biso.

Tasar cloth is manufactured in the following places :—

Indipur and Sariapada in Balarampur Biso.
Bhubon in Ganpur Biso.
Pangaitra in Palasuni Biso.
Barhiapur in Parjang Biso.

Fity persons know how to manufacture the *tasar* cloth, and they are *Patras* by caste. They are weavers and cultivators. These *Patras* buy the cocoons reared throughout the State, and occasionally the reared cocoons of Dhenkanal are bought by the weavers of Nuapatra in Tigria and Maniabund in Baramba."

CHAPTER XIX.

THE ENDI SILK INDUSTRY.

The *endi*, *eri*, or *eria* (Attacus ricini) cocoons are reared in the districts of Bogra, Rangpur, Jalpaiguri and Mymensingh. Being more easily reared and less subject to epidemics than mulberry silk-worms, it is easier to introduce the mulberry silk industry into a new locality, through the means of the *eri* silk industry. But the *eri* silk industry is not so lucrative as the mulberry silk industry, the product of the *eri* cocoon being a spun-silk and not reeled silk. All attempts to reel the *eri* cocoon have hitherto failed, and although the ultimate fibre of the *eri* cocoon is a stronger and more lasting fibre than either the mulberry or the *tasar* silk fibre, the thread spun from this cocoon is a coarse kind of thread adapted only for weaving cheap and coarse fabrics, which correspond to *matka* and *kethé* fabrics made out of pierced mulberry and *tasar* cocoons respectively. *Eri* silk cloth is, however, much more valuable than either *matka* or *kethe* cloth, as these are less lasting. In course of time *eri* cloth also gets softer and more silky looking than either *matka* or *kethe*. The demand for *eri* cloths is greater than the supply, and the demand is now being largely met by the imitation *eri* silk made out of waste mulberry silk, which has been introduced in the district of Murshidabad by the writer of this Monograph. From the specimens of silk fabrics appended to this monograph (Specimens Nos. 19 to 31) it will be seen to what diverse and beautiful uses these imitation *eri* silks might be put. They also indicate the line in which improvement might be effected in the genuine article also (*Cf.* Nos. 26 and 31 with Nos. 32 and 33). At present little skill is brought to bear on the production of *eri* silks either in Assam or in Eastern and Northern Bengal. The spinning might be more uniform in imitation of the spinning of the Rajshahi *matká*, and the weaving might be more varied and artistic. As epidemics do not seem to prevail among the *eri* silk-worms in Bengal (though they do in Assam), it is unnecessary to introduce the system of grainage, *i.e.*, organise seed-rearing nurseries for the supply of healthy seed. But improvement in another direction is feasible and desirable. The *eri* cocoons reared in Bengal are not so select as some of the *eri* cocoons of Assam, which are beautifully large and white. *Eri* cocoons reared in Bengal are of mixed colour and rather small. A large proportion of brick-coloured cocoons being mixed up among them, it makes the colour of the *eri* silk fabrics woven in Bengal less pleasing to the eye than that of the high class *eri* silk fabrics woven in Assam. The Rampur Boalia

Sericultural School may do a very useful work by popularising the beautiful white *eri* cocoons reared in this school in the neighbouring districts of Bogra, Rangpur and Jalpaiguri.

Bogra.—The following account of the *eri* silk industry of Bogra is compiled out of the district monograph. The account should be read in connection with that given for the silk-weaving industry of this district, most of the appliances and method used being common to both industries :—

"*Cultivation of the worms and preparation of the thread.*—The cultivation of the *bond* or *eri* worms is done by the same class of people as cultivate silk-worms. A cultivator may be found rearing both silk-worms and *eri* worms simultaneously. The cultivation of *eri* is now more widespread than that of the silk-worm, although both industries have dwindled away during the last 30 years. The decline is said to have begun even before the abolition of the factories owing to the fall in prices. As I have already stated, the cultivation of *eri* is more common in the eastern or *poli* tract of the district. At a time women of certain tracts wove nothing but *bond* cloth. The *bond* industry is mostly domestic. Women rear the worms by feeding and cleaning them. It is the women who boil the cocoons, arrange them in a lump, spin out the thread, and so on. The thread, when manufactured in a sufficient quantity, is made over to a Jola or Muhammadan weaver, who weaves the cloth and brings it back, charging a small amount for every cubit of the cloth woven. As the cultivators of *eri* worms are scattered over the district, and as this industry is not, and cannot be, the only source of their income, it is not possible to give an accurate estimate of their number at present. In a family of such cultivators the women are often found to possess more information about the ways, &c., of the worms than the men. This is due to the fact that they are more interested in the affair. A *bond* cloth may form an article of every day wear by a woman, whereas a man wears *bond* fabrics, as a wrapper, only in the winter.

The *eri* worms feed on the leaves of the castor-oil plant, locally called *bhelna*. The plant is grown on homestead lands, or here and there among other crops. Cultivation of castor plants as the sole crop in big areas is not very common. They are sown in small patches. The leaves are liable to destruction by various sorts of caterpillars, &c.

In the absence of *bhelna* leaves the worms eat leaves of the *papya* also. But this food does not seem to be liked by the worms. The worms are certainly more hardy than silk-worms. They have been found to go about in the room in search of food when the food given them was exhausted.

The following cycle is given for the *eri* worm :—

	Summer.	Winter.
The moths cut out of the cocoons in ...	9 days.	16 days.
Lay eggs	Same day.	Same day.
Eggs hatch	9 days	16 days.
First moulting	3 "	6 "
Second "	3 "	6 "
Third "	3 "	6 "
Fourth "	4 "	8 "
Spinning begins	8 "	14 "
Spinning	1 day.	2 "
Total ...	40 days.	74 days.

"An empty cocoon from which the worm has cut out weighs $\frac{1}{38}$th of a *tola*. The length of a cocoon is about $1\frac{3}{4}$ inches.

"The worm is bigger than the silk-worm, and the cocoon spun is also bigger. The cocoons generally have a reddish appearance, white cocoons being rare. *Eri* cocoons cannot be reeled. They have a fibrous, sticky appearance. When the worms cut out, the female ones are known by their larger appearance They are tied by threads with a string, formed by putting four or five paddy straws together. The male worms are left free to choose their mates. Eggs are laid on the above string, and then the process of hatching, &c., goes on as in the case of silk-worms.

"In the case of *eri* cocoons there is not much hurry for killing them, for it does not matter much if the worms cut out. The cocoons may be killed by exposure to the sun. For the purpose of spinning thread the cocoons are boiled in an earthen vessel closed with an earthen lid and hermetically sealed with clay. The boiling goes on for two hours or more. Then the vessel is taken off and allowed to cool. The whole thing is then kept in the same state for three or four days; after which the lid is removed and the cocoons are taken out. They give out a very nasty smell. Then the cocoons are opened at one end and the chrysalids are taken off. The cocoons are then thoroughly washed with water. Then a cocoon is turned inside out and put like a cap at the end of a small wooden stick called *kathi*. Then another cocoon is treated in the same manner and capped over the first and so on. This forms something like a knob at the end of the *kathi*. The spinning begins when the cocoons are still wet. For this purpose the woman holds the *kathi* in her left hand with the knob upwards. Some fibres are then pinched and drawn out of the knob and twisted by the instrument called *tanka*. This *tanka* consists simply of a bamboo rod fixed at the centre of a circular piece of stone or broken pot. The bamboo rod has a catch at the other extremity and is fixed firmly to the stone piece. The end of the thread to be spun is tied with the rod and wound round it a number of times. Then the whole thing is given a vigorous turn by the two fingers of the right hand The *tanka* being suspended by the thread goes on twisting it, the heavy thing below serving the purpose of a fly-wheel. More fibres are pinched up and added on to the thread which is drawn out and the twisting goes on.

From the *tanka* the thread is transferred to a *natai* of peculiar construction. It consists of a forked branch of a tree across which is tied a bamboo rod. The thread is now ready for use.

The thread so spun is far from smooth and is not of uniform thickness. So the fabrics woven out of this thread are not at all fine. They are course and thick. The woman goes on collecting her produce, till she has sufficient thread in stock for weaving a cloth. Then the thread is made over to a Jola (Muhammadan weaver) for weaving the cloth. The Jola charges for the cloth at one anna per cubit of length if the width of the cloth woven be 2 cubits. The charge is higher when the cloth is wider As I have already said, thread is spun mostly for home consumption. But when the quantity spun is too small for a cloth or larger than the quantity required for home consumption, the thread is sold to the weavers. The present price of thread is Rs. 2 per seer. A higher price may be paid for thread that is finer.

Besides the thread required for the looms of the district some thread is sent out by the Marwari merchants.

This may come to 10 maunds in the year, Taking the price Rs. 2 per seer, the price of this quantity comes to Rs. 800. The cultivators themselves bring the thread to the Marwaris for sale. Those who have to sell only very small quantities take the produce to the *hâts* and purchase vegetables or other articles of food with the sale proceeds.

Weaving.—The weaving of *bond* silk is done by people called Jolas, and also to some extent by Jogis. The Jolas are Muhammadans weavers. They are the lowest caste of Muhammadans in this part of the country. Ordinary Muhammadans do not intermarry with them, and they are looked down upon as low people. In fact the very name of Jola is used as a term of reproach by other people. The people of this class are found generally to be inferior to their neighbours in common sense. These Muhammadan weavers, in order to avoid the epithet of Jola style themselves *karigars*. The people are generally poor. They weave both *bond* cloths and cotton fabrics. But the profit from these is far from adequate, and a Jola cannot support himself by weaving only. The Jolas also keep lands and cattle and cultivate the fields The weavers do not prepare the threads from cocoons.

The other class of weavers who weave *bond* cloths are Jogis. These men style themselves Hindus. but are not recognised by Hindus as such. The number of such men weaving *bond* cloths is comparatively small. These men are also looked down upon by others. They also take to cultivation as weaving alone is not enough for maintaining a man.

The loom employed for weaving *bond* cloths is very like the looms employed by *Tantis*, but it is generally smaller. The threads obtained from the spinner or from the *hâts* are transferred to a *charkhi* and the warping can begin at once. For this purpose two posts are planted in the ground at a distance equal to the length of the cloth to be woven. Between these posts bamboo rods are planted in the ground at intervals of 1 cubit only, in a straight line with the extreme posts. The operator then knots the end of the thread from the *charkhi* to one of the two posts, and proceeds with the *charkhi* in his left hand towards the other post. He is provided with a bamboo rod in his right hand. This rod is split into two at one extremity and between these two halves of the rod a segment of a broken smooth *churi* (or glass bangle) is introduced instead of the ring mentioned in the case of the *Tantis*. The thread is passed over the concave side of this *churi*. It is drawn out as the operator walks, and he puts the thread, with the help of this instrument called *hata*, to the right of one rod and to the left of the next consecutive one. and so on. After reaching the extreme rod and turning the thread round it, he proceeds back towards the first post, the second turn of the thread intersecting the first thread between every two consecutive rods, so that these two threads enclose every one of the rods and posts. The operator goes on in the same manner till the warping is completed. The difference between the warping of the Jolas and that of the *gar .d* weavers is this—

They use only one *charkhi*, while the Tantis use two. The *hata* is separate from the *charkhi* in the case of Jolas instead of being fixed to it perpendicular to the axle. So it is evident that the process of the Tantis is more economical as regards time. The next process is that of starching the threads. This is done by applying rice gruel to the warp which is kept stretched for the purpose. The gruel is applied to the warp and when the threads are still wet a brush is applied to the warp and the superfluous gruel taken off. The brush is of peculiar construction. It is made of roots of the *khus-khus* (baina bushes). It costs Rs. 2 or so and lasts for 10 or 12 years. It is said that these brushes used to be imported from other districts. They cannot be locally prepared. In putting threads through the *sáná* the process is simpler than that of the Tantis. Instead of cutting loops at one end of the warp for the purpose, the Jolas introduce the loops themselves through the *sáná*. One loop is introduced through each interval in the *sáná* or reed. So in this case each interval contains two threads and no more. The process of forming the healds is very similar to the process of the Tantis with the following exceptions:—

(i) The *fandi* is not rounded off at one end, and it is longer.
(ii) The thin rod for knotting the loops called *moori* by Tantis is dispensed with.

Instead of this a rod with a hole on one end is used for forming the knots. A thick string is tied with this rod through the hole. The rod is drawn out and the thick string takes the place of this rod and serves the same purpose as the *moori* in *garad* looms.

There is no difference in the fitting up or working of the loom. The Jolas use only one *mantri* or bow instead of two for keeping the width of the cloth uniform.

A wooden shuttle is used instead of a metallic one.

No rods are used as treadles. Two strings tied with the rods below the healds are provided with two small square pieces of wood or bamboo at the other extremities. These squares have a hole each at the centre, and the strings passing through the holes are knotted at the ends, so that they may not run out. The operator puts each of his feet on one of these squares, the strings passing through the first two toes of each foot. These squares serve the purpose of treadles.

In *bond* cloths no ornamented borders are woven, and so there are no additional healds. For making the cloth strong at the borders, the only precaution taken is to pass two loops together through the extreme interstices in the portion of the reed to be used.

The weaving is done in the same way as by the Tantis. The Jola uses rice gruel (or water in which cooked rice has been thrown and formed into a paste) instead of *khai*, for application to the cloth woven.

The looms used by Jolas are much smaller than those used by the Tantis. They cannot prepare *bond* cloths wider than 2 cubits. This is due to the fact that they use short reeds (*sánás*). They purchase the *sánás* at 8 or 12 annas each. When a broader *bond* cloth is required, they weave the cloth of half the width, but of double the length. Then they sew up the cloth to make it of the required width. For instance, men require *bond* cloth 3 cubits wide and 12 cubits long for using it as a double *gilap* or wrapper, for use in the winter. This demand is met by weaving a cloth 1½ cubits wide and 24 cubits long and cutting and sewing it to make it of the required dimensions. There are only a few weavers who can weave *bond* cloth 3 cubits wide. They reside at and near Chandonbasia in a part of the district bordering on Mymensingh.

The industry of *bond* weaving is rapidly declining. The consumers find it more economical to purchase European cotton fabrics which are very cheap, instead of using *bond* cloths which, though very lasting, are too costly, considering everything. No *bond* cloth is exported from this district to other districts. All the fabrics woven are consumed in this district. On the other hand, gentlemen requiring *endi* cloth of better workmanship bring it from Assam by private arrangement. But this import is very small and hardly worth mentioning.

Fabrics.—The two kinds of *bond* cloths woven are *gilaps* and *dhutis*. No other variety is known, although it is possible to have a required length of cloth woven to order. *Bond* cloth is not dyed. No ornamentation is done in the cloth. There is practically no border; the only precaution taken for making the cloth stronger at the edges is to use a double pair of warp threads at each of them.

Dhuti.—*Dhutis* are said to be 2 cubits wide × 5 cubits long. But practically the width is less than 2 cubits.

	Rs.	A.	P.
Price of thread required (half a seer) is	1	0	0
The wages of the weaver	0	5	0
Total ...	1	5	0

Two such cloths are woven together by a woman. One for covering the upper part of the body and the other for covering the lower part. Generally three *dhutis* are warped at a time. The time required by the weaver for weaving them is shown below (according to the estimate of a weaver):—

Preparing the warp and brushing the threads	1 day.
Passing the threads through the reed	½ "
Making the healds	1 "
Weaving	2½ days.
Total ...	5 days.

The wages for these *dhutis* will be 15 annas. I think the time given for the whole operation is not much over-estimated. So the remuneration of the weaver is very small.

Gilaps.—A piece, 1½ cubits wide and 24 cubits long, is woven and then sewn into a double wrapper 3 cubits wide and 6 cubits long, price Rs. 6 to Rs. 7. A *bond* double wrapper, which is woven 3 cubits wide, will fetch Rs. 8 or more.

No *bond* cloth is exported from this district to other district. All the fabrics woven are consumed in this district. On the other hand, gentlemen requiring *endi* cloth of better workmanship bring it from Assam by private management. But this import is very small and hardly worth mentioning."

Rangpur.—The following account of this industry has been furnished by the Collector of Rangpur:—

"No silk industry is carried on in this district; but a rough kind of silk called *endi* is manufactured in this district by the low class Muhammadans and Rajbansis and Koeris

It is not exported, but is used by the poorer classes as wrappers. Females of well-to-do cultivators also use them as *saris*. The processes of rearing the cocoons and spinning the thread are described shortly in the annexed note prepared by Babu Sashi Bhusan Mukerjee, a Deputy Collector of this district.

Rearing and spinning of endi cocoons.—Ordinarily a family would use at the most four straw-made sticks (called *bhundias* by the people) for the purpose of getting cocoons, the process adopted for which is as follows:—Eight or ten pairs of moths or *endi* flies called *chiti*, are placed on each such stick, bound with strings, where they are kept without food for four or five days, during which they lay eggs and die. Then the eggs are taken off the stick and kept covered in a piece of cloth for five or six days, after which larvæ issue from the eggs. They are then placed inside a basket on that cloth with *redi* leaves over it, the basket being changed twice a day, that used in day-time being changed for a fresh one at night; so also the leaves. This continues for four or five days, after which the larvæ fast and fall into a state of sleep for one day. When the sleep is over they resume activity, and in this state four or five days pass. Then come two days of sleep, after which they are again active for four or five days. Then again come three days of sleep, and inactivity for the larvæ, which are then removed to a room and placed on a *machan*. This continues for five or six days, after which comes a day of fasting and sleep. Subsequently they are removed to bamboo bars within the room with the *machan* underneath. On these bars they hang for ten or twelve days on *redi* leaves on which they live. Then they spin cocoons, some on the *machans*, on which they drop down. This spinning is over in three or four days, after which they are sunned for three or four days. I may note here that the rearing of cocoons in summer takes as described above one month and-a-half, while in winter it would take double the time, the growth and development of the eggs being delayed in the latter season. Two or three per cent. (moths come out piercing through these seed-cocoons, and are utilised by being placed on the stick called *bhundia*, as described in the beginning of this report) are kept for seed, which, however, are not sunned like others. As regards those which are sunned, they are boiled with ashes of plantain trees for an hour or two. They are then pressed against a bamboo stick, one foot high and half an inch in diameter, in order that they may expand. When this is over, they are washed, kneaded and dried. Fibres are separated, spun and twisted by means of a *takua*, (*a*) the cocoons being moistened in water all the while, then the yarns are reeled on a *jhila* (*b*) and sunned. Then they are made over to a weaver.

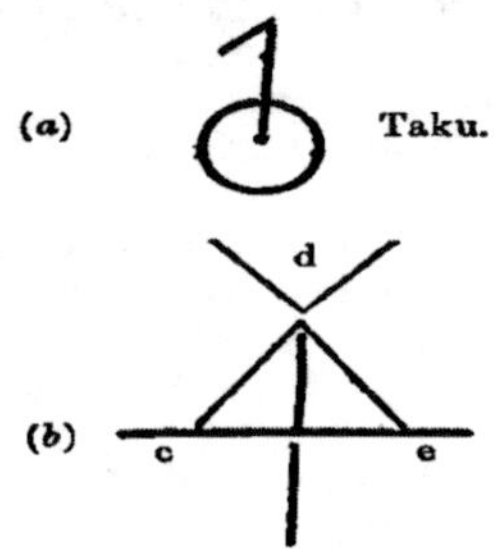

Jhila c d and d e representing the yarn reeled.

One *bhundia* would yield 1,280 caterpillars and one *pooah* of thread (one-fourth of a seer); two *bhundias* would yield yarn enough for a wearing cloth named *fota* 5 cubits by 2¼ cubits; three *bhundias* would yield three *pooahs* of thread, from which one sheet (*chadar*) 6 by 2¾ cubits, might be made. To make one *guji* of 12 by 2¾ cubits, 6 *pooahs* of thread will be required. *Guji* is seldom made. *Fota* is used by women, and would last for two or two and-a-half years. *Chadar* is used by males, and lasts for eight or ten years.

To maintain one *bhundia* of insects (moths) it would cost one rupee if *redi* leaves are to be purchased from the *hât* or villagers. Consequently one *fota* would cost Rs. 2 as well as annas 9 or 10 as cost for weaving. But it appears that people do not generally purchase *redi* leaves, the trees being grown by them in their own fields or houses, so that they have only to pay annas 9 or 10 per *fota* that women wear. A *fota* would sell for Rs. 2 to Rs. 2-8. One *chadar* would cost Re. 1 only (as cost for weaving) if *redi* leaves worth Rs. 3 can be supplied from home. One *chadar* would sell for Rs. 5 or Rs. 6 in the bazar. To carry on a regular transaction, the cost of spinning as well as other costs are to be considered. The cost of spinning is charged at 2 or 3 annas per *bhundia* or per *pooah* of thread; consequently one *fota* would cost:—

	Rs.	A.
(*a*) For *redi* leaves	2	0
(*b*) For spinning	0	6
(*c*) For weaving	0	9
(*d*) For colouring the fringes	0	1
(*e*) Two *bhundias*	0	2
Total cost ...	3	2

Similarly, one *chadar* would cost—

	Rs.	A.
(*a*) *Redi* leaves	3	0
(*b*) Spinning	0	9
(*c*) Weaving	1	0
(*d*) Colouring, no fringes or border being used	...	
(*e*) Three *bhundias*	0	3
Total ...	4	12

Now it will be seen that the making of *fota* is not profitable, the selling price being Rs. 2-8 against Rs. 3-2, the total cost incurred. But the making of *chadar* may be profitable, the total cost being Rs. 4-12 against Rs. 6, the selling price. The introduction of *markin* cloth, which is much less costly, has brought ruin on such petty industries. People no longer care to invest capital on the making of *endi* cloths, which cost much.

Low class Muhammadans and poor Rajbansis, especially the widows, still engage in the making of *endi* cloths on a small scale for their private use. The *chadars* made in Rangpur are of very coarse kind and look of earth colour; they are not liked by the genteel classes, and consequently the business is dying a natural death. It is said that *endi* cloths are not held as sacred cloths both by the Hindus and Muhammadans, and this is probably one of the causes that have diminished the use of *endi* cloths in this country. The Assam *endi* is liked by the people, as it is not so coarse as Rangpur *endi* and as it is looks better. No trade as reported before is carried on here."

Jalpaiguri.—The following account of this industry has been compiled from the report furnished by Mr. H. J. S. Forrest, C.S., Deputy Commissioner of Jalpaiguri :—

"No silk industry is carried on in this district except the manufacture of *endi* cloth, and that, too, on a very small scale and by a certain section of the people.

It is only some of the women of the Meches and Garos inhabiting parts of the Duars that manufacture *endi* cloths from a coarse kind of silk obtained from *endi* worms reared by themselves at home. The manufacturing of *endi* cloth is not followed as an industry, nor are fabrics made to any extent for purposes of trade. The women manufacture a few pieces of this cloth in a year for their personal use.

The number of the women who manufacture the fabrics may be about 400.

These people are the aborigines of the Duars, who hithorto followed a nomadic life, but are now gradually settling down in places. Their industrial position is that of cultivators.

The following is a description as to how the worms are reared, silk extracted and of the process followed in the manufacture of *endi* cloths.

The *endi* worms are like ordinary silk-worms, and are called *endi*, because they are fed with *endi* (viz., castor) plant leaves. They would not eat mulberry or any other leaves.

When very small, they are kept in a quiet place inside a house, and are every day supplied with fresh leaves, the remains of the leaves given on the previous day being carefully removed. They attain full size in about a month or a little more and then form cocoons. These cocoons are boiled for an hour or so in water in which *khar*, viz., some vegetable ash, is mixed. They are then taken out and washed well in cold water. The silk is then spun from these cocoons by means of the instrument called *takuri* (Fig. 29, No. 1). The thread is transferred from *takuri* to the instrument called *natai* (Fig. 29, No. 2) and then taken out and made into small skeins. The skeins are besmeared with *mar* (which is the milky liquid substance obtained by boiling rice in water, washed in water and dried in the sun. The thread is then arranged on *charki* (Fig. 29, No. 3). Split bamboo sticks are planted on the ground at equal distances, the entire length being the same as of the cloth to be woven. The two end sticks are flat, being about 2 inches broad; the middle ones are round—about ½ inch in diameter. The lengthwise thread of the cloth to be made is then drawn horizontally and consecutively round the entire line of the sticks and to the breadth of a little more than that of the cloth to be manufactured. This drawing of the thread is called *tana*, which means the lengthwise thread of the cloth and when fully laid looks like No. 4 of Fig. 29. The sticks with the *tana* thread on them are taken up and spread flat some height from the ground, supported by posts, to which the ends are tied. The *tana* thread is brushed by means of the instrument called *tasa* (Fig. 29, No. 5), the *tasa* which is a brush being at intervals dipped in *mar*. The *tana* thread is put through the *rash* (Fig. 29, No. 6) which is a kind of comb; each thread of the *tana* passing through each two teeth of the *rash*. The *tana* is secured at each end by a piece of wood by means of which it can be rolled up. This roller is called gonda (Fig. 29, No. 7). The *rash* is secured between two pieces of wood called sâl (Fig. 29, No. 8).

The *tana* when so arranged is fitted up on the loom. Figure 30, represents a loom fitted up in plan, section and elevation.

The cross-thread is called *poran*. The *poran* thread is wound on pieces of small tubes, and one of these tubes at a time is placed into the instrument called *maku* (Fig. 29, No. 9) and the cloth is woven on the loom by passing and repassing the *maku* through the *tana* threads by means of both the hands. The weaver works the loom all the time with his feet while he drives the *maku* from right to left and left to right with his hands. The cloth when being woven is kept stretched to its proper breadth by means of a contrivance represented by diagram No. 10, Fig. 29.

The colours used are red, black and yellow, obtained from dyes prepared by the people themselves :—

(1) The red colour is prepared by dissolving raw lac in a liquid acid obtained by boiling *thenthelang* or *mesta* in water.

(2) Indigo plants, with leaves, are cut into pieces and put in water to which *chaka*, viz., salt extracted from the ash of plantain tree barks, is mixed and left to decoct for two days. This decoction gives a black colour.

(3) Daru-haridra plants cut into pieces and *natko* fruit boiled together in water give a yellow colour.

Fig. 29.—Endi spinning appliances.

No. I.—Takuri.

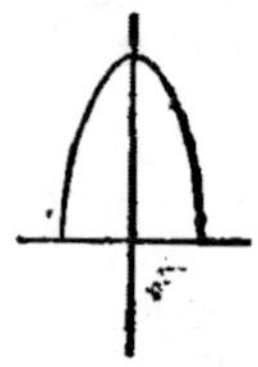

No. 2.—Natai.

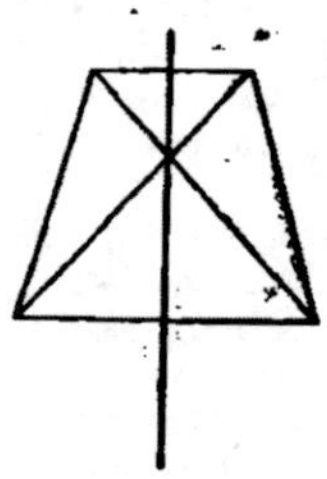

No. 3.—Charki.

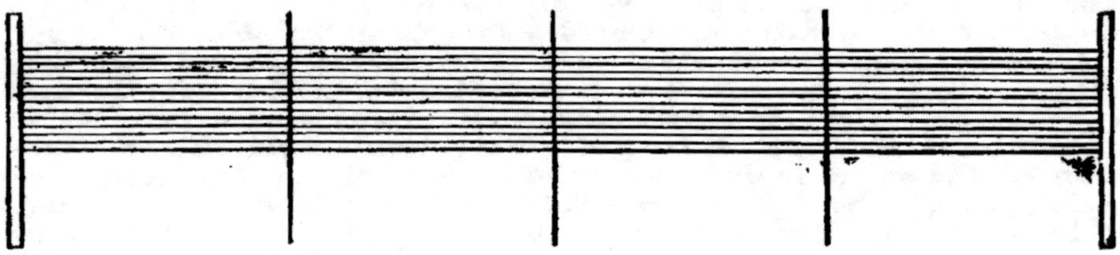

No. 4.—Warping of Endi thread.

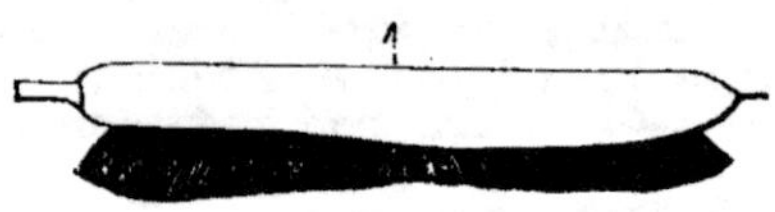

No. 5.—*Tasa* or brush.

No. 6.—*Rash* or reed.

No. 7.—*Gonda* or beam.

No. 8.—*Sal* or reed-protector.

No. 9.—Wooden shuttle (*maku*).

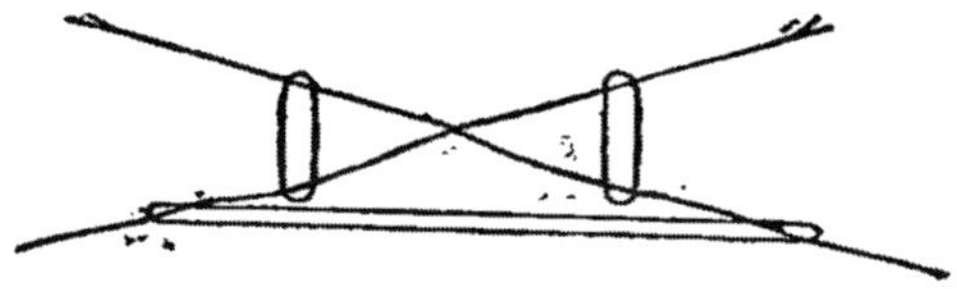

No. 10.—Bow for keeping web tight.

Fig. 30.—Endi weaving loom.

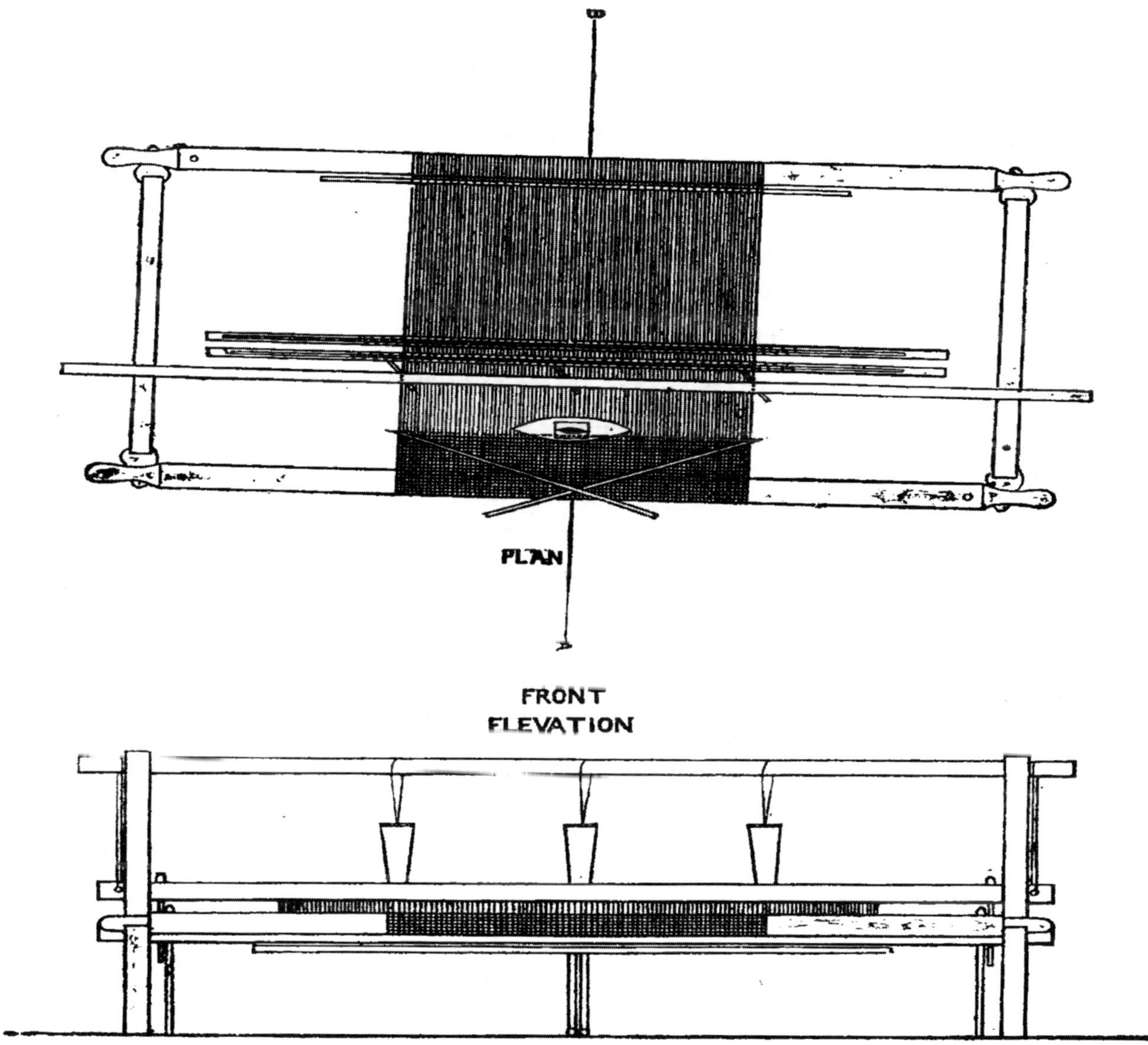

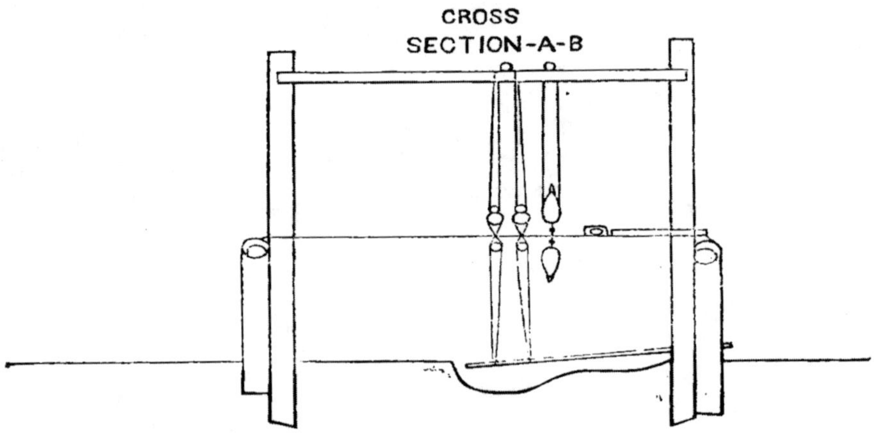

It has already been noted that the *endi* cloths are not manufactured for trade. They are prepared for the personal use of the families of the people themselves, though a few pieces can now and then be obtained from them by purchase."

Mymensingh.—The *eri* silk industry of Mymensingh is of still less importance, and the following short account of it has been furnished of it by Babu Ashutosh Dutt, Deputy Collector :—

"Strictly speaking, there is no silk industry in this district. Only within the jurisdiction of the police-stations of Dewanganj and Madarganj, in the Jamalpur subdivision, an industry in a coarse kind of cloth, locally known as *endis*, but which is far different in quality from the well-known *endis* of Assam, is carried on.

These cloths are extensively used as wrappers by the lower class of people in that subdivision. They are used as warm clothing. When used singly, they are called *tethi*, and when used in pairs they are known as *gelaps*. They are also used as waist-cloth by the women of the cultivating people. They sell ordinarily at Rs. 3-8 to Rs. 4 per piece when single, and at Rs. 7 or Rs. 8 when in pair.

They are prepared from a kind of worm which are fed by leaves of *endis* or *Bherandas* (*Ricinus Communis*). These worms are reared in the house of Muhammadan cultivators by their women throughout the year. The mother worm is kept in a kind of straw, where it lays eggs. The worms, got from these eggs, are nursed for 10 days or so. They become gradually covered with a coating of oval shape, about 1½ inches long and about an inch in circumference. These egg-shaped coatings are then soaked in water for five or six days. These, when fully wet, become soft like a lump of clay. This lump is then twined round a bamboo piece called *kati*. Threads are spun from this lump with a *takua*, a diagram of which is given in the margin. Threads are spun mostly by women. The head of the *takua* is like that of a hook : the hooked portion is thrust in the lump and then drawn : the thread comes out with it, and it is spun, and twined round the *takua*. A seer of this thread is sold for a rupee. These threads are sold to *Rajbansis* and *Tantis* who weave clothes popularly known as *endis* from this thread.

The number of women engaged in this industry in Dewanganj is about 1,000, and that in Madarganj is about half that number. They belong to low class Muhammadan families. They carry on the work of rearing the worms at home in the midst of their household duties. The threads, when ready, are sold by the male members of the family in the local markets. These cloth are sold at Char Pakarda and Golabari. About 300 men are engaged in weaving these cloths. They are men of no education, and weaving cloth is their profession. These cloths cannot be ordinarily had at bazar, but can be got prepared to order.

No silk industry is carried on in the Sadar, Tangail and Netrokona subdivisions."

B. S. Press—274J—500—17.6.1903—W. M. D'C. and N. C. R.

MURSHIDABAD GOWNPIECES.

1. TWILL GOWNPIECE
(extra thick)

2. TWILL GOWNPIECE
(ordinary)

3. GOWNPIECE
(extra thick)

4. DHALI GOWNPIECE
(superior)

5. DHALI GOWNPIECE
(ordinary)

6. LALI GOWNPIECE
(very superior)

7. LALI GOWNPIECE
(inferior)

8. PLAIN STRIPED GOWNPIECE

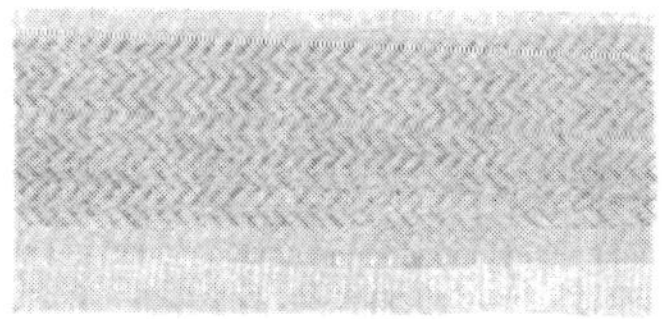

9. TWILLED AND STRIPED GOWNPIECE

10. MAYUR KANTHI GOWNPIECE
(twill)

11. RED GOWNPIECE

12. GREY GOWNPIECE
(twill)

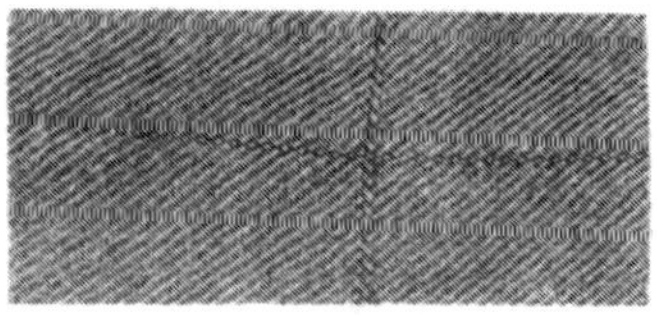

13. GREY GOWNPIECE
(thicker twill)

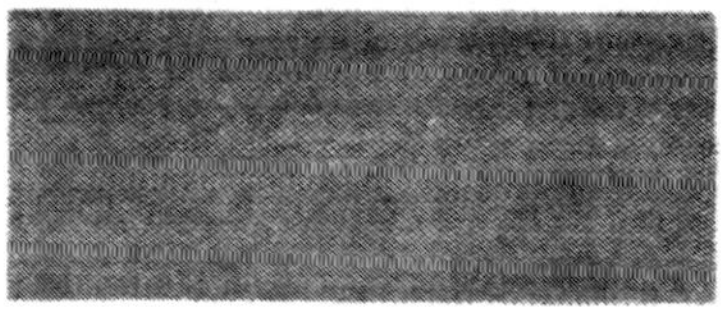

14. GREY GOWNPIECE
(plain)

15. BLACK (DEEP BLUE) GOWNPIECE

16. CORAH

17. SILK MUSLIN

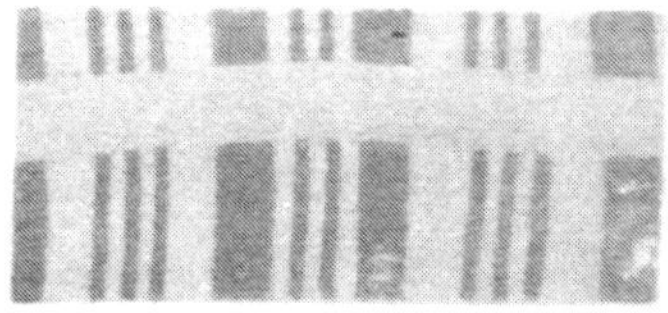

18. DURÉ SILK MUSLIN

ASSAM SILKS, IMITATION AND REAL.

19. THICK SILK, KHEJUR CHHARI
(good silk warp and matká silk weft)

20. THICK SILK, PLAIN
(good silk warp and matká silk weft)

21. IMITATION ENDI
(poor quality)

22. IMITATION ENDI
(better quality)

23. IMITATION ENDI
(better still)

24. IMITATION ENDI
(good quality)
Rs.7 for 7 yds. x 27'' piece

25. IMITATION ENDI
(good quality)
Rs.8 for 7 yds. x 27'' piece

26. THICK SILK OUT OF MATKÁ SILK ONLY
Rs.9 for 7 yds. x 27'' piece

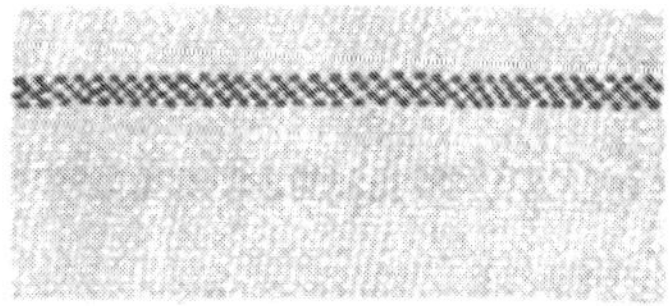

27. STRIPED IMITATION ENDI

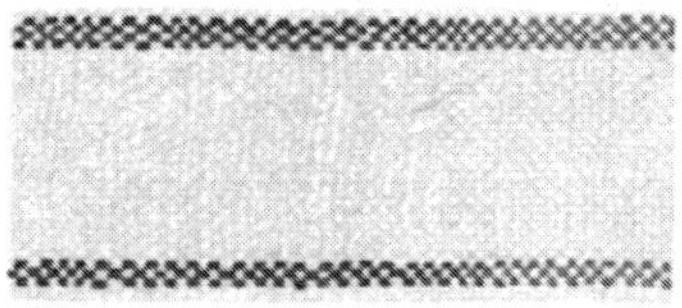

28. STRIPED IMITATION ENDI

29. CHECK IMITATION ENDI FROM MATKÁ SILK

30. CHECK IMITATION ENDI

31. DRESS PIECE FROM MATKÁ SILK ONLY
Rs.14 for 7 yds. x 27''

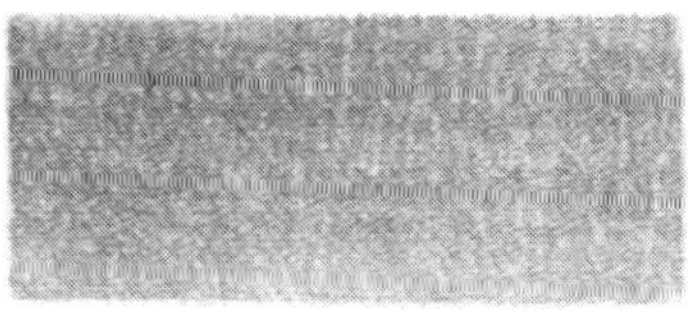

32. REAL ASSAM OR ENDI SILK

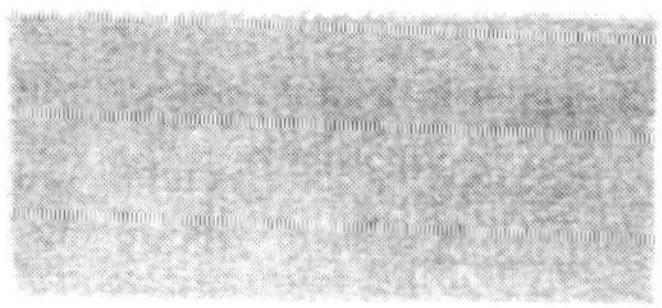

33. REAL ASSAM SILK WASHED

34. REAL ASSAM SILK
(better quality)

35. REAL ASSAM OR ENDI SILK
(superior quality)

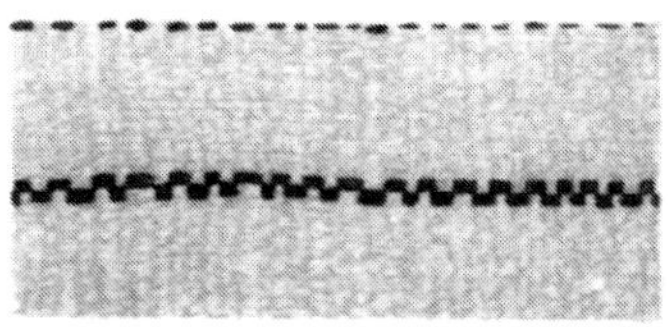

36. EXTRA THICK STRIPED ENDI
(real)

MURSHIDABAD CHECK SILKS, WHITE AND COLOURED.

50. WHITE CHECK

51. WHITE CHECK

49. TWILL CHÁRKHÁNÁ

52. MIRJAPUR CHECK

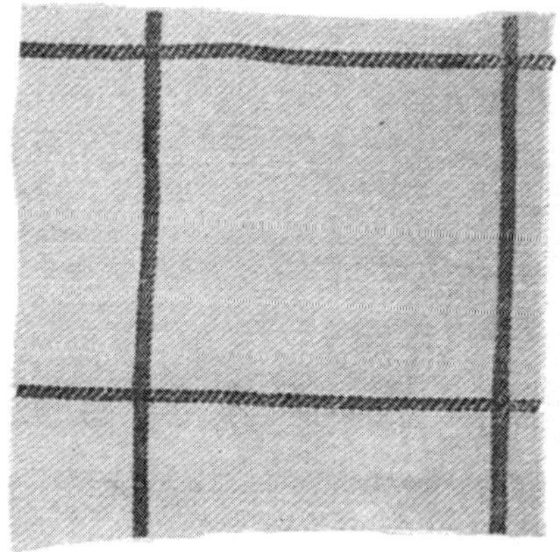

46. TWILL CHÁRKHÁNÁ

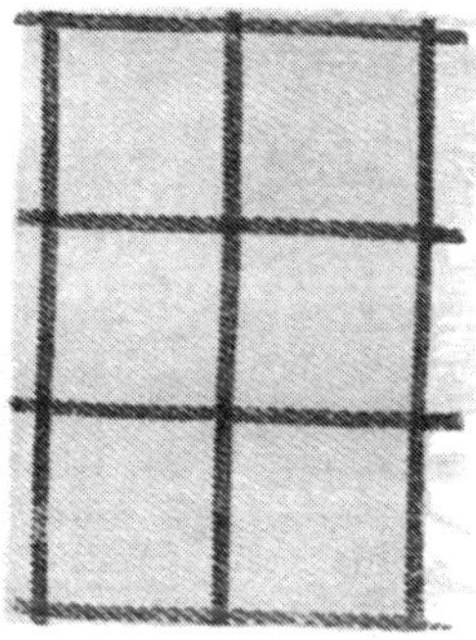

48. TWILL CHÁRKHÁNA

47. TWILL CHÁRKHÁNÁ

MURSHIDABAD BANDANNAS.

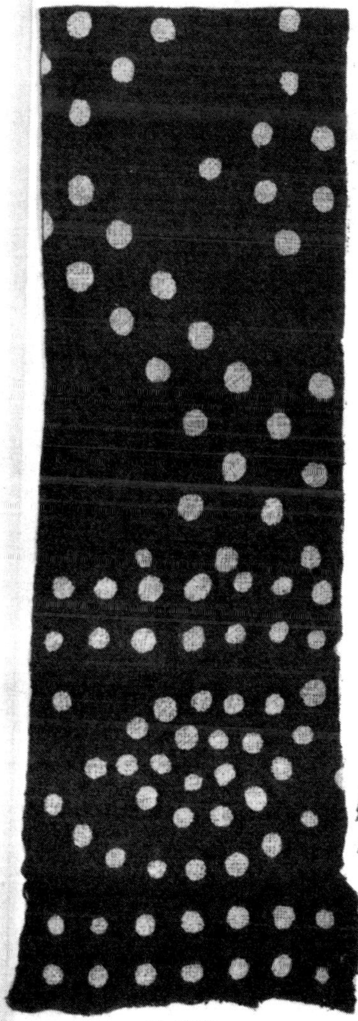

69. CHURI

70. BANDANNA OR BANHU

66(b)

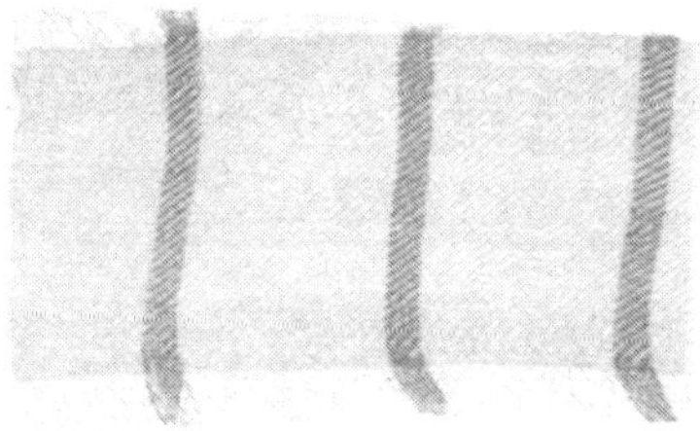

66(c)

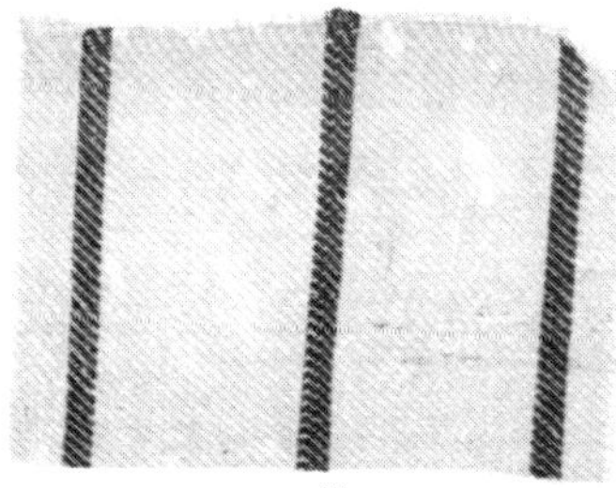

66(d)

66(e) STRIPED TWILLS

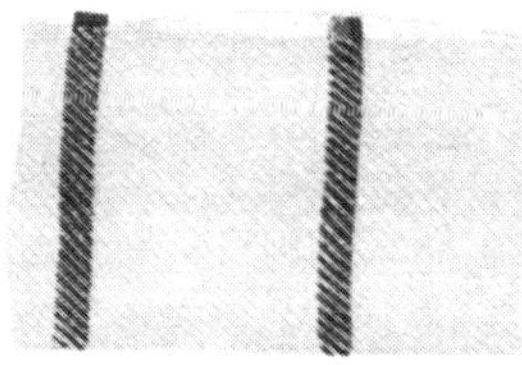

66(a)

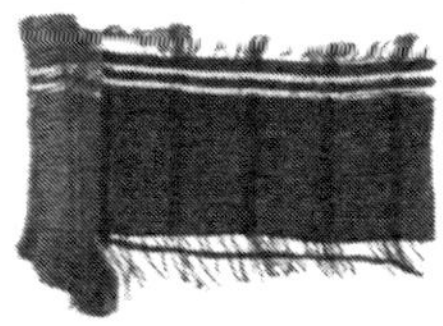

65. HIGH-COLOURED REKHI

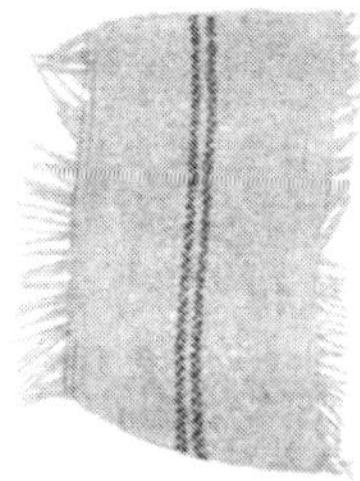

64 DOUBLE REKHI *(coloured)*

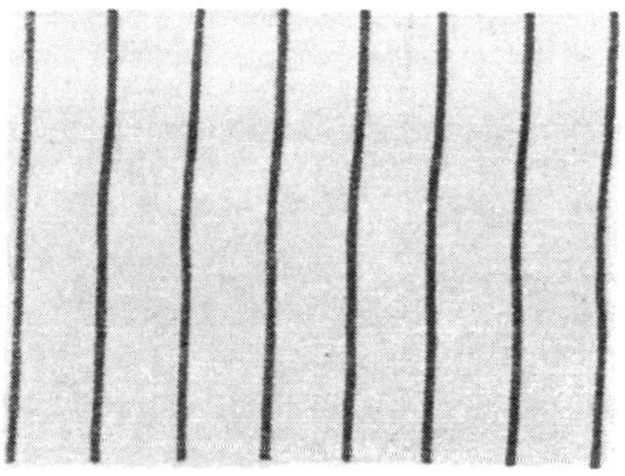

63(a) PLAIN REKHI

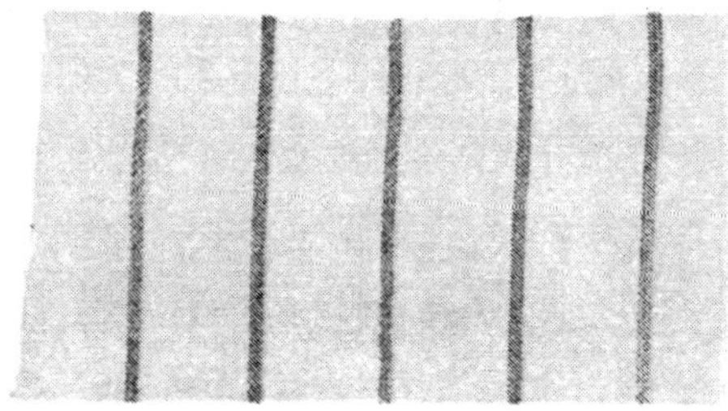

63(b) PLAIN REKHI

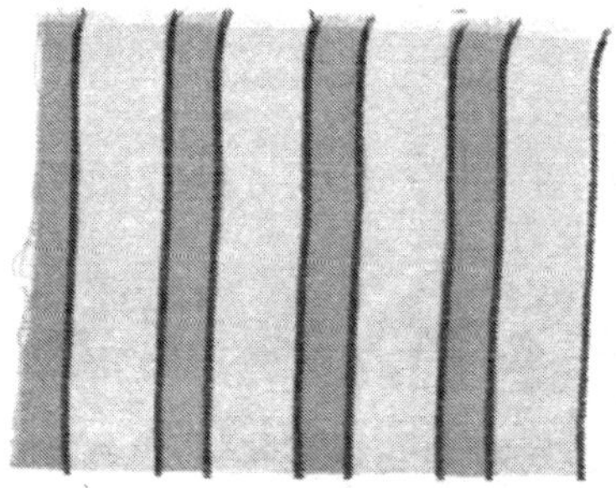

61. DHÁRI

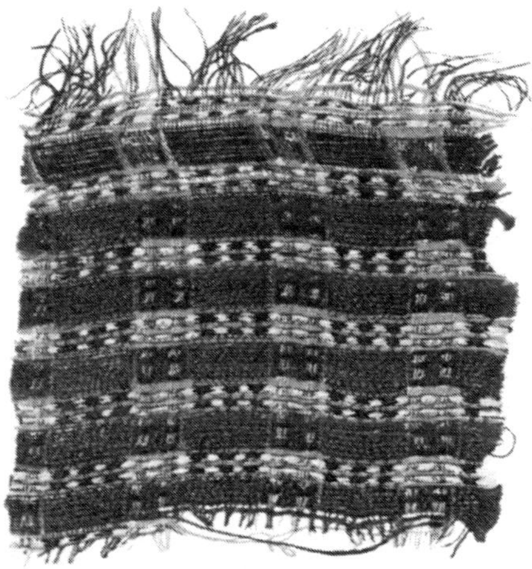

57 CHAUKARÁ

55. BALUCHAR CHEAP CHECKS

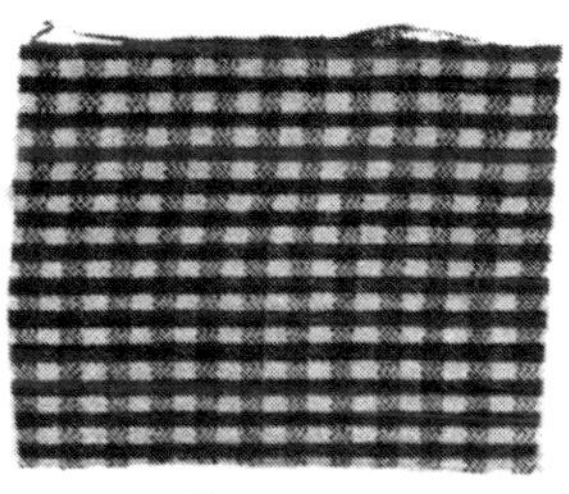

53. MIRJAPUR CHECK

54. BERHAMPORE CHECK

56(a)

56(b)

56 (a & b) BIG CHECKS MADE BY MRITYUNJAY SIRKAR OF MIRJAPUR

67. MATKÁ SÁRI EXPORTED TO MAHRATTA COUNTRY

68. BANESH PHULIKAT HANDKERCHIEF EXPORTED TO RANGOON.

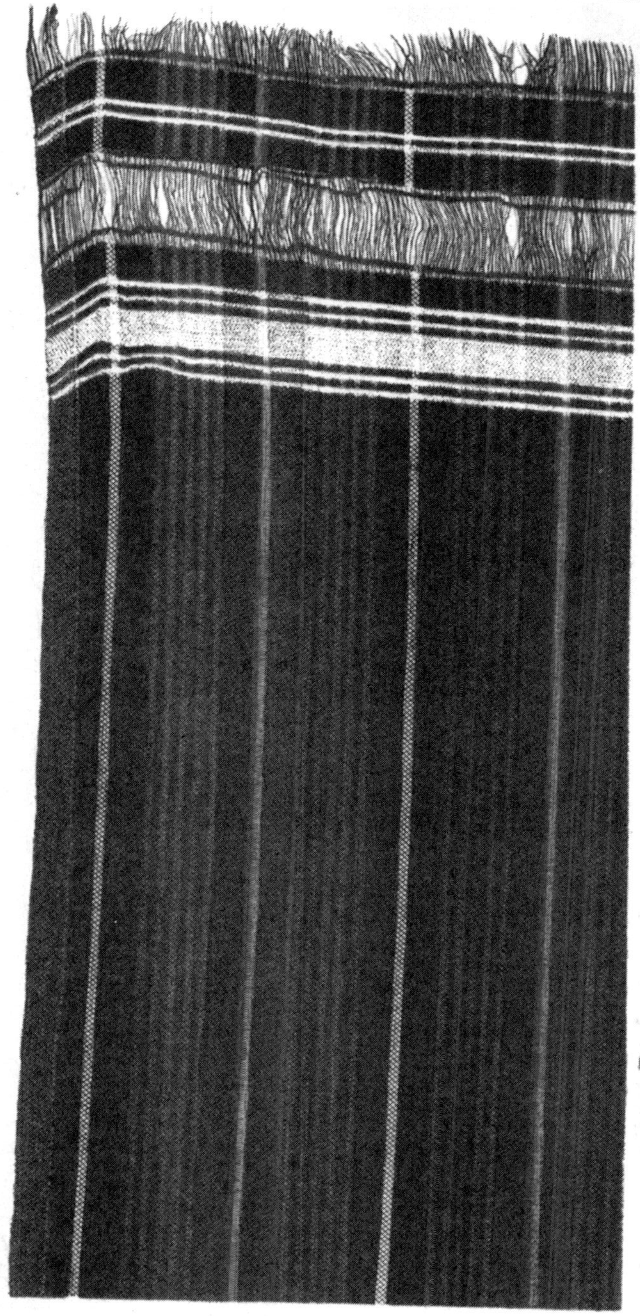
62. DHÁRI EXPORTED TO ARABIA.

71a

71b.

71 (a & b). TWO STYLES OF MURSHIDABAD PRINTED SILK HANDKERCHIEFS.

72 MURSHIDABAD SILK NAMÁBALI.

INFERIOR SILKS (TUSSER, BAFTA, AND ENDI).

73 MANBHUM TUSSER
(*thick*)

74. MANBHUM TUSSER
(*ordinary*)

75. MANBHUM TUSSER
(*extra thick*)

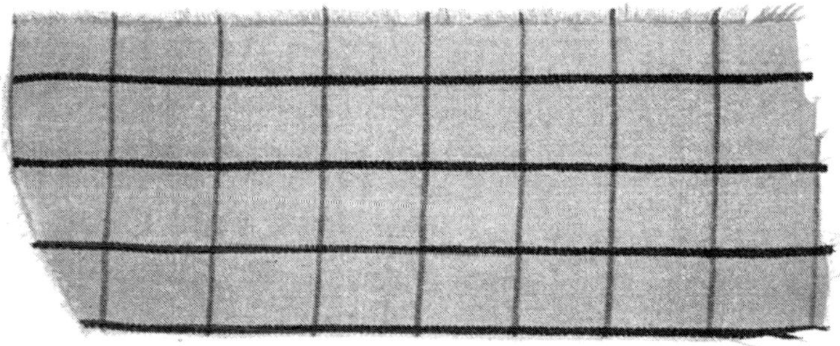

76. CHECK TUSSER FROM MANBHUM

77. MANBHUM TUSSER CHECK

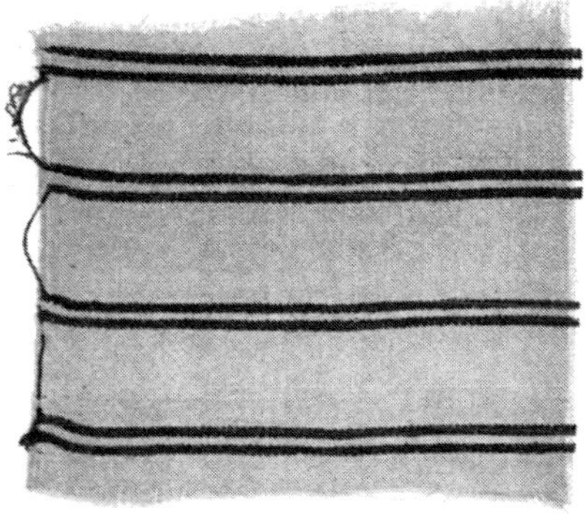

78. MANBHUM TUSSER
(*striped*)

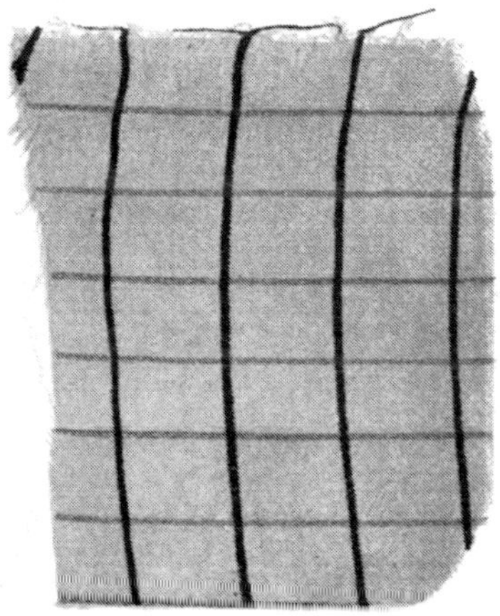

79. MANBHUM TUSSER

80. BHAGALPUR BAFTA

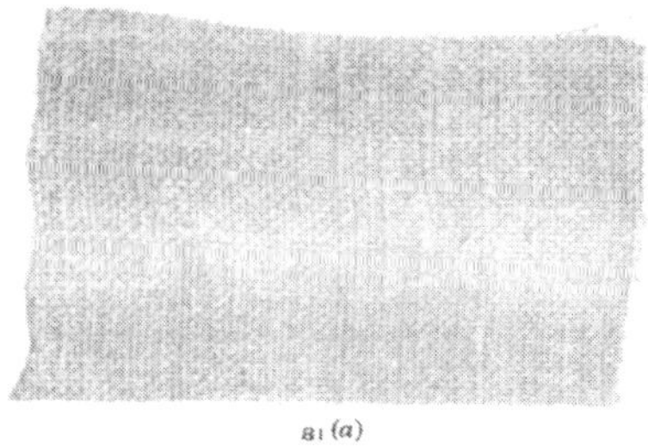

81 (*a*)

81 (*b*)

81. IMITATION ENDI
OF MURSHIDABAD

82 REAL ENDI

83. TUSSER.

84. MATKÁ DHOTI.

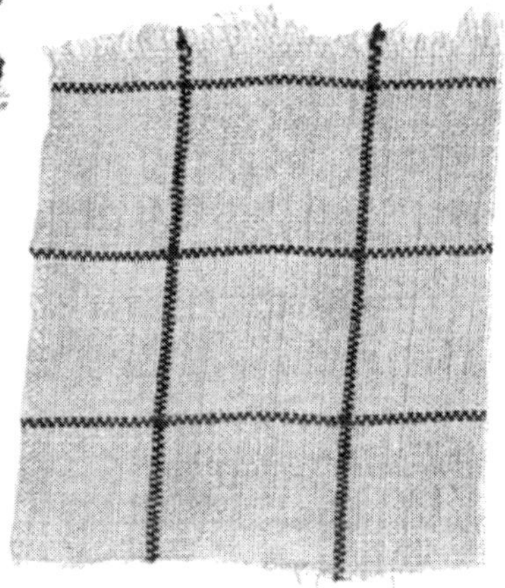

85. MATKÁ CHECK PIECE.

86. MATKÁ CHECK FOR BED COVER.

87. UNWASHED ENDI.

88. SUPERIOR ENDI
(*washed*).

89. WASHED ENDI.

N.B.—Samples Nos. 84 to 89 are from cloths woven by the pupils of the Rampur Boalia Sericultural School, and sample No. 83 is from a piece of Tusser woven by Sonthal children at the Pokhuria Industrial School (Manbhum).

MURSHIDABAD ORNAMENTAL SILKS.

90. "DHAKKA" BORDER.

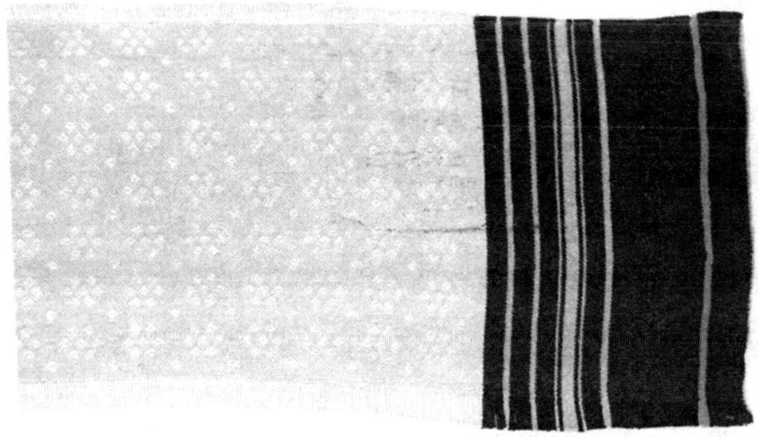

91a. MIRZAPUR SILK SARI WITH ORNAMENTAL GROUND AND "KÁSHI-PÁR" BORDER WOVEN BY MRITYUNJAY SARKAR.

←------- $12\frac{1}{2}$ *inches* -------→ ←------------------ $25\frac{1}{2}$ *inches* ------------------→

91. MIRZAPUR SILK SARI WITH THREE ORDINARY KALKÁ BORDERS

92. BALUCHAR BUTEDAR SARI (OLD STYLE)

93. BALUCHAR BUTEDAR SARI (NEW STYLE).

94. BALUCHAR SCARF (WOVEN BY DUBRÁJ).

94a. BALUCHAR ORNAMENTAL TABLE-COVER WOVEN BY DUBRAJ.

MURSHIDABAD SILK DYEING.

95. SKEIN OF BLEACHED SILK.

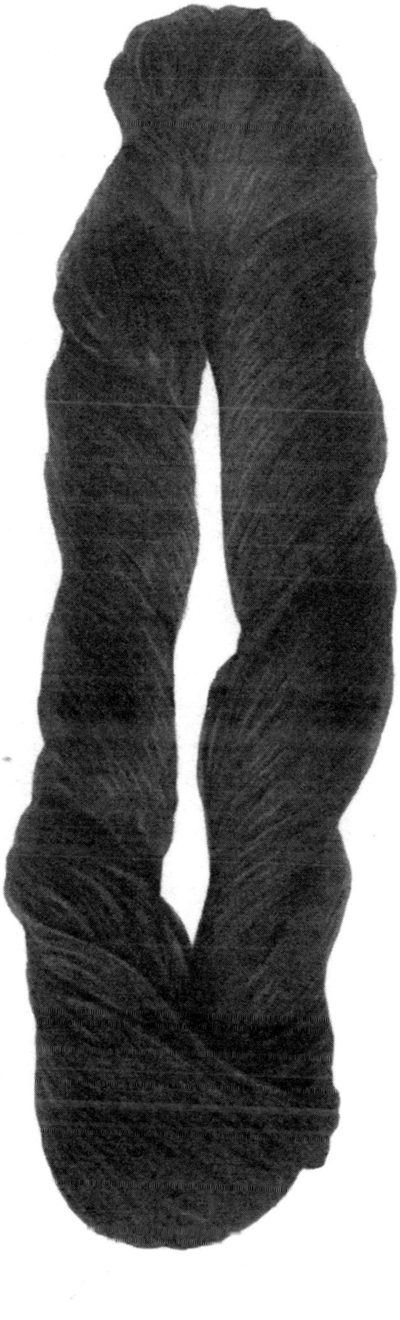

96. SKEIN OF SILK DYED ORANGE.

97. SKEIN OF SILK DYED RED.

MURSHIDABAD SILK DYES

98. DEEP BLUE OR BLACK

99. LIGHT BLUE OR GREY

100. BASANTI OR JACKWOOD YELLOW

101. KAMELA ORANGE

102. ANATTO ORANGE

103. LAC RED

104. LAC AND LODH RED

105. ANÁRDÁNÁ OR LIGHT RED

106. PURPLE

107. BANESH OR CHOCOLATE BLACK

108. DHUPCHHÁYÁ

109. MAYUR KANTHI

110. HIRÁMAN KANTHI

111. ORDINARY GREEN

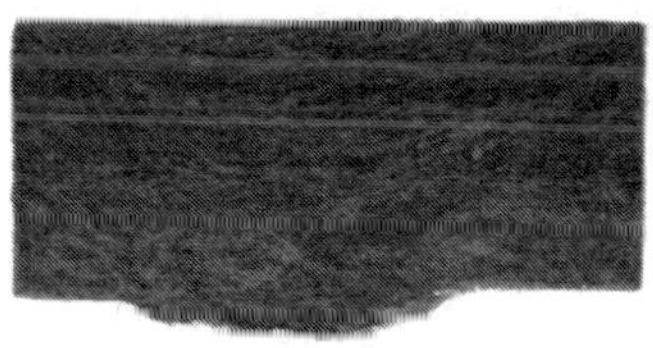
112. FAST GREEN
PRODUCED BY DUBRAJ

113. SONALI

114. AŚHMÁNI

115. PITAMBARI